Getting to Good Friday

Getting to Good Friday

*Literature and the Peace Process in
Northern Ireland*

by

MARILYNN RICHTARIK

OXFORD
UNIVERSITY PRESS

OXFORD
UNIVERSITY PRESS

Great Clarendon Street, Oxford, OX2 6DP,
United Kingdom

Oxford University Press is a department of the University of Oxford.
It furthers the University's objective of excellence in research, scholarship,
and education by publishing worldwide. Oxford is a registered trade mark of
Oxford University Press in the UK and in certain other countries

First Edition published in 2023

Impression: 1

Published in the United States of America by Oxford University Press
198 Madison Avenue, New York, NY 10016, United States of America

British Library Cataloguing in Publication Data
Data available

Library of Congress Control Number: 2022947387

ISBN 978-0-19-288640-8

DOI: 10.1093/oso/9780192886408.001.0001

Printed and bound in the UK by
Clays Ltd, Elcograf S.p.A.

*This book is dedicated to the people of Northern Ireland
and to the memory of Jonathan Bardon, the North's great chronicler.*

Acknowledgements

Countless people have assisted me with this book in various ways. My husband, Matt Bolch, and son, Declan Bolch, have been at ground zero of the work, and my most profound debt is to them. I am grateful to Richard Rankin Russell for commissioning the essay that sparked my idea for a book-length study of literature and the peace process back in 2013. And I am thankful for my agent, Jonathan Williams, who is busier in 'retirement' than most people are when fully employed and whose enthusiasm for the book has sustained me.

The writers whose work features in this book (and/or their estates) have been remarkably generous in answering my questions about their work and allowing me to quote from unpublished material. My thanks to Brian and Anne Friel, the Brian Friel Estate and Maeve Bolger, the Seamus Heaney Estate, Michael and Edna Longley, Deirdre Madden, Seamus Deane, Bernard MacLaverty, Colum McCann, and David Park. Extracts from archival material in Chapter One are © The Estate of Brian Friel and reproduced by permission of The Agency (London) Ltd, all rights reserved and enquiries to The Agency (London) Ltd, 24 Pottery Lane, London, W11 4LZ fax: 0207 727 9037. In Chapter Two, 'Ceasefire' is © Michael Longley and reproduced in full by permission of the author, with thanks to Jonathan Cape. Extracts from archival material in Chapter Four are © Bernard MacLaverty and reproduced by permission of the author c/o Rogers, Coleridge & White Ltd, 20 Powis Mews, London W11 1JN.

I owe a great debt to my first readers, whose engaged reactions and suggestions have strengthened every part of this book: Matt Bolch, Modupe Labode, Jonathan Williams, Roy Foster, Paula Hawkins, and Emily Bloom. The anonymous peer reviewers for Oxford University Press gave me expert advice in 2020, and their reports helped to shape this book at a crucial stage in its development; I am grateful to them and to senior commissioning editor Jacqueline Norton. Other readers have weighed in on a chapter or two, offering valuable commentary: Paul Arthur, Dianne Berger, Anthony Bradley, Joe Cleary, Neva Corbin, Elizabeth Cullingford, Sam Fannin, Anne Fogarty, Bowie Hagan, Edna Longley, Michael Parker, Laura Barberán Reinares, Richard Rankin Russell, and Nathan Suhr-Sytsma. Articles I published on *The Cure at Troy*, *Making History*, and *One by One in the Darkness* in *Estudios Irlandeses*, *ELH*, and the *Irish University Review*, respectively, included some material from the first three chapters of this book, and I am obliged to those journals' editors and peer reviewers for their critiques.

Many current and former Georgia State University colleagues have read and commented on parts of this book (and on the Fulbright application that preceded it), usually in the context of the Works in Progress Group of the Department of English: Christine Anlicker, Tanya Caldwell, Eddie Christie, Matt Dischinger, Lindsey Eckert, Shannon Finck, Randy Malamud, Melissa McLeod, Mark Noble, Jay Rajiva, LeeAnne Richardson, Stephanie Hassan Richardson, Renée Schatteman, and Robin Wharton. My graduate research assistant, Em Gates, offered invaluable editing suggestions in the final stage of the writing process, and the questions she asked me in the course of this work were an excellent guide to terms and concepts that someone without personal experience of Northern Ireland might need explained.

I am also exceedingly grateful to all who wrote in support of any of my (many) grant and fellowship applications, successful and unsuccessful: Anthony Bradley, Joe Cleary, Elizabeth Cullingford, Roy Foster, Paula Hawkins, Randy Malamud, Jacqueline Norton, Ronald Schuchard, and Stephen Watt. I'm particularly grateful that a few of these were funded. Most significantly, a Fulbright US Scholar Grant enabled me and my family to spend the first half of 2017 living in Belfast, where I taught a seminar at Queen's University Belfast, did research towards this book, and experienced in person a politically turbulent time in Northern Ireland.

Georgia State University, the GSU College of Arts and Sciences, and the GSU Department of English have all supported this project. Summer research awards from the Department of English enabled me to research Chapter One in 2015 and to write the 'Ceasefire' section of Chapter Two and the first half of Chapter Three in 2019. A Research-Intensive Semester funded by the College in the autumn of 2021 allowed me to write Chapter Five and the conclusion. At the University level, a Provost's Faculty Research Fellowship in 2017/18 funded two course releases, travel, computer equipment, and supplies, and a Tenured Scholarly Support Grant in 2021/22 funded a course release, a graduate research assistant, and two short-term residencies to help me finish writing this book. I am grateful to administrators at my institution, especially department chairs Lynée Gaillet and Audrey Goodman and dean Sara Rosen, for helping me to arrange my teaching responsibilities in such a way that I was able to complete this research project in a timely fashion.

Thanks are also due to helpful staff members at the various places where I researched and wrote this book, including the Stuart A. Rose Manuscript, Archives, and Rare Book Library of Emory University in Atlanta, Georgia; the National Library of Ireland in Dublin; the Newspaper Library of the Belfast Central Library; the Linen Hall Library in Belfast; the Field Day Theatre Company office in Derry (back in the twentieth century); the Hambidge Center in Rabun Gap, Georgia; the Monastery of the Holy Spirit near Conyers, Georgia; and the Lillian E. Smith Center in Clayton, Georgia. Kevin Whelan salvaged one of my research trips to Dublin by working his contacts at the National Library to speed up the rate at which I was able to access Bernard MacLaverty's uncatalogued papers. I am also especially grateful to Christine Jason and Jamie Badoud, at the Hambidge Center, and to Matthew Teutsch, director of the Lillian E. Smith Center, for facilitating my residencies in north Georgia in 2019 and 2021.

Many people associated with Oxford University Press have helped to make this book a reality. I owe special thanks to senior commissioning editor Jacqueline Norton, commissioning editor Jack McNichol, title manager Cathryn Steele, copyeditor Monica Matthews, and production manager S. Balasubramanian.

I am grateful to my students, both at Georgia State University and at Queen's University Belfast, who helped me to understand the literary texts featured in this book a little better each time I taught them, and to the members of the Atlanta Irish Studies Group (otherwise known as Irish book club), with whom I have discussed several of these works. Most of all, I am thankful to my Northern Irish friends, too numerous to attempt to list here, who have shared their perspectives with me for well over thirty years now. This book is for them.

Contents

List of Acronyms

DUP	Democratic Unionist Party
EU	European Union
INLA	Irish National Liberation Army
IRA	Irish Republican Army
LVF	Loyalist Volunteer Force
MP	Member of Parliament
NIO	Northern Ireland Office
NIWC	Northern Ireland Women's Coalition
NLI	National Library of Ireland
PSNI	Police Service of Northern Ireland
PUP	Progressive Unionist Party
RUC	Royal Ulster Constabulary
SDLP	Social Democratic and Labour Party
TRC	Truth and Reconciliation Commission
UDA	Ulster Defence Association
UDP	Ulster Democratic Party
UFF	Ulster Freedom Fighters
UK	United Kingdom
UKUP	United Kingdom Unionist Party
US	United States
UUC	Ulster Unionist Council
UUP	Ulster Unionist Party
UVF	Ulster Volunteer Force
UWC	Ulster Workers Council

Chronology

1980–1	hunger strikes by republican prisoners; Sinn Féin begins contesting elections
May '83–May '84	New Ireland Forum meets
June 1983	Gerry Adams elected MP for West Belfast
Nov. 1983	Adams elected Sinn Féin President
15 Nov. 1985	Anglo–Irish Agreement signed
May 1986	Father Alec Reid writes to SDLP leader John Hume, proposing that all nationalist parties in Ireland should unite 'in a common campaign for reconciliation and peace'
Nov. 1986	Sinn Féin ends its policy of abstentionism in the Republic, provoking a split in the party
8 Nov. 1987	an IRA bomb in Enniskillen kills eleven people assembled for a Remembrance Day ceremony and injures sixty-three others
11 Jan. 1988	first reported meeting between Hume and Adams
6 Mar. 1988	three unarmed IRA members are shot dead by the British Special Air Service in Gibraltar
16 Mar. 1988	loyalist Michael Stone kills three people and injures over sixty more in Milltown Cemetery at the funeral of the IRA activists killed in Gibraltar
19 Mar. 1988	two British Army corporals are dragged from their car and killed after driving into the funeral procession of one of Stone's victims
Mar.–Sept. 1988	formal inter-party talks between Sinn Féin and the SDLP, sponsored by the Redemptorist Order
Sept. '88–Jan. '89	Field Day Theatre Company tours throughout Ireland and to the National Theatre in London with Brian Friel's play *Making History*
Nov. 1989	Secretary of State for Northern Ireland Peter Brooke says the government would be 'imaginative' if republicans ended their military campaign
Oct.–Dec. 1990	Field Day Theatre Company tours throughout Ireland with Seamus Heaney's play *The Cure at Troy*
24 Oct. 1990	six soldiers and a civilian are killed by IRA 'human bombs'
27 Nov. 1990	John Major becomes Conservative Party leader and Prime Minister
7 Feb. 1991	the IRA fires a mortar bomb into the garden of 10 Downing Street
Mar. 1991	Brooke announces that inter-party talks will resume, with all parties accepting that discussion must focus on 'the three main relationships': 'within Northern Ireland', among 'the people of the island of Ireland', and between the British and Irish governments—these talks end inconclusively in early July, but future talks will also employ this 'three-strand' approach

Feb. 1992	Albert Reynold becomes Taoiseach of the Republic of Ireland
Apr. 1992	Sir Patrick Mayhew becomes Secretary of State for Northern Ireland
Dec. 1992	Mayhew announces that Sinn Féin could be included in political negotiations if the IRA ends its military campaign
Mar. 1993	two children die and fifty-six people are injured after two IRA bombs explode in a shopping centre in Warrington, Cheshire
Early Apr. 1993	Gordon Wilson, newly appointed an Irish Senator, meets secretly with IRA representatives to urge an end to violence; they say that first the British government must invite them to negotiate without preconditions
10 Apr. 1993	Adams is spotted entering Hume's house in Derry, arousing an uproar—two weeks later, Hume and Adams issue a joint statement that 'the Irish people as a whole have a right to national self-determination.... The exercise of self-determination is a matter for agreement between the people of Ireland. It is the search for that agreement and the means of achieving it on which we will be concentrating.'
25 Sept. 1993	Hume and Adams announce that they will be forwarding a report on their discussions to the Irish government for consideration
23 Oct. 1993	an IRA bomb in a fish shop on the Shankill Road kills ten people (including one of the bombers) and injures fifty-seven
27 Oct. 1993	Adams helps to carry the coffin of Shankill bomber Thomas Begley
29 Oct. 1993	Major and Reynolds say they will not adopt the Hume–Adams proposals
30 Oct. 1993	a loyalist attack on the Rising Sun bar in Greysteel kills seven and injures thirteen; twenty-seven people have died in the Troubles this month, more than in any month since October 1976
15 Nov. 1993	Major says that 'if the IRA end violence for good, then—after a sufficient interval to ensure the permanence of their intent—Sinn Féin can enter the political arena as a democratic party and join the dialogue'
28 Nov. 1993	the *Observer* reveals that the British government has had a secret channel of communication with Sinn Féin and the IRA for three years
15 Dec. 1993	Major and Reynolds issue a Joint Declaration on Northern Ireland, the Downing Street Declaration, which emphasizes a three-strand approach to negotiations, the importance of majority consent in Northern Ireland to any constitutional change, the British government's lack of 'selfish strategic or economic interest in Northern Ireland', and the right of 'the people of Ireland' to self-determination
20 Dec. 1993	in a radio interview, UUP leader James Molyneaux rejects the idea that the Declaration represents a 'sell out' of unionists
21 Dec. 1993	Adams asserts that the Declaration 'needs to be clarified'
29 Jan. 1994	US President Bill Clinton approves a visa for Gerry Adams against the advice of the British government and the US State Department
Mar. 1994	the IRA launches three mortar attacks on Heathrow Airport
19 May 1994	the NIO publishes a 21-page 'commentary' on twenty questions submitted to the British government by Reynolds on behalf of Sinn Féin
29 Aug. 1994	Adams says he has told the IRA Army Council that he believes the conditions now exist for advancing the peace process

31 Aug. 1994	the IRA announces a 'complete cessation of military operations'
3 Sept. 1994	Michael Longley's poem 'Ceasefire' published in the *Irish Times*
13 Oct. 1994	the Combined Loyalist Military Command announces its ceasefire
17 Nov. 1994	Reynolds resigns as Taoiseach
1 Dec. 1994	President Clinton appoints George Mitchell (former US Senate majority leader) as an economic adviser on Ireland from January 1995
9 Dec. 1994	British civil servants meet Sinn Féin representatives at Stormont for the first time in over twenty years—the British want to discuss decommissioning, while Sinn Féin want 'parity of esteem' for their party
Dec. 1994	John Bruton (a strong critic of the IRA) becomes Taoiseach, warning soon after that the peace process should not get stuck on decommissioning
22 Feb. 1995	the British and Irish governments publish *Frameworks for the Future* documents: one with proposals for governance in Northern Ireland, and one on North–South relations; the latter is quickly rejected by unionists
7 Mar. 1995	Mayhew outlines a three-point plan for IRA decommissioning that proves unacceptable to both republicans and unionists
9 July 1995	the 'siege of Drumcree': police prevent Orangemen from marching down a nationalist stretch of Portadown's Garvaghy Road—DUP leader Ian Paisley and local MP David Trimble try unsuccessfully to negotiate a compromise, and the RUC and Orangemen confront each other
11 July 1995	a compromise allows 500 Orangemen to march down the road despite residents' protests but without any loyalist bands; Paisley and Trimble celebrate with marchers
8 Sept. 1995	Trimble elected UUP leader
28 Nov. 1995	the British and Irish governments issue a joint communiqué launching their new 'twin-track' approach; the governments note their 'firm aim' of all-party talks by late February 1996 and invite the parties for preparatory talks—an 'international body' will be established to advise on decommissioning: George Mitchell is asked to chair this body (later called the Mitchell Commission); former Prime Minister of Finland Harri Holkeri and Canadian General John de Chastelain are also invited to serve
30 Nov. 1995	President Clinton visits Northern Ireland
24 Jan. 1996	the Mitchell Commission's report suggests that decommissioning might happen *during* all-party negotiations rather than before or after (as unionists and republicans, respectively, demand) and lays out the Mitchell Principles of democracy and non-violence; Major tells the House of Commons there are two ways in which all-party negotiations can begin: paramilitaries can start decommissioning, or elections can be held to 'secure a democratic mandate for all-party negotiations'
9 Feb. 1996	the IRA ends its ceasefire with a bombing in London's Docklands that kills two, injures more than a hundred, and causes an estimated £100 million worth of damage
21 Mar. 1996	the British government announces plans for Forum elections to be held 30 May: votes will be for parties rather than individuals, with two extra seats allocated to each of the ten most successful parties in Northern Ireland

May 1996	Deirdre Madden's novel *One by One in the Darkness* published
6 June 1996	a joint British–Irish paper gives Mitchell the jobs of chairing both plenary sessions of the talks and a sub-committee dealing with decommissioning—his colleagues on the international body will also participate in the negotiations; this plan is welcomed by nationalists but greeted suspiciously by unionists, who object to Mitchell as chair
10 June 1996	multi-party talks begin at Stormont; Sinn Féin is barred because of the continuing IRA campaign
15 June 1996	a huge IRA bomb in Manchester injures two hundred people and causes extensive damage to the city centre
Summer 1996	Seamus Deane's novel *Reading in the Dark* published
7 July 1996	police and marchers confront each other after the RUC bans an Orange march along the Garvaghy Road from Drumcree Parish Church to Portadown
11 July 1996	after the RUC allows the Orange march to proceed, days of rioting follow in nationalist areas
15 July 1996	a BBC television programme reveals that Trimble talked with loyalist leader Billy Wright during the Drumcree confrontation
22 July 1996	fears grow that the loyalist ceasefire is about to break down
5 Mar. 1997	the deadlocked multi-party talks adjourn until June
1 May 1997	a British general election results in a landslide victory for the Labour Party, led by Tony Blair; Mo Mowlam becomes Secretary of State for Northern Ireland
16 May 1997	in a speech in Northern Ireland, Prime Minister Blair says his 'agenda is not a united Ireland'; he offers immediate talks between Sinn Féin representatives and British government officials but says the 'settlement train' is leaving with or without Sinn Féin
3 June 1997	multi-party talks resume
6 June 1997	a general election in the Republic leads to a coalition government headed by Bertie Ahern of Fianna Fáil
16 June 1997	the IRA murders two RUC men on foot patrol in Lurgan
24 June 1997	British and Irish government proposals presented to the plenary talks suggest parallel talks and decommissioning
25 June 1997	Blair says he expects substantive talks by September, with a settlement by the following May
June 1997	Bernard MacLaverty's novel *Grace Notes* published
6 July 1997	there is widespread rioting in nationalist areas after police clear protesters to allow Orangemen down the Garvaghy Road in Portadown
19 July 1997	the IRA announces a restoration of its 1994 ceasefire, with a 'complete cessation of military operations' from midday on 20 July—the renewed ceasefire permits Sinn Féin to join the talks process two days later
21 July 1997	Trimble initiates consultations between the UUP and Northern Ireland's citizens; after Sinn Féin representatives are allowed to prepare their offices, the DUP and UKUP withdraw permanently from the talks

29 Aug. 1997	Mowlam in the House of Commons accepts the IRA ceasefire as genuine and invites Sinn Féin into negotiations from September
15 Sept. 1997	all-party talks formally begin, with Mitchell chairing—the UUP, PUP, and UDP join the talks on 17 September
24 Sept. 1997	the International Commission on Decommissioning is formally launched, and passage of a detailed procedural motion allows the start of substantive political talks
27 Dec. 1997	LVF leader Billy Wright is shot dead by INLA prisoners in the Maze, setting off a spate of sectarian killings early in 1998
12 Jan. 1998	after a weekend of phone calls between Ahern, Blair, and Trimble, the governments present the parties with proposed 'Heads of Agreement'
19 Jan. 1998	Adams says the 'Heads of Agreement' document does not offer a pathway to peace
26 Jan. 1998	the British and Irish governments present the parties with a paper on possible North–South structures, which is rejected by unionists
3 Apr. 1998	after the third meeting in three days between Blair and Ahern, there are still significant differences between the British and Irish governments
7 Apr. 1998	Mitchell presents a draft to help the parties reach agreement, but unionist rejection of its North–South provisions (negotiated by the British and Irish governments) brings the process close to collapse; Blair flies to Belfast
8 Apr. 1998	on the eve of the talks deadline, Ahern also joins the negotiations in Belfast
9 Apr. 1998	on the final official day of talks, bilateral discussions continue
10 Apr. 1998	on Good Friday, negotiators approve the Belfast Agreement
Feb. 2008	David Park's novel *The Truth Commissioner* published

This chronology is based substantially, but not exclusively, on Paul Bew and Gordon Gillespie's invaluable *Northern Ireland: A Chronology of the Troubles 1968–1999* (Lanham, Maryland: The Scarecrow Press, 1999).

Introduction

Lucy Caldwell's novel *All the Beggars Riding* explores metaphorically the experience of living in the aftermath of Northern Ireland's late-twentieth-century Troubles. Born in Belfast in 1981, Caldwell believes in fiction's ability to develop empathy in writers and readers alike, and her belief suffuses the novel, which was featured as Belfast's One City One Book selection upon its publication in 2013. Using the tabloidy premise of a Northern Irish surgeon who has a wife and two children in Belfast and a mistress and two children in London, Caldwell constructs a touching account of one woman's quest to come to terms with a troubled personal history. Protagonist Lara's discovery, upon entering puberty, that her parents had never been married—and that her father had another, legitimate, family—initiated a self-destructive rebellion, intensified a few months later when her father was killed in a helicopter crash. Decades later, her mother's death prompts Lara, nearing 40, to attempt to write her life story to 'set the past to rights and to rest, and to understand'. Above all, she seeks 'to be truthful'. Because her life 'was a whole tissue of deception and lies', she feels that 'somehow getting to the truth, or towards it', is all that matters.[1]

Lara quickly runs up against the limits of her knowledge, however. Halfway through *All the Beggars Riding*, she is ready to give up, lamenting that 'I haven't managed to write even one single episode without it breaking down midway into hypothetical questions and holes, things I don't know and have no way of knowing. Pathetic, isn't it? Even our own stories, we're unequipped and essentially unable to tell' (123). At this point, her creative writing instructor urges Lara to try writing her mother's story as fiction. The teacher insists that any kind of narrative (even a 'true' one) is a 'story', consciously structured and bounded by the writer, and argues that fiction is the only avenue to certain kinds of truth. 'We can never know what it's like to be someone else, ever, except through fiction', she explains, which makes it not only 'an escape from the world' but 'an escape out of ourselves and into the world, too' (124).

Initially hesitant, Lara decides to try writing her mother's story instead of her own and soon finds herself imagining her father's perspective as well, which is even more difficult. Just when she feels she is 'getting into the swing of things', though, she is surprised to discover that she no longer feels the need 'to write them' (201–2). The anger she once felt towards her parents has turned to pity. Lara has no idea if any of the history she has imagined for them resembles what really happened: 'Perhaps it didn't happen like any of that at all. It probably didn't.

Getting to Good Friday: Literature and the Peace Process in Northern Ireland. Marilynn Richtarik, Oxford University Press. © Marilynn Richtarik 2023. DOI: 10.1093/oso/9780192886408.003.0001

But I understand how it could have' (202). Writing, she comes to believe, 'isn't self-expression, vomiting self-pity onto the page. It's the taking and shaping of things, carefully, again and again, until they make a sort of sense that not only you but others can understand, and maybe benefit from.... I've come to realise that you can never know; but you can understand, and that's what fiction does, or tries to do' (238). After writing her mother's story, Lara decides to reach out to her father's Northern Irish children; although her advance is rebuffed by one of them, she becomes friends with the other. She even allows her half-brother to read what she has written, which helps him, too, 'to let the past go' (238). In *All the Beggars Riding*, the act of writing enables reconciliation, both internal and external.

Bernard MacLaverty, one of the writers whose work features in this book, agrees with the notion that 'Narrative is a way of thinking.'[2] In keeping with that idea, *Getting to Good Friday* is a narrative account of Northern Ireland's peace process which grew out of my attempt to answer a question that had long puzzled me, despite the fact that I had already written two books about Northern Irish literature (*Acting Between the Lines*, which describes the formative years of the Field Day Theatre Company, and *Stewart Parker*, a biography of the Belfast playwright).[3] Throughout the twenty-plus years during which I was researching and writing those books (and reading and teaching British and Irish literature), the Troubles appeared to be an eternal feature of life in Northern Ireland. In their late-twentieth-century form, they had been ongoing since at least 1969 and bid fair to continue indefinitely, so how was peace made there—suddenly, as it then seemed to me—in the spring of 1998?

I conceived of this book in 2013, while working on a commissioned essay about MacLaverty's novel *Grace Notes*.[4] My early research revealed that most of what I had intended to say about the novel's political resonance had already been said by other critics, so I had to find a different way into it, and I began looking closely at what was happening in Northern Ireland while MacLaverty was writing. This exercise revealed that, although the novel was written after the 1994 paramilitary ceasefires had signalled an important advance in the peace process, the two years that elapsed between these ceasefires and September 1996, when MacLaverty sent a complete draft of *Grace Notes* to his agent, were filled with tension, uncertainty, and scant political progress. The contemporary lack of resolution had formal implications for the novel, which has a 'happy ending' that occurs, chronologically, halfway through the events depicted in the book. As a result of writing this essay, I had two realizations: 1) my densely historicized approach to literary texts could reveal things that even critics with similar interests had missed, and 2) because Stewart Parker died in 1988 and my Field Day book focused mainly on the early 1980s, I had not previously *studied* the 1990s in Northern Ireland, the very decade during which I had most frequently visited as a researcher. As T. S. Eliot writes in *Four Quartets*, I had had the experience but missed the meaning—partly because much of what was happening in this period was not publicly known at the time.

Getting to Good Friday represents my personal search for that meaning, conducted through texts significant to me for a long time, the import of which shifted as I became more aware of the circumstances under which they were written. The sections on Brian Friel's play *Making History* and Seamus Heaney's play *The Cure at Troy* are a continuation of my work on Field Day. In writing these chapters, I drew on archival research conducted in the Field Day office in Derry in the early 1990s, in addition to more recent primary research at Emory University's Stuart A. Rose Manuscript, Archives, and Rare Book Library in Atlanta, Georgia, and the National Library of Ireland (NLI) in Dublin. In these archives, I took advantage of sources such as authors' notes and unpublished correspondence that were not available when I wrote my Field Day book.

I met Michael Longley at the John Hewitt Summer School in 1991 and crossed paths with him regularly after that. I distinctly remember the thrill I felt reading his poem 'Ceasefire' for the first time in the *New Yorker* in 1995. I hosted Seamus Deane (whom I had first met in 1989, when I began researching the Field Day book) in Atlanta in 1997, the year after *Reading in the Dark* was published. MacLaverty (whom I had interviewed in 1994 as part of my research for the Parker biography) was my guest there in 1998, the year after *Grace Notes* came out. I remained in contact with both writers and have also consulted their archives in the Rose Library and the NLI.

I first read Deirdre Madden's *One by One in the Darkness* some time ago, inspired by a Northern Irish friend's enthusiasm for it, but I did not meet Madden herself until the summer of 2017. My personal encounter with her changed my view of the novel: I had always assumed it was written in response to the cease-fires, but she emphasized that she had begun writing the book before the cease-fires were announced, when peace had seemed a distant prospect to her. I have met Colum McCann only once to date, at a conference in New York City late in 2019, but our brief conversation concerning his approach to writing about real people informs my reading of his fiction.

I read David Park's first book, a collection of short stories called *Oranges from Spain* (1990), in the 1990s but had no accurate mental image of its author until years later, when, after being mightily impressed by his 2008 novel, *The Truth Commissioner*, I asked another Northern Irish novelist, Glenn Patterson, to introduce us via e-mail. Park and I met in person for the first time in July 2013 and corresponded afterwards. I got to know both him and Longley better when I lived in Belfast during the first half of 2017.

Much of what matters to me about these texts is my personal relationship with them and with their authors over a long period. If there is a principle of selection at work, it is that these are texts I read differently now because I have learned more about the historical and political situation in Northern Ireland at the time of their composition, and they have helped me to understand that context. The most distinctive feature of *Getting to Good Friday* is the way in which I intertwine literary and historical analysis. Literary critics who sketch historical backgrounds are not uncommon, and historians might illustrate their points with examples from literary texts. My approach is unusual, however, in the degree to which I employ literary analysis to illuminate historical events and processes. I contend that literature *as literature* (that is, in its formal properties, in addition to anything it might have to 'say' about a given subject) can enrich our historical understanding.

Getting to Good Friday centres on literary reactions and contributions to progress towards peace in Northern Ireland during the fifteen years preceding the 1998 Belfast/Good Friday Agreement, which officially ended three decades of political and sectarian violence between unionists, primarily Protestant, who wish Northern Ireland to remain permanently part of the United Kingdom (UK), and nationalists, mainly Catholic, who favour the idea of an Irish state consisting of the whole island of Ireland. Rather than surveying literary production in this time span, I focus on selected literary works as part of an effort to craft an accessible narrative about the shifts in thinking and talking about Northern Ireland's still-divided society which made the Agreement possible. I argue that history and literature in this time and place are so intertwined that a genuine understanding of either requires that they be considered together, and I hope that increased public awareness of how the peace was made might inform ongoing debates about Northern Ireland's future and the role of creative writers in the crucial projects of achieving social reconciliation and a more inclusive sense of Northern Irish identity.

John Hume—leader of the nationalist Social Democratic and Labour Party (SDLP), member of both the British and European Parliaments, and a prime mover of the peace process—once remarked that 'political leadership' involves 'changing the language of others', and scholar and filmmaker Maurice Fitzpatrick has highlighted 'Hume's abiding belief that modifying the language of others would establish peace in Northern Ireland'.[5] Such a belief chimes with Friel's 1982 framing of the problem of Ireland's relation with Britain as a problem of language: 'we are in fact talking about accommodation or marrying of two cultures here, which are ostensibly speaking the same language but which in fact aren't'. Because Friel believed that the political crisis manifesting itself in the Troubles had originated in language, he also believed it might be 'solved by language in some kind of way'.[6] His claim struck me as hyperbolic when I first encountered it in the early 1990s, but it seems less so in retrospect. Eugene McNamee, Head of the School of Law at the University of Ulster, argues persuasively that Field Day and its critics in the 1980s and 1990s engaged in 'a productive antagonistic cultural politics' characterized by 'its lack of resolution', which helped to create 'the conditions of possibility for political change'. Specifically, the disputants' 'decoupling of the idea of citizenship from the idea of defined territory' (a concept also central to Hume's thinking about possible solutions to Northern Ireland's enduring Troubles) prepared the way for the Agreement approved in April 1998.[7]

Similarities between Hume's analysis of Northern Ireland's situation in the 1980s and 1990s and that of writers connected with Field Day were probably not coincidental. He was, after all, close friends with both Friel and Heaney and socially acquainted with Deane, and he regularly attended Field Day opening nights.[8] Nor were these relationships between Field Day members and Hume the only link between authors whose works feature in this book and prominent political figures. Deane, who taught secondary school in Derry immediately after completing his undergraduate degree at Queen's University Belfast, had a pupil named Martin McGuinness. McGuinness—who went on to become a leader of the Irish Republican Army (IRA) and, later, of Sinn Féin, the party which eventually convinced militant republicans to trade arms for politics—ended his career by serving for a decade as Deputy First Minister of the Northern Ireland Executive.[9] Although I cannot prove direct influence, I believe there was productive interaction between political and literary spheres in Northern Ireland during the period (the early 1980s through 1998) primarily under examination here. My evidence for this conviction comes from the literary works discussed in this book, which, I argue, were clearly written with political intent. By analysing literary texts within a detailed historical frame, I illuminate aspects of these works that have hitherto been obscured by critical underestimation of the extent to which their authors were motivated by a desire both to comment on and to intervene in unfolding political situations. I also use these texts to enhance readers' understanding of historical developments and to help inform their assessment of the present.

To people unfamiliar with Irish history, examining creative writing to glean political insights may seem an odd tactic. However, in the case of the Belfast Agreement signed on Good Friday in 1998, progress hinged on the negotiators' ability to revise the terms used to discuss the conflict. As cultural commentator Fintan O'Toole remarked shortly after the Agreement was approved, the British and Irish governments, in nudging the parties towards consensus, were required 'to act more like poets and novelists than like politicians: massaging fixed meanings so that they become supple and fluid; complicating the definitions of words so that they become open and ambiguous'.[10] Albert Reynolds, Taoiseach (prime minister) of the Republic of Ireland from 1992 to 1994, confirms O'Toole's insight in his autobiography, asserting that 'Archaic language was the problem, the expression of ideologies buried in history.' He believed at the time that resolving unionists' and nationalists' 'opposing views on the principles of consent and self-determination' would be 'central to any agreement'.[11]

Describing an important stage of the peace process, during which he and his top adviser on Northern Ireland, Martin Mansergh, were secretly exchanging documents with the Sinn Féin leadership, Reynolds recounts how 'With painstaking care phrases, words, the placing of a comma, a full stop, would be analysed so that they exactly and meticulously expressed the philosophy, policy and aspirations of Sinn Féin. At the same time they needed to take into account the concerns of the Unionists, the demands and rigours of the British and Irish constitutions, and the innumerable agendas and agreements at the root of the Troubles. Everything was challenged, amended, suspended in a hundred different ways as progress alternately inched forward and stalled'. This high-stakes writerly negotiation between Irish nationalists and republicans was itself the prelude to an even more strenuous one between the British and Irish governments over the wording of what would become known as the Downing Street Declaration of December 1993. On the final day of these intergovernmental talks, Reynolds recalled, 'tensions were high as we battled with revising, refining, balancing and counter-balancing the text of the joint declaration. It was imperative it was acceptable to both Republicans and Unionists or all our aspirations for peace would be lost, our hopes for an end to violence would be dashed—all our efforts wasted.'[12]

A vital element of the peace process involved framing an agreement that could be interpreted in different ways by unionists and nationalists. Literary writers and critics are comfortable with precisely this kind of ambiguity, and expert in creating and analysing texts that support divergent readings. On 22 May 1998, the day it was endorsed by referendums in Northern Ireland and the Republic, Michael Longley stated that 'In its language the Good Friday Agreement depended on an almost poetic precision and suggestiveness to get its complicated message across.'[13] Additionally, the literary works I scrutinize in *Getting to Good Friday* offer an emotional chronicle of a fraught time in Northern Ireland, showing present-day readers how people in the period leading up to the 1998 Agreement felt and thought about contemporary events. Attitudes were changing rapidly then, but often by minute degrees. Brief factual accounts of what happened in the late 1980s and early 1990s often do not address *how* and *why* it happened. Literature can help to answer such questions.

The peace process in Northern Ireland remains unfinished business, as events in recent years have emphasized. The 2016 Brexit referendum undermined a key basis of the Agreement—the European Union (EU) membership of both the Republic of Ireland and the UK—and reopened questions that had long been regarded as closed by raising the spectre of a hard border once again dividing the island of Ireland.[14] This threat exacerbated problems inherent in the Northern Ireland governmental bodies created by the Agreement, which, as historian Ian McBride notes, '[b]y institutionalizing cross-community consensus as the basis of decision making…also inadvertently institutionalized the communal division deplored by so many of the individuals and groups who actively tried to make

Northern Ireland a more equal, tolerant, and peaceful society'.[15] The predictable result of this 'consociational' governmental design has been aptly described as a 'sectarian carve-up' rather than genuine co-operation between unionist and nationalist members of coalition governments there, and practical difficulties with the institutions' operation have resulted in the Agreement being amended on five separate occasions—most recently in 2020, after a three-year suspension of the regional arrangements caused by an impasse between the largest unionist and nationalist parties in the Northern Ireland Assembly, the Democratic Unionist Party (DUP) and Sinn Féin, which had controlled the Northern Ireland Executive since 2007.[16] That 2017 suspension was triggered by Sinn Féin's withdrawal from the Executive. As I write this introduction, the DUP has just collapsed the Executive by withdrawing from it to protest post-Brexit customs checks on goods coming into Northern Ireland from Britain.[17] It remains to be seen what longer-term effects this action might have on Northern Ireland's institutions or constitutional status.

The fact that 'the devolved institutions that were supposed to be its principal achievement remained in cold storage' when the Belfast Agreement marked its twentieth anniversary probably contributed to the ambivalent tone of some appraisals of it at that time and shortly afterwards, as social scientists Colin Coulter, Niall Gilmartin, Katy Hayward, and Peter Shirlow point out. Their own 2021 book, *Northern Ireland a Generation After Good Friday*, draws attention to the discrepancy between the rosy lens through which Northern Ireland's peace agreement tends to be viewed internationally and its messy workings at home.[18] In *The Good Friday Agreement* (2018), journalist Siobhan Fenton similarly stressed the extent to which the establishment of peace in Northern Ireland had not resulted in a cohesive society. Catholics and Protestants still, for the most part, lived, worked, and socialized separately. More than 90 per cent of primary and secondary schools were identified with one side or the other, and a similar percentage of people married within their community. 'Peace walls' still divided Protestant and Catholic areas from each other in the parts of Belfast where Troubles-era violence had been most pervasive. Meanwhile, the crude division of political influence between Catholic nationalists and Protestant unionists took little account of other kinds of identity and politics (environmental, economic, feminist, LGBT, and generational, for example) existing in Northern Ireland. Moreover, the general lack of political will to deal definitively with so-called 'legacy issues' pertaining to the Troubles meant that the conflict continued to play out in the cultural and political arenas. Fenton's work covering efforts by the families of Troubles-era victims to learn exactly what happened to their loved ones or to see the perpetrators prosecuted led her to the conclusion that 'Although the civil war has ended, it cannot be said to be truly over.'[19]

Notwithstanding the justice of such critiques, however, one overwhelming fact remains: the Belfast/Good Friday Agreement, as Fenton allowed, had 'proven a phenomenal success in doing what had previously been thought impossible by ending the horrors of the Troubles'.[20] Indeed, Coulter and his co-authors cite an estimate that 'at the time of its twentieth anniversary there were approximately 2,400 Northern Irish people alive and well who would have been long since cold in the grave had the peace deal never materialised'.[21] My book's title reflects my appreciation of this achievement, together with my sense that Northern Ireland has not yet reaped the full benefits of the peace. For Christian readers (Catholic and Protestant alike), Good Friday has a specific penitential resonance. It is a step on the road to a better dispensation, not a desired destination itself.

My experience of living in Belfast as a US Fulbright Scholar during the first seven months of 2017 showed me both how much things have changed in the North since I began visiting in the late 1980s and how they have remained the same. At Queen's University Belfast, I taught an undergraduate seminar on literary responses to the peace process in Northern Ireland and found, to my surprise, that I knew more about the Troubles than my students did. They had been toddlers when the Agreement was signed and had heard little about the conflict from their elders. It was obvious that class members were deeply divided along the old sectarian/political lines yet also extremely reluctant to discuss their different experiences and assumptions. My older friends in Belfast were voting for the more moderate nationalist and unionist parties or for unaligned parties, but my students could not seem to imagine any alternative to the hardline parties (Sinn Féin and the DUP) that had dominated politics in the North for over a decade—even though Northern Ireland's power-sharing executive had just fallen apart over the partners' manifest inability or unwillingness to continue to work together. Outside the classroom, visits to the working-class areas where Troubles-era violence had been most intense gave me the dispiriting sense that much popular commemoration of that period in those places was of a sort more likely to nurture partisan resentment than a future in which the two sides could once again cooperate for their common good. Recovering that hopeful possibility will require a better public understanding of the concessions and mental adjustments made by both unionists and nationalists to enable peace to be established in 1998. This book is my contribution towards that end.

Getting to Good Friday is informed by archival research and personal communication with the writers whose work I examine in it, so it contains much that I hope will interest scholars approaching the field of Irish Studies from various disciplines. However, I also want this book to be useful to readers who have not been pondering Northern Ireland for years, so a few definitions are in order. The first and most important thing to know is that practically everything having to do with politics in Northern Ireland is contentious. The basic political obstacle there is that unionists think of themselves as British and want Northern Ireland to stay in the UK, while nationalists think of themselves as Irish and would prefer that it become part of the Republic of Ireland. For a heady couple of decades, it looked like the whole issue of nationality could be finessed by the fact that both the UK and Ireland belonged to the EU, which was pursuing a path of greater integration among its member states. Sadly, that is no longer the case, as the UK left the EU in 2020 and, in the process, reinvigorated the old 'national question' in (Northern) Ireland.

An Irish nationalist is someone who views Ireland as culturally distinct from Great Britain and believes that this cultural difference should be given political expression of some sort. An Irish republican favours the complete independence of Ireland from Britain, regards the entire island of Ireland as one natural political unit, and advocates a republican form of government. All Irish republicans are Irish nationalists, but not all Irish nationalists are Irish republicans. Irish republicans take a harder position on the national question, but not all of them believe that violence is justified in the republican cause—I use the term 'militant republicans' to refer to those who do. 'Constitutional nationalists', on the other hand, support the idea of a united Ireland but advocate working for constitutional change only through democratic and diplomatic means. In the period covered by *Getting to Good Friday* (primarily the early 1980s through 1998), the constitutional nationalist label applied to the SDLP in Northern Ireland, led by John Hume throughout this time, as well as to most political parties in the rest of Ireland. Sinn Féin, a republican party operating throughout the island of Ireland, was associated with the IRA and led by Gerry Adams and Martin McGuinness during these years.

On the unionist side, the largest party in this period was the Ulster Unionist Party (UUP), led by James Molyneaux before early September 1995 and by David Trimble afterwards. The DUP, its main rival, was more uncompromising on the national question as well as more socially conservative; it was led throughout the period covered in this book (and, indeed, throughout the first thirty-seven years of its existence) by Ian Paisley, also the founder and leader of the fundamentalist Free Presbyterian Church of Ulster. The term 'loyalist' denotes a harder-line unionist, much as a 'republican' is a harder-line nationalist; thus, it is customary to speak of republican and loyalist paramilitary groups rather than nationalist and unionist ones. The Northern Ireland Office (NIO) is a UK government department based in London and Belfast and responsible for Northern Ireland affairs; during the period discussed in this book, it ran Northern Ireland under 'direct rule' until 1999 and at intervals thereafter when local political arrangements ceased to function. The Secretary of State for Northern Ireland, who oversees the NIO, is a cabinet member of the British government.

The political situation was and remains so fraught that unionists and nationalists cannot even agree on what to call the place in which they live. The island of Ireland contains thirty-two counties: twenty-six of these are in the country known today as 'Ireland' (I usually refer to this country as 'the Republic', short for 'the Republic of Ireland', to distinguish it from Northern Ireland), and the other six constitute Northern Ireland (part of the United Kingdom of Great Britain and Northern Ireland). Ulster is one of the four historic provinces of Ireland. It consisted of nine counties, only six of which make up Northern Ireland. Nevertheless, many Protestants/unionists refer to Northern Ireland as 'Ulster'—a label I have learned to avoid because (like 'the province') it is so clearly identified with a unionist perspective. A 'republican' name for Northern Ireland is 'the six counties' (or, more polemically, 'the occupied six counties'). 'Northern Ireland' is a unionist-tinged term, while 'the North (of Ireland)' is nationalist-tinged, but both are more neutral than the names discussed above, and I use them interchangeably.

An Ulster Protestant is simply a Protestant from Ulster. Such people can be found in both Northern Ireland and the Republic. More commonly, though, the term refers to a Protestant living in Northern Ireland—who might, or might not, be a unionist. (Protestant nationalists have long played a significant role in Irish history. Catholic unionists tend to be less prominent and vocal, but they also exist.) Green is the Irish national colour (one name for Ireland is the Emerald Isle). Hence, to call something 'green' is to imply that it is nationalist. Similarly, orange is the colour associated with Irish Protestants since the Protestant Dutch prince William of Orange (who became the English monarch William III after the Glorious Revolution of 1688) defeated the deposed Catholic King James II at the Battle of the Boyne in Ireland in 1690, an event commemorated annually in Northern Ireland (and elsewhere) by the Protestant and unionist Orange Order.[22]

In the interest of readability, I have tried to limit references to one or two per paragraph; all my sources are documented in endnotes. The introduction to a scholarly book (which this is, although I wrote it to be accessible to non-academics) typically includes an overview of its contents. Readers wishing to preserve the suspense of the narrative should feel free to skip the next couple of pages.

Chapter One ('Storytelling') focuses on constitutional nationalists' search in the mid-1980s for a way out of the deadlock of typical Northern Irish politics, with special attention given to *Making History* (1988), Friel's play about Hugh O'Neill, leader of an Irish rebellion against Queen Elizabeth I. Friel emphasizes O'Neill's English education, marriage to the daughter of an English colonist, and policy of co-operating with colonial authority, which alternated with armed resistance to England. I contend that this depiction of the nationalist icon complemented John Hume's contemporaneous efforts to demonstrate to Protestants that they had nothing to fear from a united Ireland and to persuade republicans to engage politically rather than militarily. Historical events discussed include the New Ireland Forum (1983–4) and the Anglo–Irish Agreement (1985), both of which, I suggest, helped to shape the development of the play. I draw extensively in this chapter on the National Library of Ireland's Friel archive to illustrate the dynamic interplay between authorial intent and circumstance in the work of a politically engaged and motivated writer at a crucial juncture in Ireland's history.

The narrative arc of Chapter Two ('Understanding') concerns attempts by constitutional nationalists, some republican leaders, and the British and Irish governments, from 1986 through 1994, to convince the IRA to end its military campaign. I examine key issues involved, with reference to works by Seamus Heaney and Michael Longley which approach the then contemporary politics of Northern Ireland through the classics. Heaney's *The Cure at Troy* (1990), a Northern Irish vernacular version of a Sophocles play, centres on the feud between the Greek hero Philoctetes and former comrades who abandoned him on their way to the Trojan War. I argue that their rapprochement can be interpreted as a metaphor for the uniting of militant and constitutional nationalists at this time, although unionist allegorical readings are equally plausible. The chapter also highlights the hope and anxiety that seized Northern Ireland's people during the lead-up to the IRA's 'cessation of military operations' in August 1994 through Longley's Homeric poem 'Ceasefire'. The title of Longley's poem, arguably its only topical feature, perfectly encapsulates the uncertainty of the moment.

Chapter Three ('Grieving') opens with a description of reactions to the paramilitary ceasefires announced in the summer and autumn of 1994. Along with relief and joy at the suspension of the fighting, people felt anger about the lengthy conflict and sorrow for lost loved ones. In lieu of the historical narrative that grounds the previous chapters, this one explores Deirdre Madden's *One by One in the Darkness* and Seamus Deane's *Reading in the Dark*, texts dealing with the lingering effects of personal and political trauma. These novels, conceived as responses to the Troubles and written largely before 1994, were both published in 1996. I argue that they express the grief felt by many in the North, after the exhilaration that greeted the ceasefires faded, for the human cost of the decades of conflict. Madden's novel focuses on the late twentieth-century Troubles and Deane's on the shadows cast by the Troubles of the 1920s, but both illustrate the scale of the damage caused by political injustice and civil strife, as well as the stakes of the peace process.

Chapter Four ('Repeating') examines Bernard MacLaverty's novel *Grace Notes* (1997), about a female composer from Northern Ireland, to shed light on the political impasse that persisted for several years after the 1994 ceasefires. The book contains some overt political commentary—the composer, a Catholic like MacLaverty, writes music that incorporates traditional Protestant drums, thus weaving a symbol of unionist oppression of the Catholic minority into a harmonious representation of Northern Irish identity. However, most of the novel seems more personal in nature, focusing on the protagonist's difficult relationships with her mother, dead father, and the father of her child. Set at an unspecified time in the 1980s, *Grace Notes* refers only obliquely to the Troubles and not at all to the peace process. Nonetheless, it reflects through its form the tensions of the period in which it was written (1994-6), with personal interactions serving as metaphors for the tense political situation and the kind of honest and respectful communication that would be required to improve it. The narrative sections of this chapter introduce another important historical figure: David Trimble, who would go on to lead the UUP in the negotiations and head the first power-sharing government created by the Belfast Agreement. These actions could hardly have been predicted in the period covered by Chapter Four, however, when Trimble rose to prominence as a spokesman for hardline unionists during the contentious 'marching seasons' of 1995 and 1996.

Chapter Five ('Drafting') describes the political negotiations that resulted in the Belfast Agreement signed on Good Friday in 1998. Colum McCann's novel *TransAtlantic* (2013), which includes American mediator George Mitchell among its characters, highlights the role of writing as both the medium of and a metaphor for the peace process—a literary insight confirmed in autobiographical accounts by talks participants, as well as in histories and scholarly analyses of the negotiations. While celebrating what the negotiators achieved, this chapter also indicates issues left unresolved by the Agreement.

The conclusion ('Truth-Seeking') focuses on Northern Ireland's immediate post-conflict milieu and the lingering effects of the Troubles through a close examination of David Park's novel *The Truth Commissioner* (2008), which employs five distinct points of view and a limited third-person narration to emphasize the difference perspective makes to any individual's experience and assessment of Northern Ireland's late-twentieth-century history. During the decade following the approval of the Belfast Agreement, there was considerable public speculation about the possibility of Northern Ireland implementing a comprehensive truth-recovery process along the lines of South Africa's Truth and Reconciliation Commission. *The Truth Commissioner* presents Park's ambivalent vision of how such a body might function in practice. I end my discussion of it by suggesting that a novel may be more effective than a truth commission in reaching certain kinds of truth and promoting social understanding.

The 1998 Belfast/Good Friday Agreement accomplished the remarkable feat of establishing peace in Northern Ireland, but it should be seen as the beginning rather than the end of the challenging task of imagining a shared Northern Irish identity. In this endeavour, the contributions of artists will continue to be at least as important as initiatives by politicians. Creative writers tend to approach intractable problems with more questions than answers, and this disposition enables them to produce literary works that invite readers to explore perspectives very different from their own. My own methods in writing this book resembled those of the writers whose works I examine in it: I was writing towards understanding of something (how peace was made in Northern Ireland) that had baffled me at the start of the process. Like them, I did not know what I intended to say until I grappled with the concrete task of trying to say it. *Getting to Good Friday* does not have a thesis that can be neatly summarized in a sentence, but its form testifies to my faith in narrative as a means of comprehending complexity.

February 2022

1

Storytelling

Brian Friel, one of Ireland's best-known and highly regarded playwrights, surprised the theatre establishments of several countries in May 1980 when he announced that his next play would open, not in Dublin, London, or New York City, but in Derry, Northern Ireland, a city so disadvantaged that it lacked a dedicated theatre building. The production of *Translations* later that year launched the Field Day Theatre Company, founded by Friel and actor Stephen Rea. Immediately hailed as a national classic, *Translations* was soon claimed as a seminal work of postcolonial literature as well, and Field Day, a critical as well as an artistic enterprise, set the agenda for cultural discussion in Ireland for more than a decade, attracting both fervent support and fierce criticism.[1] *Making History*, Friel's last script for Field Day, premièred on 20 September 1988. By then, Field Day openings were renowned for their ability, against a backdrop of civil unrest, to attract political, religious, artistic, and media celebrities from both sides of the Irish border, Britain, and places even farther afield to Derry's Victorian Guildhall, which for these occasions took on 'an aura of first-night magnificence' at odds with 'its total unsuitability as a…performance venue'.[2] Among the dignitaries assembled that night in September were two Derry natives integral to the peace process, already tentatively underway.[3] One, Friel's friend John Hume, was a member of both the British and European parliaments and would be a principal architect of the Good Friday Agreement of 1998, which ended three decades of violence in Northern Ireland. The other, Martin McGuinness, had formerly been an Irish Republican Army (IRA) commander but would later serve as Deputy First Minister in a power-sharing Northern Ireland government. Let their mutual inclusion in Field Day's audience serve as a reminder, if one is needed, that the literary and political realms of Irish public life, like the natural and supernatural worlds of Irish folklore, lie close together and frequently intersect—and that those seeking to understand both must examine them together.

Making History is both a history and a meta-history play, both a popular historical drama with a political subtext and a self-reflexive meditation on history as storytelling. Friel takes as his subject the bicultural early modern Irish leader Hugh O'Neill, a Gaelic chieftain who also held an English title and represented, for a time, the best hope of the European Counter-Reformation. O'Neill is celebrated by Irish nationalists as the mastermind of the Gaelic aristocracy's last stand against English colonization; his 1601 defeat at the Battle of Kinsale and subsequent exile from Ireland cleared the way for the seventeenth-century Plantation

Getting to Good Friday: Literature and the Peace Process in Northern Ireland. Marilynn Richtarik, Oxford University Press.
© Marilynn Richtarik 2023. DOI: 10.1093/oso/9780192886408.003.0002

of Ulster, to which may be traced the roots of Northern Ireland's divided society. Friel's drama, however, focuses on his brief marriage to an English settler named Mabel Bagenal. Academic critics of *Making History* have observed that, far from replacing heroic myth with less heroic truth (as a naïve reading of it might suggest), Friel deliberately replaced one historical myth with another.[4] Friel's factual distortions in the play are neither incidental nor accidental, but there has been insufficient attention paid to the nature of the story he used the play to tell and to his reasons for telling it. A fuller understanding of *Making History* will result from the recognition that Friel wanted not only to consider the writing of history, or to rewrite it himself, but to help *make* it through storytelling. Friel's dramaturgical decisions during the four years he spent writing *Making History* also advanced his political aim of demonstrating that division along sectarian lines need not be a defining feature of political life in Ireland. As another Northern Irish playwright, Stewart Parker, remarked about his own play *Northern Star* (1984), centred on a leader of another failed Irish rebellion, 'this is not an historical play', although set centuries in the past, but 'very much a play about today'.[5]

Friel sought, as James Joyce had done before him, 'to forge in the smithy of my soul the uncreated conscience of my race'.[6] Field Day, for him, offered a way to channel both his own and other artists' efforts towards that end. Friel once described his writing process as a means of thinking through subjects about which he felt radically uncertain: 'You don't have anything to say about anything. You delve into a particular corner of yourself that's dark and uneasy, and you articulate the confusions and the unease of that particular period'.[7] His papers, donated to the National Library of Ireland (NLI) in 2000, corroborate this self-assessment. Friel drafted individual scenes of *Making History* by hand, shifting to typescript only at an advanced stage of composition, and the NLI archive also preserves Friel's extensive notes towards the play, which show how his thinking about it evolved. His working papers thus bear witness to the dynamic interplay between authorial intent and circumstance in the work of a politically engaged and motivated writer at a crucial juncture in his country's history. Friel's notes reveal him to be feeling his way through a particularly volatile period, often unsure about where he was headed both politically and artistically. His relentless self-questioning allowed him to write a play that spoke to disparate publics during a critical time.

Like the Irish Literary Revival at the turn of the twentieth century, the artistic and critical collective known as Field Day emerged largely as a response to political stagnation. Since the 1974 collapse of the first power-sharing government in Northern Ireland, there had been no plausible initiative to bridge the gap between unionists, who favoured the continuation of the union with Great Britain, and nationalists, who instead saw their desired future in terms of a united Ireland.[8] As bleak as the situation had seemed then, it looked much worse by 1981, when Friel and Rea invited filmmaker David Hammond and poet-critics Seamus Heaney,

Seamus Deane, and Tom Paulin to join them on Field Day's board of directors. Between October 1980 and October 1981, two protracted hunger strikes by republican prisoners intended to underline their demand for political status had had the effect of greatly increasing sympathy, if not support, for the IRA among Northern Catholics, as the striking prisoners (ten of whom eventually died) 'articulated a tribal voice of martyrdom, deeply embedded in the Gaelic, Catholic Nationalist tradition'.[9] Constitutional nationalists like Friel, who did not consider violence conducive to achieving any positive political end, regarded this development with alarm. In a letter to the new Field Day directors in September 1981, Friel noted that one of the ideas he and Rea had for the company was that it might find 'some means of celebrating the best of the Northern Protestant tradition'.[10] Garret FitzGerald, then Taoiseach (prime minister) of the Republic of Ireland, seemed to be thinking along similar lines when he announced on 27 September 1981 his intent to lead 'a republican crusade, to make this a genuine republic'. He regarded as a basic obstacle to a united Ireland the fact that the Irish state 'is itself sectarian—not in the acutely sectarian way Northern Ireland was, in which Catholics were repressed', but in the sense that 'our laws and our constitution, our practices, our attitudes reflect those of a majority ethos and are not acceptable to Protestants in Northern Ireland'. Changing these could create a basis 'on which many Protestants in Northern Ireland would be willing to consider a relationship with us'.[11]

During the hunger strikes, Sinn Féin had begun contesting elections, soon afterwards formally adopting a policy of fielding candidates for Westminster and Northern Ireland elections, while at the same time continuing to endorse the IRA's military campaign. Both the British government and the constitutional nationalist Social Democratic and Labour Party (SDLP) began to fear a scenario in which Sinn Féin would surpass the SDLP as the voice of Northern nationalists. SDLP leader John Hume approached FitzGerald (Taoiseach again after a hiatus through most of 1982) with the idea for a forum 'where all constitutional politicians committed to a new Ireland would together define what we really wish this new Ireland to be'. Specifically, Hume asked parties in the Republic to 'join with us in abandoning rhetoric and, by placing their cards on the table, show what sort of role there will be for the Protestant community'.[12]

The New Ireland Forum met for a year between May 1983 and May 1984. The four major constitutional nationalist parties on the island—Fine Gael, Labour, Fianna Fáil, and the SDLP—participated, representing over 90 per cent of nationalists in Ireland as a whole. The body's deliberation on ways to unify Ireland peacefully was theoretical rather than practical because it excluded Sinn Féin for refusing to renounce violence as a tactic and because the various unionist parties declined to take part. Nevertheless, it manifested a new pragmatism among nationalists about the actual barriers to a united Ireland. Thinking in concrete terms about what a reconstituted Ireland might realistically look like, forum participants shifted the debate, as historian Jeremy Smith remarks, 'away from notions of ownership and conquest, towards reconciliation and accommodation'.[13] Hume later commented, 'We had for too long stressed this essential unity of Ireland but forgotten about its equally essential diversity.' The forum, therefore, needed 'to forge a new, unheard-of, generous definition of Irishness which would include—not exclude—everything that was encompassed in being a Northern Protestant, including a sense of British identity'.[14]

Field Day, too, had publicly committed itself to creating a sense of Irishness which could gain assent throughout the island. A distinctive feature of the company was its symbolic rejection of both the Republic of Ireland and the United Kingdom in favour of a political entity that did not yet exist. As Friel explained to Fintan O'Toole in 1982, 'You can't deposit fealty to a situation like the Northern situation that you don't believe in. Then you look south of the border and that enterprise is in so many ways distasteful.' He thought the Republic 'could be adjusted and...could be made very exciting. But...it requires the Northern thing to complete it. I'm talking about the whole Northern thing.' Declaring his faith in 'the possibility of a cultural whole available to us', Friel elaborated, 'How to achieve that and how to contribute to that is one of the big problems'. When O'Toole asked directly if Field Day's project depended on 'political nationalism and on the achievement of a united Ireland', Friel replied coyly, 'I think it should lead to a cultural state, not a political state. And I think out of that cultural state, a possibility of a political state follows.'[15]

In keeping with the welcoming spirit that also animated the New Ireland Forum, Field Day devoted considerable energy in the mid-1980s to efforts to reach Northern Protestants, although, owing to the delay between deciding to do something and the fruits of that decision, many of these initiatives were not apparent at the time. By the spring of 1982, for example, Field Day had commissioned a play from David Rudkin, a Protestant residing in England who had strong family connections to Northern Ireland, for the company's 1983 tour. Unfortunately, the play Rudkin wrote, *The Saxon Shore*, unnerved several of the directors with both its technical demands and its nationalist message, which seemed too overt to them to serve their purpose, and, at its June 1983 meeting, the board decided not to produce the play.[16] That November, however, the company published Heaney's *Sweeney Astray*, a translation of the medieval Irish narrative *Buile Suibhne*, which annoyed some purists owing to the poet's decision to use Anglicized place-names because he 'wanted the Unionist population to feel that they could adhere to it, that something could be shared', if only names and landscapes.[17]

Field Day had begun publishing pamphlets, as well, by 1983. The first three of these, issued in 1983, were received as nationalist statements, leading Friel to worry that Field Day was not successfully reaching a Northern Protestant and/or unionist readership and to ask how the company might change that.[18] Accordingly, at its September 1984 meeting, the board decided to focus on the Protestant idea of liberty in Field Day's third set of pamphlets, published in 1985.[19] By the mid-1980s, Friel and Rea were also concerned about the fact that predominantly Protestant venues were dropping off the Field Day tour route. In an effort to reverse this trend, they urged Stewart Parker in March 1984 to write a play for the company; when his *Pentecost* was eventually produced, in 1987, it proved to be one of Field Day's most successful productions, both critically and financially.[20] These various Field Day initiatives preoccupied Friel during the period he was working on *Making History*, and that play expressed his desire to help persuade Northern Protestants that they had more in common with Northern Catholics than with the rest of the British population—even, ideally, to help them recognize that, in some ways at least, they were Irish themselves.

The inspiration for *Making History* probably came to Friel in the spring of 1983, when he read Seamus Deane's contribution to the first set of Field Day pamphlets, *Civilians and Barbarians*.[21] Deane traces the colonialist imagery of English 'civilization' versus Irish 'barbarism' from the sixteenth through the late twentieth century, and his analysis likely reminded Friel of Sean O'Faolain's book *The Great O'Neill*, which had made a significant impression on him years before.[22] In this biography of O'Neill, O'Faolain anticipates the attitudes of revisionist historians and cultural critics, as well as those of scholars with a postcolonial perspective. Initially attracted by O'Neill's status as a nationalist hero, O'Faolain proclaims in his preface that his investigation led him to the conclusion that 'The traditional picture of the patriot O'Neill, locked into the Gaelic world, eager to assault England, is not supported by the facts and must be acknowledged a complete fantasy.' He instead told a more complicated story about an intelligent leader intimately acquainted with both English and Irish culture, using O'Neill's life to illustrate 'the fact that in England's decision to make Ireland her first real colony two civilizations became interlocked that were in spirit utterly divergent':

> It is the same forced juncture of modernity and antiquity that comes with every imperial conquest, whether it is the conquest of Mexico by the Spaniards, or the colonization of India by the Hanoverians, or the plantation of Ireland by the Tudors.... In the final stage of all nothing remains but the oversimplified story of the victor and the oversimplified memories of the defeated, both of them unfaithful to the always confused and occasionally troubled split-mindedness of the time.[23]

O'Faolain saw O'Neill as the prototypical modern Irishman, 'painfully caught in a dual loyalty.'[24] The English, vastly outnumbered in Ireland, maintained their position as a colonial power through a policy of co-opting Gaelic aristocrats known as Surrender and Regrant (as Friel's O'Neill explains this in the play, in return for the 'token gesture' of 'a public profession of...loyalty and obedience', the English monarch offered local leaders 'formal acknowledgement and recognition' of their authority) coupled with careful attention to the balance of power among these proxies.[25] O'Neill, who lived from about 1550 to 1616, held both English and Irish titles. In 1587, Queen Elizabeth I proclaimed him Earl of Tyrone and gave him control of a territory encompassing much of present-day Northern Ireland; in 1595, after openly rebelling against his English masters, he became The O'Neill, leader of a legendary line of Gaelic chieftains, and the nucleus for the first groping movements of the Irish towards a concept of national identity.[26] Ironically, it was O'Neill's early and extensive exposure to English thought and culture that gave him the perspective to imagine a similar status for Ireland.

O'Faolain's narrative focuses on his subject's self-division, the way in which O'Neill was torn between his respectful comprehension of English Renaissance modes of social and political organization and his abiding fondness for Gaelic culture. In some of his earliest notes towards his play, Friel registers O'Neill's understanding that 'The persistent & mostly genuinely held English belief was that they were leading a medieval people to "civility"—to modernise their customs, to introduce the Protestant faith, to make a modern state—all three notions being in part synonymous.' Reflecting on O'Faolain's indictment of the Gaelic culture's 'inflexibility', which made it vulnerable to obliteration in the dawning modern era, Friel decided that 'this must be close to the kernel of the play: the recognition of—and indeed the demonstrated (theatrically) love for—the old ways & the recognition of the demands of change.'[27]

O'Faolain saw O'Neill's political wiliness as integral to his achievements as a military strategist because—with one fateful exception—he did not let his desire to win battles obscure his larger long-term goal of achieving security and autonomy for himself and his allies. Thus, repeatedly during the Nine Years War he led against the English in Ireland from 1595 to 1603, he sued for peace and pardon just when he seemed to be winning. O'Faolain perceived that 'His tactic was that of a leader of armies which fought in comparatively small groups as guerillas wasting the enemy. He wasted their energy, their money, their time. A military victory in the sense of a vast overthrow of numbers by numbers was always out of the question.' O'Neill 'was the first to grasp this fact: an able politician and an able general, and the only big man in all Irish history from beginning to end of that dual order'.[28] Queen Elizabeth I accepted these hypocritical surrenders because, while O'Neill maintained control of his own territory, his nominal allegiance represented her only claim to that part of Ulster. Sadly, from this perspective, O'Neill is best known for his uncharacteristic decision to launch a frontal assault on English forces at the Battle of Kinsale in December 1601, resulting in a disastrous defeat that determined the outcome of the war—and sounded the death knell for the old Gaelic order in Ireland. Contemplating this loss in January 1984, Friel wondered, 'If Kinsale marked the end of Irish independence in any form for three centuries, what was determining about the event?' He decided at this time that his

O'Neill would 'have to discuss the pursuit of his aims by diplomacy (politics) & arms'.[29]

In December 1601, much of the pressure on O'Neill stemmed from the invading Spanish fleet's choice of Kinsale, in the extreme south of Ireland, as its landing point. O'Neill's hopes for an outright military victory hinged on such foreign intervention, but Spain's interests and his own did not entirely align. If the Spanish had been as focused as he on consolidating control of Ireland, they would have landed in the north or west of the island, where the native population was already roused against the English colonists. Instead, they were thinking beyond the Irish campaign to an intended invasion of England.[30] The incident illustrates the ambiguous position in which O'Neill found himself by the end of the sixteenth century as a leader of the Counter-Reformation because the financial and military aid he received from both Spain and the Pope came with strings attached.

Nevertheless, O'Faolain saw Catholicism in this period as a useful 'coagulant' of O'Neill's Irish confederacy and a conduit to broader streams of thought. As a Europeanist who deplored the insular nationalism of his own newly independent Ireland, O'Faolain waxed poetic on this aspect of O'Neill's career:

> Fortunately for his country...he associated his struggle for independence with the whole movement of the Counter-Reformation, and that was a European idea and a European link, and it gave his people access to a great heritage of culture and tradition from which the principle of Development has never been absent. And whether or not they have exploited that European heritage to the full, so enlarging and fructifying, so colourful, so rich in urbanity and tolerance and discipline, and even in the hoary wisdom of the world, he did at any rate spin them that thread, and he did colour all future nationalism with its purple and gold.[31]

Here, more than on any other point, Friel found himself resisting O'Faolain's assessment of O'Neill's leadership, having observed in his own time and place how the amalgamation of Irish nationalism and Catholicism had deepened cultural and political divisions within Ireland. Whatever the merits of O'Neill's strategy in his time, Friel did not consider the continuing identification likely to result in any desirable future. This attitude would shape his own approach to O'Neill's biography in *Making History*.

Friel loved *The Great O'Neill*, which brings the Elizabethan world to life in all its complexity. Though not a professional historian, O'Faolain proved adept at reading between the lines of the surviving written record and describing the perceptions of O'Neill and his contemporaries. Skills developed as a fiction writer served him as a biographer, and his account of O'Neill's life is full of human interest: vivid settings, suspenseful action, penetrating psychological insights, and convincing characters. Unfortunately, as Friel discovered soon after deciding to write a play about him, O'Neill's life was dramatic in every way except the literal one. Its events sprawled over an awkwardly long period of time, involved a huge cast of characters from multiple countries, and took place in a series of milieus unfamiliar to modern audiences. Moreover, and most important, the conflict that primarily interested Friel was an internal one, played out within O'Neill's hybrid mind. The chieftain, in short, would make a compelling protagonist—for a novel.

The encyclopedic knowledge of O'Neill's life and times that informed Friel's thinking about the play also made it hard for him to render his subject's career intelligibly.[32] The more he knew about O'Neill, the less he could decide what to think about him; he had far too many conflicting ideas about the man to fit coherently into a two-hour drama. Friel's notes towards the play consist, to an extraordinary degree, of questions. Many of these recur at regular intervals, indicating that they remained open until a very late stage of the writing process. Apart from queries about his main characters' motivations, the most important concern structure and style. Friel wanted to convey both O'Neill's power at its height and his abjection in defeat, and he was attracted to both linear and retrospective modes of storytelling; the former had the advantage of suspense and immediacy, while the latter would afford audiences the critical hindsight with which to assess O'Neill's actions.

In his first set of notes, dated 7 December 1983, Friel hit upon the idea of setting Act 1 in O'Neill's 'pre-Kinsale full-power' and Act 2 'post-Kinsale'—the form the finished play eventually took—yet he continued to revisit the structural question for almost three additional years, until at least early October 1986, repeatedly weighing the possibility of setting the play after O'Neill's defeat and presenting events from earlier in his life through flashbacks. He returned frequently to a scene suggested by O'Faolain, in which an aged, drunken O'Neill, stranded in Rome after fleeing Ireland in 1607 with another Gaelic leader (an event known in Irish nationalist mythology as The Flight of the Earls), watches 'helplessly' as a Church official sharing his living quarters, Archbishop Lombard, writes a history that turns him 'into a star in the face of all the facts that had reduced him to poverty, exile, and defeat'.[33] Friel struggled to decide, however, what the main action of his drama should be. Stylistic questions also preoccupied him, and he considered various non-naturalistic modes of presentation to make his audience think as hard about O'Neill and his relevance to modern Ireland as he was doing.

After a few months of making notes towards his O'Neill play, Friel fastened on the dramatic possibilities represented by the chieftain's third wife, Mabel, who stood out from the others by virtue of her non-Gaelic lineage and upbringing. Half O'Neill's age and the daughter of the former Queen's Marshal in Ireland, Sir Nicholas Bagenal, who for nearly twenty years had blocked O'Neill's advancement within the English colonial system, a less likely mate for him could hardly have been imagined. Her brother Henry, the current Queen's Marshal, vehemently opposed the match, but the couple eloped in August 1591, less than eight months after O'Neill's second wife died. O'Faolain devotes a mere half-dozen pages to this marriage, characterizing it as a rare lapse in a life marked by self-discipline and self-interest and speculating that 'this inexperienced English girl may finally have seemed to [O'Neill's] humiliated eyes nothing but a silly little weakling when he realized that his passion had betrayed his pride into a mesalliance'.[34] Nicholas Canny, an academic authority on Irish history of the period, with whom Friel corresponded as part of the research for his drama, regards the marriage differently, as a failed power play—an attempt by O'Neill to align his interests with those of the Bagenal family that backfired because Henry never accepted the union.[35]

Friel thus deliberately departed from his sources in depicting O'Neill's marriage to Mabel as a genuine love match in *Making History*. This portrayal developed gradually, over several years. Adding Mabel to his contemplated cast of characters early in 1984 served less to introduce a love interest than as a way for Friel to externalize psychic action. Including a colonist who was also on intimate terms with O'Neill allowed the playwright to convey the cultural divisions of Elizabethan Ireland, and O'Neill's self-division, to an audience likely ignorant of both. At times, he focused on familiar binaries in thinking about the pair, musing in late February 1984 that 'If the heart of the play is the Mabel–Hugh relationship', she would have to represent 'Protestant', 'Ulster', 'England', while he stood for 'Catholic', 'Gaelic', 'Ireland'. But Friel also saw them as individuals 'subject to complementary historical imperatives', reflecting a month or so later that 'She is poised somewhere between her Newry colony and England', while 'He is poised somewhere between the dying Gaelic past and an unknowable future'.[36] By mid-April 1985, Friel had hit upon the idea of including Mabel's sister Mary as a character and shifting the burden of representing the official colonial attitude onto her, freeing Mabel to become a more complex, hybrid character like O'Neill.

The longer Friel thought about his O'Neill drama, the more convinced he became that 'Whatever historical burden the play has' would have to be 'carried by O'N & Mabel and indicated through their relationship. The play lives—or dies—in these two'.[37] His decision to centre the play on this relationship, however, entailed a seemingly intractable technical challenge because Mabel had died in 1595, when O'Neill's storied career as an Irish rebel and Counter-Reformation leader was effectively just beginning. From the time Friel decided to include Mabel as a primary character, he associated the end of O'Neill's marriage to her with the lost chance of a cultural synthesis in Ireland between the Gaels and the so-called New English similar to that which had taken place long before between Irish natives and the Old English settlers who had arrived in Ireland before the Reformation and intermarried with the locals. 'Why did she die in her fifth year of marriage?' he asked himself in late February 1984. The historical record provided no answer, but he imagined that she might have expired in childbirth or, perhaps, in attempting to abort the 'offspring of O'N. & herself'.[38] Discussion of abortion had dominated the Irish news throughout the spring and summer of 1983 after Fianna Fáil, then in opposition, proposed an amendment to the Constitution of Ireland banning abortion—already illegal in the country. The Dáil approved the proposal by eighty-seven votes to thirteen, and it was put to a referendum in early September, passing with a two-thirds majority and the strong support of the Catholic Church. This debate had thus provided a constant counterpoint to the proceedings of the New Ireland Forum during the first few months of its deliberations. The episode did not bode well for FitzGerald's call to make the Republic's laws and constitution more acceptable to Northern Protestants.[39]

Friel ultimately rejected the abortion possibility as 'too symbolic', but he assumed a breach between husband and wife over O'Neill's decision to fight against English rule in Ireland and to do so under the banner of the Counter-Reformation. He liked the idea of Mabel's confronting O'Neill after the Battle of the Yellow Ford in 1598 (a victory for O'Neill's forces in which her brother Henry was killed), seeing him off to Kinsale ('with curses'), or parting with him after his rout there. The problem with these notions, a significant one for Friel, was that 'Violence would have to be done to certain historical facts'.[40] In early April 1985, Friel still sought an actual span of O'Neill's life that would allow him to address the themes that interested him, and he returned to the year 1595, in which O'Neill had been proclaimed a traitor by the English and The O'Neill by the Irish, and at the end of which Mabel had died. He flirted with the idea of setting the play, or at least ending it, in the woods, after O'Neill, 'in powerful rebellion', destroyed his home to keep it from the English forces.[41] The difficulty this schema posed for him was that it did not encompass the aftermath of the war and O'Neill's humiliating defeat—in 1595, he enjoyed the upper hand.

Friel's indecision about how to proceed derailed the writing process at this juncture, but notes made in March 1985 reveal the way in which he then thought of O'Neill's marriage to Mabel, as

> an emblem of his being caught between Gaelic & New English, Gaelic & England, old order & new. Each trying & failing to understand the other....The marriage reflects the strains in the public, political & religious life. The marriage is the theatrical barometer. How far can he distance himself from the Gaelic order? How far from the English? To begin with, fairly distant from both—able to handle both. Then, as the situation deteriorates, he moves closer to Gaeldom— declared traitor, battles, The O'Neill, Tullyhogue; burning house; abortion; collapse of marriage etc.[42]

Without a clear vision of the structure within which this story of the marriage would fit, however, Friel stopped work on the play for the better part of ten months. He glanced at it in late November 1985, at which point he seemed to be leaning towards a 'retrospective' frame, but quickly concluded that 'The play has lost its centre, if it ever had one. It was being drawn into a Biography of O'Neill; too ambitious, too diffuse.' Moreover, 'It was inclining to the notion that the end of the Gaelic era, the Flight of the Earls etc. was due to a transient fling with Mabel, an insignificant daughter of a marshal.'[43]

This extended suspension of composition came at an opportune time, encompassing a period of rapid change on the political front initiated by the signing of the Anglo–Irish Agreement on 15 November 1985.[44] The agreement, which inaugurated what political scientists Paul Bew and Gordon Gillespie term 'an era of direct rule with a green tinge',[45] gave the Republic a say in Northern Ireland's affairs by establishing an Inter-Governmental Conference, headed by the British Secretary of State for Northern Ireland and the Irish Foreign Minister, to promote cross-border initiatives and deal with security, legal, and political issues affecting the North. Designed to overcome the alienation many Northern Catholics felt from British rule, this mechanism authorized the government of the Republic to represent the interests of the North's nationalist minority in such matters as discrimination and cultural expression. The British government affirmed that no change in the constitutional status of Northern Ireland would take place without the express consent of a majority of the population there and declared its eagerness to devolve authority to a power-sharing government in Northern Ireland.

As John Hume saw it, the accord 'gave recognition in an international agreement to the Irish identity of people living in Northern Ireland', 'committed the two sovereign governments to a process of ensuring equality between the two traditions', and 'contained an undertaking from the British government to comply fully with any wish for a united Ireland expressed by a majority of citizens there.'[46] Seamus Heaney later commented that ' "the spirit of the agreement" seemed to require and sponsor a candid coming and going between the domains of Britishness and Irishness'.[47] Sinn Féin, however, immediately denounced the pact as endorsing partition and the status quo in Northern Ireland, and the IRA intensified its military campaign in response. If some more moderate nationalists also felt suspicious or unsure about the agreement at first, the horrified reaction of most unionists offered reassurance that there must be something in it for them.

No unionist parties had been consulted or informed about the progress of the talks; indeed, the agreement was designed to be impervious to the sort of pressure that had toppled the short-lived power-sharing government brought down by a loyalist strike in 1974, and its workings relied on the cooperation of the British and Irish governments alone. Unionists were appalled that what they regarded as a foreign government would have any role in Northern Ireland and shocked that Margaret Thatcher, of all people, had entered into such an arrangement. They immediately began a lengthy protest campaign against the agreement: staging gigantic rallies, mounting unsuccessful legal challenges, and engaging in acts of civil disobedience which often crossed the line into outright lawlessness. Nothing unionists did had any appreciable effect on the British government, but they raged futilely against the Anglo–Irish Agreement throughout the rest of the time that Friel worked on his play, and the perceived change in the North's balance of power and upsurge in violence as a result had an impact on the script he was writing.

Another decisive influence on the play's development was Friel's reading of a review essay by Hayden White published in the *Times Literary Supplement* in late January 1986. In his survey of four books (by Paul Veyne, C. Behan McCullagh, José Ortega y Gasset, and Dominick La Capra) on the writing and philosophy of history, White emphasized the rhetorical, discursive elements of historical writing, the extent to which historians *construct* the past by narrative means rather than merely interpreting it. He summed up his analysis of the authors' reflections on the nature of historical knowledge thus:

> Historians have not in general been willing to acknowledge that their discourses may be more symbolic or, more precisely, more symbolizing operations than simply informative or explanatory.... [The] notion that historical facts were to be 'found' in the documents blocked a proper appreciation of the extent to which 'facts' are constructed out of reflection on 'events' by discursive means. In short, it is events that belong to objective reality; facts are constructions created by the subjection of events to the protocols of different discursive characterizations. This means that there can be as many valid, adequate, or even 'true' interpretations as there are different discursive protocols recognized in any given culture as permissible ways of making sense of the world. In this respect, even fiction can be said to deal in 'facts' even when the 'events' of which it speaks are openly admitted to be 'imaginary'. [48]

Friel must have found this last assertion reassuring because his 1980 play *Translations* had, over the past few years, been criticized for historical inaccuracy—a circumstance that likely exacerbated his misgivings about trying to write another history play, this time one based explicitly on a named historical figure.[49] At a symposium on *Translations* held in January 1983, Friel's best riposte had been that 'Drama is first a fiction, with the authority of fiction. You don't go to *Macbeth* for history.' White's insistence on the common grounding of history and fiction in subjective narrative offered a more subtle justification for the playwright's urge to bend the past to what he called 'the imperatives of fiction'.[50]

White's essay inspired Friel to muse anew on his O'Neill play. On 20 February 1986, he decided to call it *Making History*, a title alluding both to O'Neill's life and to the stories told about it. 'The play itself', he declared in his notes, 'is a form of fictional historiography. The acknowledgement of this seems to release it into a different kind of discourse, to offer it a new form, even to afford it an attitude.' Now he began to conceive of 'The play as history—the form of the play as methodologies of writing history' and to think through the implications of this adjustment to his conception of the drama. 'The conflict becomes dual', he observed: 'the drama of the "events" and the structuring of those events into "facts", and then the interpretation of those "facts" into a comprehensive "explanation" that claims to correspond with some objective truth. In other words: the events of the play constitute one drama; the historian's use/abuse/reading of those events a second drama.' Armed with this new vision of his play's subject, Friel immediately began drafting speeches for Archbishop Lombard in which the biographer explains his rationale and procedure to the audience, several of which made it practically intact into the final version of the script. 'We may have lost the war', Lombard declares in one of these draft speeches, but 'Its telling may still be a victory.' 'The heart of the play', Friel commented in the margin.[51] The next day, reading through his earlier notes, Friel added 'as historiography' to a list of possible non-naturalistic approaches he had made in early November 1984.

Political developments during the summer of 1986 added urgency to Friel's plans to finish his play, as unionist outrage over the Anglo–Irish Agreement made for an especially tense 'marching season'. Defiant Orange marches through predominantly Catholic areas in Belfast and Portadown provoked almost a week of rioting and hand-to-hand fighting in July, with more than a hundred people injured in sectarian clashes. On 10 July about four thousand loyalists occupied Hillsborough, County Down, to protest the agreement, and on 7 August five hundred of them invaded the Republic, temporarily taking over the village of Clontibret, County Monaghan (site of one of O'Neill's most famous victories against the English, in 1595). The IRA, for its part, expanded its list of targets to include anyone working for the army or police in any capacity whatsoever, an edict resented by nationalists as well as unionists at a time when jobs of any kind were hard to get—that October, unemployment in Northern Ireland would reach 23 per cent.[52] On 26 June, voters in the Republic rejected by referendum an amendment, part of FitzGerald's continuing campaign to make the Irish constitution less overtly sectarian, that would have allowed a restricted form of divorce; with Catholic bishops outspokenly opposed, this failed by a large margin, with 63.5 per cent voting to retain the ban. As FitzGerald wearily conceded, 'It cannot reasonably be denied that we have a long way to go before we create in this part of Ireland a society that would seem welcoming to, open to and attractive to people of the Northern Unionist tradition.'[53]

That autumn, Friel was still considering several different experimental forms for the play, still weighing the relative benefits of a linear versus a retrospective structure, still wondering if he could keep the historiographical focus while limiting the story to the actual period of O'Neill's marriage to Mabel (1591–5). Despite all the thinking he had done about the process of 'making history', however, it hit Friel with the force of a revelation on 1 October 1986 that 'Lombard writing about ON is like Friel writing about Lombard & ON—fashioning events-facts into an acceptable fiction—inventing a plot that will endow the events with intelligibility.'

Friel underlined this sentence in his notes and annotated it with a '?!' but continued to fret over the same stylistic and structural questions that had preoccupied him for almost three years.

In the early months of 1987, Friel at last began writing again, tinkering with the two scenes he had thus far drafted, back in the spring of 1985. Only at this point did he decide (or, perhaps, decide not to decide) between telling the story as it happened and telling it in retrospect. He kept both scenes, probably conceived as alternative openings for the play, making one in which O'Neill announces his marriage the first scene of Act 1 and one with Lombard in Rome the second (and final) scene of Act 2. Because this last scene revolves around the biography Lombard is writing, the characters reflect explicitly on the past that audiences have just seen dramatized, but Friel ultimately abandoned the idea of incorporating flashbacks. He wanted *Making History* to be alienating in the Brechtian sense of provoking thought—but not *too* alienating. Critic Anthony Roche points out that telling the story chronologically also 'has the effect of stressing the parallel between the activities of O'Neill and Lombard' as history-makers.[54] Friel settled, as well, on a suitably ambiguous ending for the play: O'Neill 'reciting his submission' while 'at the same time, or in counterpoint, Lombard begins to read aloud his history. Both utterances "inaccurate", "untruthful"; but both history as symbol—the creation of myth, of acceptable fiction.'[55]

Friel used a combination of outright distortion of the historical record and ingenious stagecraft to keep Mabel, and the modern resonances evoked by her, at the forefront of the audience's consciousness throughout the drama. In the final version of *Making History*, Act 1, Scene 1, set in August 1591, depicts O'Neill, Lombard, O'Neill's secretary Harry,[56] and his chief co-conspirator Hugh O'Donnell discussing their attempts to recruit Spain and Rome to support them in a fight against England. O'Neill shares the news of his marriage, and his colleagues react disapprovingly, treating Mabel coldly when they are introduced. Act 1, Scene 2, set '[a]lmost a year' later (that is, in the summer of 1592),[57] begins with an exchange between Mabel and Mary establishing that the Bagenal family remains unreconciled to Mabel's marriage and revealing the extent to which Mabel has adopted the values of her husband. O'Neill enters and talks about the awkward position he has been put in by the refusal of one of his most important Gaelic allies, Maguire, to take an oath of allegiance to the English crown, since he will now have to choose publicly between the two systems he has hitherto managed to keep in precarious balance. Later, O'Donnell and Lombard appear and tell O'Neill that the Spanish are coming at last, and Mabel urges O'Neill not to chance an open war against the English before announcing her pregnancy. Act 2, Scene 1, set roughly eight months later (that is, in the spring of 1593), shows the aftermath of Kinsale. O'Neill and O'Donnell, on the run, discuss the devastation of the country some months after the battle and compare their plans: O'Donnell will try to enlist support outside Ireland for another attempt against the English, while

O'Neill is composing a speech of unconditional surrender and loyalty to Queen Elizabeth in the hope of being restored to his territory. At the end of the scene, Harry arrives and reveals that Mabel has just died, shortly after giving birth, and that the child did not survive. Act 2, Scene 2, set in Rome 'many years later' (54), presents an argument between O'Neill and Lombard over the biography the latter is writing, focusing on O'Neill's insistence that Mabel's role in his life should be presented as '[c]entral to it' (62) and Lombard's view of her as incidental to his 'story of a hero' (67).

Numerous scholars have pointed out the inaccuracy of dates and other details in *Making History*, which a partial list of Friel's most significant misrepresentations will illustrate. O'Neill could not have met with O'Donnell in 1591 because O'Donnell was imprisoned at the time.[58] Lombard did not write a biography of O'Neill; his *De regno Hiberniae, sanctorum insula, commentarius* (written in 1600, although in Friel's play Lombard is already working on it in 1591) made the case for papal support of an Irish rebellion in the name of Catholicism and includes some discussion of O'Neill's leadership qualities.[59] The correspondence with the Spanish king read out in the play's first scene is authentic, but this exchange of letters happened in 1595–6, not 1591.[60] Maguire's rebellion, which in Friel's play forces O'Neill's hand in 1592, actually reached its crisis in 1593, and the historical O'Neill fought on the English side in that campaign, though the play implies otherwise.[61] The submission to the queen that O'Neill rehearses with O'Donnell in 1593 in the play was actually delivered in 1603, at which point O'Donnell was already dead.[62] In short, Friel's presentation of O'Neill's career is consistently, even at times gratuitously, counter-factual, and anyone taking it at face value as an account of his rebellion risks looking as silly as the *Guardian* writer who solemnly informed his readers that the defeat at Kinsale occurred in 1592[63]—at least to those familiar with Irish history, although *Making History*'s initial reception raises the question of how many such people exist.

Friel compounded his audiences' puzzlement with a programme note he wrote for the Field Day production, later scrutinized by scholars. *Making History*, he explained,

is a dramatic fiction that uses some actual and some imagined events in the life of Hugh O'Neill to make a story. I have tried to be objective and faithful—after my artistic fashion—to the empirical method. But when there was tension between historical 'fact' and the imperative of the fiction, I'm glad to say I kept faith with the narrative. For example, even though Mabel, Hugh's wife, died in 1591, it suited my story to keep her alive for another ten years. Part of me regrets taking these occasional liberties. But then I remind myself that history and fiction are related and comparable forms of discourse and that an historical text is a kind of literary artifact. And then I am grateful that these regrets were never inhibiting.[64]

Historian Sean Connolly has remarked of this note that it 'would make sense if the battle of Kinsale had been presented as occurring, as in real life, in 1601. But in the play Kinsale has happened, and Mabel is dead, by Spring 1593. The second problem is that the real Mabel Bagenal died, not in 1591, or in 1601, but in 1595. Contradiction is piled on contradiction.' Connolly rightly rejects as 'unlikely' the possibility that 'there has been a mistake', speculating that 'Friel has deliberately chosen to confuse the picture: partly…to advertise even more clearly his liberation from the constraints of the historical record; partly…to reinforce the play's satirical treatment of the pretensions of history, by means of a subtle practical joke at the expense of the hapless academic fact checker'.[65]

Both Connolly's explanations have much to recommend them, but one might also interpret this blatantly false information in Friel's note as a coded signal to commentators inclined to examine the history the play purports to represent that there is more to his seemingly cavalier treatment of the past than might immediately meet the eye. Friel knew what he was doing and did it on purpose, and he wanted his scholarly critics to understand that.[66] Knowledge of the ambivalent state of mind in which he wrote the play allows us to see, as well, that a bigger falsehood than the wrong date Friel gives for Mabel's death is the statement that his 'regrets' about the 'occasional liberties' he had found it necessary to take with the facts 'were never inhibiting'.[67] Despite his private doubts, however, Friel's apology for these liberties appears to have been offered in the same spirit as O'Neill's repeated submissions to Queen Elizabeth I: perhaps 90 per cent tongue-in-cheek and 10 per cent hoping to be taken literally.

The 'imperative of the fiction' did demand numerous adjustments to what most people would call facts and what Hayden White would term 'events'. As Connolly sums up their overall effect, the playwright 'compressed the events of ten years, from 1591 to 1601, into somewhere under two' for the sake of 'dramatic continuity'.[68] Does this matter? On the one hand, of course it does. A few years can make an immense difference in social and political terms—Northern Ireland in the 1980s affords a striking example of this truism. In 1981, the alienation of Northern Catholics from the British government had become almost total in reaction to Margaret Thatcher's intransigent handling of the hunger strikes by republican prisoners. After the 1985 Anglo–Irish Agreement, however, it was unionists who were praying (sometimes literally) for the end of her tenure as prime minister. By the summer of 1987, as Friel prepared to finish writing *Making History*, constitutional nationalist leaders were stating on the record before a British general election that it would be to the advantage of 'nationalist Ireland' if Thatcher remained in power 'for a limited period of time'.[69] So when Friel presents the events of 1600 or 1601 as if they happened in the early 1590s, the change is not a trivial one.

On the other hand, giving a fine-grained and accurate account of the 1590s in Ireland was not Friel's primary purpose in writing *Making History*. Rather, he wanted to offer his audiences an alternative picture of the past that would prompt them to reconsider what they thought they knew about the legendary figures of O'Neill and O'Donnell, but, as he remarked in notes made during the writing of the play,

> I don't think my function is to provide a flowing & logical chronology. I think my function is satisfied if I provide a half-a-dozen key episodes—stepping-stones—dramatic points-of-reference so that, for example, when the Flight of the Earls is mentioned, what images does it conjure up? Defeated men scuttling away, deserting their people, betraying their trust.[70]

Friel cared what his audiences thought about the Flight of the Earls because their beliefs about the Gaelic confederacy's leaders had the power to influence their attitudes and actions in the late twentieth century. He wrote *Making History* as a disciple of his Archbishop Lombard, telling an engaging story with a political moral for his own time. The first three scenes of the play present the 'facts' he manufactured from the 'events' of the historical O'Neill's life, and the last, a coda rather than a frame, comments on them.

Friel sought to influence events in his own Ireland by demonstrating the futility of violence as a means of achieving the nationalist ideal of Irish independence and integrity. At a time when he knew the republican movement was riven by debates between those who favoured engaging in the political process and those who saw armed struggle as the only way to achieve a sovereign, united Ireland, he wished to bolster the position of the former. As a liberal Irish nationalist, Friel believed that the only realistic path to a united Ireland would be to persuade con-temporary unionists that their cultural differences would be accepted and their rights respected in a reconstituted Irish state. Thus, he wanted his audiences to believe in the possibility of a new cultural synthesis in Ireland, which would include both Protestants and Catholics in 'the overall thing' (39, 69) that—like the 'cultural whole' he had advocated for in 1982—he shrewdly left undefined in the play. To that end, he wished to show a more positive side of Northern Protestantism than nationalist members of his Irish audiences might previously have encountered and to give unionist members of those audiences sympathetic characters with whom to identify. He wanted to illustrate both the challenges and the promise of cultural cross-fertilization. Because none of these goals could be achieved unless the play was widely seen and discussed, Friel also wanted to write a popular play and worked hard to avoid a polemical or didactic tone. *Making History* served his rhetorical purposes best when audiences received it primarily as an engaging story.

Read with these aims in mind, Friel's version of O'Neill's career brims with political relevance, but the dramatist makes his case with the tools appropriate to his own trade. Instead of telling audiences things, he shows them. In Act 1, we see O'Neill happy, rich, and powerful, in a position of authority in both Gaelic and

English systems and engaged in a loving relationship with a Protestant woman of New English stock. In Act 2, after he has resorted to war on behalf of Ireland and Catholicism, we see him hunted, reviled by his own people, stripped of his power and wealth, and existing in a depressing, all-male void. Although we cannot know what would have happened had O'Neill continued his established policy of strategic surrender and cooperation with the English (i.e. peace and power-sharing), we can see clear parallels between the wasted, famine-ridden land he leaves behind when he goes into exile and Northern Ireland in the late 1980s—parallels reinforced in the Field Day production by the set used for Act 2, Scene 1, in which, as the *Ulster Herald*'s reviewer observed, 'The pillars and columns of the castle have become the rubble of a blasted edifice, the wire protrusions calling to mind modern, urban building blocks in a ravaged city (Derry? Belfast?).'[71]

The marriage between O'Neill and Mabel serves as the play's primary vehicle for Friel's ideas about Ireland's best future. Although both journalistic and academic critics invariably refer to Mabel as English, a proper understanding of the play's political subtext requires the recognition that she is more accurately described as an Ulster Protestant. Establishing this identity is an important purpose of her conversation with Mary in Act 1, scene 2, in which the sisters discuss in loving detail the landscape surrounding their childhood home in Newry: the only home besides O'Neill's house that Mabel has ever known. Friel's portrayal of her relationship with O'Neill is both a realistic depiction of a functional marriage and a powerful metaphor for the sort of partnership that might be possible between nationalists and unionists in Northern Ireland.

From the beginning of *Making History*, Friel takes pains to establish Mabel as a person of substance. Any initial impression that O'Neill is just another middle-aged man besotted with a woman young enough to be his daughter is dispelled by her first appearance, when she meets his openly hostile co-conspirators. Despite her youth and inexperience, she displays an impressive composure in this difficult situation, as Friel's stage directions emphasize. '*She holds out her hand*', and O'Donnell is forced to take it but '*does not speak*'. After an awkward pause, O'Neill introduces her to Lombard, and '*Again she holds out her hand.*' He takes it '*After a pause*' but also '*does not speak*' (15). These actions, as Roche observes, are reminiscent 'of the symbolic force of a handshake in Irish politics when it was many years before a constitutional politician would shake a Sinn Féin leader's hand'.[72] Later, alone with O'Neill, Mabel admits to having been terrified: 'Hugh O'Donnell and a popish priest all in a couple of minutes! Did you not see my hand?—it was shaking!' (17). O'Neill teasingly informs her that all the gory rumours she has heard about O'Donnell are true and that an archbishop like Lombard is '[m]uch worse' than a priest, advising her to look at her hand, which he says is 'turning black'. She reacts with exaggerated alarm, then, when she '*realizes she has been fooled*', responds unexpectedly with '*a great whoop of laughter*' and '*punches him*' (17–18). By the end of the scene, O'Neill's insistence that 'I have married a very talented, a very spirited, a very beautiful young woman' seems a plain statement of fact (14).

Significantly, their marriage is harmonious in the musical rather than the colloquial sense. In notes dating from the spring of 1984, Friel had worried about centring the play on this relationship because O'Neill and Mabel would be 'in a kind of unison', whereas 'drama requires the depth & richness of harmonies'.[73] He overcomes this challenge in the finished script of *Making History* by highlighting their differences of opinion, major and minor. O'Neill and Mabel are on stage together for only about a quarter of the play, and they spend at least a quarter of that time at odds. If one looks exclusively at exchanges in which they are focused on conversation with each other, more than half their dialogue is devoted to arguing or fighting. In Act 2, although Mabel never appears in person, O'Neill describes to O'Donnell a debate he has been having with her.

This depiction of the marriage as contentious has some basis in the historical record. O'Faolain cites an incident early in their married life when Mabel 'refused to countenance his mistresses any longer' and 'laid public complaint against him'. He also includes 'one clear, sinister glimpse' of their relationship a couple of years after the elopement, when an informant reported a bitter altercation between husband and wife, apparently over O'Neill's condoning of a clansman's murder.[74] From such evidence as this, O'Faolain concludes that the marriage must have been unhappy, but Friel had the imagination to infer, instead, a woman with both self-respect and political instinct. A discreet and dutiful wife, Friel's Mabel is nevertheless unafraid to challenge her aristocratic husband on his own ground, and he values her advice even when he fails to take it.

Their most heated dispute comes at the end of Act 1. Mabel waits until O'Donnell, Lombard, and Harry have left the room before urging O'Neill to stop the impending Spanish invasion because 'this isn't what you really want to happen' (37). Here, as elsewhere, her primary role is to tell O'Neill, for the benefit of the audience, things he already knows. She reminds him, for instance, that

> you're the only Irish chieftain who understands the political method.... That's why the Queen is never *quite* sure how to deal with you—you're the antithesis of what she expects a Gaelic chieftain to be. That's your strength. And that's why your instinct now is not to gamble everything on one big throw that is more than risky.   (38)

She is right, but the implication that she knows her husband better than he knows himself annoys him.

O'Neill insists that with Spain and Rome behind the Gaelic forces the confederacy has an excellent chance of success, but Mabel counters with the argument that Spain and the papacy are only using Ireland's war against England to advance their own agendas and will move on as soon as they encounter difficulties.

England, in contrast, 'will throw everything she has into this war', a war 'England must win because her very survival is at stake' (38–9). Compared to this 'nation state that is united and determined and powerful and led by a very resolute woman' (Friel's Field Day audiences would undoubtedly have been thinking of Margaret Thatcher as well as Queen Elizabeth I at this point), O'Neill's compatriots are merely 'an impromptu alliance of squabbling tribesmen...grabbing at religion as a coagulant only because they have no other idea to inform them or give them cohesion' (38). Mabel's diagnosis of O'Neill's essential problem derives from O'Faolain, who summarized it as '[d]isunity among the people, a unified purpose in the invader',[75] but her critique of his solution ('religion as a coagulant') is Friel's. Precisely because O'Neill suspects she is correct, however, he lashes out at Mabel after conceding most of her points (and immediately after she demonstrates where her loyalties truly lie by passing on military intelligence that her sister had made her promise not to share with him), raging that 'for you to suggest that religion is the only coagulant that holds us together is to grossly and ignorantly overlook an age-old civilization'. He intensifies the argument by urging her to 'look at what the alternative is: the buccaneering, vulgar, material code of the new colonials' (40).

At this juncture, their political dispute turns personal, with devastating results. '*She swings back and glares at him in hatred*' before announcing that she refuses any longer to live in the same house as his mistresses (whose presence she had earlier defended to her sister as 'part of his culture'), an ultimatum O'Neill scornfully rejects (41, 25). When she tells him about her pregnancy, he feigns indifference, and Mabel runs from the room—her final exit in the play. O'Neill is filled with '*instant remorse*', but O'Donnell interrupts his attempt to apologize with news that the Spanish fleet will land at Kinsale, a location identified earlier in this scene as an utterly inappropriate launching point for an attack (41–2). Friel thus connects O'Neill's harsh rejection of Mabel with the military campaign, doomed before it begins.

The marriage, however, proves more resilient, illustrating a crucial difference between the kind of love that leads people to get married and the kind that keeps them together through good times and bad. The first relies on the illusion that the parties have everything in common, or that the strength of their mutual attraction renders any differences unimportant. The second, more enduring, entails the recognition of each other as independent subjects—with histories, mentalities, and ends of their own—who choose to work together and compromise for the sake of the goals they share and the life they are building together.

Despite Mabel's non-appearance in Act 2 of the play, she remains notably present in her absence. The first scene begins months after the defeat at Kinsale with O'Donnell returning from a scouting expedition to O'Neill's hiding place in the mountains. Almost as soon as he enters, he asks about Mabel. O'Neill reports that Harry has taken her to an ally's home to give birth because 'She wasn't able to keep moving about any more'. O'Donnell, unbidden, remarks that 'She's been terrific....Not a whimper out of her all these months—and us skulking about like tramps', and O'Neill concurs (44). After the two men discuss the dire state of the country, their conversation turns to the future. O'Donnell has delegated his title to his brother and will be leaving Ireland. O'Neill has not yet decided what he will do but confesses that 'My instinct is to leave like you'. O'Donnell confirms his changed opinion of O'Neill's marriage by asking, 'What does Mabel think?', and O'Neill's reply underscores the fact that their marriage has not been salvaged at the expense of Mabel's independent thought or voice: 'She's urging me to hang on, pick up the pieces, start all over again'. O'Donnell allows that she may be right, but his resistance grows when he hears the specifics of Mabel's advice, which involve O'Neill publicly pledging loyalty to the queen and asking her to reinstate him to his lands with only 'nominal authority'. When O'Donnell wonders why Elizabeth would entertain such a proposal, O'Neill explains, 'Because she knows that the only way she can rule Ireland at this point is by *using* someone like me. She hates me—but she can rule through me provided she has control over me. At least that's Mabel's argument. I think I could get enough of my people behind me and she thinks some of the New English would back it—those that are sick of England'. O'Donnell, aware that O'Neill is already writing his submission, remarks that he is a 'tenacious bugger', adding, 'You and Mabel are well met' (46–8).

After O'Neill and O'Donnell rehearse O'Neill's submission, Harry arrives with the distressing report that Mabel died immediately after giving birth to a son who lived little more than an hour himself. He waits until the end of the scene to break this news, however, allowing Friel to keep Mabel alive from the audience's perspective through the recounting of various developments that vindicate her opinion of the war: Lombard has fled to Rome, another archbishop who encouraged the Irish rebels has gone to London to meet with the authorities there to try to prevent 'a backlash against the Catholics in England', and the English government 'wants to explore what areas of common interest might still exist between you and the crown' (51–2). Most significant, politically, is Harry's account of a conversation with their hostess just before Mabel went into labour. When asked if her husband was considering exile, Mabel 'got very agitated' and said, 'Hugh?...Hugh would never betray his people' (53). At a stroke, Friel reverses the traditional nationalist valuation of the Flight of the Earls: in *Making History*, pragmatic accommodation with the colonial power of the sort that Mabel advocates represents a chance to protect Gaelic culture, while clinging to ideological purity is a form of betrayal.[76] The history lesson had an obvious application to Ireland in the late 1980s, where contemporary republicans had a similar decision to make between political engagement with the enemy and continuing the war, even at the expense of their own people and ultimate goals.

Mabel's last reported words hang over the final scene of the play as a judgement upon O'Neill's decision to flee Ireland. Although Mabel's death is now years in the past, Friel keeps her memory to the fore in ways that indicate his protagonist's feelings of guilt about failing to follow her advice to live with the consequences of his actions and make whatever concessions would be necessary to retain some authority in Ulster. The missing Mabel becomes an explicit subject of this scene in its second half, as the play's closing debate between O'Neill and Lombard over what should be included in the latter's history focuses on her role in O'Neill's life. Lombard, who plans an exemplary account of a Gaelic and Catholic leader, seeks to expunge the English and Protestant influences on his hero, including the time O'Neill spent in England as a child and young man, his pledges of loyalty to Queen Elizabeth, and his New English wife. O'Neill, though, keeps returning the conversation to the question of how Mabel will be portrayed, with Lombard insisting repeatedly that she will have her place in his narrative, along with O'Neill's other three wives. Mabel, he declares, 'had her own value, her own importance. And at some future time and in a mode we can't imagine now I have no doubt that story will be told fully and sympathetically. It will be a domestic story, Hugh; a love story; and a very beautiful love story it will be' (69). Lombard's attitude is hardly surprising in a Catholic archbishop, but critics who cite these lines as a description of Friel's play itself only advertise how little they have understood it.[77]

In Ireland in the 1980s—where debates on abortion, divorce, and contraception highlighted the difficulties that many women and Protestants alike had with the Catholic-inflected version of Irish nationalism represented by the Republic—*Making History*'s depiction of women's roles made a decidedly feminist statement, although this has gone largely unremarked upon by scholars. Far from serving primarily as a 'domestic' distraction and love object, Mabel acts as her husband's confidante and political adviser, and the action of the play validates her insights. It is precisely because audience members have witnessed Mabel's active engagement in O'Neill's deliberations regarding the wider world that his tacit acceptance of Lombard's attempt to limit her part in his life story strikes them as a betrayal. The other woman who appears on stage, Mabel's sister Mary, is similarly unafraid to challenge O'Neill to his face, and, as in O'Faolain's book about O'Neill, Elizabeth I features as an intelligent and powerful force on the margins of the onstage action. Furthermore, Roche points out that Mabel and the queen 'are consistently doubled throughout the play, from the moment O'Neill gives his wife a wedding present of a watch and declares that only Elizabeth has its like'.[78]

Commentators who find *Making History* wordy or static generally emphasize its last scene, but here the effect is deliberate. Audiences are made to *feel*, on a visceral level, Mabel's absence from the stage. On the symbolic level, O'Neill and the ideal of an independent and united Ireland he represents are diminished without the Ulster Protestant element embodied in the play by Mabel. Lombard and O'Neill alternate lines in *Making History*'s antiphonal ending, with the former reciting the opening of *The History of Hugh O'Neill* he is supposedly composing and the latter quoting from his own abject apology to Queen Elizabeth. O'Neill's speech gradually blurs into an appeal to Mabel, though, culminating in his final utterance: 'Mabel, I am sorry...please forgive me, Mabel...' (71). Against his better judgment, O'Neill has acquiesced for the second time in the play to a vision of Ireland, as essentially Gaelic and Catholic, which excludes her. The negative effects of his first capitulation are apparent in Act 2; Friel's original audiences were living in the bleak situation created by the second.

In a programme note for the Field Day production entitled 'The Search for a Usable Past', Declan Kiberd interpreted the marriage between O'Neill and Mabel as emblematic of the '*impossible* but desirable fusion of Gaelic and English tradition' [emphasis added]. This reading, however, is defeatist in a way the Field Day enterprise was not. Critic Christopher Murray comes closer to the mark in positing that Mabel signifies 'reconciliation and integration', both an opportunity lost in the past and a possibility for the future.[79] By portraying Mabel as a pragmatist and endorsing her ideas about the political course O'Neill should have taken, Friel prompted both unionists and nationalists to recognize the value of thinking strategically and long-term, rather than focusing on sentimental identification or the desire for a decisive partisan victory. Friel's ambiguous conclusion also invited audience members to dwell upon the questions raised by the dispute between O'Neill and Lombard about what should be remembered, and how.

These were questions that Friel and his fellow Field Day directors had been pondering for years by the time he completed the script, a fact reflected in Seamus Heaney's excited reaction to the play upon first reading it in January 1988. Heaney recognized *Making History* as a work that both expressed Friel's innermost musings and spoke to contemporary public debates, praising it simultaneously as an intellectual statement and as a moving and immersive piece for theatrical performance.[80] The Northern nationalist heritage they shared allowed Heaney to perceive that Friel's willingness to question his own assumptions enabled him to challenge his audiences' preconceptions as well. We might usefully adapt Yeats's dictum about rhetoric and poetry: a playwright makes agitprop out of the argument with others, but drama out of the argument with himself.

Irish reviews of Field Day's *Making History* production register the shocking contrast between the traditional nationalist image of Hugh O'Neill and Friel's portrait. The reviewer for the *Ulster Herald* informed its predominantly nationalist readers that 'The audience in Omagh were visibly taken aback' by O'Neill's English accent, an effect made 'all the more startling when the actor quite consciously lapses into the occasional line in the Tyrone dialect'. A critic in Galway agreed that 'misconception about such a legendary figure initially made the character...almost implausible, for he had a rich English accent, appeared fickle and pre-occupied by domestic affairs while Irish chieftains under him fought with one another long before turning any attention to England', although 'the rich thread of Friel's work soon weaves an intricate account of O'Neill that is entirely plausible and real'. A writer for the *Cork Examiner* identified the play's theme as the 'apparent tension between what actually happened and history's version of the events', proffering a few examples of Friel's re-reading of the past: 'Hugh O'Neill, a soured émigré [sic], lonely and besotted with drink, turning on his closest friend, would not be the traditional, school-text image of the man who led the Irish in the glorious Battle of Kinsale....It shouldn't be, but it was discomfiting for this reviewer, educated in the fifties, to be told by O'Neill...that Kinsale was a one hour rout; that the Irish ran away and that the Flight of the Earls was more...*running away*'. Timothy O'Grady opined in the *Evening Press* that *Making History* 'is a cautionary tale about national self-delusion. It takes a national hero, removes his debilitating romantic patina and celebrates his depth and honesty and courage of mind.'[81]

Nicholas Canny, asked by the *Galway Advertiser* to comment on the play's treatment of history and historians, tactfully refrained from discussing Friel's dating of key events. Instead, he interpreted the play in the context of current debates about the nature of history, with Lombard appearing 'not as an historian in any professional sense but as a custodian of the Catholic nationalist *version* of our past that was inculcated in some of us as children' and O'Neill standing for 'the contemporary revisionist who would discredit the myth that has been constructed by presenting evidence that exposes its inadequacy as a historical explanation'. In Canny's view, 'What Friel is saying is that such exposure by itself will never attain its purpose unless it is accompanied by some new narrative of the past that will prove more convincing than that which has been discredited.'[82]

Making History represented Friel's attempt to provide such a narrative, and its initial reception demonstrates that he achieved his purpose. While nationalist critics usually focused on O'Neill himself, other commentators tended to home in on the character of Mabel. Jim Patton, reviewing the play for the unionist *Belfast Telegraph*, wrote that she evokes 'sympathy and compassion as she struggles, in vain, to come to terms with her adopted culture'. This reviewer regarded the marriage between O'Neill and Mabel as 'doomed', with her death in childbirth and the loss of their son echoing the way that 'O'Neill himself is unable to synthesize his Gaelic instincts and his formative English training'. Other unionist viewers managed to extract a more positive meaning from O'Neill's New English wife, whose tragically early death Friel presents as forestalling a wiser course of action after Kinsale. Charles Fitzgerald, long-time drama critic for Belfast's *News Letter*, pronounced *Making History* 'Friel's greatest play to date', seeing in Mabel a woman who 'with her intelligence and intelligences' had a value for O'Neill surpassing that of 'loved spouse'. He believed the play explored 'how the influence of people upon a central historical character can alter what might have been the course of history'. A reviewer in the border county of Cavan concurred, arguing that Mabel's 'pragmatic though softened view of Anglo/Irish relations' ensures that her advice 'contains logic, balance, sympathy'—the reason, in this writer's opinion, that 'O'Neill's final gesture is to demand that she be given a central role in his own particular history'.[83]

Although many of these original reviewers described the play's subject in terms of 'myth' versus 'reality', at least some popular-press critics understood that Friel was, in effect, replacing one subjective narrative version of the past with another. Jane Coyle wondered in the *Sunday Press* if the seeming hesitancy of first-night audience members could be attributed to their grappling with the implications of storytelling both inside and outside the drama, if 'the very nature of Friel's theme—the dubious methods by which history is shaped—became its own obstacle, leaving the audience wondering whether what we were watching was any more substantial and valid than Archbishop Peter Lombard's "official history" of O'Neill'. As the *Ulster Herald* reviewer described the play's dynamic, the audience understands that Friel 'may be creating a fiction' but 'in a subtle way, he is also an historian'. The Cavan reviewer, for one, recognized the play itself as 'a rewriting of history', Friel's 'own imaginative reshaping of facts'. *Sunday Independent* critic Brian Brennan cited Friel's programme note in support of a similar reading: 'By embracing the belief that an "historical text is a kind of literary artifact," Friel is repeating, indeed celebrating the very process which poor old Hugh O'Neill deplores within the play. And this lovely existential joke will be repeated with every performance of the play.'[84]

Not everyone got the joke, of course. This was particularly true in London because English critics had not grown up with the heroic version of O'Neill's story and had few, if any, preconceptions about him. Right after its tour of Ireland ended, the National Theatre hosted Field Day's production of *Making History* for twenty-one performances, which were met with mixed reviews. The *Evening Standard*'s drama critic, Milton Shulman, saw Friel as 'merely reiterating Henry Ford's dictum that history is bunk' and found the characterization of O'Neill 'confusing, inconsistent and unconvincing'. The *Guardian*'s Michael Billington regarded the dramatic 'conflict' as one 'between prosaic fact and heroic myth'. He argued that 'It would be an intellectually tougher play, however, if Friel admitted that Lombard had a point', apparently not noticing that Friel's drama itself illustrates Lombard's theory of history.[85]

The predictable difficulty of impressing upon English audiences the relevance of O'Neill's centuries-old dilemmas to current events caused different Field Day directors to discuss Friel's political intent more openly in the English press than they did in Ireland. In a substantial article about Field Day published in *The Times* to coincide with *Making History*'s opening at the National Theatre, Heaney presented an overview of O'Neill's career along with a partial listing of Friel's revisions to the traditional nationalist image of him. Friel, Heaney observed, like Sean O'Casey before him, wrote amid 'the omnipresent fact of political violence, so the scrutiny of the relation between myth-making and action…attains a special urgency. For them, drama comes to be a factor in the re-reading and rewriting of history, a way of reshaping the consciousness of the audience in posterity, if not in the stalls'. Stephen Rea commented on the play's politics even more explicitly in an interview for the *Guardian* published the same day: 'History for the Irish is something that has not yet been completed because of the conflict we live in. Obviously if it can't be completed it has to be re-examined all the time, to find ways that we can move on. The pleasing irony is that Friel is making his own version of history that is useful to us today, a history...of reconciliation'.[86]

The more perceptive English reviewers either took such hints or knew enough about Ireland to see the play's political subtext for themselves. Irving Wardle, for example, declared in *The Times* that *Making History* 'is emphatically not a debunking exercise....Friel, no less than Lombard, is chiefly telling a good story. What he offers is not the "truth" about O'Neill, but a seventeenth-century figure who reflects our own need for Anglo–Irish understanding'. *Financial Times* critic Michael Coveney, who described *Making History* as 'taut and compelling', 'Friel's most accomplished and important play since *Translations*', remarked of the Hugh–Mabel marriage that 'Their relationship in the play, tough and argumentative, embodies a hope for their country that dies with O'Neill's capitulation and flight'.[87]

Overall, *Making History*'s original reception can be fairly described as overwhelmingly positive, summed up well by O'Grady's declaration in the *Evening Press* that 'The writing has lightness and energy, far-reaching ironies and wit. The production has enough warmth and buoyancy and realism to bring us in and enough abstraction to allow us to hear the debate'. Reviews like this make it hard to account for the curious reputation *Making History* has acquired in academic circles as 'a problem play'.[88] Much of the responsibility for this persistent assessment lies with influential critic Fintan O'Toole, who pronounced the play 'not sufficiently dramatic' in a review of the Field Day production for the *Irish Times* and expanded his critique in a later essay, insisting that '*Making History* is so reflexive that it ceases to have any dramatic tension or much theatrical force'.[89] Richard Pine agrees that it lacks 'dramatic impact', as well as 'form', 'content', and 'an authorial voice', going so far as to ask if it should even be termed a play at all. F. C. McGrath views it as 'a staged treatise on poststructural history' that fails as theatre, and Ulf Dantanus describes *Making History* as 'a play of ideas that fits nicely into the Field Day program and the context of the revisionist 1980s in Ireland' but 'does not do justice to [Friel's] creative powers' as 'a piece of dramatic literature'. Aidan O'Malley, who examines the play in the context of a comprehensive study of the Field Day project, seems to endorse such analysis but acknowledges, in a note, that 'transcripts of...brief interviews with audience members after the first performances of the play in the North...would tend to dispute the dominant critical view of the play, as the audiences show a great appreciation of the complexities of the drama', with most seeing it 'as a salutary act of historical demythologising' and reflecting on 'its connections with the "Troubles"'.[90] Yvonne Lysandrou suggests a plausible reason for the discrepant reactions of scholars and rank-and-file audience members, arguing that 'It is because many critics...treat *Making History* as essentially a staged poststructuralist text that they give a largely negative assessment of it as drama. Focusing attention on what is being said in the play rather than on what it projects in its entirety through the dramatic medium, critical opinion effectively misses the play's artistic force.'[91]

Critics who question *Making History*'s effectiveness as drama should consider Field Day's box office receipts—always, as Friel knew only too well, a more reliable indicator than reviews of audiences' judgement on any of the company's productions. At a board meeting held the month before *Making History* opened in Derry, the directors learned that Field Day's budget shortfall for the tour was projected to be £10,000 and that hopes for obtaining sponsorship were rapidly dwindling. Friel expressed the opinion that they might yet break even if they managed to sell 80 per cent of the tickets, an ambitious target.[92] During the play's run, attendance averaged 84 per cent during the Irish tour and 88 per cent at the National Theatre.[93]

Friel did not measure success merely in money, however, so a letter he received in the spring of 1989 from a writer identifying himself as a republican prisoner undoubtedly gave him great satisfaction. This correspondent reported that, over the past few years, a group of inmates including himself had been performing plays for their fellow prisoners. Although forced to fill the female roles with male actors, they had 'the ultimate in captive audiences', and he hoped Friel would not mind that they had recently presented his play *The Freedom of the City* ('we didn't change a word of it'). After these preliminaries, the man explained why he had decided to get in touch:

> Because we are Republican Prisoners our interest naturally leans towards Political/historical themes....I recently read the reviews, and saw a Television documentary, on your play 'Making History'. It sounds very interesting and hopefully I will get to see it performed professionally sometime. For now though, how might I go about getting a copy of the script?...It seems like the type of play we would be interested in performing, given its historical nature and also that you seem to have challenged some of the accepted notions of the period in question. We find that plays which challenge our thinking generate more interest and are more beneficial all round.[94]

The Field Day Theatre Company made intense physical and psychological demands on Brian Friel, both as a playwright and as a person, and health concerns would shortly force him to scale back his involvement with it.[95] Reading this letter, though, it is easy to see why he devoted himself to Field Day for over a decade. The company created the opportunity, during a crucial period, to reach audiences hungry for more than just a good night out. And *Making History* epitomizes the ways in which Friel sought to contribute through his art to the creation of a new Irish consciousness.

2

Understanding

After reading Brian Friel's *Making History* for the first time in late January 1988, Seamus Heaney responded from the United States, where he spent each spring teaching at Harvard University, with a letter praising the play in both political and aesthetic terms and proudly anticipating that autumn's Field Day tour of it. Along with his '[c]onviction that I have been at the edge of great events', Heaney confessed to having 'an acute sense of my distance, and a feeling that this is a critical time'. 'I do need to get back closer in', he concluded.[1]

Hindsight makes it even clearer than it seemed to Heaney at the time that this was, indeed, a crucial juncture. Less than two weeks earlier, on 11 January 1988, his and Friel's mutual friend John Hume, leader of the constitutional nationalist Social Democratic and Labour Party (SDLP), had met with Gerry Adams, President of Sinn Féin. Because Sinn Féin refused to condemn the use of force by the Irish Republican Army (IRA) in pursuit of their shared republican aims, the party had long been treated as a pariah by those who renounced violence in Northern Ireland. Thus, Hume's willingness to talk with Adams represented a notable departure from his party's position and provoked, as Adams recalls, 'an immediate and generally hostile response from the [British and Irish] governments, the other political parties and sections of the media'. As the two men hastened to quash rumours that the meeting might portend an imminent IRA ceasefire, Hume 'found himself increasingly and uncharacteristically barracked during interviews'.[2]

The chorus of condemnation would no doubt have been louder still had Hume's critics known that, before this reported meeting, he had already been conversing secretly with Adams for some time. In May 1986, Hume had received a letter from Father Alex Reid, a priest belonging to the Redemptorist Order based at Clonard Monastery in west Belfast. From the start of the Troubles in 1969, Father Reid declared, he had devoted himself to 'the processes of peacemaking'. To this end, he maintained contact with people from all sectors of Northern Irish society—especially, owing to his location, with nationalists. He had known Adams since the mid-1970s, when he helped negotiate an end to a feud within the republican movement, and he believed the Northern Sinn Féin leadership to be genuinely committed to presenting militant republicans with an 'alternative' course to armed struggle in pursuit of their goal of a united Ireland. The gist of Father Reid's proposal to Hume, laid out in his letter, was that 'the nationalist parties, North and South, would agree…to formulate and, then, to

Getting to Good Friday: Literature and the Peace Process in Northern Ireland. Marilynn Richtarik, Oxford University Press.
© Marilynn Richtarik 2023. DOI: 10.1093/oso/9780192886408.003.0003

co-operate in a common Nationalist policy of aims and methods for resolving the conflict and establishing a just and lasting peace'. The theory behind this 'alternative method' was that 'the creation of a powerful, combined political force on the Nationalist side' would prompt the IRA to 'respond by ending "the armed struggle"'.[3]

The 'crucial exercise in the whole enterprise', Father Reid stressed, 'would be ongoing, open-ended dialogue between all the parties concerned': 'the representatives of the Church as the initiators and co-ordinators of the discussions, the representatives of the constitutional Nationalist parties as the holders of the main political authority in the situation and the representatives of Sinn Féin as the party directly related to "the armed struggle"'. Hume had always promoted dialogue, but he would naturally worry that any talks between himself and Adams would be exposed and subjected to misinterpretation by unionists and the British government. Father Reid assured him of absolute confidentiality, and he allowed himself to be persuaded. As Mark Durkan, then Hume's Westminster assistant, recalls, 'Even a consummate politician found it hard to argue carefully with someone invoking the Holy Spirit with both regularity and conviction.'[4]

According to Adams's account of the peace process, he and Hume met privately for the first time in September 1986. He describes this encounter as 'friendly and constructive', although this did not distract either of them from fundamental differences of opinion.[5] Hume pointed to the 1985 Anglo–Irish Agreement, in which the Irish and British governments affirmed that 'any change in the status of Northern Ireland would only come about with the consent of a majority of the people of Northern Ireland', as evidence that the British government had no interest in managing Northern Ireland's affairs indefinitely and would have no objection to a united Ireland if unionists could be persuaded to accept the idea. The very suggestion that the constitutional status of Northern Ireland *could* change had been enough to provoke a frenzied unionist reaction, but Adams argued that Britain's lack of proprietorial interest in Northern Ireland was merely implied in the agreement and would need to be stated explicitly before militant republicans would believe in it. He advocated instead for a united nationalist front to pressure the British government to withdraw from the North. Despite their divergent viewpoints, Adams felt heartened by the fact that the meeting had taken place, emphasizing in his narrative the courage Hume had shown in engaging with him at all when the political systems in both Ireland and the United Kingdom, including many members of Hume's own party, demonized Sinn Féin members. He attributed Hume's relative openness to his roots in Derry, a republican stronghold where some of the SDLP leader's own neighbours belonged to Sinn Féin. He might not agree with republicans, but he knew they 'could not be ostracised out of existence'. Adams and Hume continued to meet in secret and presented each other's positions to their respective contacts to try to reach a consensus.[6]

Adams allows that their interactions were complicated by the 'high level of armed activity during this period', which involved the security forces and loyalists as well as the IRA. One notorious example of republican violence, the Enniskillen bombing of 8 November 1987, resulted in the deaths of eleven people and the injury of over sixty others who had gathered for a Remembrance Day observance. Historian Jonathan Bardon notes that the IRA's standing among Catholics 'plunged to an all-time low' after this attack. Barely a week before the Enniskillen atrocity, 150 tons of arms and ammunition destined for the IRA had been seized from a trawler off the coast of France; however, several prior shipments had already gotten through. Though both these incidents intensified hatred for and fear of militant republicans, the IRA also experienced military losses in 1987. On 8 May, eight IRA members had been killed during an attack on an RUC station in County Armagh—their highest death toll in a single incident.[7] This violent back-drop made the project of identifying an 'alternative' means of republican struggle ever more urgent, from the perspective of republicans as well as everyone else.

As old friends of Hume, Heaney and Friel surely took a keen interest in the early Hume–Adams encounters. Heaney had known Hume since the early 1950s, when they were both pupils at St Columb's College in Derry. Friel had also attended St Columb's, in an earlier student generation, and he and Hume had both worked as teachers in the city; their stints as professional educators over-lapped towards the end of that decade. Heaney observed that the 'Derry/ St Columb's context' played a 'very important' role in their friendships. These youthful relationships deepened during the 1970s, when all three of them took holidays with their families over the border in the Republic and 'there was virtu-ally a West Donegal Summer School in action'. Heaney recalled that 'Everybody was highly conscious of the crisis over the border, but everybody was on holiday and ready for revels: public houses, the singing of songs, the reciting of poems, the raking over of all matters of current concern, literary and political.'[8] Given the length and closeness of their association with him, Heaney and Friel's attention must have been riveted on Hume in January 1988, when his private relationship with Adams became a controversial public one.

The meeting between Hume and Adams that month, widely reported in the news media, had been occasioned by their decision at the end of 1987 to include their parties in their discussions; these party-to-party meetings would begin in March. Before they did, though, Northern Irish people would absorb a series of shocks that rivalled any felt during the Troubles. On 6 March, three unarmed IRA members in Gibraltar planning an attack on British soldiers stationed there were shot dead at point-blank range by British undercover agents. The incident con-firmed the opinion of many, especially nationalists, that the government was pur-suing a 'shoot-to-kill' policy against militant republicans. The passions aroused by these killings were compounded ten days later, at the funeral of the three dead activists. The police, unusually, stayed clear of the mourners, who were attacked by a loyalist with guns and grenades. Three people were killed and over sixty others wounded, and republicans suspected collusion between loyalists and the security forces. Three days later, as mourners gathered for the funeral of an IRA member who was one of those murdered at Milltown Cemetery, two British Army corporals inexplicably drove their car into the funeral procession and could not extricate themselves. One of them brandished a gun and fired a warning shot, and members of the crowd, fearing another attack, pulled them from the car, beat, stripped, and shot them. Father Reid, who had worked so hard for so long to get people with opposing views to talk with one another, suddenly attained world-wide notoriety when he rushed to offer last rites to the dying soldiers. Footage of the incident appeared on television screens globally, and Reid lamented that 'Our parish is seen as dripping in the blood of the murders.' Adams, more combatively, remembers the outrage republicans felt at commentary that branded the soldiers' killers 'savages' and 'animals'.[9]

Tensions on all sides were running so high after this terrifying fortnight that even Seamus Heaney attracted negative attention to himself at a banquet where he accepted the *Sunday Times* Award for Literary Excellence. He regarded the killing of the soldiers as '[b]arbaric IRA stuff, but not my fault, nor the fault of Irish people in general, although the *Sunday Times* and the British press in general had come out with the usual anti-Irish slabber' and recalls, 'I just didn't think I could stand up and receive their award without making clear my attitude to that kind of xenophobia.' The *Boston Globe* published excerpts from Heaney's speech a few months after he delivered it. Invoking T. S. Eliot's distinction between the 'detachment' necessary for artistic creation and actual 'indifference', Heaney had taken the opportunity to comment on Irish nationalists' growing disillusionment with the Anglo–Irish Agreement. This had, at first, seemed to him to imply 'an eye-level equilibrium between the British government and the Irish government, an abdication by both sides of the moral high ground, a recognition by Britain that the haughty fiction that the internal affairs of Northern Ireland were a matter of domestic British concern only was indeed a fiction'. Recent events, however, appeared to demonstrate that the British government regarded the agreement chiefly as a security measure. Commenting on the double standard by which military funerals taking place on the Falls Road were regarded as 'a tribal and undesir-able form of solidarity', while those in which 'the victims were British soldiers' and 'the mourners were British parents' were 'somehow immunized against tribal significance', Heaney remarked that

> The so-called 'spirit of the agreement' is not against the solemnization in public
> of national sorrows, but it is surely against the gradual obliteration from public
> British awareness of a realization that policies which Downing Street presum-
> ably regard as a hard line against terrorism can feel like a high-handed disregard
> for the self-respect of the Irish people in general; and it should be against any

downplaying of the fact that local Belfast paranoia—generated by a recent grave-yard bombing and shooting—played some part in the shamefully automatic cruelty and horror of the two British soldiers' deaths which followed.

Asserting that the 'caution rightly induced by detachment has its limits', Heaney recalled instead W. B. Yeats's 'challenge to the writer…to hold in a single thought reality and justice'. Some in attendance shouted 'rubbish' after Heaney's comments, an unusual if not unprecedented response to his words.[10]

In an atmosphere in which it took some fortitude for Heaney to align himself publicly with an Irish nationalist position in criticizing 'mainland' British complacency, Father Reid was not wrong to suppose that republicans and constitutional nationalists should be able to identify broad areas of agreement. Nonetheless, the three encounters between Sinn Féin and SDLP representatives in 1988 (the first of which took place just days after the last Gibraltar-related funeral) resembled strained arguments more than the exploratory discussions previously conducted by the parties' leaders and gave the participants a clearer sense of their differences than of what they might have in common. Although they agreed in principle on Ireland's right to 'self-determination' and opposed any purely internal solution to Northern Ireland's problems, Sinn Féin equated self-determination with a united Ireland and held to this as a firm objective. The SDLP, following Hume's reasoning, pointed out that unionists, too, were part of Ireland's population and thus shared in the right to self-determination. Because the British government in the Anglo–Irish Agreement had effectively stated 'that Irish unity and independence are entirely a matter for those Irish people who want it persuading those Irish people who don't', it seemed clear to SDLP members that 'In this context the "armed struggle" can only be a negative factor'. Because republicans did not share this view of the British government's neutrality, the parties largely talked past each other, but Adams believed the eight months of 'detailed debate' had served a useful purpose. In any case, although few knew it at the time, the Hume–Adams dialogue, which now involved the Irish government as well as Father Reid, continued after the SDLP–Sinn Féin talks ended.[11]

Since at least November 1985, even longer than Hume had been talking with Adams, Heaney had been thinking about writing a version of Sophocles's play *Philoctetes*. He might have considered the prospect indefinitely if not for a post-card from Friel in the spring of 1989 imploring him, in terms he could hardly refuse, to contribute a play to Field Day for 1990. In January 1990, Heaney finally yielded to 'peer pressure' from his colleagues on the Field Day board and committed himself to writing the play. Relying primarily on three English translations because he did not know Greek, Heaney worked 'line by line' on his version of the play through the first half of the year. Field Day produced *The Cure at Troy* that autumn, touring throughout Ireland during October, November, and early December.[12]

Academic commentary on *The Cure at Troy* has tended to focus on the most Heaneyesque elements of it: how the poet made the Sophocles text his own and its relationship to the rest of his oeuvre.[13] The avenue of inquiry I will follow here, however, pursues the question of what made Heaney decide that this relatively obscure Greek drama was appropriate for the pivotal period of Irish history in which he was writing his play and in which it would be seen by a diverse cross-section of the population of Ireland, north and south of the border. After all, Heaney insisted (truthfully) that his version of *Philoctetes* was essentially conservative, calling it 'just my homework for Field Day' and stating that his foremost concern in writing it had been to be faithful to the original while rendering it more accessible to those who would see it on tour.[14] So what associations did he expect the play to evoke for contemporary Irish (and especially contemporary Northern Irish) audiences? What meaning did it have for Heaney? Critics have called attention to the way in which the play's most famous Chorus speeches captured the global sense of political possibility at the time of its première and to the enthusiastic appropriation of Heaney's words by politicians of various political stripes, including Irish President Mary Robinson, US President Bill Clinton, and Gerry Adams (who borrowed from the play for the titles of both the European and the American editions of his personal account of events leading up to the Good Friday Agreement of 1998).[15] Though the close relationship between *The Cure at Troy* and the peace process in Northern Ireland is now common knowledge, it is usually conceived abstractly. I wish to put this general insight into concrete terms.

Many in *The Cure at Troy*'s first audiences found Field Day's decision to produce a classical Greek drama in 1990 puzzling.[16] Heaney himself, though, saw clear political relevance in its action. He had an advantage over most of Field Day's patrons in knowing a great deal both about Sophocles's original and about other classical sources touching on the story the play presents. For instance, Homer mentions the Greek archer Philoctetes in the 'catalogue of the ships' passage of his *Iliad*, relaying the information that seven ships full of his men were assembled at Troy,

> But he, their captain, lay on Lemnos isle
> in anguish, where the Akhaians had marooned him,
> bearing the black wound of a deadly snake.
> He languished there, but soon, beside the ships,
> the Argives would remember and call him back.[17]

The passage hints that the Greeks will have good reasons (known to Homer's listeners) to 'remember' Philoctetes, but, because he does not participate in the Trojan War until after the period covered by the *Iliad*, this is the only extant Homeric reference to him, apart from an offhand report in the *Odyssey* that he reached his home safely after the war ended.

Works by other classical authors, some writing before Sophocles and some after him, reveal other aspects of his legend. Scholar and playwright Oscar Mandel collates many of these references in a chapter on the traditional lore regarding Philoctetes in his 1981 book *Philoctetes and the Fall of Troy*, which Heaney likely consulted while working on his version of the play.[18] In some accounts, Philoctetes had been an Argonaut, serving alongside Hercules in Jason's famous expedition. When, after being poisoned, Hercules decided to die on his own terms, he asked Philoctetes to light his funeral pyre and bequeathed him, as a reward, his magical bow and arrows; as his body burned, Hercules attained god-like status. The link with Hercules was significant, Mandel points out, because he had led a successful assault on Troy during the reign of the Trojan King Priam's father. Although Hercules died before the Trojan War depicted in the *Iliad* began, his legendary weapon, wielded by Philoctetes, could have a share in the eventual Greek victory. In all the stories, Philoctetes is bitten by a snake during a stop the Greek forces make on their way to Troy. The snakebite is so disabling that Philoctetes is left behind on the island of Lemnos (populated in most versions of the legend) when the Greeks continue their journey to Troy. In some, though not all, of the stories, his companions abandon Philoctetes because they find the stink of his infected foot and his cries of pain intolerable. In some, but not all, of these accounts, Philoctetes bitterly resents their action. Ten years into the war, the Greeks capture a Trojan soothsayer who informs them that Troy cannot be taken without the assistance of Philoctetes and Neoptolemus (son of the pre-eminent Greek warrior, Achilles). The two men are brought to Troy, Philoctetes is cured of his wound, and the Greeks proceed to win the war. Traditionally, Philoctetes is credited with killing Paris, whose abduction of the Greek hero Menelaus's wife Helen initiated the conflict, and Neoptolemus with the death of King Priam, father of the Trojan hero Hector, who had been killed by his own father.[19]

In a chapter comparing Sophocles's *Philoctetes* with earlier plays about him by Aeschylus and Euripides, now lost but doubtless known to Sophocles, Mandel highlights Sophocles's distinctive treatment of the traditional material. All three dramas featured Odysseus, the Greek hero most renowned for cunning, as the emissary to Lemnos. All three presented him as having been personally responsible for abandoning Philoctetes there ten years earlier, and all depicted Philoctetes as implacably angry about how he had been treated and dreaming of revenge. Surviving commentaries suggest that, in the Aeschylus and Euripides plays, the drama centred on whether Philoctetes would be brought back into the Greek war effort and, if so, how. In these earlier dramatic treatments, Odysseus employed both deceit and theft to obtain the magic bow. *After* Philoctetes had been rendered helpless by the loss of his weapon, Odysseus in both versions induced him to rejoin the Greek forces.[20]

Sophocles's great innovation was to introduce a third major character, Neoptolemus, and to change the stakes of the action. As Mandel explains:

For Aeschylus and Euripides, the question posed by the play had been, 'Will Philoctetes yield to Odysseus?' But Sophocles...decided from the beginning that Philoctetes would *not* yield to Odysseus or any other mortal. He turned Philoctetes into a fixed and ultimately unproblematic character, and wrote instead a Neoptolemus play dealing with a movement from lie to truth in the mind and action of his new hero.[21]

In *Philoctetes*, Odysseus, with Neoptolemus in tow, arrives on the deserted island of Lemnos determined to obtain the bow belonging to Philoctetes by any means necessary (whether or not he believes Philoctetes himself to be equally indispensable to the Greek cause is a point left notably ambiguous in Sophocles's play). Rather than confront his erstwhile comrade directly, he proposes that Neoptolemus, who was not a member of the original expedition to Troy, should approach Philoctetes, gain his trust by telling his own story of mistreatment at the hands of Odysseus (the Aeschylus and Euripides plays had featured similar tall tales about Odysseus's perfidy), and take the bow when he lets down his guard. Neoptolemus reluctantly agrees, meets Philoctetes, and lies to him along the lines suggested by Odysseus. Instead of seizing the bow, however, he befriends (or pretends to befriend) the outcast, agreeing to take him home to trick the older warrior into coming with him of his own accord. Trusting him completely, Philoctetes allows Neoptolemus to hold the bow shortly before being overcome by a paroxysm of pain that pushes him to the limits of his endurance. While he sleeps after this fit, the Chorus urges Neoptolemus to slip away with the bow, but he insists that it will be useless without its owner, that Philoctetes himself must be given his destined share in the Greek victory to fulfil the oracle.

When Philoctetes wakes, the two warriors start walking to the ship, but Neoptolemus, overcome with remorse about deceiving the injured man, feels compelled to tell him the truth about where they are going and why. Philoctetes then angrily refuses to leave, demanding that Neoptolemus return the bow. He is about to do so when Odysseus enters and commandeers it. After a heated argument between Philoctetes and Odysseus, the latter orders Neoptolemus back to the ship with him. The Chorus urges Philoctetes to reconsider and come to Troy of his own free will to be healed and win glory, but he remains adamant in his refusal. Neoptolemus and Odysseus come back, and, in direct defiance of his commanding officer, Neoptolemus returns the bow to Philoctetes. When Odysseus leaves to summon the rest of the Greeks to punish the insubordinate youth, Neoptolemus, who has just proved his goodwill towards Philoctetes, pleads with him one last time to put aside his grievance and come with them. The older man refuses still and reminds him of his earlier promise to take Philoctetes home, and Neoptolemus agrees to keep it despite his fear of his comrades' retribution. As they prepare to depart, Hercules appears and orders Philoctetes to go to Troy to fulfil his destiny.

The intrusion of the *deus ex machina* at the end of Sophocles's play comes as a resounding anticlimax. Mandel argues persuasively, however, that the question of whether Philoctetes would go to Troy was not the question that interested Sophocles. His play 'is a drama of human ethics and politics from which the gods stand aside, if only temporarily'. Thus,

> the gods have permitted Neoptolemus just enough objective freedom to make the two authentic moral choices which constitute the play....Neoptolemus discovers that the most fluent eloquence cannot repair an injustice; justice must be *done*; it demands action....For a moment he had thought that returning the life-sustaining bow would do. But Justice is an exacting mistress. Neoptolemus must carry the injured man home: the false invitation must become a true one; and Sophocles underscores its consequences—the Greeks outraged, their cause ruined, a massive revenge threatened. When Neoptolemus makes the second and greater of his decisions, he does so fully conscious that he will become a hounded outcast. His moral victory is complete.

As in Shakespeare's late romances, tragedy is only narrowly averted by supernatural intervention, and Heaney's version of the text draws explicit parallels between Philoctetes and the character of Caliban in *The Tempest*.[22] The point of the play, for Heaney as for Sophocles, lay in the difficult decisions Neoptolemus must make without foreknowledge of their outcome.

Neoptolemus's moral quandary—'the crunch that comes when the political solidarity required from him by the Greeks is at odds with the conduct he requires from himself if he's to maintain his self-respect'—was what initially drew Heaney to *Philoctetes*, for reasons that had everything to do with his Northern Irish upbringing. 'That kind of dilemma', he observed, 'was familiar to people on both sides of the political fence in Northern Ireland', where 'to speak freely and truly on certain occasions would be regarded as letting down the side'. Heaney felt, as a consequence of having grown up there, 'a fascination with the conflict between the integrity of the personal bond and the exactions of the group's demands for loyalty'.[23] Neoptolemus is the only one of the play's three main characters able to acknowledge the legitimacy of both sides of this conflict. The dramatic interest resides in watching him move between the fixed poles represented by Odysseus and Philoctetes, who cling tenaciously to their belief in the righteousness of their respective positions. Neoptolemus is also the only character to change significantly during the drama. At first, although he deplores the deceitful methods advocated by Odysseus, he does not doubt their right to deprive Philoctetes of his bow to win the war. He even suggests that they should simply overpower the crippled man and take it by force. By the end of the play, he has become, effectively, a traitor to the Greek cause through his unwillingness to lie to Philoctetes. This does not mean, however, that Neoptolemus thinks Philoctetes is right to refuse to help the Greeks. Rather, he feels personally obligated to keep his promise to the older man and not to take advantage of his trust or force him to come to Troy against his wishes.

On one level, *The Cure at Troy* can be read as Heaney's defence of a political stance that involves seeking to understand various positions on an issue, whatever one's own opinion about it may be. As Neoptolemus's case demonstrates, this attitude is not without risk. A genuine willingness to listen to different points of view and seek common ground can leave one '[d]angerously out between' opposing factions, as Heaney wrote about his friend Sean Armstrong, a social worker killed in 1973 because of his activity on both sides of the sectarian divide. John Hume also left himself open to charges of double-dealing or worse as he continued to meet secretly with Gerry Adams throughout the period when Heaney was working on his play, while at the same time participating in an initiative by Peter Brooke, appointed Secretary of State for Northern Ireland in July 1989, to convene talks involving the British and Irish governments and the four main constitutional parties in the North: the SDLP, the Ulster Unionist Party (UUP), the Democratic Unionist Party (DUP), and the centrist Alliance Party. Brooke's 'talks about talks' continued through late 1989 and all of 1990 before actual negotiations got haltingly underway in 1991—only to collapse within months without making much progress. Hume's then assistant Mark Durkan, one of the few people who knew about both sets of conversations, recalls that Hume regarded them both 'as necessary, compatible and potentially complementary' and that he sought to build 'layers of understanding in both dialogue channels so that a convergence could be achieved'. He walked the tightrope between the two processes via a rigorous commitment to personal honesty, though there was 'obviously potential tension in trying to ensure that the SDLP did not adopt language or propositions in either channel that could confound or be seen to contradict understandings in the other'.[24]

Empathy features prominently in a mentality open to others' perspectives. Critic Michael Parker notes that Neoptolemus's 'observation first-hand of the excruciating agonies visited on his host' is a 'key factor' in his transformation. His witnessing of Philoctetes's suffering awakens his compassion and leads him to attempt to put things right. For Neoptolemus, just action is its own reward, although he understands that it is unlikely to be rewarding in the worldly sense of the word. The only thing that saves the situation for him is the reaction his understanding inspires in Philoctetes, who, Heaney wrote in a programme note for the Field Day production, 'suffers a division in himself between a sense of personal grievance and an inner command (which he keeps repressing) to comprehend his own experience, however painful, in the light of a more generous, less self-centred vision'.[25]

At the end of *The Cure at Troy*, as Heaney later explained, the speech of 'Hercules' (delivered by the Chorus in Heaney's play) 'is an expression of recognition which Philoctetes has repressed': 'the Chorus is the voice of his unconscious'.

In positing a psychological alternative to the *deus ex machina*, Heaney followed Edmund Wilson, whose essay 'The Wound and the Bow' had introduced him to *Philoctetes* when he was an undergraduate. Wilson states that the god's appearance 'may of course figure a change of heart which has taken place in Philoctetes as the result of his having found a man who recognizes the wrong that has been done him and who is willing to champion his cause in defiance of all the Greek forces'. So the change in Neoptolemus produces a change in Philoctetes, too, although Heaney noted the irony that, in surrendering his grievance, 'Philoctetes is "cured" but cured into the very loyalty and solidarity which Neoptolemus had to flout in order to bring the cure about'.[26]

Thus, as Mandel observes, by the end of his play Sophocles 'has managed to uphold both the principles of justice and of historical necessity, though they were contradictory up to this point'. He agrees, however, with another scholar who declared that 'nowhere in the whole of Sophocles is there a speech less impressive' than the one he wrote for Hercules.[27] Mandel explains the lapse by stressing that the god's speech was merely a formality to make the action of the play conform with what a classical Greek audience believed to have happened. From Sophocles's perspective, 'The chief point, that there is something superior to all this, has been made outside [the god's] jurisdiction.'[28] If Heaney read Mandel's book, one can imagine him finding permission in this passage to try to improve on Sophocles at this point in his own drama.

Heaney took more liberties with the Chorus speeches than with the dialogue passages in *The Cure at Troy*. The moment at which he decided to use the Chorus to highlight the relevance of the action to contemporary Irish concerns is discernible in his initial draft of the play. This consists at first of a straightforward rendering, albeit in Northern Irish vernacular speech, of the corresponding dialogue in *Philoctetes*. About a third of the way through Heaney's first notebook, though, in the middle of a conversation between Neoptolemus and the Chorus about why the apparently innocent Philoctetes has been doomed to such terrible suffering, words start to appear, upside down, on the facing page, as if Heaney had suddenly turned the book over and begun scribbling.[29]

This burst of lines contained the germ of what would become Heaney's invented prologue to the action, the Chorus speech that opens *The Cure at Troy* by reflecting on

> People so deep into
> Their own self-pity self-pity buoys them up.
> People so staunch and true, they're fixated,
> Shining with self-regard like polished stones.[30]

Heaney saw Philoctetes as 'an aspect of *every* intransigence, republican as well as Unionist, a manifestation of the swank of victimhood, the righteous refusal, the wounded one whose identity has become dependent upon the wound, the betrayed one whose energy and pride is a morbid symptom'. He sensed that the archer's 'pride in the wound is stronger than the desire for a cure' and confessed, moreover, to feeling a certain 'sympathy with that reluctance to shed the haughti-ness of the hurt spirit for the humdrum and *caritas* of renewal', with the 'intoxica-tion of defiance over the civic, sober path of adjustment'.[31]

Much commentary on Heaney's play, including that of the author himself, has drawn attention to the parallel he establishes in that opening speech between the role of the Chorus and the role of poetry ('the voice / Of reality and justice') because both operate on the interface 'Between / The gods' and human beings' sense of things' (2).[32] A didactic impulse also prompted Heaney to add the prologue because he knew the play would be performed for audiences whose familiarity with the lore concerning Philoctetes or the conventions of classical Greek drama could not be assumed. Thus, his Chorus, after describing people who spend their time 'Licking their wounds / And flashing them around like decorations', adds the words

I hate it, I always hated it, and I am
A part of it myself.
                          And a part of you,
For my part is the chorus, and the chorus
Is more or less a borderline between
The you and the me and the it of it.   (2)

Heaney's emphasis on the Chorus's function as a representative of the audience on stage gains significance as the action unfolds because the Chorus expresses a great deal of uncertainty throughout the play, strongly sympathizing with Philoctetes in his pain and resentment at some points and, at others, encouraging Neoptolemus to follow Odysseus's directives and urging Philoctetes to remember that the gods have foreordained that he should fight at Troy. In this way, both Sophocles and Heaney prompt the audience to acknowledge right on both sides.

What topical resonances might Field Day's audiences have seen in *The Cure at Troy*? Heaney insisted to Northern Irish journalist and political commentator Barry White that 'it is not a political allegory about solutions to the problems of Ireland', adding, 'My interest in the play was not in terms of putting a grid of its plot to equal the grid of the forces in the North.' Nevertheless, he understood that people who attended a Field Day production expected political commentary, however oblique. Hence, Heaney took the further precaution of specifically dis-avowing readings he considered 'entirely wrong'. Despite Edmund Wilson's use of Philoctetes to illustrate the romantic image of the artist, Heaney categorically denied that he saw himself as 'the wounded artist, turning his hurt into some-thing redemptive'. He also emphatically rejected 'any interpretation that the walled city of Troy equates to Londonderry and that the Greeks are the Catholics and the Trojans the Protestants' and denied that 'the taking of Troy is like the taking of the North'.[33] *The Cure at Troy* is certainly not an allegory in the sense of having only one 'correct' interpretation, but I concur with critic Hugh Denard's contention that 'Heaney's version often realizes the possibility of polyvalent allegorical alignments'. In fact, in attempting to foreclose interpretations he considered obviously mistaken, Heaney sometimes resorted to allegorical readings himself. At a seminar in 1995, for instance, he stated that 'Troy would be, not an United Ireland, as such, but an integrated possibility...a possible future.'[34]

The most obvious political readings of *The Cure at Troy* centre on Philoctetes as a unionist, with his magic bow representing the so-called unionist veto over constitutional change in Northern Ireland, which historically had been underwritten by loyalist paramilitary action as well as by political recalcitrance. Heaney acknowledged that he intended the association, while denying that the character should be interpreted as 'a trimly allegorical representation of hardline Unionism'. Self-exiled to the political wilderness since their categorical rejection of the Anglo–Irish Agreement in November 1985, unionists had defied the predictions of people like John Hume who had believed that the accord between the British and Irish governments would provoke a 'catharsis within unionism [that] would lead to a necessary adjustment to not having all power in its own hands'.[35] Instead, for the ensuing five years, unionists had clung to a futile resistance and to slogans including 'Ulster Says No!' and 'No Surrender!'

From the opening speech of *The Cure at Troy*, when the Chorus uses the word 'staunch' (often paired with 'unionist' in Northern Irish political discourse) to describe people smothered in self-pity, Heaney draws parallels between this mindset and Philoctetes's festering grievance (1). Audiences hearing Philoctetes denounce the Greek commanders—'Gods curse them all! / I ask for the retribution I deserve. / I solemnly beseech the gods to strike / The sons of Atreus in retaliation' (19)—might well have been reminded of DUP leader Ian Paisley's equally theatrical appeal to his God to 'deal with' British Prime Minister Margaret Thatcher shortly after she signed the hated agreement: 'O God, in wrath take vengeance upon this wicked, treacherous, lying woman; take vengeance upon her, Oh Lord, and grant that we shall see a demonstration of thy power.' Philoctetes's plaintive remarks about Lemnos—'a home where I never was at home' (29), 'The island's all there is / That'll stand to me' (51)—recall the passionate attachment to the physical landscape of Ireland that, for many unionists, can coexist with their denial of any cultural affiliation. His outraged reaction to the Chorus's suggestion that, deep down, he *wants* to come to Troy takes the form of a compact metaphor for the famed 'siege mentality' of Ulster Protestants: 'Never. No. No matter how I'm besieged. / I'll be my own Troy. The Greeks will never take me' (63). When Neoptolemus asks him point-blank, 'Are you going to stay here saying no for ever / Or do you come in with us?', Philoctetes rebuffs him before retorting with a question of his own: 'What sort of a surrender do you want?' (69). Scholar Nathan Wallace notes that such echoes of 'unionist rhetoric' were amplified in the Field Day production by the fact that Des McAleer, who played Philoctetes, 'growled and hollered his lines so that they sounded like Paisley'. Indeed, 'some in Field Day started to call the play "Ulcer Says No"'.[36]

Readings of Heaney's Philoctetes as a hardline unionist sometimes assume that Odysseus and Neoptolemus must represent nationalists or republicans and interpret the play as a symbolic depiction of reconciliation between Catholics/nationalists and Protestants/unionists in Northern Ireland.[37] This approach, however, misses the element of betrayal that Heaney regarded as central to the drama.[38] Philoctetes's grudge is not against a traditional enemy, but against former allies. As Michael Parker observes, his pus-filled wound is not his only agony: 'the callousness and injustice of fellow-countrymen acts as an additional, gnawing source of pain'. A more precise analogy might associate Odysseus with Thatcher and Neoptolemus with Peter Brooke, who, mere months into his tenure as Secretary of State for Northern Ireland, in November 1989, had stated publicly his belief that it was not possible to defeat the IRA by military means and that the British government 'would need to be imaginative' if the 'terrorists were to decide the moment had come when they wished to withdraw from their activities'.[39]

Brooke's remarks had an inflammatory effect on unionist opinion, but he got more positive attention from the Sinn Féin leadership. Hume had so far been disappointed in his hope that the Anglo–Irish Agreement would promote a new reasonableness on the unionist side, but Durkan relates that he had always given 'equal significance to the agreement's potential to refute the residual rationale for armed struggle'. Hume's ongoing discussions with Adams would have reinforced his sense of possible change at this time. Heaney's comment to Denard that Philoctetes's position could 'suit a Sinn Féiner' indicates that he, too, was alert to division on the nationalist side and mindful of the contemporary effort to forge a pan-nationalist consensus about ends and means that would preclude the threat or use of force—the magic bow of militant republicans.[40] In this scenario, Odysseus might represent the Irish government (also involved in the secret conversations), which had, from the republican point of view, marooned Northern Catholics in a repressive Protestant statelet at the time of partition, while Hume fits neatly into the mediating role of Neoptolemus.

In this context, Hume's developing personal relationship with Adams acquires a significance akin to that between Neoptolemus and Philoctetes in the play, and it is worth remembering that Hume's emotional insight and integrity were the qualities Heaney chose to emphasize in a November 1969 essay about his friend. 'What other politician has Hume's attentive intelligence and sympathy for his opponent?', he asked, adding that 'it seems to me that Hume has made the life-enhancing connection between vision and practice'. Adams, who understood that 'We were more the "enemy" than the British and the unionists for some of the

SDLP leadership', appreciated that Hume risked his reputation by continuing to meet and talk with him. Like Neoptolemus, Hume sometimes acted in ways that seemed contrary to his own party's interests in pursuit of what he regarded as higher aims, and political scientist Cathy Gormley-Heenan writes that 'hindsight has shown that Hume's sustained and successful attempts at engaging Adams in the [peace] process were undertaken at the expense of the SDLP's electoral successes in later years'. Hume himself likely understood and accepted that this would be the case; this was, after all, a man said to have told colleagues who disagreed with his tactics that 'If it's a choice between the party and peace, do you think I give a fuck for the party?'[41]

Heaney departs most decisively from the Sophoclean text at the end of *The Cure at Troy*, adding an original long speech before the lines attributed to Hercules. In a classical Greek production of the play, performed by three actors in masks, the actor playing Odysseus would also have played Hercules.[42] At least as significant as Heaney's insertion of his own lines at this juncture is the fact that he assigns them, as well as the Hercules speech, to the Chorus, so that the attitudes expressed seem to emanate directly from the consciousness of the audience. After vacillating throughout the drama, the Chorus finally speaks with conviction, exhorting both the characters on stage and the audience in the theatre to

> …hope for a great sea-change
> On the far side of revenge.
> Believe that a further shore
> Is reachable from here.
> Believe in miracles
> And cures and healing wells.   (77)

Female actors played the three Chorus members in the Field Day production, chanting lines both individually and in unison and accompanying them with stylized movement. The women's performances, notably effective, increased the Chorus speeches' impact.[43]

Eileen Battersby reported in the *Irish Times* before *The Cure at Troy*'s first performance that Heaney 'would be impatient with the idea that there is a coded message about Northern Ireland contained in the play or any inference that the play is an analogy for how the troubles could be resolved', quoting him as saying, 'I'm not a political writer and I don't see literature as a way of solving political problems....I don't think any miracle is going to happen in the North.' Though reviewers like Michael Coveney of the *Observer* seized on this Chorus speech as 'Heaney's first overtly political statement', the poet himself commented that 'The Chorus's sense of suffering is absolutely true, I think. No song or poem, they say, will ever right a wrong inflicted and endured. The rest…isn't politics. It's *sentiment*.'[44]

As sentiment, though, the Chorus's climactic speech staked its claim to the specific kind of efficacy that Heaney believed literature could have in the world. As early as 1972, he had stated that he did not subscribe to the view that 'poetry makes nothing happen': 'It can eventually make new feelings, or feelings about feelings, happen, and anybody can see that in this country for a long time to come a refinement of feelings will be more urgent than a re-framing of policies or of constitutions.' This speech expressed less a political position than a *disposition*: to focus on the future rather than the past, to believe that something better is possible. In the words of Heaney's friend and fellow Field Day board member Seamus Deane, 'The turn in his poetry that is matched by *The Cure at Troy* is not simply a turn from ground to air; it is a turn from place to time, from a past that was literally grounded...to a mobile future' that is 'not a preordained destiny into which the past, history, snugly fits' but 'a future the past could not imagine when it was embedded in its apparently inescapable stereotypes'.[45]

Heaney described *The Cure at Troy* as 'a kind of "post-cease-fire" writing *avant la lettre*', although he understood that the uplifting attitudes expressed by his Chorus remained 'in the realm of pious aspiration'.[46] The very title of Heaney's play points beyond the frame of the drama: towards the desirable future that Philoctetes finally decides to set his sights on, the end of his physical pain, the end of the Trojan War. The vision Heaney presents at the conclusion of *The Cure at Troy* seemed utopian in 1990, but it would be realized before the end of the decade to an extent that no one could have predicted when the play was touring.

Meanwhile, though, the war continued unabated. In fact, the level and intensity of violence increased around this time. During 1989, sixty-two people had died in Troubles-related incidents, but that number climbed to seventy-six in 1990 and ninety-four in 1991. The IRA had also resumed its bombing campaign aimed at economic targets, planting hundreds of bombs and incendiary devices in 1990 and 1991.[47] Both in Northern Ireland and in Britain these explosions were intended to cause extensive property damage and wreak havoc on the British economy. Naturally, though, the economic impact was felt most acutely in the North, already depressed after more than twenty years of political unrest.

These developments highlighted the tension within the republican movement between its political and military wings. Given the regularity with which, in the early 1990s, ill-timed and brutal attacks by the IRA undermined the credibility of Sinn Féin leaders who expressed the earnest desire of republicans for peace, there seems little reason to doubt Adams's assertion that they operated autonomously by the mid-1980s. Elected MP for West Belfast in 1983, Adams, in keeping with Sinn Féin's long-standing abstentionist policy, had refused to take his seat at Westminster. 'However,' he recounts, 'I was resolved that our interpretation of abstentionism would be for active abstentionism', explaining that Sinn Féin

leaders initiated or supported ongoing efforts to improve housing and social welfare in the areas they represented and that he himself 'tried to ensure that my status as MP could be used by local campaigners to get access to the agencies and
institutions which generally locked them out'. As historian Jeremy Smith points
out, though, this approach exposed a basic contradiction in republican thinking
because Sinn Féin's politics 'were about making the present state more bearable
for some of its most downtrodden victims' by 'working within the existing structures of power' and focusing on 'local and community-related questions', whereas
the IRA's leaders, with their exclusive focus on the national question, sought to
advance their aims by 'making the northern state unbearable' and collapsing
existing structures. This contradiction must have been frustrating for the Sinn
Féin leadership, and it certainly did not go unnoticed by others. In early January
1991, for instance, after IRA incendiary devices destroyed a factory and six shops,
the Northern Ireland Office minister responsible for the economy asked angrily if
jobs created in west Belfast as a result of investment demanded by Sinn Féin
would likewise be fire-bombed; later that month, after attacks on two additional
shops, he announced that £25 million earmarked for social and economic programmes would instead be used to pay for damage caused by the IRA.[48]

As IRA bombings and killings continued, so, too, did the war of words between
constitutional nationalists and republicans. This focused primarily on the legitimacy
and efficacy of political violence. As SDLP leader, John Hume consistently argued
that IRA attacks perpetuated partition by deepening divisions among Ireland's
people. He insisted, moreover, that most injustices suffered by the nationalist
community were, by then, directly attributable to the IRA campaign and would
be alleviated if that ended. In a speech to his party's annual conference in 1988,
for example, he stated that 'If I were to lead a civil rights campaign in Northern
Ireland today the major target of that campaign would be the IRA. It is they who
carry out the greatest infringements of human and civil rights, whether it is their
murders, their executions without trial, their kneecappings and punishment
shootings, their bombings of jobs and people.' On this occasion, and many others,
Hume also reminded his listeners of who bore responsibility for most Troubles
deaths, with the IRA having killed more people (including many Catholics) than
loyalists and the security forces combined.[49]

Some might see hypocrisy in Hume's forthright criticism of Sinn Féin and the
IRA in his speeches and writings at the same time as he was secretly developing a
working relationship with Sinn Féin's leader, but it's a safe bet that he was not saying anything publicly that he was not also saying, more vehemently, to Adams in
private. The odds are also good that Adams agreed with him because it was
becoming increasingly clear that Sinn Féin's support for the IRA prevented it
from increasing its share of the Northern Catholic electorate and even threatened
to erode its base in strongly republican areas. Having conceded, if only in his own
mind, Hume's fundamental argument that the only way to achieve a just and

peaceful united Ireland would be to persuade a majority in Northern Ireland—including, by necessity, many Protestants—to embrace the idea, Adams faced the even more urgent task of convincing militant republicans that an exclusively political approach offered a surer path to their shared goal than violence did. Essentially, 'The Sinn Féin leadership had to persuade the army leadership of the merits of the strategy we were developing.' This would be no easy feat: in a September 1990 interview with the London *Independent*, an IRA spokesperson had declared on the record that 'There will be no ceasefire, no truce, no cessation of violence short of British withdrawal.'[50]

In the late 1980s and early 1990s, IRA activity reinforced the impression that hardliners remained in charge. Republicans had from the start of the Troubles regarded members of the security forces as 'legitimate targets', but in August 1985 the IRA extended this designation to all people, Catholics as well as Protestants, who worked for or provided goods to the police or army. The category of those deemed deserving of death continued to expand in subsequent years. British military personnel serving in Germany and their families made soft targets, for example: in July 1989, a car bomb that killed a British soldier also injured his wife and children; barely two months later, the German wife of another British soldier was murdered; that October, both a Royal Air Force corporal and his six-month-old daughter were shot dead at a petrol station. Other deaths, like that of the Catholic nun killed by an IRA bomb that also blew up three policemen near Armagh in July 1990, were regarded by the IRA as regrettable collateral damage, but they hurt the republican cause nonetheless.[51] When, in May 1990, the IRA killed two Australian lawyers on holiday in the Netherlands after mistaking them for off-duty British servicemen, contributions from republican sympathizers in Australia dropped sharply.[52]

Although Adams stated publicly that the June 1990 car-bomb killing of a retired police reservist and his wife could not be condoned, he also reaffirmed that Sinn Féin's relationship with the IRA remained one of 'critical support'. To condemn such attacks outright would have been to invite a split in the republican movement between those seeking political progress toward a sovereign and united Ireland and those convinced that one last military push could induce the British government to yield control of the North. The republican movement was, historically, much given to schism, and Adams had already experienced one such split on his watch as Sinn Féin's president when, in 1986, he persuaded the requisite two-thirds majority of delegates to the party's annual convention to end its abstentionist policy in the Republic of Ireland and allow Sinn Féin candidates who won election to the Irish parliament to participate fully in it. The motion carried because the IRA had, unexpectedly, voted a couple of weeks earlier to amend its own constitution to remove the ban on supporting successful republican candidates who took their seats in the Dáil. However, the revised policy provoked a walkout led by the party's former president, who formed a new organization called Republican Sinn Féin.[53] Adams survived this challenge to his leadership, but he knew that a similar split on the *military* wing of the republican movement would spell disaster for anyone hoping to see an early end to the armed conflict.

An IRA operation during the run of *The Cure at Troy*, especially the part of it that took place just outside Derry—home of Field Day, John Hume, and Martin McGuinness alike—epitomized various tensions at the time. In the wee hours of 24 October, Patsy Gillespie, a 42-year-old father of three from Derry who worked as a kitchen assistant for the Ministry of Defence, was ordered by the IRA to drive a van loaded with 1,400 pounds of explosives into the search-bay area of a permanent vehicle check-point on the border between Northern Ireland and the Republic while his wife and 12-year-old daughter were held hostage at their home. Although the IRA told Gillespie's wife that he would return safely, the bomb was set to explode as soon as he arrived, killing him along with five soldiers and wounding at least seventeen other servicemen and more than thirty civilians. A similar 'human bomb' attack at a check-point near Newry resulted in the death of one soldier (who happened to be a Catholic from Northern Ireland), while the driver managed to escape with a broken leg; a third such bomb, at an army camp in Omagh, failed to explode.[54]

More than two thousand people from both sides of Derry's sectarian divide attended Gillespie's funeral. Catholic bishop Edward Daly decried the IRA's recent actions, which he said had crossed 'a new threshold of evil': 'Over the years the Provisional IRA have used people's homes to launch their vile attacks and they have used people's cars to launch other vile attacks. Now they have descended a step lower to use people's lives to launch their vile attacks....Jesus Christ said "By their fruit you shall know them" and the fruits of the IRA are strewn all over Europe from a murdered infant in West Germany and murdered Australian tourists in Holland to murdered pensioners in Enniskillen'. Coming from Bishop Daly—who had lived in Derry throughout the Troubles and whose photo waving a bloodstained handkerchief over the body of one of the unarmed demonstrators shot by British paratroopers on Bloody Sunday in 1972 had become an iconic image of the nationalist struggle in the North—these words struck close to home. Hume also denounced the human bomb tactic as both cowardly and incapable of achieving its objective because 'There is no way that any government in the western world today, because of the implications for international terrorism, could surrender to this type of activity'.[55]

Many in the British government had already concluded that the only way to establish peace in Northern Ireland would be to negotiate with republicans, but they could not afford to do so while the IRA was committing atrocities such as these. Aware of the debate within republican ranks over the best means of advancing a republican agenda, however, they wanted to fortify those leaning towards an exclusively political approach. In the autumn of 1990, Northern Ireland

Secretary Peter Brooke, who had already scandalized unionists with his comment a year earlier that the government would need to be 'imaginative' if republicans ever abjured the use of force, authorized the reactivation of a 'line of contact' between the British government and republicans involving three go-betweens of neutral status in and near Derry. This gave high-level British officials insight into the thought processes of militant republicans and an opportunity to share their own while allowing them to maintain the notion that the government was not talking with terrorists. Brooke sent up another trial balloon on 9 November, stating in a speech that the British government had 'no selfish strategic or economic interests in Northern Ireland': 'Britain's purpose...is not to occupy, oppress or exploit but to ensure democratic debate and free democratic choice'. The Sinn Féin leadership hearkened to both his words and their subtext, as Adams recalls. They did not accept Brooke's 'explanation of British strategy in Ireland', but 'his remarks did suggest possibilities worth exploring'. After all, Adams reflected (calling to mind the fall of the Berlin Wall and the reunification of Germany, democratic elections in former Eastern Bloc countries, and the freeing of Nelson Mandela in South Africa), 'Unfolding events on the world stage were evidence that governments, and apparently intractable situations, could change.' By the end of that month, John Major had succeeded Margaret Thatcher as Conservative Party leader and Prime Minister, further enabling a reorientation of British policy.[56]

Hume's decision to engage with Adams had been motivated by his reassessment of the prevailing assumption that a political agreement on Northern Ireland's future would lead to peace. Instead, he had come to believe that peace itself would be a necessary precondition to any viable agreement—and achieving it would have to involve talking with those making or supporting war.[57] Now the British government seemed to share his view of the situation. It had previously focused on trying to isolate 'the men of violence' by seeking consensus among representatives of the constitutional parties in Northern Ireland (SDLP, UUP, DUP, and Alliance). This approach had not achieved much, for two reasons. First, these politicians agreed on little apart from their hatred of the IRA. Second, against a backdrop of violence on both sides, all parties remained defensive, making real compromise unlikely if not impossible.

Adams thought that 'The only possible reason London wanted any dialogue with republicans was to achieve an IRA ceasefire', an objective the Sinn Féin leadership would not be induced to adopt unless it was convinced that ending the armed struggle would help to realize republican aims. Even then, Sinn Féin in turn would have to make a successful case to the IRA leadership 'that the republican cause would be advanced [in] this way, that it was the Army's responsibility to assist such a development and encourage such a process', a prospect that still seemed distant in 1990. Despite unhappy experiences of communicating indirectly with past British officials, however, Adams and McGuinness reasoned that the possible benefits of contact outweighed the risks. Thus began an extended period of 'private teasing out and public semaphore' between republicans and the British government.[58]

Such 'semaphore' politics, in which public actions and statements were also directed at particular people, were not limited to these two participants. For example, the IRA announced its first Christmas truce in fifteen years on 23 December 1990, three days after a record number of prisoners in Northern Ireland were released on parole over Christmas. The truce's 'message of goodwill' was intended for the British government as well as for the population at large—and especially, Adams recounts, for Father Reid, John Hume, and others 'working with the Sinn Féin leadership'—offering 'evidence that the IRA leadership was able to think outside the frame when it wanted to'. Most of the time, though, it appeared that it did not want to, as demonstrated barely six weeks later by a mortar fired at the British prime minister's residence at 10 Downing Street, which landed less than fifteen yards from where Major was chairing a cabinet meeting.[59]

Conflicting signals abounded in the early 1990s, and ordinary citizens in Northern Ireland, whose lives and livelihoods depended on their coded meanings, strove to decipher the visible signs of a largely invisible process. Speculation-filled news reports and commentary about the motives behind the contradictory gestures and remarks of various political actors reflected the pervasive sense at the time that established ground was shifting, but also acute uncertainty about the direction of the shift. Most of the questions being asked could not be answered by outside observers. Which IRA faction currently had the upper hand? Did moderate or extreme unionist leaders better reflect the views of most Northern Protestants? Why was the SDLP taking a harder nationalist line in the interparty talks that took place intermittently throughout this period? What, on any given day, was the state of relations between the British and Irish governments? Was Northern Ireland moving towards peace or all-out civil war?

Fear of the latter possibility grew pronounced through 1991 and 1992, as the North experienced a terrifying upsurge in violence perpetrated by loyalists as well as republicans. In addition to indiscriminate bombing attacks, which by November 1992 had induced many municipalities to begin closing security gates around their town centres for the first time since the 1970s, tit-for-tat killings by paramilitaries on both sides dominated the news cycle. On 17 January 1992, for instance, seven Protestants who had done construction work for the security forces were killed on their drive home by a huge IRA bomb at Teebane Crossroads, near Cookstown, County Tyrone; an eighth man died a few days later. The following month, an off-duty policeman shot three people dead in the Sinn Féin office on the Falls Road just one day before the murder of five Catholics in a bookmaker's shop on the Ormeau Road in Belfast—the loyalist Ulster Freedom Fighters (UFF) concluded the message in which they claimed responsibility for the latter attack with the words 'Remember Teebane'.[60]

Many of the people killed in incidents such as these were previously unin-volved in the conflict. More civilians died in 1991 than in any year since 1976, and by the end of February 1992 the civilian death toll had already reached thirty-one. In early November 1992, in response to IRA bombs that had damaged hun-dreds of Protestant homes, the UFF announced that it would be expanding its campaign to include 'the entire republican community'. An associated paramili-tary, the Ulster Defence Association (UDA), declared its intention that New Year's Eve to intensify its activities 'to a ferocity never imagined', detailing later its plans to attack a 'pan-nationalist front' which would include members of the SDLP, Gaelic Athletic Association, and the Irish government, as well as the IRA and Sinn Féin.[61]

Meanwhile, unionist politicians continued to fixate on the 1985 Anglo–Irish Agreement, which they (in stark contrast to republicans) regarded as the first step towards a united Ireland.[62] Having maintained for years after the agreement's adoption that they could not talk with Irish nationalists or even do business with British ministers as long as it remained in effect, many were, by the end of the decade, starting to look for some way out of the corner into which they had painted themselves. Perceiving this, Brooke managed by 1991 to get unionists around a negotiating table with the SDLP and the Alliance Party via a creative re-interpretation of their demand for 'suspension' of the Inter-Governmental Conference (by which they had meant a permanent shut-down) as an extended recess and by repeatedly reminding them that the only way to get rid of the hated agreement would be to help the governments devise a better 'replacement' for it. In preparation for these talks, unionists agreed in principle that they should pro-ceed along three fronts, originally described by Hume, which focused on different aspects of the problem: Strand One dealing with the internal government of Northern Ireland, Strand Two with relations between Belfast and Dublin, and Strand Three with relations between the Republic of Ireland and Britain. This first round of discussions quickly fell apart over procedural questions, but it set an important precedent that Brooke's successor as Secretary of State for Northern Ireland, Patrick Mayhew, exploited in 1992. Again, unionists (at least the more moderate UUP) made some small steps towards engagement with Irish national-ists in both Northern Ireland and the Republic, but, as political scientists Paul Bew and Gordon Gillespie put it, despite an investment of two years and £5 mil-lion, the talks overall 'served only to emphasise the seemingly irreconcilable dif-ferences between nationalism and unionism'.[63]

Given a choice between Northern Ireland's unionists and republicans, the British government might well have suspected by the end of 1992 that the latter could prove marginally more flexible. At any rate, its back-channel communica-tion with the Sinn Féin leadership increased around this time. That autumn, the British representative briefed republican contacts on the progress of the Mayhew talks ('going nowhere') and gave them a preview of a speech Mayhew would deliver in Coleraine in December, in which he created controversy by saying that the British government had 'no pre-selected constitutional outcome' in mind for Northern Ireland and that Sinn Féin would be eligible to take part in talks about its future if the IRA ended its military campaign. In a public response to Mayhew's speech, Adams maintained that his party had a 'democratic mandate' to participate in negotiations regardless of what the IRA did, arguing that such preconditions served 'only to delay' its 'inevitable involvement'; privately, Sinn Féin's leaders continued to press for face-to-face meetings with British government officials. They seemed tantalizingly close to achieving this intermediate goal by 19 March 1993, when the government sent, via the Derry link, an offer of exploratory talks with Sinn Féin if the violence were halted—with the British representative hinting that an unannounced suspension of two to three weeks might be enough to facilitate such a dialogue.[64]

The Sinn Féin leadership, both optimistic and sceptical about the British overture, passed the information on to the IRA, which proffered a response of sorts the next day with two bombs detonated in a shopping centre in the English town of Warrington on a busy Saturday. The attack left a 3-year-old boy dead and fifty-six others wounded; the five most critically injured were young people, including a 12-year-old boy who died a few days later. The arbitrariness of the target, the youth of the victims, and the fact that the explosions took place outside Northern Ireland all contributed to what Bew and Gillespie term 'a wave of revulsion throughout Britain and Ireland against terrorist killings'. This intensified on 25 March, when the UFF killed five Catholics in the North within twelve hours. On 1 April, the unionist Belfast *News Letter* reported that 42 per cent of four thousand readers it polled had expressed some support for loyalist paramilitary violence, with 80 per cent regarding this as a reaction to republican killings which would 'wither away if the IRA ended its bloody campaign'.[65]

An elderly man named Gordon Wilson felt the horror of all these developments more keenly than most. He had been present at the war memorial in Enniskillen in November 1987 when an IRA bomb exploded just before the annual wreath-laying ceremony was due to begin, crushing members of the assembled crowd, including Wilson himself, under the rubble of a collapsed building; his 20-year-old daughter, Marie, was among those killed. Speaking to a BBC reporter that evening, Wilson had insisted that 'I bear no ill will. I bear no grudge. Dirty sort of talk is not going to bring her back to life', adding that he forgave the bombers: 'I shall pray for those people tonight and every night.' Wilson became a reluctant celebrity after this broadcast, credited with forestalling immediate loyalist retaliation.[66]

Owing to his prominence as a peace campaigner after the Enniskillen bombing, Wilson had been invited by Taoiseach Albert Reynolds (who succeeded Charles Haughey as leader of Fianna Fáil in February 1992) to join the Irish senate. On 25 March 1993, in his first speech to Seanad Éireann, Wilson announced that the IRA had granted his request for a personal meeting, the time and place of which would remain secret, and urged other senators to support his individual plea to the organization to end its military campaign, 'which seems from the outside more and more to have become a campaign for continued political stagnation'. He planned to tell the IRA that 'In the eyes of all but a small percentage of Irish people the so-called armed struggle has degenerated into a campaign of sickening sectarian killing of fellow Irish men and women'. He looked forward to the conversation, he informed his colleagues, although he suspected that others might accuse him of 'naivety'—after all, 'The IRA are composed of human beings like ourselves, and they have suffered too, just as we have because of them.'[67]

A thin man with a heavily lined face, prominent ears, and large horn-rimmed spectacles, Wilson seemed an unlikely challenger to the IRA, but many must have shared his belief that if anyone could get through to militant republicans, he could. His personal peace mission, however, ended in disappointment. The two IRA representatives he met with merely delivered a message from the IRA leadership apologizing for the loss of his daughter and reiterating their contention that 'peace will only come about as the result of a process which takes as its starting point the proven failure of partition and which accepts the fundamental right of the Irish people to self-determination'. 'They told me the British Government must invite them to the table without pre-conditions', Wilson reported, expressing his own opinion that 'They can't have it both ways, they want to talk with a gun in one hand and a pencil in the other. It's just not on.' 'I appealed to them', he said, 'to forget the past and think about the future of this lovely land and they said they could not. Instead they must continue to do what they have done.'[68]

Wilson was so disheartened by the IRA's apparent unwillingness to reconsider its tactics that he joined the growing chorus of people in Britain, Northern Ireland, and the Republic calling for internment of terrorist suspects—a demand Adams terms 'the equivalent of using petrol to put out a fire'. For nearly four and a half years by the spring of 1993, he and Hume had been conferring privately to try to articulate a formula that would give the IRA a positive reason to end its military operations. In the autumn of 1991, they had hit upon the idea of 'a joint declaration between the two governments' to make explicit the ideas about British neutrality and the possibility of Irish unity by negotiation and consent that republicans felt were only implied in the Anglo–Irish Agreement. Hume wrote the first draft of such a declaration in October 1991 and submitted it to the Irish government for consideration. An 'amended document' emerged from this process which Hume brought back to Adams, who found it revised out of recognition and thus 'totally unacceptable' to republicans. From the Sinn Féin leadership's perspective, 'The argument we had put consistently about the need for an alternative to armed struggle was valid. The problem was that those we were dealing with on the Irish side did not seem capable of producing such an alternative. Increasingly, we would have to spell out to them what was required. We would also have to figure that out for ourselves.'[69]

At the February 1992 Sinn Féin party conference, members had debated a manifesto called *Towards a Lasting Peace in Ireland*, which the leadership had been working on for 'almost a year'. This paper called on the British and Irish governments to work to convince unionists of the potential benefits of Irish unity and on the international community to support these efforts. Taken in context, Adams asserts, it represented 'a major shift in Sinn Féin thinking', which had previously assumed that any settlement would come from bilateral discussions between republicans and the British government: 'Now the onus for progress was being put very much on the two governments with sovereign power and authority.' Adams remembers that, during the debate on the paper, 'I remarked that republicans might have to accept interim phases and interim arrangements while still working for a united Ireland'. In the British general election of April 1992, though, Adams had been unseated as MP for West Belfast. The SDLP outflanked Sinn Féin partly by convincing unionists to vote for their candidate, Joe Hendron, instead of for unionist candidates who would lose in that constituency anyway. There were private compensations for this public humiliation, however. Hume told Adams later that 'it was this event that persuaded him that I was serious about our discussions and my desire to build a peace process' because 'my refusal to break confidence and exploit our discussions for party political or personal reasons convinced him of my good faith'.[70]

Trust between the two men would prove essential when, in early April 1993 (days after Gordon Wilson's discouraging interview with IRA representatives), Adams was spotted by an acquaintance of local journalist Eamonn McCann entering Hume's house in Derry. McCann had been doing freelance work for the *Sunday Tribune* newspaper and passed this gossip on to the Belfast correspondent for that paper, who phoned Hume to ask if the story was true. Hume first denied the report, McCann recalls, but about 'two minutes later...phoned back and said, "Look, I don't want to be telling you lies, yes it is true." ' While acknowledging that a meeting had taken place, Hume and Adams initially refused to elaborate on what they had discussed, prompting unionist accusations that the SDLP leader was 'engaging in a futile initiative which would only fuel the IRA's propaganda machine'. Adams believed that Hume found the revelation unsettling in part because few of his party colleagues (unlike the Sinn Féin inner circle) had even known the dialogue was taking place and did not appreciate learning about it in this way.[71] As Hume's then assistant Mark Durkan recalls, 'people just felt that John had lost his way, lost his judgement and was throwing away his reputation and was throwing away his long pedigree of non-violence and his claims to statesmanship. There was very strident and very negative criticism and a lot of friends shrank back from him in that time.'[72]

As in January 1988, when the news that Hume and Adams had been talking seemed especially shocking to many observers because it came barely two months after the Enniskillen atrocity, so this meeting, just three weeks after the

Warrington bombs, appeared to some to be calculated to bolster the IRA's standing at a time when its support was dwindling. Deputy DUP leader Peter Robinson expressed the view that no 'self-respecting unionist would be involved in any talks while the SDLP was engaged in the twin process of having discussions with Provisional IRA representatives.... It seems almost as if John Hume has come to the aid of the IRA at a time when their spirits were low.' Many unionists, though, had long regarded Hume as 'a respectable front for a sinister terrorist campaign'. Nationalists were inclined to withhold judgement until they saw what results the dialogue between Hume and Adams might yield. As a leader writer for the *Irish News* commented, 'The simple fact of the matter is that there will never be peace until so-called unconstitutional forces are persuaded that there is a better way to achieve change than through violence.'[73]

As the Sinn Féin leadership assessed the impact of the news story, they came to believe that 'a public debate around a peace initiative could be productive': 'The popularity of a peace initiative could help inject a momentum that might make progress easier.' Hume and Adams discussed the matter and agreed on the desirability of revealing more about the substance of their talks, and Hume convinced his SDLP colleagues to set aside their suspicion of Adams by promising 'that if this initiative failed or proved folly, he would personally take the consequences, and not the party'. On 24 April, the two nationalist leaders issued a joint statement describing the scope and purpose of their ongoing conversations. This began with the observation that 'the most pressing issue facing the people of Ireland and Britain today is the question of lasting peace and how it can best be achieved', relating this to their own project:

> In striving for that end we accept that an internal settlement is not a solution because it obviously does not deal with all the relationships at the heart of the problem.
>
> We accept that the Irish people as a whole have a right to national self-determination. This is a view shared by a majority of the people of this island though not by all its people.
>
> The exercise of self-determination is a matter for agreement between the people of Ireland. It is the search for that agreement and the means of achieving it on which we will be concentrating.[74]

This statement registered, albeit in coded form, the evolution in Sinn Féin thinking that had taken place over the previous couple of years. The distance between the party's position in the spring of 1993 and traditional republican assumptions can be seen in the subtle but critical difference between the IRA's insistence on 'the fundamental right of the Irish people to self-determination' and the Hume–Adams definition of self-determination as 'a matter for agreement between the people of Ireland'. Whereas the 'Irish people' of the first formula could be, and was, taken to refer only to those who considered themselves to be Irish (i.e. Irish nationalists), the second pointedly extended the franchise to the Irish people 'as a whole' (as in *all* 'the people of this island'). The emphasis on agreement, which implied negotiation and consent, was of similarly recent vintage. These shifts reflected the Sinn Féin leadership's growing recognition that a million Northern Protestants would not disappear merely because the border did—significant because the republican movement had not, historically, let that reality get in the way of its aspirations. Unionists generally failed to appreciate such fine distinctions, but definite signs of progress were apparent to those skilled at close reading.

What this joint statement did not say was as important as what it did. Durkan explains: 'While the concept of possible Hume–Adams proposals was now in common political parlance, none of this revealed that they were really drafting an intended joint declaration, not for themselves but for the British Prime Minister and the Taoiseach. Both governments were fully aware of this but for their own reasons did little to reflect this or relieve any of the excoriating criticism that was being heaped on Hume.'[75] An agreed draft of such a declaration was arrived at by early June 1993 and was delivered to the British and Irish governments with the expectation, Durkan writes, that they would 'concentrate on working together to bring the project of a joint declaration forward (to herald a ceasefire and subsequent inclusive negotiations)'. Throughout that summer, though, amid continuing violence on both sides, Hume and Adams awaited developments with increasing impatience. John Major's majority in the British parliament was so small that he needed the nine UUP MPs to support his government's policy regarding the Maastricht Treaty for greater European integration (as they eventually did in a critical vote of confidence in late July), so he could not afford to upset them by appearing to respond positively to an initiative coming from Northern nationalists. Moreover, the type and scale of IRA violence at the time seemed, in historian Jeremy Smith's words, 'if not actually designed to push the British backwards then to appease those Republican hardliners who stood against a cease-fire'.[76]

On 25 September, Hume and Adams pressured the two governments to move on the joint declaration by announcing that their meetings had resulted in a report 'on the position reached to date', designed for 'wider consideration' between London and Dublin. Without providing any details about the substance of this report, they stated that 'We are convinced from our discussions that a process can be designed to lead to agreement among the divided people of this island, which will provide a solid basis for peace. Such a process would obviously also be designed to ensure that any new agreement that might emerge respects the diversity of our different traditions and earns their allegiance and agreement.' A remarkable feature of the debate their statement provoked is that it took place in the absence of any public knowledge of what the report it referenced contained. Unionist politicians voiced some negative responses, but Adams recollects that the 'general reaction reflected the heartfelt desire of the vast majority of Irish people for progress towards real peace'. British and Irish government officials remained non-committal, but the IRA (having been informed of 'the broad principles' contained in the Hume–Adams paper) issued its own statement welcoming the initiative.[77]

The IRA's stated 'vested interest in seeking a just and lasting peace in Ireland' was hard to square, however, with its contemporaneous actions, which included bombs in Belfast city centre, south Belfast, and London. By the autumn of 1993, news of the latest sectarian killings in Ireland had jostled for space in British and Irish newspapers with dispatches on the civil war in Bosnia for more than a year and a half, with Bosnia serving as a constant reminder of how much worse things could get. That October, which would prove to be the deadliest single month of the Troubles since the same month in 1976, many must have feared that Northern Ireland was on the brink of outright chaos. On 23 October—the day after Hume in the House of Commons called his dialogue with Adams 'the most hopeful sign of lasting peace that I have seen in twenty years' and urged the British govern-ment once again to '[h]urry up and deal with' their report—the IRA planted a bomb in a fish shop on the Protestant Shankill Road which killed ten people, including one of the bombers, and injured fifty-seven. The no-warning attack missed its intended target, members of a loyalist paramilitary group who sometimes met in an upstairs office, but took 'a heavy toll of shoppers'; an early news report observed that, even if the bombing had gone according to plan, 'injuries to other people were inevitable because the offices adjoin shops on a busy stretch of the road', adding that it appeared 'to have been designed to draw the maximum violent response from loyalists'. Predictably, in the five days following the Shankill Road bombing, loyalist paramilitaries killed four Catholics and wounded five others.[78]

Adams felt 'shattered' by news of the Shankill explosion, 'conscious of how damaging this was going to be to our efforts to breathe life into a peace initiative that appeared close to collapse'. Nevertheless, he attended the dead bomber's funeral and even helped to carry the coffin, an action for which he was denounced. To do otherwise would have been to risk forfeiting any ability he had to influence militant republicans, but the consensus, according to the British *Independent on Sunday*, was that the 'Shankill bomb outrage' had 'all but extinguished hopes that a settlement of the 25-year-old "Troubles" might emerge from the SDLP–Sinn Féin dialogue'. This gloomy assessment seemed confirmed by a statement Reynolds and Major issued on 29 October, in which they emphasized their gov-ernments' refusal to negotiate with those who used, threatened, or supported violence; although they described Hume's efforts as 'courageous and imaginative', they publicly rejected the Hume–Adams proposals.[79] Adams, recalling the differ-ence between this public stance and what had been happening privately, remarks indignantly that 'All of this was spun to the media as "no talks with Sinn Féin". It ignored the reality that each government had been talking to republicans for years, in the Irish government's case, only a few days earlier.' Reynolds, however, explains that he and Major 'agreed that we had to distance ourselves from the Hume–Adams initiative, that it was now so tainted as to be unusable; the only way forward was for the two governments to take matters into their own hands'. The prime ministers reasoned that 'the Hume–Adams initiative was being declared dead in order to keep it alive'.[80]

The violence of that horrific month continued and presaged worse to come when members of the UFF stormed into the Rising Sun bar in the village of Greysteel and opened fire on a crowd of locals celebrating Halloween, killing seven and injuring more than a dozen others; the paramilitary described its random attack as revenge on the 'nationalist electorate' for the Shankill bombing. Martin McGuinness made a public appeal for calm, though his words were also directed specifically to militant republicans: 'Emotions are running very high in the present climate and the Protestant community may now fear a possible retaliatory attack. I readily understand these feelings and I am stating with all of the authority of my position with Sinn Féin that such actions are totally contrary to republican philosophy'.[81] Hume broke down and wept at the funeral of one of the Greysteel victims after the daughter of the deceased told him that 'when we said the rosary around my daddy's coffin we prayed for you, for what you're trying to do to bring peace'. 'The pressure on both of us was intense,' Adams remembers, 'but it was John's instinctive, emotional and tearful response ... which in many ways captured the public mood'. Despite the dismissal by the governments and sometimes 'vitriolic' criticism from sections of the media, 'broad nationalist popular endorsement of Hume/Adams grew by leaps and bounds'. This groundswell of public support derived from the respect and trust the two leaders commanded in their respective constituencies rather than from any popular knowledge of what the so-called Hume–Adams approach actually entailed, but it encouraged them both to keep talking, with Hume on 4 November going so far as to declare ('rashly' in Durkan's view) that there could be peace within a week if the governments moved on the lines suggested in the Hume–Adams report.[82]

Albert Reynolds, at any rate, was not immune to the popular nationalist sentiment, especially as it manifested itself within his own party, and he hinted both publicly and privately that the British and Irish governments were in fact seriously considering the Hume–Adams proposals while also indicating that 'other soundings' would likewise inform their deliberations; Durkan notes that this second point reflected the effort by the two governments 'to include paragraphs more customized to unionist and loyalist perceptions alongside the worthy terms in the Hume–Adams draft declaration'.[83] 'Behind the scenes', Jeremy Smith writes, the governments were working 'hard and at times acrimoniously to compose their joint statement', a project lent urgency by the spiralling violence on both sides. Little of this frantic activity showed on the surface, however, and Hume and Adams, like everybody else, had to guess at what was really happening. Major's public comment on 15 November (that 'if the IRA end violence for good, then—after a sufficient interval to ensure the permanence of their intent—Sinn Féin can enter the political arena as a democratic party and join the dialogue on the way ahead') would not have reassured them that his government was prepared to act in a manner capable of convincing militant republicans that politics would pay better dividends than violence.[84]

To 'maintain the public focus and pressure on John Major', Hume and Adams issued yet another joint statement on 20 November, expressing their hope that the British government would 'respond positively and quickly to the clear opportunity for peace' offered by their initiative. The IRA also 'again welcomed the Hume/Adams initiative and reiterated both its support and desire for a peace process'. Unionists and loyalists strove to apply their own pressure on the British prime minister, and matters were further complicated for him, Smith observes, by 'an Irish Foreign Affairs document on the future of Northern Ireland, with a distinctly "green" hue, [which] mysteriously found its way into the Irish press, enraging Unionists', and by other press leaks about the secret British contacts with Sinn Féin dating back to 1990. After all this exhortation, speculation, revelation, and recrimination, it came almost as an anticlimax when, on 15 December 1993, Reynolds and Major issued their long-awaited Joint Declaration on Northern Ireland.[85]

The Downing Street Declaration, as it came to be called, committed the two governments to working together towards a new, consent-based political framework comprising institutional arrangements within Northern Ireland, on the island of Ireland, and between Britain and Ireland: Hume's three-strand approach. The British government repeated its assertion that it had 'no selfish strategic or economic interest in Northern Ireland' and restated its aim of seeing peace, stability, and reconciliation achieved by agreement among all the people of Ireland. If a majority both North and South agreed that they wanted a united Ireland, the British government would introduce the legislation necessary to give effect to that wish—or, indeed, to any other constitutional arrangement arrived at by agreement of the people living in Ireland. The Irish government accepted that 'the democratic right of self-determination by the people of Ireland as a whole must be achieved and exercised with and subject to the agreement and consent of a majority of the people of Northern Ireland' and pledged, following any settlement, to propose changes to the Constitution of Ireland reflecting the principle of consent in Northern Ireland—thus accommodating a long-standing unionist demand that the Republic should repeal the constitutional clauses, of huge symbolic and negligible practical importance, that officially laid claim to the territory of Northern Ireland. Both governments confirmed that 'democratically mandated parties which establish a commitment to exclusively peaceful methods and which have shown that they abide by the democratic process, are free to participate fully in democratic politics and join in dialogue in due course between the

Governments and the political parties on the way ahead'. In short, as Bew and Gillespie explain, 'The self-determination of the Irish people was conceded by Britain, but solely on the basis that the Irish Government only wished to operate that principle in favour of Irish unity with the support of a majority in the North.'[86]

Smith describes the Downing Street Declaration as 'an Anglo–Irish "mission statement" that sought to appeal to the broadest cross-section of Northern Irish politics', less a matter of 'saying something new' than of 'saying it at the right time'. The governments' strategy involved 'wording the declaration so that it could be read differently by both sides.... *Both* Nationalists and Unionists had to feel the same document offered them enough of what they wanted, without alarming the other. Thus plenty of textual mist was required through which messages were sent in code or wrapped in loaded words and meaningful phrases or signalled by the position of a comma or full stop.'[87] Nonetheless, according to Durkan, Hume quickly determined that the governments' declaration preserved the essential features of his vision:

> John could not say so publicly but could show colleagues just how substantively the Hume–Adams draft had been transposed into the two premiers' joint statement. The more unionist-facing paragraphs did not detract from this. Indeed the balance and roundedness of the Major–Reynolds paper allowed party colleagues to reaffirm confidence that the process ahead could not only entail inclusive talks under a ceasefire, but could recruit relevant understandings already developed in the Brooke/Mayhew talks.

Major, whose own political survival as well as that of the peace process depended upon avoiding the kind of histrionic unionist reaction that had greeted the Anglo–Irish Agreement eight years earlier, had stayed in close touch with the leader of the UUP, James Molyneaux, throughout the drafting process, and Reynolds had solicited help from Northern Protestant clergy in writing his government's sections; their efforts at inclusion paid off when Molyneaux, in a radio interview, dismissed the idea that the declaration represented a 'sell out' of unionists.[88]

Republicans' suspicions, however, were aroused by Major's attempt in the House of Commons to reassure unionists by emphasizing what had been left out of the declaration:

> What is not in the declaration is any suggestion that the British Government should join the ranks of persuaders of the 'value' or 'legitimacy' of a united Ireland.... Nor is there any suggestion that the future status of Northern Ireland should be decided by a single act of self-determination by the people of Ireland

as a whole....Nor is there any timetable for constitutional change, or any arrangement for joint authority over Northern Ireland.

Because these omissions had previously been key republican demands, the movement's rank and file felt understandably bewildered.[89] Within a week of the declaration, Adams called publicly for 'direct and unconditional dialogue' with the British and Irish governments and stated his belief that the document needed to be 'clarified'. He had realized almost immediately that 'Internally, within Sinn Féin and our activist base, we also had to seriously engage in a wide-ranging process of briefings and discussion.' The scale of this challenge became evident after about four hundred republican activists met in County Tyrone to discuss the declaration, with most or all who attended reportedly opposed to it. In early January 1994, Adams wrote to Major to personally request clarification of the Downing Street Declaration, but he was rebuffed with a reply from the prime minister's private secretary a couple of weeks later to say there could be 'no question of [its] renegotiation'.[90]

Durkan found 'Sinn Féin's move to "clarification" mode' both 'somewhat confusing and increasingly frustrating', but Hume advised patience for the leadership's conversations with its base and need to prove 'their own standing as potential negotiators in a new approach'. Hume's understanding of the tricky position Adams found himself in prompted him to do what he could to buttress the Sinn Féin leader's standing within the republican movement by engaging Irish-American support to demonstrate the practical benefits that an exclusively peaceful strategy might provide. Adams, along with other leaders of Northern Ireland's political parties, had been invited to a peace conference focused on the North in New York City at the beginning of February 1994, but, because he represented an organization associated with terrorism, his attendance would require a special visa waiver. A much-publicized battle followed this invitation between the British government and its allies in the US State Department, who opposed giving Adams a visa, and powerful members of the Irish-American lobby in the US Congress together with some of President Clinton's advisers, who supported it. Ultimately, positive urging from Hume, the US Ambassador to Ireland, Jean Kennedy Smith, and the Irish government influenced Clinton's decision to grant the waiver. Adams obliged his benefactors by concluding his speech at the conference with the statement that 'It is our intention to see the gun removed permanently from Irish politics', but those in the US administration who had hoped for a ceasefire by St Patrick's Day were sorely disappointed.[91]

Adams found the peace process 'in crisis' upon his return from the US, with the British government, still reliant on the nine unionist votes in parliament, steadfastly refusing to offer the 'clarification' sought by republicans. He describes the Sinn Féin annual conference later that month as 'a crucial juncture in the

internal politics of Irish republicanism'. He seized the occasion—his 'first opportunity...to speak to such a widespread representative gathering of activists since
the Hume/Adams initiative had become public, since the secret negotiations with
the British had been revealed and since the Downing Street Declaration'—to
emphasize, for the benefit of both party members and the public, 'the pivotal role
we had played in all of this'. While arguing that the declaration did indeed indicate a shift in British policy with its explicit recognition of a right to national self-
determination in Ireland, he also earned an ovation by asking 'does anyone really
expect the IRA to cease its activities so that British civil servants can discuss with
Sinn Féin the surrender of IRA weapons after we have been "decontaminated"?'[92]

In truth, no reasonably well-informed person could have expected such a
development, a point the IRA underscored with a series of mortar attacks on
Heathrow Airport in early March; these bombs failed to explode but caused
immense disruption and consternation nonetheless. Adams recounts that he and
McGuinness 'held a number of meetings with the IRA leadership during this
period to update it on current developments within the [peace] process and to
put to them our views on the potential of all of these'. They consistently found that
'The IRA's position was to continue the war. The Army Council had no other
position.' Any debate about the peace process was 'informal', with most volunteers
'sceptical about any notion of a ceasefire'. One thing seemed certain to them:
'there was no possibility of an IRA ceasefire on the back of the Downing Street
Declaration'.[93]

People who relied on print and broadcast media for their sense of the situation
could have inferred as much, and disillusionment with the peace initiative grew
as a result. In March 1994, Northern Ireland's independent political and cultural
review *Fortnight* published an arts feature in which three dozen artists, intellec-
tuals, and arts administrators from both the Republic and Northern Ireland
commented on the peace process. Whether they blamed the stubbornness of the
British government or the intransigence of the IRA for the present impasse, only
two of them seemed to feel any appreciable optimism about the initiative's
immediate prospects, while twenty-one voiced opposition, doubt, or pessimism.
The remaining thirteen cultural leaders expressed an attitude, best summed up by
novelist and playwright Jennifer Johnston, that conveyed support because the
only alternative appeared to be acceptance of an unacceptable status quo: 'We
must clarify; we must negotiate; we must speak together, speak aloud so that the
public ear can hear the words that are being spoken....Some common ground of
trust and understanding has to be reached before the secret armies will put
away their guns....There should be no more hole-in-the-corner talks, no more
lies, slogans, equivocations; we are masters at using and manipulating words, we
must now learn the art of listening.'[94]

Seamus Heaney, in his contribution, cited writer, dissident, and then
Czechoslovakian president Václav Havel's useful distinction between hope and

optimism. Hope 'is different from investing in enterprises that are likely to succeed. It is rather the conviction that a thing is worth working for in itself.' It was in
this sense, Heaney said, that the Downing Street Declaration had 'created hope'
by reminding 'people on all sides that there are other options besides stoical
endurance' and encouraging 'imagination to press back against the pressure of
reality. And this reorientation, whatever about the outcome of "negotiations" and
"clarifications", is an achievement in itself.'[95]

Poet Michael Longley kept his own response more direct and topical, stating
forthrightly that 'I publicly supported the Hume–Adams initiative. I feel disappointed. I hope I shall not feel betrayed.' After describing the declaration as 'com-
passionate, imaginative, nimble—the fruit of deep thought and huge care', he
asked, 'Does the differential between the initiative and the declaration warrant
the loss of a finger, let alone a life?' Urging 'Less talk, please, about "our divided
people", and more talk about our differences', Longley ended his piece by quoting
English poet W. H. Auden: 'All real unity commences / In consciousness of
differences.'[96]

Like Heaney (one of his closest friends), Longley was a liberal Irish nationalist.
Unlike him, he had not inherited this political perspective. Raised in Belfast by
English parents, whose easy-going Anglican agnosticism insulated him in early
childhood from the corrosive sectarianism endemic to the North, Longley's
inclination to identify with Ireland as a cultural whole was both illustrated and
reinforced by his decision to attend university in the Republic rather than in
Northern Ireland or Britain. After earning a degree in Classics at Trinity College
Dublin, he returned home when his wife, literary critic Edna Longley, joined the
English faculty of Queen's University Belfast, and the couple had remained in
the city throughout the Troubles. Longley had none of the superstitious fear of
the Catholic Church or the Irish state that bedevilled many Northern Protestants,
but, because of his family background and upbringing, he naturally thought of
himself as Irish *and* British, in the same way someone else might be Welsh or
Scottish and British; he did not feel compelled to choose between these identities
and would chafe at any political dispensation that required him to do so. Before
quitting his day job in 1991 to devote himself more fully to writing, Longley spent
two decades working in the British civil service as an administrator for the Arts
Council of Northern Ireland. In this capacity, though, he consistently sought to
nourish local talent and promote activities that distinguished the Northern Irish
arts from those elsewhere in the United Kingdom. Although he abhorred the
tactics of the IRA, which had killed several of his friends, he did not consider its
members to be beyond reason and had sympathized with republican prisoners'
demands for political status.[97]

Longley identified with the regionalist ethos of John Hewitt, an older Northern
Irish poet and arts administrator. He liked to tell the story of watching, with
Hewitt, a television report on the IRA's latest atrocity: 'A British Army officer was

dismissing the perpetrators as subhuman animals', and Hewitt, 'who was vehemently opposed to the IRA's campaign (as was I), turned to me and said: "That young man is talking about *our* terrorists." They were just as much products of our society as we were. They were not complete strangers'[98]

From his own perspective, Longley would follow the events of the next few months, parsing news bulletins for signs of movement on the part of people who were in a position to advance the peace process. By this point, Adams hardly felt himself to be one of these people, but, believing that the Sinn Féin leadership 'needed to take initiatives', if only to signify that 'we had not given up', he 'began a letter-writing campaign to Major and other British political leaders'. The IRA, for its part (and despite actions that often seemed to imply the opposite), had not rejected Sinn Féin's peace strategy outright. On 13 March 1994, the day of the group's final mortar attack on Heathrow, IRA leaders announced that 'our positive and flexible attitude to the peace process is an abiding and enduring one'. This statement gave Hume an opening to urge the British government to take risks that might help end the violence. Speaking to the *Boston Globe*, Hume remarked, 'Given that the British government would talk to [the IRA] secretly when peace wasn't on the table, I am asking, why not talk to them publicly when peace is, in fact, on the table': 'If the British government believes the IRA is bluffing, they should call their bluff'[99]

An opportunity to do so presented itself on 30 March, when the IRA announced an Easter ceasefire for 5–8 April. Adams describes this as 'more than a gesture': 'For the first time in twenty years, the IRA had decided on a unilateral suspension of hostilities for the express purpose of creating space for political developments to take place' and, moreover, had announced it six days in advance so the British government had a chance to offer the 'clarification' republicans had been requesting for more than three months. Major, however, still under siege from the right wing of his own party, dismissed the announcement as 'a brief public relations gesture', insisting that 'What people in Northern Ireland want is not a ceasefire over two or three days but a permanent end to violence'. It was not until 19 May that the Northern Ireland Office finally issued a lengthy 'commentary' on twenty questions that Reynolds had delivered to the British government on behalf of Sinn Féin in late April. This reiterated the government's intent to 'encourage, facilitate and enable . . . a process of dialogue and co-operation based on full respect for the rights and identities of both traditions in Ireland' and its pledge 'to give effect to any measure of agreement on future relationships which the people of Ireland may freely determine'. The government recognized all electoral mandates, including Sinn Féin's, but reiterated its position that 'all who join in political dialogue should demonstrate a commitment to exclusively peaceful methods and to the democratic process'[100]

Although the commentary was a far cry from the 'direct and immediate talks between Sinn Féin and the Government' that Adams had demanded at the end of

March, he privately viewed it as 'a small but important step in the slowly evolving peace process'. However, 'for anyone who was following the story closely it was obvious that the package was still not in place for Martin and me to take to the IRA'. The Sinn Féin leadership decided to convene a special delegate conference in late July 'to examine the Downing Street Declaration in detail and agree our formal attitude to it'.[101] This gathering attracted much public interest, but few observers would have been encouraged by Adams's public pronouncement at the conference that the Downing Street Declaration, while suggesting a 'potentially significant change in the approach of the two governments to resolving the conflict in Ireland', did not 'deal adequately with some of the core issues'. 'For most of the media,' he remembers, 'our considered position spelt rejection', but the meeting served an important internal purpose for Sinn Féin in giving party leaders a chance to brief members on the less public aspects of the new strategy: 'Now that we were driving a process, our activists had a real sense of being agents of change, and of the party being at the centre of developments.'[102]

Adams recalls that 'It was coming to the point of deciding if this was the right time to start putting the jigsaw together. Timing was critical. If we pulled everything together and the army said no, the process was over before it really started.' He and McGuinness met with the IRA leadership early in August to report progress to achieve a political agenda that the Irish government, the SDLP, and Sinn Féin could all agree upon and that prominent Irish-American business and political leaders believed the US government could be persuaded to champion. This meeting, he recalls, 'had a new, different quality':

> It was obvious that matters were coming to a head.... What was not so clear was how the Army Council would formally deal with a proposition for a cessation. Some were prepared to support the idea if it was a launching pad to drive the struggle forward.... They could see the political landscape changing as a result of Hume/Adams and other initiatives.... But short-term tactical initiatives, even risky ones, were nothing compared to a decision to call a halt to operations.

Along with such qualified endorsement of Sinn Féin's proposal, Adams knew that some other members of the IRA leadership were frankly opposed to the idea of a cessation: 'It was going to be a close call.'[103]

The Sinn Féin leaders would meet with the Army Council again soon. In the meantime, they sought to orchestrate a series of statements ('more public initiatives than statements', Adams remarks) 'which would actually signal the coming together of the different pieces of the package'. These 'public manifestations of support for an alternative approach' were intended to convince militant republicans 'that there really was the possibility of another way forward'. Thus, for example, the London *Independent* newspaper reported on 21 August that an Irish-American delegation with contacts high in the Clinton administration would be visiting Belfast to conduct 'behind-the-scenes talks with Gerry Adams aimed at persuading the IRA to announce a permanent ceasefire'. Niall O'Dowd, publisher of New York's *Irish Voice* newspaper, commented publicly on the group's aims and the situation as its members saw it: 'We believe the time has never been more opportune for a peace initiative. There is an understanding between Hume and Adams, sympathetic governments in Dublin and London, a reasonable leader of the Ulster Unionist Party in James Molyneaux and an American president who has taken a personal interest in the issue. There is also a new level of sophistication in Irish America which can help smooth the peace process and events afterwards.'[104] By late August 1994, largely owing to news stories like this one, a large percentage of the general public probably felt more confident than Adams himself that an end to the long conflict in Northern Ireland was imminent.

Other contemporary coverage, even when sympathetic, conformed less closely to Sinn Féin's purposes. The *Guardian* reported on 22 August that 'indications are that the IRA's army council has taken the decision to call an open-ended ceasefire which falls short of London and Dublin's demand for a permanent cessation'; such a move would strain relations between the British and Irish governments, which would then have to decide whether to allow Sinn Féin to join talks about Northern Ireland's future based on it. The writer of this piece also speculated about divisions within the Irish government and the SDLP, as well as within the republican movement, and a leader in the same issue of the newspaper warned that 'it would be unwise to assume that the IRA ceasefire alone will bring peace to Northern Ireland. Loyalists might join in, but they might be just as likely to escalate their attacks.' Six days later, when an end to the IRA's campaign seemed less rather than more likely, Mary Holland acknowledged in the *Observer* that 'Last week in Belfast there was anticipation, but for most people the hope that Northern Ireland might be on the verge of a significant breakthrough was tempered by nervousness and the fear that, if this initiative were to fail, the situation could worsen.'[105]

Amid conflicting reports, interpretations, and predictions, an analysis by Tom McGurk in the *Sunday Business Post* on 28 August seems, with hindsight, notably well-informed. According to him, the IRA was expected to announce 'an indefinite cessation of hostilities' from midnight on 31 August, called 'in the clear and real expectation that it will prove to be permanent'. Although McGurk believed there to be 'sufficient agreement within the republican movement that the "Armalite and ballot box" strategy can be superseded by the "argument and ballot box" strategy', his account also included the disquieting detail that 'one important Northern member of the Army Council has continued to express his unhappiness at what is proposed'. Reports such as this one inspired Michael Longley, as he recalled in 1997, to attempt his own version of semaphore politics to try to make a 'tiny, tiny, minuscule, unimportant contribution to the drift towards a ceasefire' with a poem distilling an episode from the final book of Homer's *Iliad*. He wrote

'Ceasefire', he said, 'because I do have some sense of the magic of poetry in the world', and he sent the poem to the *Irish Times* 'in the hope that if they did print it somebody might read it and it might change the mind of one ditherer on the IRA council'.[106]

That summer, Longley had been putting the finishing touches to his book *The Ghost Orchid*, a collection unified by the theme of metamorphosis. This preoccupation, as critic Fran Brearton explains, manifests itself in the volume as transformation through supernatural or imaginative means 'as well as the natural process of growth and change in humans and animals and . . . the possible changes in a society's condition and character'. Nearly a third of its poems, she points out, are 'free translations, versions, or part borrowings'—not coincidentally, because translation itself involves 'transformation into and out of another language, time, and place'.[107] Latin and Greek works feature prominently in this collection: in addition to seven poems reworking or responding to stories in Ovid's *Metamorphoses*, *The Ghost Orchid* contains seven poems derived from Homer.

A self-described 'very lazy scholar at Trinity', Longley believed that it was only in his mid-forties that he had 'started to read Homer properly, and that was a revelation'. In his 1991 collection, *Gorse Fires*, revising episodes from the *Odyssey* had allowed Longley, as he confided later, 'to give expression to sorrows and toxins' as moments in the epic 'chimed with emotions that I would have found almost impossible to deal with otherwise: heartbreak, paranoia, bitterness, hatred, fear'. Now he was trawling the *Iliad* in search of episodes that could help him express his feelings about the prospect of an end to what he thought of as 'our tawdry little civil war'.[108] As Brearton observes, 'the *Odyssey* provides [Longley with] a framework for poems that illuminate a personal journey, the *Iliad* for poems about social conflict'. He read the *Odyssey* like a 'picaresque novel', seeing the *Iliad* as 'altogether darker and deeper—a huge lamentation, really, a painful exploration of war, a gigantic poem about death'. As a craftsman, though, Longley responded similarly to both: 'Inside epics such as the *Iliad* there are lots of little works of art waiting to be set free. I wade in against the narrative flow and freeze-frame telling moments to make what I hope are self-contained lyric poems'.[109]

Brearton comments on the significant timing of the change in Longley's focus from the *Odyssey* to the *Iliad*. She argues that the 'war of attrition' depicted in the latter might have been expected to 'speak more immediately to the poet at a time when Northern Ireland's own conflict seemed to have no end in view—that is, during the 1970s and 1980s'. Instead, 'the shift towards the *Iliad* at a point when a ceasefire is imminent relates to Longley's sense of how the poet's negotiations between public and private have to be acutely sensitive to context. If the *Iliad* were to serve, in Longley's poems, merely as a reflection of one war in another, it might prove more problematical than helpful' by conferring on the Troubles 'precisely the kind of inevitability and inescapability that the poetry should, in Longley's terms, work against'.[110] (Heaney's 1990 decision to rework *Philoctetes*, which centres on an incident related to the same long and wasteful struggle but concerns the question of how to bring it to an end, may be usefully regarded in the same light.)

Longley believed in 'inspiration, the breathing into the mind of some idea'. Certain passages from classical texts, he said, 'hit me between the eyes, much the same way as seeing a bird out the window or hearing some terrible news on the radio or being in the company of friends or relatives. They're emotional epiphanies, spiritual epiphanies, rather than literary events in my life, therefore they fit into the flow of where ever it is I happen to be going, at any particular time.' One day in late August 1994, Longley was on a train journey from Dublin to Belfast thinking about the episode in Book 24 of the *Iliad* in which the elderly Trojan king, Priam, secretly visits the Greek hero Achilles to plead for the return of his son Hector's body.[111] Twelve days earlier, in retaliation for Hector's slaying of Achilles's closest companion, Achilles had killed Hector. Since then, sacrilegiously, he had repeatedly attempted to mutilate the corpse by dragging it behind his chariot. In this climactic scene, Achilles is startled to find Hector's father in his tent, clasping his knees in supplication. Their ensuing encounter, which Longley regarded as 'the soul' of the epic, struck him as 'very modern, psychologically speaking' because 'Priam in his fragility awakens in Achilles memories of his own father and rekindles the gentler emotions he has had to suppress in order to be a general.' When Longley pictured the scene to himself, he gave Priam the face of Gordon Wilson.[112]

The bereaved father's real-life appeal to the IRA in April 1993 had ended in bitter disappointment, but, with Homer's help, Longley imagined a different sort of meeting. The first lines he decided on would become the most famous ones in 'Ceasefire': '"I get down on my knees and do what must be done / And kiss Achilles' hand, the killer of my son."'[113] Normally, Longley said, he subjected his work to 'an awful lot of revision', but in his experience there were also times 'when lines present[ed] themselves' to him 'more or less perfect'. In this instance, the gift must have seemed an especially good omen because it came in the form of a rhyming couplet, which Longley regarded as 'the ultimate stanza'. Priam makes this statement near the beginning of his scene with Achilles, but Longley wanted to save the satisfying full rhymes for the end of his poem. He eventually solved this technical problem with 'the idea that...I could put that at the end of the poem and refer it back, which *does* make it all seem fated and so forth. And then I thought, well, if I can take three moments, three milestones, in this really quite long scene and make a quatrain out of each one I'll have a sonnet.' As he explained, 'The formal aspect of a poem is really just taking tendencies in the story or the raw material and tendencies in the language, and letting them interact in a way which seems...to be preordained'.[114]

Shortly after *The Ghost Orchid* was published, Longley described the three discrete elements of the encounter that he chose to highlight: 'When he grabs his knees in supplication Priam reminds Achilles of his own aging father, and the two men weep together. Achilles himself supervises the washing and wrapping of the corpse so that Priam won't have to see it. They're both emotionally drained by this time, so Achilles invites his old adversary to eat with him.' Thus, Longley concluded, 'I concentrated into a sonnet all that I wanted to borrow' from this 'heart-stopping scene in which the balance of power gradually shifts from the great warrior to the old king'. 'For me', he would later tell an interviewer, 'the form, the stanzaic shape, is an endorsement, proof that I'm engaged with the Latin or Greek at an original level, that my versions are explorations.'[115]

Longley knew that, in isolating intimate moments from the *Iliad* to draw attention to the human cost of war, he was merely amplifying what was already in the original. His reading of Homer's epic accorded with the interpretation presented by Simone Weil in her essay 'The Iliad or the Poem of Force', written in 1940 in response to the fall of France. Weil argues that *force*, 'that x that turns anybody who is subjected to it into a thing', is 'the true subject' of the *Iliad*. Homer, in her view, demonstrates that 'Force is as pitiless to the man who possesses it, or thinks he does, as it is to its victims; the second it crushes, the first it intoxicates.' In fact, 'nobody really possesses it', Weil writes, adding that 'those who have force on loan from fate count on it too much and are destroyed.'[116]

Noting that both the Greeks and the Trojans in the *Iliad* have chances to win honorably by settling for less than everything but fail to take them, Weil comments on the deranging effect that armed conflict has on the human psyche. By effacing 'all conceptions of purpose or goal, including even its own "war aims"', it 'effaces the very notion of war's being brought to an end. To be outside a situation so violent as this is to find it inconceivable; to be inside it is to be unable to conceive its end. Consequently, nobody does anything to bring this end about.' Homer's portrayal of war's devastating momentum impressed Weil as both utterly realistic and disheartening, a vision redeemed only by the very episodes that attracted Longley's attention:

The wantonness of the conqueror that knows no respect for any creature or thing that is at its mercy or is imagined to be so, the despair of the soldier that drives him on to destruction, the obliteration of the slave or the conquered man, the wholesale slaughter—all these elements combine in the *Iliad* to make a picture of uniform horror, of which force is the sole hero. A monotonous desolation would result were it not for those few luminous moments, scattered here and there throughout the poem, those brief, celestial moments in which man possesses his soul.

Weil concedes that 'moments of grace are rare in the *Iliad*' but asserts 'they are enough to make us feel with sharp regret what it is that violence has killed and will kill again'. For her, as for Longley, the meeting between Priam and Achilles in the epic's final book represents the prime example of such a moment, epitomizing as it does 'the purest triumph of love,…the friendship that floods the heart of mortal enemies': 'Before it a murdered son or a murdered friend no longer cries out for vengeance. Before it…the distance between benefactor and supplicant, between victor and vanquished, shrinks to nothing'.[117]

In Homer's epic, the exchange between Priam and Achilles gains resonance and poignancy both from what came before and what will come after it. As translator and Greek scholar Richmond Lattimore notes, the *Iliad* is not simply the story of the Trojan War (neither the beginning nor the end of which are presented in it) but 'a work of art evolved within the scope of a chronicle'. Homer's art was one of 'selection within limits': he could emphasize some parts of the story and downplay or omit others, 'But he could not contradict the legends'.[118] Within these parameters, Homer repeatedly underscores the futility and waste of war. Warriors on both sides are resentfully aware of the paltriness of the cause for which they are fighting, and Achilles, who sits out most of the battles depicted in the *Iliad* after quarrelling with the Greek commander, seriously considers withdrawing his army and going home, choosing a long life without glory over the short life with glory he has been told awaits him if he fights at Troy (Book 9, lines 410–20). It is only after his dearest friend's death that he resolves to rejoin the war effort and kill Hector, although he knows it has been decreed that his own death will quickly follow (Book 18, lines 90–6). The dying Hector begs Achilles ('by your life, by your knees, by your parents') to accept the ransom his father and mother will surely offer for his body, but Achilles refuses: 'I wish only that my spirit and fury would drive me / to hack your meat away and eat it raw for the things that / you have done to me' (Book 22, lines 338–48). His reaction to Priam, then, represents a dramatic reversal, but it does not change the course of events. After the two men grieve, talk, and eat together, Achilles asks Priam exactly how many days the Trojans require for Hector's funeral rites, and Priam asks for eleven, offering to fight again on the twelfth day 'if so we must do' (Book 24, lines 656–67). The *Iliad* ends with Hector's burial, but the war would continue, as Homer's listeners knew. That struggle would claim the life of Achilles and many other heroes and would not end before the complete destruction of Troy.

In Homeric terms, the 'ceasefire' of Longley's title (which, like the 'cure' of Heaney's, gestures beyond the frame of the work itself) must refer to the truce Achilles and Priam arrange to allow for the proper disposition of Hector's corpse. Negotiated pauses in the fighting for various purposes and lengths of time are scattered throughout the *Iliad*, calling attention to the fact that the two sides could stop the war at any time but choose not to do so. Weil analyses the psychological reason for the nearly unstoppable momentum long conflicts acquire:

> [T]he soul that is enslaved by war cries out for deliverance, but deliverance itself appears to it in an extreme and tragic aspect, the aspect of destruction. Any

other solution, more moderate, more reasonable in character, would expose the mind to suffering so naked, so violent that it could not be borne, even as memory....The idea that an unlimited effort should bring in only a limited profit or no profit at all is terribly painful.

The pain of admitting war's pointlessness is so great, in fact, that it renders almost unthinkable the rational calculations of risk and reward that make a peace settlement possible.[119]

Significantly, then, the encounter between Priam and Achilles proceeds via emotion rather than reason, and the feeling that unites the men is sorrow. The important shift in Book 24 is the change from two warriors mourning separately to their mourning together. Whereas the first nourishes the desire for retribution, the second enables an interlude of communion. Mourning separately, they see the other as responsible for their own pain. Mourning together, they recognize each other as human beings who have suffered in the same way as themselves and thus can understand their hurt. In the *Iliad*, Priam has one purpose alone in visiting Achilles: to retrieve Hector's body, which Achilles has been desecrating. He 'must' go privately to Achilles's camp in the dead of night to beg for his son's corpse because Zeus has sent word that this is the only way to obtain what he wants. Zeus has also instructed Achilles to honour the old king's request. (Like Heaney does in *The Cure at Troy*, Longley downplays the god's involvement in the story— while divine intervention may be helpful in such fraught circumstances, he did not want to imply that it was essential.) What transforms their meeting and lifts the encounter above the purely transactional one commanded by Zeus is the reaction of Achilles to Priam's plea, and surely one reason Achilles thinks of his own father when he sees the grieving Priam is his foreknowledge that he himself will die at Troy.

The popular critical view of 'Ceasefire' as offering a blueprint for peace in Northern Ireland may be summed up in Richard Rankin Russell's assertion that the sonnet 'articulates a heart-rending, complex process of Christian forgiveness in which the pagan Priam swallows his urge for vengeance and kisses the hand of his son's killer as a step toward future reconciliation'. However, forgiveness and reconciliation are concepts that play no part in the Homeric action. Critic Sarah Broom notes that Longley excluded from his poem the passage in the *Iliad* in which Achilles instructs his serving-maids to keep Hector's body out of Priam's sight as they prepare it, for fear that the old king 'might see his son and in the heart's sorrow not hold in his anger / at the sight, and the deep heart in Achilleus be shaken to anger; / that he might not kill Priam and be guilty before the god's orders' (Book 24, lines 581–6).[120] And, even after they share a convivial meal and come to an agreement regarding a suspension of the fighting, neither Achilles nor Priam seriously suggests that they might decide between them to end the war altogether. The thought of suing for peace *had* crossed Hector's mind just before he met Achilles on the battlefield, but he had quickly rejected it as fanciful: 'I might go up to him, and he take no pity upon me / nor respect my position, but kill me naked so, as if I were / a woman, once I stripped my armour from me' (Book 22, lines 123–5).

Unlike many of his readers, Longley was intimately familiar with the Homeric context of the interaction he presents in 'Ceasefire'. In the epic, as Broom observes, 'The encounter between Priam and Achilles gains its potency because its placement at the end of the *Iliad* necessitates a doubleness in our thinking of it: at one moment we can envisage its symmetry and harmony as permanent, final, conclusive, but at the next we are compelled to imagine it breaking apart hopelessly into the very same chaos of war that went before.' The most (arguably the only) topical aspect of Longley's poem is its title, but this perfectly captures the ambiguity of the original scene as well as the tensions impinging on the sonnet's composition. In August 1994, the announcement of an IRA ceasefire was both eagerly awaited and anxiously dreaded in the knowledge that it would not be enough to convince unionists and the British government that republicans genuinely wanted peace. Thus, as Russell points out, 'Longley's political prescience lies not so much in anticipating the cease-fire, which was in the air anyway, as in realizing that "cease-fire," with its implications of a possible resumption of violence, was more appropriate to the situation than a poem about the final end of an armed struggle.' Given the dynamic political situation at the time, Brearton finds it 'unsurprising that Longley's awareness of the possibility of change carries within it awareness of the possibility of failure and stagnation.'[121]

Like Homer, Longley understood his art as one of selection within limits. He could not rewrite the story of the *Iliad*, but he could choose which parts of it to include in his own work. 'Ceasefire' depicts an emotion-charged meeting of bodies:

I

Put in mind of his own father and moved to tears
Achilles took him by the hand and pushed the old king
Gently away, but Priam curled up at his feet and
Wept with him until their sadness filled the building.

II

Taking Hector's corpse into his own hands Achilles
Made sure it was washed and, for the old king's sake,
Laid out in uniform, ready for Priam to carry
Wrapped like a present home to Troy at daybreak.

III

When they had eaten together, it pleased them both
To stare at each other's beauty as lovers might,

Achilles built like a god, Priam good-looking still
And full of conversation, who earlier had sighed:

IV

'I get down on my knees and do what must be done
And kiss Achilles' hand, the killer of my son.'

When Priam suddenly appears in his shelter, Achilles is jolted into an awareness of the old king as a fellow human being and, as such, kin to him. What happens after that—weeping together, sharing a meal, conversing familiarly, even staring 'at each other's beauty as lovers might'—derives from the simple fact of their being together in the same room. In framing these exchanges for examination, Longley offered readers a concrete vision of what might be found, in Heaney's words, on 'the far side of revenge'. Because Priam's humbling of himself to establish personal contact makes everything else possible, Longley's sonnet ends appropriately with a resounding reminder of the action that initiates their encounter. As Classics scholar Lorna Hardwick comments, the poet's concluding couplet compels readers to recognize 'the necessity of such gestures, metaphorical or literal, in processes of negotiation'.[122]

That summer of 1994, the fervently hoped-for halt to IRA operations was regarded both as desirable for its own sake and as a necessary prelude to face-to-face negotiations involving Sinn Féin and Northern Ireland's other political parties. Thus, Longley's focus on the potential benefits of personal proximity was calculated to appeal to the poem's primary intended audience: the IRA leadership. Between Longley's writing of 'Ceasefire' and its publication, the Army Council was inching towards a decision on whether or not to end its campaign. On 29 August, Gerry Adams announced that he had informed the body that the conditions now existed for advancing the peace process. He did not then reveal that 'The meeting was inconclusive. People needed more time to cogitate over all the issues.' Arguing for Sinn Féin's proposal before the Army Council again a day or two later, Adams still found it 'impossible to predict the outcome'.[123]

The IRA leadership finally issued a statement on 31 August declaring that 'to enhance the democratic peace process and underline our definitive commitment to its success' there would be, as of midnight, 'a complete cessation of military operations'. Adams records that the announcement inaugurated 'a busy, unsettling time for the people involved'. He had argued before the Army Council that continuing to fight would be 'the easy decision' but urged instead the 'high-risk option' of stopping, although this meant 'uncharted waters': 'It would involve compromises. It could mean risking—and losing—everything.... But we could also be the generation who would win freedom.'[124]

'Ceasefire' was first published in the *Irish Times* on Saturday, 3 September, and it created an immediate sensation, as Longley recalled in 1997: 'The coincidence struck people, and the poem...had some kind of public life in as much as priests and politicians picked it up. I found that a refreshment.' Despite the elation that possessed many, however, he remained mindful of the continuing uncertainty, including doubts as to whether the IRA's 'complete cessation' would suffice to gain Sinn Féin's entry into talks on the future of Northern Ireland. In the days, weeks, and months that followed, he remembered, 'when I went here and there', he would be asked to read 'Ceasefire': 'and what I should have said when I read the poem—but I didn't, you see, because I didn't want to put a jinx on the peace process—I should have said, of course, this is only a twelve-day ceasefire and the Trojan war resumes. And Achilles himself gets killed.'[125]

3

Grieving

After meeting in Dublin on 6 September 1994, John Hume, Gerry Adams, and Albert Reynolds issued a joint statement hailing the IRA's 'complete cessation of military operations' with the words, 'We are at the beginning of a new era in which we are totally and absolutely committed to democratic and peaceful methods of resolving our political problems.' As much as Northern Ireland's people might have wished to share the sentiment, however, the situation was not as simple as this formula implied. In an essay published in the *Sunday Tribune* two days earlier, Seamus Heaney had shared his own reaction to the IRA's announcement. This had, he acknowledged, 'changed everything for the better': 'I felt 25 years younger. I remembered what things had felt like in those early days of political ferment in the late '60s. How we all were brought beyond our highly-developed caution to believe that the effort to create new movement and language in the Northern context was a viable project.' At the same time, 'as well as feeling freed up, I felt angry also. The quarter century we have lived through was a terrible black hole, and the inestimable suffering inflicted and endured by every party to the conflict has only brought the situation to a point that is politically less promising than things were in 1968.' Two and a half decades of political and sectarian violence had taken a toll on the entire population, deepening pre-existing divisions in society. Both the IRA ceasefire and the loyalist one announced in mid-October were cause for celebration, but also for sorrowful contemplation.[1]

After Michael Longley's 'Ceasefire' appeared in the *Irish Times* on 3 September 1994, the poet was approached on the Lisburn Road by an acquaintance who told him that he admired Longley's 'Achilles poem' but added, 'I'm not ready for it.' His son, he said, had been subjected to a 'vicious paramilitary punishment beating' and might never fully recover. This encounter made Longley question his poem's 'redemptive symmetries' and reflect anew on the repercussions of the conflict. He understood that '"Each neighbourly murder"—Seamus Heaney's devastating phrase—destroys family, poisons the futures of the bereaved, overwhelms small communities.'[2] Robin Wilson, editor of Northern Ireland's current affairs magazine *Fortnight*, similarly observed that 'If the "troubles" are coming to an end, one of the paradoxical outcomes will be that the suffering of the bereaved will be heightened by new hopes for the future which they can not fully share, and by a desire to draw a line under a past which for them is always present.'[3]

In a separate piece in the same issue of the magazine, Marie Smyth, whose academic research on the aftermath of political violence included interviewing the

Getting to Good Friday: Literature and the Peace Process in Northern Ireland. Marilynn Richtarik, Oxford University Press.
© Marilynn Richtarik 2023. DOI: 10.1093/oso/9780192886408.003.0004

families of those killed in Derry by the British Army in January 1972, reported that 'More than 20 years on, over half had psychological symptoms which could be directly connected to the episode. The overwhelming majority re-experienced pain, distress, or fear when they saw or heard media coverage of other "troubles" deaths, when they saw a soldier or when the anniversary came around.' These findings did not make her sanguine about the prospect of any rapid return to normality in Northern Ireland: 'Fourteen people were killed on Bloody Sunday. There are some 200 immediate family members. Yet this does not include extended family links, close friends, those wounded on the day, eyewitnesses and so on. And Bloody Sunday was only one of thousands of violent incidents in the last 25 years.' Another scholar had recently argued that 'in a year only those crucially involved would have much of a memory' of the violence, but Smyth wondered in response how many of Northern Ireland's inhabitants had *not* been 'crucially involved'. Many people in her study had 'survived all these years by minimising traumas, and not talking about them': 'There is little space to grieve, mourn, question, search for answers, adjust and accept. And one trauma barely waits upon the next, as people experience multiple losses.' Smyth suggested that, in the Northern context, 'It is at best naïve to say that the aftermath of violence will disappear, left to its own devices. Indeed, the psychological costs may only now begin to emerge to their full extent.... The end of violence is only the tip of the "peace process" iceberg.'[4] Later research has demonstrated the accuracy of Smyth's prediction.[5] One measure of distress is the startling fact that suicide rates in Northern Ireland rose sharply after the Belfast Agreement was approved; in the sixteen years immediately following it, more people killed themselves there than had lost their lives in Troubles-related violence between 1969 and 1998.[6]

That summer and autumn of 1994, Deirdre Madden and Seamus Deane were both working on novels they had begun before an end to the violence had seemed a remotely realistic prospect to most people. These books, Madden's *One by One in the Darkness* and Deane's *Reading in the Dark*, would not be published until 1996, yet the ceasefires did little to mitigate their sombre tones. Both novels focus on the lingering effects of trauma on individuals and families, underlining the fact that even when Northern Ireland's Troubles fade from popular consciousness, a great many people will still be grieving.

Madden started planning *One by One in the Darkness* during the summer of 1993 and finished writing it in July 1995. This book, which she describes as her most 'personal', was likely conceived in anticipation of the twenty-fifth anniversary of the conflict looming in 1994; Madden recalls that she wanted to write about her own time and place and show 'what it was like to live through the Troubles'. One of the novel's characters, after watching a television documentary about the start of the violence a quarter-century previously, wonders 'how you ever got to the essence of things, of your time, your society, your self', and there can be little doubt that Madden aimed to do just that.[7] Although she thought of her subject as the Troubles themselves, it is also probable that the ongoing Hume–Adams initiative (the existence of which, excluding the details, had become public knowledge in April 1993) was at least subconsciously on her mind as well.[8] Nevertheless, in Madden's recollection of the period in which she wrote the novel, it felt like the Troubles had been going on for ever and would continue indefinitely. Given the heightened tensions of 1993 and the first eight months of 1994, she did not feel hopeful about the prospects for peace at that time.[9]

Madden left Ireland in 1988 and would spend most of the next sixteen years living away from it: in Italy, England, Switzerland, Germany, and France. During the 1994/95 academic year, however, she was Writer-in-Residence at University College Cork, living closer to Northern Ireland than she had since 1988 while still in a place distinctly different from it.[10] Her relationship to the North resembled that of her character Cate Quinn, whose week-long visit in June 1994 to her family in County Antrim provides the backbone for the present-day sections of *One by One in the Darkness*. Cate leads a cosmopolitan life as a fashion editor in London, but on trips home she makes a habit of 'driving for hours through the countryside alone, trying to fathom Northern Ireland in a way which wasn't, if you still lived there, necessary. Or advisable, she thought. Or possible, even' (82).[11] Cate's gaze lingers on places where the sectarian polarization of Northern Irish life is most visible: 'pinched villages where the edges of the footpaths were painted red, white and blue, where there were Orange Lodges and locked churches' and 'villages where unemployed men stood on street corners and dragged on cigarettes, or ambled up and down between the chip shop and the bookie's, past walls which bore Republican graffiti or incongruously glamorous advertisements on huge hoardings' (82). During these solitary drives, Cate sees

> signposts for places which had once held no particular significance but whose names were now tainted by the memory of things which had been done there: Claudy, Enniskillen, Ballykelly.... The towns and fields slipped past her until she felt that she was watching a film, and then she realised that if she had been asked to pick a single word to sum up her feelings towards Northern Ireland she would be at a complete loss, so much so that she didn't even know whether a negative or a positive word would have been more apt.   (83)

Cate is the middle of three Quinn sisters, the eldest of whom, Helen, was born in 1959 (97). Madden's 1960 birth made her about the same age as this generation of her characters. All are old enough to remember life before the Troubles flared up in the late 1960s, although they were young children when that conflict began. Madden has acknowledged that her thoughts 'about Ireland and about home' are 'inextricably bound up with the impulse to write, and with the act of writing', stating that 'For me, writing is a way not just of getting at something, but of getting back to something.'[12] One of her achievements in *One by One in the Darkness* is to document, in meticulous detail, the slow degrees by which the sisters' childish innocence gives way to a 'dark knowledge' as the latent divisions in their society begin to manifest themselves in acts of horrific violence.

The divisions themselves, of course, were always there. Madden describes the girls' primal sense of their environment in nostalgic terms, emphasizing that 'The physical bounds of their world were confined to little more than a few fields and houses, but they knew these places with the deep, unconscious knowledge that a bird or a fox might have for its habitat. The idea of home was something they lived so completely that they would have been at a loss to define it' (74–5). In the same passage, however, Madden makes it clear, as critic Michael Parker puts it, that 'this sense of wholeness and homeliness has been achieved only by conscious, willed acts of exclusion'.[13] The next paragraph begins with the words 'And yet for all this they knew that their lives, so complete in themselves, were off centre in relation to the society beyond those few fields and houses' (75). For the young sisters, this fact impinges on their awareness only during the summer marching season, when the predominantly Protestant towns in the area are decorated with Union Jacks, bunting, and arches over streets. They know that Orange marches are taking place from pictures in the newspaper or reports on television, but they never see one because 'their parents always made a point of staying at home on that day, complaining bitterly that you were made a prisoner in your own home whether you liked it or not' (75). The girls understand instinctively that this public celebration is not 'for them': 'For the most part, they didn't even think about it, for their lives were complete as they were' (75).

Madden in this passage hints at something she will soon develop more fully: the different perspectives of the adults and children in the extended Quinn family on the events of the 1960s and early 1970s. The burden of adult understanding is revealed most directly in the recollections of Emily, the sisters' mother, about how the world had appeared to her as a young woman:

At that time 'politics' meant Stormont, meant a Protestant government for a Protestant people, so if you happened to be a Catholic, the message was clear. You just worked as hard as possible within the tiny scope that was allowed to you, and that in itself was so time consuming and difficult that few, and certainly not Emily, had the insight or the necessary energy to begin even to think of how things ought to be, or might be, changed. Education was the only hope, it was like a rope that you struggled to cling to, in the hope of pulling yourself up to a position less disadvantaged than the one in which you started out. Keep your head down, look to your own, and don't expect too much in any case: nobody ever said those words explicitly to her, but then nobody needed to, because the world around her wordlessly insisted on this every single day of her life.   (115)

Emily's father had died unexpectedly when she was still a child, and in the ensuing years her 'rage' at this bereavement would 'occasionally make itself felt': 'Her spirit was broken by the time she was twelve, but spirits, whether those of a child or a society, never break cleanly, and the people who didn't understand this were shocked when the dull, quiet girl, so eager to please, suddenly displayed a violent temper. They thought these two sides of her were at odds; couldn't understand that the malevolence was the logical corollary to the obsequiousness' (114). Emily's personal perspective here represents that of the whole Northern Catholic population prior to the civil rights movement, and Madden's analysis of her psychology also sheds light on the rapidity with which civil rights demands, when met with unionist stonewalling or outright reaction, yielded to traditional republican aims and increasingly militant means of seeking change.

Madden centres *One by One in the Darkness* on the story of the Quinn family, but she also conveys through flashbacks a wider narrative about Northern Ireland in the latter half of the twentieth century. The novel presents an emotional history of the civil rights movement and subsequent Troubles in Northern Ireland from a rural, Catholic, and nationalist point of view. Odd-numbered chapters, set in the present day, are each narrated from the limited third-person perspective of one or more of the Quinn women: Emily, the matriarch; Helen, a solicitor on the Falls Road in Belfast, whose clients include people accused of terrorist offences; Cate; and the youngest sister, Sally, who lives in the family home with Emily and teaches at the primary school the girls attended. These alternate with chapters set in the past and adopting a more ambiguous, collective point of view. The flashback chapters, which rely heavily on anecdote and contain a great deal of dialogue, illustrate the reactions of the local Catholic community to the developing political situation.

This community is not monolithic, as Parker stresses, and Madden carefully delineates tensions within the family and in the area.[14] Adult attitudes towards the shifting status quo are conveyed mainly through the girls' father, Charlie, and his two brothers, Brian and Peter. Each has a different way of coping with the official and unofficial restrictions placed on Northern Catholics at that time. Brian, who drives a bread van, is politically engaged and rails against the injustices of the Stormont system, joining the civil rights movement as soon as it begins and, later, Sinn Féin. Peter—whose mother explains that 'He thinks too much, and then he drinks too much' (16)—retreats into alcoholism. Charlie, a farmer, focuses on caring for his own family as best he can.

Politically quietist by habit, the girls' parents at first respond warily to the civil rights protests, but soon they are caught up in the general 'defiant excitement' (76): 'all the talk at home now was about civil rights, and how things would have to change' (71). To introduce even more diversity of Catholic opinion, Madden contrasts the Quinn family's responses with those of Emily's mother and brother, who, from a securely middle-class position, disparage the efforts of civil rights leaders and warn that 'It'll end in a bloodbath' (79). As the Quinn sisters grow up, their own life choices demonstrate a similar diversity of reactions to the Troubles: Helen becomes a lawyer in Belfast out of a sense of duty to the Northern Catholic community; Cate leaves Northern Ireland as soon as she can (changing her name from 'Kate' to 'Cate' in the process); and Sally remains at home, her unbroken attachment to which, Madden implies, mirrors her co-dependent relationship with their mother.

Chapters Two and Four of *One by One in the Darkness* establish the baseline of the Quinn family's existence before the late 1960s. Subsequent even-numbered chapters present milestones of the next quarter century in Northern Ireland through their eyes: the first big civil rights march from Coalisland to Dungannon in August 1968; a banned civil rights demonstration on 5 October 1968 in Derry, where marchers were beaten by police and the everyday violence of the Stormont regime finally attracted international attention; the student-led march from Belfast to Derry in January 1969 that was viciously attacked by loyalists; the election of student civil rights leader Bernadette Devlin to Parliament in April 1969; the resignation of the reformist Northern Ireland Prime Minister Terence O'Neill later the same month; the rioting in Belfast and Derry in August 1969 which prompted the deployment of British troops to Northern Ireland; the introduction of internment without trial of suspected republican activists in August 1971, which caused a huge upsurge in paramilitary recruitment and attacks; Bloody Sunday; and Bloody Friday, 21 July 1972, when the IRA detonated at least twenty bombs across Belfast in just over an hour, killing eleven people, most of whom simply happened to be in the wrong place at the wrong time, and injuring 130 others.[15] Alongside descriptions of these historically significant events in the flashback chapters are stories illustrating their local ramifications: Brian is wounded at the Derry demonstration; he and Peter are briefly detained in August 1971, angering the entire extended family; British soldiers are stationed in the area and quickly alienate locals, even the pacific Charlie, with intrusive searches and harassment at security check-points; a local boy is killed while attempting to plant an IRA bomb; Charlie is distressed because Protestant tradesmen he had considered friends grow afraid to work in such a republican area. Each successive even-numbered chapter advances the historical narrative chronologically towards the present day. Cumulatively, they illustrate the ways in which the Troubles gradually encroached on daily life, and how, despite them, life went on. 'You can get used to anything, can't you? That's what people say', Sally remarks to Cate near the end of the novel, adding, 'Maybe it's true' (139).

This historical narrative, intimately familiar to any Catholic who grew up in Northern Ireland outside the urban centres of Derry and Belfast during the 1960s and 1970s, gains poignancy through being relayed from the point of view of maturing children, who acquire much of their awareness of the unfolding action via overheard and imperfectly understood adult conversations. Because the grown-ups in their lives are newly obsessed with hearing and talking about current events, 'The sisters quickly learnt not to interrupt any of these discussions, nor to make a noise while the news was on the radio or television', though their own lives still revolve more around 'a spelling test at school, or a trip to the dentist's, or the prospect of an outing to the cinema in Magherafelt or Ballymena' (94). Helen, 13 in 1972, crosses the line between innocence and a dreadful understanding shortly after Bloody Friday. She witnesses an argument between her father and Peter and their brother Brian, who, as a republican, is less willing to blame the IRA for its actions.[16] Late the next night, Helen hears her father go downstairs and, 'after what seemed to her like a long period of time', slips out of bed to join him. She finds him smoking alone in the dark kitchen, and he calls her to his side and hugs her tightly:

> 'What if…?' he said eventually, and he embraced her harder. 'What if…?' but he couldn't finish what he was trying to say, and she realised that he was crying. She knew now, all in a rush, what he was thinking; and there, in the darkness, it was as if she had already lost him, as if his loved body had already been violently destroyed. They clung to each other like people who had been saved from a shipwreck, or a burning building; but it was no use, the disaster had already happened. All over the country, people were living out the nightmare which she now dreaded more than anything else. Who was she to think she deserved to be spared? He took her back up to her room and tucked the blankets tightly around her in the bed; he stroked her face and told her he loved her; he told her to sleep. But she gained a dark knowledge that night which would never leave her.   (130–1)

The incident illustrates the traumatic effect the Troubles had even on people as yet physically unscathed by political and sectarian violence. After it, Helen can put her own worst fears into words. Even more terrifying, she realizes that her parents recognize their own inability to protect her from what she fears.

The knowledge of how quickly and arbitrarily lives could be ended or blighted lurked in the minds of all Northern Irish people of adult awareness during the Troubles. Madden makes this point with striking directness through present-day Sally's unwilling recollection of a 'strange incident' that occurred about six months before Cate's visit. She had been with her pupils in her classroom when a van stopped at the school gates and a man she did not recognize ran towards the school. 'Something closed in her heart', and, convinced that the school was about to be attacked, she ordered the children to put their heads on their arms and close their eyes. She knew this to be 'a wholly inadequate response' but even in retrospect could not imagine 'what she should have done instead'. She had waited tensely for the man to 'burst in' and start shooting, but nothing happened, and then she had noticed him outside again running away from the school and towards his van 'through the steady rain…the rain!' When the children left at the end of the day, she had 'put her head on her folded arms and wept uncontrollably'. Madden writes,

> She cried because she might not have been wrong. Over the past twenty-odd years, all kinds of people had been killed or maimed. Many of them might have thought that the tasks in which they were engaged would have nullified their risk of danger, but they would have been wrong. Bricklayers and binmen on their tea break had been shot. They'd killed a man driving a school bus full of children; opened fire on supporters at a football match; and shot people sitting in a bookie's watching horse racing on television. Men lying in bed asleep beside their wives or girlfriends had been woken up and murdered. At each new variation, Sally had shared in the shock of those around her. To kill the members of a showband! How could anyone go into a church and start shooting at the congregation? And yet each event seemed to be no preparation, no warning for the next. Until someone attacked mourners at a funeral, and threw hand grenades at them, it seemed impossible that this should ever happen. So no one had ever gone into a primary school in Northern Ireland and opened fire on a gaggle of five-year-olds and their female teacher: what did that prove? Nothing, Sally thought. Just because a thing hasn't happened doesn't mean that it never will.   (146–7)

Sally does not share this story with her sister: 'It would have upset her too much to try to explain all of this to Cate; possibly it would have upset Cate too, and there was no point in that' (147).

Sally's reluctance to speak on this occasion exemplifies an evasion that characterizes all the Quinn women's thoughts and conversation. Readers gradually learn that it is not merely the Troubles in general that they avoid talking about, but a more personal and specific tragedy: in October 1991, roughly two and a half years before the novel's present-day action, Charlie had been assassinated in Brian's house by loyalist gunmen who mistook him for his republican brother. Veiled allusions to this event appear throughout the novel. Near the end of Chapter One, for example, we are told that the sisters and their mother are 'bound' by 'the thing that had happened to their father': 'Cate felt that just by looking at them, people might have guessed that something was wrong, that something had frightened them; and that fear was like a wire which connected them with each other and isolated them from everyone else' (9). Details are added, indirectly and incrementally, as the narrative progresses on its twin tracks of past and present, but it is not until the closing paragraphs of the book that we are given a vivid picture of the circumstances of Charlie's death. Thus, the flashback scenes move closer and closer to this essential darkness, reaching it just when we may be thinking it might be avoided because the concluding Chapter Fourteen, breaking with the pattern established in the rest of the novel, focuses on present-day rather than past action. In this 'final recreation of the scene with its terrible inevitability', critic Geraldine Higgins remarks, readers are 'locked into experiencing the murder which has been the insistent undertow of the book'.[17]

Reviewing *One by One in the Darkness* for the *Spectator*, James Simmons complained, obtusely, about Madden's 'withholding' of information: 'obviously all the characters in this novel know that the father was murdered, and nothing is achieved by the reader not being told this at the beginning'. As Higgins points out, however, 'This is to misunderstand the crucial connection between "withholding" and distancing mechanisms in Madden's work.' Madden establishes that time has passed since the murder and that the characters try not to dwell on it because 'she is primarily concerned with grief and survival rather than the representation of violence itself'. In Higgins's words, 'Rather than staging the violence directly in a realistic narrative and mapping the reactions of the survivors after the event, Madden delays and replays the traumatic event as part of the grieving process', with the 'tension between what must be remembered and what must be avoided...played out through dreams and nightmares'. This narrative strategy means that the novel is far more artfully constructed than may be apparent on a first reading. As Higgins explains, Madden 'pulls off the difficult task of maintaining a linear time structure while suggesting a psychic alternative which tugs the attention of the reader in another direction. Indeed, all the "happy childhood" memories are suffused by the loss that is to come', as Charlie's sudden and unnatural death 'has retroactive consequences'. In Higgins's astute reading, the novel explores 'the differences between the experiencing of violent events and the telling or remembering of them, whether in public or private forums.... In filtering the violence through the controlling desires and dreams of her protagonists, Madden reveals the architecture of the grieving process. Grief, unlike time, is non-linear—it ripples in concentric circles from the death of a loved one, echoing always the lost centre at its core.'[18]

Another early reviewer, Patricia Craig, commented wryly that Madden's 'approach to the terrorist element in Northern Irish life is the opposite of a thriller-writer's'. This is true. For one thing, the perpetrators of violence merit only a few sentences in *One by One in the Darkness*; instead, Madden keeps her attention squarely on its victims. Moreover, whereas most thrillers centre on 'the public domain of men and war rather than the private domain of women and home' and stereotype the few female characters they include, this novel concentrates on the experiences and impressions of a mother and three daughters. Superficial appearances to the contrary, Madden also eschews the kind of realism that typifies the thriller genre.[19] She opts instead for exploration of her characters' subjective thought processes.

The psychological effects of traumatic loss are evident everywhere in *One by One in the Darkness*. Noting that 'much of the worst violence of the Troubles took place in domestic spaces, such as homes, pubs, or shopping centres', critic

Daniel W. Ross argues persuasively that Madden deliberately invokes Sigmund Freud's concept of the uncanny. Freud posited that 'the familiar can, under circumstances like trauma, become unfamiliar and even haunting', so that an experience of the uncanny is 'one in which things which are most familiar and comforting suddenly seem to be concealing something, long hidden from view, that is terrifying'. Sadly, 'once a familiar place becomes uncanny to its residents, they are not likely to find comfort there again'. The novel begins with Cate's vision of her family home: 'Home was a huge sky; it was flat fields of poor land fringed with hawthorn and alder. It was birds in flight; it was columns of midges like smoke in a summer dusk. It was grey water; it was a mad wind; it was a solid stone house where the silence was uncanny' (1). The book's penultimate sentence, moreover, alludes to the uncanny once again: 'In the solid stone house, the silence was uncanny' (181). Critic Elmer Kennedy-Andrews observes that, for the novel's characters, 'Returning home means facing the demons of violence and terror, recognising the strangeness of the familiar world. Homecoming is to experience the loss of home, to approach the existential awareness of death.'[20]

Helen tells Cate that she returns to the country most weekends because she feels the need to get out of the city: 'It's a safety valve' (6). The reality, she privately realizes, resembles instead 'an entry into a danger zone, as though there were a hairline crack in her otherwise steely self-containment, and to go home was to push against that crack with her fingers and feel it yield and fear that some day it would split open completely' (24). For her, 'the horror of what had happened to their father had been compounded by it having taken place in Brian's house', which had been like a second home to the sisters when they were growing up, and she purposefully refrains from fully furnishing or personalizing her new townhouse in Belfast, preferring to keep it, 'psychically, a blank' (44). Brian and his wife Lucy, despite having completely renovated their kitchen about a year and a half after Charlie was killed there, can still hardly bear to sit in it—'The place is desecrated', Cate remembers Lucy saying (143). Sally, who had once wanted to emigrate but stayed because she feared she would lose the intimacy of her connection to the North without making any comparable connection elsewhere, now, since their father's death, wants out again. 'If it wasn't for Mammy, I'd leave tomorrow', she tells Cate: 'I can't stand being in Northern Ireland' (139). Emily, for her part, is tormented by her inability even to want to forgive her husband's killers: 'To be a woman in her late sixties, to have prayed to God every day of her life, and to be left so that she could feel no compassion, no mercy, only bitterness and hate, was a kind of horror she had never imagined' (125). Even Cate, who had established a once-fulfilling existence for herself in a different place, feels a new sense of vulnerability after losing her father, 'like a tightrope walker suddenly aware of the abyss into which she could fall at any moment' (4). In the immediate aftermath of his death, 'she'd flung herself back' into life in London 'as if her own life depended on it': 'And yet, for all of that, her life had gone sour' (91). Her recognition of this fact is entangled with her sudden desire 'to have children', but 'The only explanation she would ever be able to give was this: "I wanted something real"' (93).

Cate's decision to become a single parent and her (initially) secret pregnancy, which have motivated her trip home, provoke a family crisis that inevitably stirs up memories of the one that accompanied Charlie's murder, never truly dormant anyway—the only good thing about *that* crisis, Sally remarks, is that 'nothing can ever be so bad again' (177). The unborn baby can be read as a metaphor for the peace process itself: embryonic, still uncertain, even, in the conservative context of Northern Ireland, a bit illicit. Sally, despite the tension inherent in the situation, is 'delighted' by the news and tells Cate as much, but she also knows that 'To say how much she felt the family needed something like this would have been to point up how haunted and threatened she had felt herself to be over the past two years' (145–6). The prospect of a child concentrates the women's focus on the future, although this is one that, for Emily at least, will take some getting used to. She is oppressed by her sense of 'how bad a show it is for the child to have no father' and confides to Sally that 'I won't be able to feel the way I ought to or indeed want to for a while yet....I know what's required of me, but it'll take time' (128).

Significantly, Cate is the only character to express any optimism about present-day politics, alluding vaguely to 'articles in the papers from time to time which suggest that there's far more going on behind the scenes than we're being told, and that things could suddenly change' (149). Sally meets this comment with scepticism, saying, 'I wish I could believe it. Living here, you see too much to expect anything to change quickly' (149). She does, however, testify to shifting attitudes in their own community and family that might pave the way for progress. Uncle Brian, for example, 'had his doubts for a long time before Daddy was killed': 'he still is a Republican, he always will be; it's too deep with him for that ever to change. But there are things he can't stomach now, things he won't defend' (142).

Despite the tentative hope offered by the peace process, Madden remained keenly aware that peace, if or when it came to Northern Ireland, would not erase the pain of the past or end the sorrow of those who suffered losses during the years of civil strife. She had not lost any close family members during the Troubles herself, but Northern Ireland is a small place, she says, and almost everyone living there in 1994 knew *someone* personally affected by them.[21] Emily in *One by One in the Darkness* still mourns her father, who died of natural causes during her childhood; the pain of violent bereavement is even more acute. Given her sense of Northern Ireland as a society filled with such pain, Madden wanted her novel to show how grief lasts indefinitely—as one of her characters remarks, 'There's something about it that...that never stops or ends' (52). In the chapter narrated from her point of view, Emily reflects that 'There'd been well over three thousand people killed since the start of the Troubles, and every single one of them had parents or husbands and wives and children whose lives had been wrecked. It would be written about in the paper for two days, but as soon as the funeral was over it was as if that was the end, when it was really only the beginning' (127).

Early in the novel, Helen critiques journalism about the Troubles, charging that it amounts to 'making up stories out of a few facts, and presenting them as though that interpretation was the absolute truth'. Although one of her closest friends is a journalist, she insists that many reporters 'have no empathy, no imagination' and describes the 'medium' as 'a blunt weapon': 'It isn't fitted to dealing with complexity, it isn't comfortable with paradox or contradiction, and that's the heart of the problem' (50–1). This passage demands to be read self-reflexively because literature is, or can be at least, everything that Helen says journalism is not.

The IRA announced its cessation of operations on 31 August 1994, while Madden was still writing *One by One in the Darkness*, but she chose nonetheless to retain a pre-ceasefire setting for it.[22] Her own sense of her subject dictated the exclusion from the novel of hopeful speculation about a possible end to hostilities. Madden also concluded the book on a carefully ambiguous note, which she says Northern Irish readers would have sensed at the time.[23] After an evening spent enjoying each other's company and joyfully anticipating the birth of Cate's baby, the Quinn women, one by one, retire for the night. This scene of cozy domesticity is undercut by what follows, as the centre of consciousness returns to Helen. Lying in bed, she remembers how comfortable she used to feel as a child waiting for sleep, secure in her sense of a marvelous universe overseen by a benign God. Her childish view of the cosmos had been mirrored in her own experience of a happy home tended by loving parents, and 'Helen could see herself, as though she were looking down on her own bed, ... so safe and so happy, not knowing that when she was a woman, it would break her heart to remember all this' (180). Now, the vision that visits her nightly, 'repeated constantly, like a loop of film but sharper than that, more vivid', is her recreation of her father's last moments. Now, she is 'aware of the cold light of dead stars; the graceless immensity of a dark universe', and 'Sometimes she felt that all she had was her grief, a grief she could scarcely bear' (180–1).

The Quinn women's excitement about welcoming new life does not cancel out their mourning for Charlie, and the final sentence of Madden's novel—'One by one in the darkness, the sisters slept'—suggests that each may be, like Helen, left alone with her grief, despite their physical and emotional closeness. Readers have little reason to suppose that the 'uncanny' silence will be broken any time soon, and the women's common constraint carries ominous implications for the future. Mental health professionals in Northern Ireland have warned that, as psychologist Siobhan O'Neill puts it, 'when one person is traumatised, it will affect how they relate to everybody else', including their children and grandchildren, and researchers are now investigating the mechanisms by which the effects of stress and trauma might even be transmitted biologically from parents to offspring.

Northern Irish journalist Lyra McKee cited several studies of such 'intergenerational transmission of trauma' in a celebrated 2016 article about Northern Ireland's high suicide rate and the curious fact that almost a fifth of those who had killed themselves there between 1999 and 2014 were 'ceasefire babies' like herself—people born, as Cate's baby will be, during the final years of the conflict, with little first-hand knowledge of Troubles violence.[24] In *One by One in the Darkness*, Madden underscores the reverberations of traumatic experience that continue to threaten the peace.

Silence and sorrow connect *One by One in the Darkness* with Seamus Deane's *Reading in the Dark*, but the two books share more than these themes. Both novels contrast two generations, use the experiences of one family to tell a wider story about Catholic nationalists in Northern Ireland, focus on the reverberations in the present of past loss, and revolve around absences. While Madden concentrates on the late-twentieth-century Troubles, Deane examines the belated effects of the Troubles of the 1920s, revealing the two conflicts to be part of a continuum. Whereas darkness slowly encroaches on the awareness of Madden's young female protagonists, the narrator of Deane's novel searches it out and actively seeks to plumb its depths, only to discover, to his cost, that he has always been immersed in it. In *Reading in the Dark*, Deane explores, from a position of radical uncertainty, the question of how best to deal with a painful past.

Like Madden, Deane grew up in Northern Ireland but left it as a young adult. Born in Derry in 1940, he earned bachelor's and master's degrees from Queen's University Belfast before moving to England for doctoral study at the University of Cambridge, followed by short-term teaching positions in the United States, a country to which he would return regularly for extended periods in the ensuing decades. He spent much of his academic career at University College Dublin, becoming Professor of Modern English and American Literature there before departing in 1993 to head the Irish Studies programme at the University of Notre Dame in Indiana. By then, he had been recognized for some time, in scholar Joe Cleary's words, as 'one of the most charismatic and authoritative figures in the Irish humanities'.[25]

Deane served on the Field Day Theatre Company's board of directors alongside his friends Brian Friel and Seamus Heaney. He played a primary, and frequently controversial, role in articulating the group's mission and developing its activities in the publishing realm, first through a series of pamphlets and later with the landmark *Field Day Anthology of Irish Writing*.[26] This anthology project, which Deane headed as general editor, engrossed his attention from 1984 until the first three volumes were published in 1991; it continued to require his involvement thereafter as he oversaw the compilation of an additional two volumes, concentrating on Irish women's writing and traditions, under the editorship of a feminist collective helmed by Angela Bourke. Deane wrote *Reading in the Dark* during the same period, beginning in 1984 and continuing until at least October 1994.[27] That he managed to write it at all while absorbed in a scholarly undertaking as ambitious and demanding as *The Field Day Anthology* indicates its great personal significance to him.[28] Notably, and in stark contrast to most first-time novelists, Deane was a prominent public figure by the time *Reading in the Dark* appeared, one especially well-known among critics and scholars of Irish literature.

The novel originated in an invitation from Bill Buford, editor of the literary magazine *Granta*, to contribute to an issue devoted to autobiography. Then unacquainted with Deane, Buford wrote at the recommendation of English poet Craig Raine, who had described to him a gathering at Heaney's house where Deane regaled the assembled guests for two hours with stories about their school-days at St Columb's College in Derry. Buford wanted to publish Deane's work on the strength of this account, but the issue would be going to the printers in a mere five or six weeks. *Granta*, which published the most distinguished contemporary writers in the world, had, as Buford explained to Deane, a circulation exceeding those of the *Times Literary Supplement*, the *London Review of Books*, the *Spectator*, and the *New Statesman*, so Deane agreed to try to produce something despite the tight deadline. He eventually submitted a piece, although not in time for the auto-biography issue.[29]

Buford probably hoped for an amusing, anecdote-filled account of Deane's long friendship with Heaney—something along the lines of 'The Famous Seamus', an essay Deane would publish in the *New Yorker* years later.[30] Deane gave him something altogether darker and deeper, a collection of reminiscences entitled 'Haunted'. This piece, which *Granta* published in March 1985, comprised a series of sharply delineated memories from Deane's childhood and youth, most of which he would later include in *Reading in the Dark*.[31] The sole vignette not set in Derry is also the only one to appear exclusively in *Granta*. In it, Deane describes his 'first bad haunting'. After a fight outside a university dance that turned into a sectarian brawl, some students, including Deane, had been picked up by the police and detained for several hours. Released around four in the morning, he went home and 'fell over a cliff into sleep', where he 'relived an earlier haunting': the episode described in the novel's 'Pistol', wherein the protagonist's family home is ransacked by police, who then question and beat him, his brother Liam, and his father at the local police station. As a university student in Belfast, Deane 're-lived the police at our house as a haunting', panicking as he woke under the repeated interrogation: 'Where was the gun? I had had it, I was seen with it—where was it? I needed it now, for defence.' When he finally managed to stumble downstairs, 'I found I was in a kitchen, years later, and I moved among its orderliness in a daze, taking the sleep and fear off my face like cobwebs'. The incident illustrates Deane's statement in the next paragraph to the effect that, in the Northern Ireland in which he had come of age, 'Politics was a grief'.[32]

Despite the surprising nature of Deane's first contribution to *Granta*, Buford responded with enormous enthusiasm, urging him via telephone call and letter to write an entire book on similar lines. Deane demurred, conscious of the fact that his family history did not belong to him alone. The predictably appalled reaction of his mother, who would feature prominently in any longer story he might write about his own journey to adult understanding, would be one (although far from the only) inhibiting factor. Buford brushed off such objections, insisting that the book could be honest while still obscuring details Deane felt might implicate other people and encouraging the reluctant author to think of autobiography as 'fabricated truthfulness'. Over the next fifteen months or so, Buford communicated with Deane at regular intervals, entreating him to write additional autobiographical sketches and submit them for comment and possible inclusion in the magazine, while also returning repeatedly to the idea that Deane should really be writing a book. *Granta* was preparing to launch an imprint, with plans to publish six titles annually to be promoted and distributed by Penguin, and Buford thought a book by Deane would be a worthy addition to the launch list. He stressed, though, that the most important quality of any such work would have to be uncompromising honesty, urging Deane not to censor himself or withhold any secrets.[33]

Faced with unexpected expenses in the spring of 1986, Deane finally yielded to Buford's persuasion and signed a contract for a work to be published by Granta Books. After accepting an advance that summer, he was obliged either to write the book or to return the money, but he remained deeply ambivalent about the project.[34] It would be another decade before *Reading in the Dark*'s publication—by Jonathan Cape, not Granta Books. In the meantime, Buford, who had rejected an initial draft in early 1987, pressed Deane for fuller disclosure, suggesting in January 1988 that he forget about genre and regard his text as a *book* rather than as a novel or an autobiography but insisting that it needed a clearer chronology and plot. He believed that Deane's story should be one about leaving Northern Ireland. Deane, probably suspecting that (spiritually at least) he never *had* left the North, considered fictionalizing the story further to render it more coherent.[35]

Buford, still hoping to include Deane's book among the first titles to be published by Granta Books in August 1989, wrote him increasingly plaintive letters requesting status reports. Frustrated by the apparent lack of progress, an obvious explanation for it seemingly never occurred to Buford: Deane's mother remained alive through 1988 and into 1989. Her death in March of that year must have encouraged Deane to think he could finish *Reading in the Dark* at last. That, at least, was the impression he gave Buford, who scheduled the book with Penguin around the same time. This publication plan appears to have been abandoned by late spring, however, when it became clear that Deane would not manage to complete the writing in time.[36]

Much the same thing would happen repeatedly over the next several years. *Reading in the Dark*'s appearance seemed so imminent in 1990 that, in May,

Deane read from his work-in-progress at the Booksellers Association Conference and was asked to review a proof of the cover.[37] A four-page letter from Buford to Deane dated 11 June, however, made it abundantly clear that he did not consider the book ready to meet its public. While pleased with much of the rewriting Deane had done, Buford was not satisfied with the chapters that departed most significantly from Deane's actual experiences; these struck him as artificial and sensational, and he urged Deane to stick closely to his own truth. Publication was scheduled (or rescheduled) for January 1991 despite the lack of an agreed-upon draft, but Deane became increasingly elusive as summer gave way to autumn, and the project was put on the back burner once more.[38]

No one familiar with the complicated history of *The Field Day Anthology of Irish Writing* will be shocked to hear that it interfered with Deane's efforts to write a novel. Originally proposed by Deane in 1984 as 'a definition, in the form of a comprehensive anthology, of what writing in this country has been for the last 300–500 years', it had grown to three volumes (4,044 pages) covering 1,500 years by the time Deane, Heaney, Friel, and Taoiseach Charles Haughey launched the boxed sets on Halloween night in 1991.[39] *Reading in the Dark* was supposed to appear shortly afterwards.[40] This plan, though, likely fell victim to the anthology's tumultuous reception. The Field Day directors had expected it to be attacked on the grounds of political nationalism, and reviews were by no means wholly negative, but a robust feminist critique of the volumes caught them off guard. *Irish Times* columnist Nuala O'Faolain raised the issue of male bias barely a week into November during a televised interview with Deane, pointing both to the under-representation of female writers and the absence—in a self-consciously political collection of Irish *writing* (not literature)—of texts related to Irish feminism. She developed her observations about the anthology's omissions more fully in her widely read column a few days later, expressing her disappointment and surprise 'that Seamus Deane, a Northern Catholic, should not be alert to what it's like to be treated as a second-class citizen'.[41]

Debate over Field Day's anthology raged in Ireland and in Irish Studies circles internationally for the better part of a year and dominated cultural discussion about Ireland for an extended period thereafter.[42] Deane, who knew all too well 'what it's like to be treated as a second-class citizen', resented the way in which feminist arguments about the anthology were seized upon by people critical of Field Day for other reasons, but he also admitted forthrightly the 'serious weakness' of the anthology as it stood.[43] His immediate response to O'Faolain during their televised exchange reflected both regret and recognition of responsibility: 'To my astonishment and dismay, I have found that I myself have been subject to the same kind of critique to which I have subjected colonialism...I find that I exemplify some of the faults and erasures which I analyze and characterize in the earlier period.' Deane first proposed to rectify the original anthology's omissions by incorporating feminist documents in the paperback edition that was supposed to appear in a year or two, but by early August 1992 he had committed Field Day to the production of a fourth volume devoted to women's writing and edited by a feminist collective. Deane's practical and moral support over the ensuing decade ultimately enabled the 2002 publication of *two* additional volumes focused chiefly on Irish women's writing and experience, which were hailed by reviewer Catriona Crowe as 'one of the triumphs of the Irish feminist movement, as important in their way as the achievement of access to contraception or equal pay'.[44]

In the autumn of 1992, though, Deane remained sunk in depression. He had spent seven years of his professional life intent on a scholarly project he regarded as having national importance, but, rather than receiving the heartfelt thanks of a grateful nation, he had been subjected to criticism he recognized as legitimate. There was a special irony in the fact that Deane had been charged with being oblivious of the social controversies then roiling the Republic because the deterioration of his own long marriage coincided unhappily with a protracted dispute about whether the Irish constitution should be amended to allow for a restricted form of divorce (63.5 per cent of voters in a June 1986 referendum on the issue had rebuffed an effort to remove the prohibition, and Deane's marriage was one of many left in limbo until a second referendum to allow divorce in certain circumstances finally passed by a slim margin in November 1995). Long discontented at University College Dublin, Deane was pursuing job opportunities in the US and contemplating drastic changes to his life in every sphere, but both public and private stresses left him feeling trapped and unable to work—and especially to write.[45] By the summer of 1993, Deane spoke facetiously about his abortive career as a novelist, telling an interviewer in June that he had 'written a novel about the North and finished it several times, then refused to publish it, called *Reading in the Dark*. You may have seen this advertised. It was supposed to come out about six times, but now everyone's so embarrassed they're not going to mention it again.'[46]

That autumn, Deane took up a new post as Donald and Marilyn Keough Professor of Irish Studies at the University of Notre Dame. This presumably paid enough that he could, if he wished, have refunded his Granta advance and put the whole episode behind him. Instead, for reasons that may have been as much therapeutic as artistic or commercial, he returned to the work of refining *Reading in the Dark*. The furore over silent and silenced Irish women occasioned by the original Field Day anthology might well have prompted him to reconsider his mother's refusal to speak about subjects that had once preoccupied him. Deane sent Buford a revised draft in late October 1994, with a note intimating strongly that this was the last one he was going to get.[47] The intention was to publish the book in 1995, but Buford's departure that spring to become the fiction and literary editor of the *New Yorker* delayed the process once again. When it began to appear likely that publication would be pushed into 1997, Deane and his agent convinced Granta to release him from his contract and took the book to Jonathan Cape, which published it within months, in the summer of 1996.[48]

Questions of genre that had perplexed Deane as author also confounded his readers. A persistent theme in commentary regarding *Reading in the Dark*, from the first reviews on, has been a query posed succinctly by critic Stephen Regan: 'Should [it] be read as fiction, autobiography or memoir?' The cover of the first edition appeared designed to stoke uncertainty on the subject, as Regan observed: 'The faded photograph on the dust jacket shows Seamus Deane and his brother, arms folded, celebrating their first holy communion. As if simultaneously inviting and denying the suggestion of autobiography, the book cover also reveals a cracked photographic plate.' Deane's own statements about the book make it difficult, if not impossible, to answer Regan's question conclusively. Shortly after *Reading in the Dark*'s initial publication, Deane asserted that 'some of it did happen, and some of it didn't' but acknowledged that he had found it hard to finish writing the book because he believed his siblings would be annoyed if it was published before their mother died. He later explained that his immediate family's reaction had not been his only worry, stating that 'I couldn't publish it when other people were alive, not only my parents. I could have written it, but I couldn't have *published* it before their death.' Later still, while confirming that he did have a grandfather and an uncle who fought in the IRA, Deane evaded a question about the book's factuality with the comment that '*Reading in the Dark* is as accurate as can be when we are speaking of fiction, however autobiographical.'[49]

In Deane's most substantial interview about the book, he emphasized its emotional rather than literal truth ('I felt how the child in the fiction feels') and said he had tried to deal with 'this strange and elusive thing called the truth' to show the reader that 'there's certainly a connection between knowing the facts of a situation and knowing the truth of a situation, but...the facts and the truth are not entirely coincident'.[50] I have argued elsewhere that Deane, paradoxically, wrote *Reading in the Dark* in the first person to distance himself from the story being told, as allusions throughout the book to Henry James's ambiguous novella *The Turn of the Screw* should have reminded readers of its famously unreliable first-person narrator.[51] This literary strategy, however, proved overly subtle for Deane's readership, the most sophisticated members of which were personally acquainted with him. Instead of calling the narrator's tale into question, the use of the first person served to underwrite his version of the story owing to Deane's established authority as a teacher and scholar. Thus, for example, when *Reading in the Dark* was short-listed for the Booker Prize, awarded to the 'best' novel of the year written in English and published in the UK, the book critic for the *Irish Times* questioned if it should even be competing for a fiction prize, writing that 'This book has been widely celebrated and became something of an enigma in the years leading up to its belated publication. However, exactly why it was published as a novel rather than the memoir it so patently is remains in itself a further mystery.'[52]

Reading in the Dark consists chiefly of short, vivid vignettes, each entitled and dated. Deane, who grew up in the same part of Derry at the same time as the narrator, describes the book's composition in revealing terms. Strikingly, his account of the writing process begins with passive voice constructions that downplay his own agency in that process: 'It began as a series of flash memories that were recounted. Those memories accumulated, and as they accumulated they were written and re-written.' Deane then relates that he tried 'to put the images in certain kinds of sequence that would both make them more powerful in themselves' and 'attract or seduce the reader into wondering not only what happens next, but what is the relationship between these parts'. He sought to capture 'the strange experience of the young boy in actually uncovering something piece by piece by piece, and then only towards the end being able to see the whole thing in perspective'. Deane's use of the word 'memories' indicates the origin of the book in personal reminiscence, while the addition of the adjective 'flash' hints at the involuntary, perhaps even unwilling, nature of the recollection. Significantly, the reflections that make up the book were shared as oral stories before they were committed to paper. At that point, the shards of memory were 'written and re-written', at least partly with the aim of mastering experience. Deane recalls that 'I wanted to write about the process of discovery, but the writing about the process of discovery was itself another form of discovery. It was both retrieval of something that I have known and I had experienced [and] also finally coming to terms with it'.[53]

Reading in the Dark's protagonist is an unnamed boy growing up in Derry during the 1940s and 1950s in the Catholic ghetto known as the Bogside. Deane presents him interacting with his parents, siblings, and other relatives; attending school; exploring the area around his home; dodging danger in the streets; coping with the arbitrary authority of priests and policemen; listening to countless stories; and beginning to ask awkward questions about why things are the way they are. Many of his childhood and adolescent experiences are, like those of the sisters in *One by One in the Darkness*, typical of his time and place, but it is a grimmer place than the Quinn family farm. Moreover, his family's fortunes are bleaker, dogged by disease, death, deprivation, and discrimination. The reader of Deane's novel, like that of Madden's, also quickly learns that this family carries its personal burden of Northern Ireland's dark history. Deane gradually reveals the nature of that burden as the boy learns more about his family's past.

In contrast to Madden's novel, Deane's has one controlling consciousness: a first-person narrator who is an older version of the curious boy protagonist. The boy's pivotal discovery comes midway through the book when he is about 12 years old. He tricks his mother's dying father into sharing with him a secret that had obviously upset her some weeks earlier. In 1922, the grandfather, an IRA commander, had ordered the execution of a volunteer, Eddie, suspected of being an informer. Several years later, the grandfather learned that the real informer was a man named McIlhenny who was married by then to his younger daughter, Katie. Meanwhile, his older daughter (the narrator's mother) had married Eddie's brother Frank (the narrator's father). The boy, his entire world rendered uncanny by his grandfather's revelation, goes 'straight home' after it: 'home, where I could never talk to my father or my mother properly again'.[54]

The narrator's determined but ultimately unsuccessful efforts to learn the *whole* truth about Uncle Eddie's fate are threaded through the rest of the novel, which is dominated by his recurring inner debates about whether or not to confront his parents with the parts of the story he knows and demand further details. The question of what each of them knew when they got married especially obsesses him. Not long after the boy's fateful conversation with his grandfather, his father, who believes that his brother was an informer, tells the narrator and *his* brother Liam that Eddie was killed by his own side, although the narrator is perturbed to hear that he did not confide this belief to his wife until after their wedding. His mother, the narrator decides, could not have known that her father ordered Eddie's assassination until his deathbed confidence, which clearly devastated her, but his suspicions about what other information she might be withholding multiply after his Aunt Katie mentions that her husband (McIlhenny) had courted the narrator's mother before he married her. He thinks his father ought to be told that Eddie was killed in error rather than in consequence of his own treachery, but he regards this secret as properly belonging to his mother. She, for her part, shows no inclination to share it with her husband and silently forbids the narrator to say anything, either, although letting mysteries lie runs contrary to his nature.

The narrator is convinced that his mother could, if she wished, tell him everything he longs to know:

> She knew it all now. She knew I knew it too. And she wasn't going to tell any of it. Nor was I. But she didn't like me for knowing it. And my father thought he had told me everything. I could tell him nothing, though I hated him not knowing. But only my mother could tell him. No one else. Was it her way of loving him, not telling him? It was my way of loving them both, not telling either. But knowing what I did separated me from them both.   (194)

The narrator's estrangement from his parents grows throughout the remainder of his teenage years. He distances himself from his father in fear that he will blurt out the secret about his grandfather's responsibility for Eddie's death. And, despite his mute entreaties, his mother never either confirms or denies his private speculation that she refuses to enlighten her husband because she still harbours romantic feelings for McIlhenny (who fled Derry for Chicago, leaving his pregnant wife Katie behind, after being unmasked as the real traitor). The narrator eventually attends university in Belfast and then, at his mother's request, embarks on his adult life away from Derry, which enables a détente between them. The novel ends, in the early 1970s, with his father's death from heart failure against the backdrop of resurgent Troubles in Northern Ireland.

Notwithstanding the uncertainty about *Reading in the Dark*'s status as a factual record, commentators have rarely hesitated to identify its narrator with Deane himself in a way that has limited their ability to analyse the text on its own terms. Deane's formidable critical achievement and reputation have shaped the reception of his novel. As cultural historian Gerry Smyth observed in 2001, Deane 'has been at the forefront of most of the major issues and debates which have animated Irish cultural criticism since the 1970s', 'responsible in large part for setting the agenda of the latter discourse as it is currently practised'. Key items on that agenda include 'the appropriateness of (post-)colonialism as a theoretical paradigm for island history', 'the confrontation between tradition and modernity in modern Ireland', and 'the function of [Irish historical] revisionism'. Thus, 'certain connotations and expectations, elicited from prior enunciations and alternative contexts, attend upon any text published under the authorship of "Seamus Deane". *Reading in the Dark* could thus be read as an engagement with the issues associated with that name—that is, as an apology for postcolonialism, as a dramatisation of the confrontation between tradition and modernity, or as a refutation of revisionism'.[55] Deane the critic, in short, bequeathed to Deane the novelist an exceedingly long paper trail, as dubious an asset to a literary author as it is to a political candidate.

Most academic analyses of *Reading in the Dark* situate it in the context of Deane's critical publications and reflect his own scholarly interests.[56] Deane himself regarded his novel as 'connected' with his critical writings, especially those on Edmund Burke and the essays collected in his volume *Strange Country*. He simultaneously wondered, however, if his own sense of his entire body of work as 'coherent' might be a consoling fantasy. Perhaps, he mused, his many texts in different genres embody instead 'a series of splintered reactions' to his experience.[57] For the purpose of this discussion of *Reading in the Dark*, I will argue that critical and creative writings are fundamentally different in kind. As a critic, Deane had many things he wanted to say and rarely gave the impression of being in doubt as to what those were. As an autobiographical novelist, he was grappling with unresolved questions. Friel, Deane's mentor as well as his friend, memorably described his own writing process thus: 'You don't have anything to say about anything. You delve into a particular corner of yourself that's dark and uneasy, and you articulate the confusions and the unease of that particular period.'[58] During the decade in which he wrote *Reading in the Dark*, Deane, I believe, was tormented both by the question of how best to handle a traumatic past and by the suspicion that this question has no good answer.

The central conflict in *Reading in the Dark* is that between the protagonist's overwhelming urge to uncover family secrets and his parents' equally fervent desire to conceal them. Deane highlights this tension in the opening pages of the book, when the narrator's mother, described later as having 'a touch of the other world about her' (50), senses the 'shadow' of '[s]omebody unhappy' on the stairs and orders her son (then about 5 years old) not to cross it. Instead of being frightened, he is 'enthralled' by the idea that 'We had a ghost, even in the middle of the afternoon.' He longs to approach the spot but is young enough that his mother can still compel his obedience, saying, 'It's bad enough me feeling it; I don't want you to as well' (3-4). Over the next several years, the protagonist becomes fascinated by a more specific shade: that of his Uncle Eddie, who joined the IRA around the time of Ireland's partition but 'disappeared' in April 1922 (8). The narrator's maternal uncles explain Eddie's absence by saying that he emigrated, although his whereabouts and circumstances are unknown, but the boy notices that his father 'would not speak of it at all' (8). When he asks his mother about Eddie, she responds with a question of her own: 'Can't you just let the past be the past?' (42).

The boy pursues his inquiries against his parents' increasingly adamant resistance because he yearns to know and to understand them better and feels oppressed by a '[s]ilence everywhere' that conditions his own existence: 'My father knowing something about Eddie, not saying it, not talking but sometimes nearly talking, signalling. I felt we lived in an empty space with a long cry from him ramifying through it. At other times, it appeared to be as cunning and articulate as a labyrinth, closely designed, with someone sobbing at the heart of it' (42).

As a child, an instinct for self-preservation tempers the protagonist's curiosity about the reasons for his father's unspoken grief. The narrator reflects that 'I knew then he was going to tell me something terrible some day, and, in sudden fright, didn't want him to; keep your secrets, I said to him inside my closed mouth, keep your secrets, and I won't mind. But, at the same time, I wanted to know everything' (45). When the boy becomes an adolescent, this second desire overwhelms his qualms.

Both the boy's parents seek to shield him from the darker aspects of their own past, and that of Ireland. As Deane commented in 1997,

> there's an element in the novel where the older generation is looking at this young child growing up and trying to dig it all up again, and saying 'Oh for Christ's sake stop, stop, let's get rid of that history, let's find some way of leaving it behind.' The only way out is by…keeping things secret.…There's no talking-cure, no implication that by revealing everything you will somehow overcome it![59]

In his remarks about *Reading in the Dark*, Deane consistently emphasized the impact on Northern Irish people his age of 'socialist legislation' enacted by the British Labour government in the mid-1940s, 'especially the Free Education Act'. Extended to Northern Ireland in 1947, this law mandated free and compulsory secondary education, including, for the most 'able' 20 per cent (selected by competitive examination around the age of 11), state-subsidized placement at the exclusive grammar schools that could prepare them for university, also paid for by the state. This gave Northern Ireland's parents—especially members of the disproportionately disadvantaged Catholic minority—hope that their children might transcend, and eventually transform, the demeaning conditions that had stifled their own generation. Even as a child, Deane understood that his parents 'recognised that a cohort of Catholic kids going to school was what was going to break the Northern Irish state'.[60] With their eyes firmly focused on the future, the parents in *Reading in the Dark* are intent on the narrator's prospects and thus terrified of anything that might distract him from his studies. Living in a republican enclave, the last thing they want is for him to romanticize an uncle who fought in the IRA. The fact that they both know Eddie to have been executed as an informer (a stigma that continues to influence the way some of their neighbours view the family) only strengthens their determination to prevent the protagonist from learning too much about him.

The contest of wills between the boy and his father comes to a head in the first half of the novel. After the boy throws a stone at a police car to evade a beating by local bullies, an action interpreted in the Bogside as 'going to the police' (102), he is framed as an informer by a Catholic policeman named Sergeant Burke. On this occasion, Burke makes cryptic comments about Eddie, implying both that he has a reputation as an informer and that those who view him as such are mistaken. Following this incident, the boy and his family are ostracized for some time. On a day when the narrator's father has been 'insulted' on the boy's account, he berates his son, provoking a quarrel between them: 'Was there something amiss with me? No, I told him, there's something amiss with the family. The police were on top of us long before I was born. If he wanted to blame someone, let him blame Eddie, not me.' The father responds ('so fast, I saw nothing') by punching his son, who 'got up, hating him' (104). Not long after this argument, the boy systematically destroys his father's prized rose bushes.

Seamus Deane ruined his father's rose garden as a child, an act of wanton vandalism he regretted for the rest of his life. He alludes to this event in two paragraphs of 'Haunted' and in a poem entitled 'The Birthday Gift' from *Rumours*, a poetry collection dedicated to his father's memory.[61] His treatment of it in *Reading in the Dark* is distinctly different, however. In the two earlier autobiographical accounts, the boy's action is unmotivated; the speaker seems as mystified by it as readers are likely to be. Moreover, the boy's father does not reprimand him or demand an explanation—in fact, in both earlier versions of the story, he says nothing about it at all, either at the time or afterwards.

In the novel, in contrast, Deane turns the episode into a rite of passage. The speaker of 'The Birthday Gift' says he was 10 years old when he destroyed his father's garden. In *Reading in the Dark*, the 'Roses' vignette is dated July 1952, making the protagonist about 12. *Reading in the Dark*'s dates are among its most fictive elements. The precise dating of episodes, as Regan observes in his review, creates 'the impression of a diary or journal'.[62] This perception, however, is an illusion—Deane, who probably did not recall exactly when many of the events described in the book happened, added the dates to clarify its narrative arc and to create the chronological framework demanded by Buford. In this case, he deliberately shifted an act of childish rebellion forward in time to push it closer to an age more commonly regarded as the threshold of adolescence. Age 12 also had another importance in Northern Ireland at the time. 'That autumn', the narrator notes, 'I would start secondary school and was enchanted by the notion that I would be reading new languages—especially Latin and French. I was trying to read a prose translation of *The Aeneid*, but the strange English and the confusion of names left me stranded' (108). By emphasizing the boy's pending initiation into the rarefied grammar school atmosphere, Deane references his own education, which would both free him from his parents' poverty-stricken circumstances and further alienate him from them and the world they inhabited.

Deane's naming of *The Aeneid* as the protagonist's reading matter at this pivotal time holds special significance because of its political and cultural associations. Virgil's Latin epic, which attributes the founding of Rome to the Trojan warrior Aeneas, resonated with British imperialists, who compared their empire with the Roman one; during Deane's schooldays, it remained a central text in British elite education. Deane was also aware of a competing identification between Ireland and Carthage—destroyed by Rome like the founding Queen of Carthage, Dido, is destroyed in Virgil's account by her love affair with Aeneas. The Ireland–Carthage analogy had been used since the eighteenth century to express Irish resistance to colonial rule, and several writers associated with Field Day had evoked this association in their own work.[63] Rome, moreover, loomed large in an Irish Catholic context as the centre of the Church, and masses were celebrated in Latin throughout Deane's childhood and early youth. As a pupil at St Columb's College in Derry, Deane, like James Joyce's Stephen Dedalus, was emphatically subject to two masters (the 'imperial British state...and the holy Roman catholic and apostolic church'), and the study of Latin was intimately connected with both.[64]

While composing this vignette devoted to a painful memory involving his beloved father, Deane might also have been remembering Richard Kearney's comments on *The Aeneid* in his Field Day pamphlet *Myth and Motherland*, edited by Deane and first published in 1984:

> Aeneas is repeatedly described by Virgil as 'pious' not only because he is a quasi-divine hero...but also and more importantly because he is an agent of ancestral continuity carrying the past into the present (as he bears his father, Anchises, on his back out of burning Troy into the new land of Rome). The message of Virgil's myth is, therefore, one of filial piety towards the father.... That is what tradition means—*tradere*, carrying or transferring the past into the present and the present into the past.[65]

In writing *Reading in the Dark*, Deane was, figuratively, bearing his parents out of the Derry in which they spent their entire lives: a place that, effectively, no longer existed. Completing the text required him to re-enter that vanished time and space to try to understand his own behaviour as well as other people's.

Placing the 'Roses' vignette directly after 'Informer' (dated June 1952), which includes the boy's fight with his father, has the effect of providing him with a clear reason for targeting his father's pride and joy. The rose bushes themselves, moreover, are described much more fully than in the earlier works. They are sickly despite the attention and care the father lavishes on them, their leaves dotted with black spots and their stems encased in greenfly. The roses represent what the father has managed to make of his life in Northern Ireland through immense love and effort, but their stunted nature symbolizes the official and unofficial restrictions on Catholics that have limited his potential. The narrator also details the actions of the boy, bent on destruction. After uprooting one bush with great difficulty, he resorts to cruder methods, sprinkling cement dust over the remaining fifteen bushes and then beating them flat with a spade. This act recalls an earlier vignette, 'Pistol' (dated January 1949), in which police raid the narrator's family home after he shows neighbourhood boys a gun that had been given to his father by a German prisoner of war. The policemen, like the boy in 'Roses', seem intent on causing as much damage as possible, with one emptying a tin of peaches onto the kitchen floor and another splitting open a bag of cement during his search of the shed. This second policeman 'came walking through in a white cloud, his boots sticking to the slimy lino and the cement falling from him in white flakes' (29). Thus, Deane aligns the protagonist with the oppressive forces harassing his father.

Although he does not say much about his son's attack, the father in *Reading in the Dark* says more than Deane's own father evidently had. When the protagonist's mother arrives on the scene and asks him, tearfully, what he has done and why, he replies, 'Ask Father. He'll know' (107). In 'Haunted', Deane writes that 'my shoes were removed, my clothes confiscated, and I was put to bed to wait for my father'. The protagonist of *Reading in the Dark*, in contrast, 'clumped angrily up the stairs, stripped naked, got into bed and lay there waiting'. When his father comes home, he looks at the boy for some time before speaking,

> 'So I know, do I?'
> I nodded.
> 'Tomorrow, and the day after, and the day after that, and every other day that comes, you'll know.'   (108)

The next day, assisted by the narrator's maternal uncles and some workmen, the father uproots and discards the damaged rose bushes and covers the area where they had stood with cement. The narrator comments, 'I think that was the first time my father ever missed a day's work' (109).

As in a coming-of-age ritual, the boy spends two and a half days alone in the room he usually shares with siblings (in his large family, probably the first extended period he has ever *been* alone), going without food apart from some bread and butter he takes from the kitchen on the second morning. On the evening of the second full day following his assault on the rose bushes, he is allowed to join the others for dinner, and his father invites him back into the family on new terms: 'You ask me no more questions. Talk to me no more. Just stay out of my way and out of trouble' (110). In this family (and this society), becoming an adult means learning to keep one's mouth shut. The narrator recounts that he went back upstairs, 'still angry, but more horrified', and 'half-cried, half-cursed myself to sleep'. Later that night, he wakes to the realization that '[s]omeone had touched me' but pretends to sleep while his father bends over and kisses his hair. 'That more or less ended it', he remembers (110). In 'Haunted', Deane recounts that 'We played a version of miniature football on that cemented stretch for years afterwards', a detail epitomizing the way his father sacrificed his own dreams for his children's welfare. The protagonist of *Reading in the Dark* benefits in similar fashion but periodically suffers searing pangs of guilt: 'When I kicked a football there, I could see it bounce sometimes where the rose petals had fallen and I would briefly see them again, staining the ground. Walking on that concreted patch where the bushes had been was like walking on hot ground below which voices and roses were burning, burning' (110–11).

The father eventually relents, breaking his silence regarding Eddie in February 1953, about seven months after the events of 'Roses'. He takes the narrator and Liam on an outing across the river to see an area he used to visit with his parents and siblings which is about to be 'industrialised', and during it he reveals that Eddie was killed as an informer. Frank's reason for confiding his appalling secret to his oldest sons at this time probably had something to do with the IRA's resurgence in preparation for the border campaign it would launch a few years later.[66] Two months before this conversation, though, the narrator had heard the truth about Eddie's wrongful execution from his dying grandfather. Thus, his father's attempt to explain why Eddie is a sore subject for him only makes the boy feel worse. He thinks, 'Now he had said it all, and a great shame and sorrow was weighing his head down....I should stop this. Mother, I should stop this. You should stop this. Would it be worse? "Daddy," I said internally, "I know it's too late but go back a few minutes...and say nothing. Never say. Never say"' (139).

As a child on the brink of adolescence, the narrator had blindly pitted himself against his father's silence; during his teenage years, his mother becomes his wilier antagonist. The boy is with her in his grandfather's house right after she learns about her father's role in Eddie's death, and her exclamation on that occasion—'"Eddie," she said, "dear God, Eddie. This will kill us all"' (123)—gives him just enough information to extract the secret from his grandfather himself some weeks later. She quickly recovers her composure, however, warning her son to 'Pay no attention to what he says and don't, whatever you do, don't repeat it. Not even to me' (124). After his grandfather dies, the boy hopes that 'the effect of what he had told me would magically pass away or reduce', but on some level he already knows 'it could not but re-embed itself in my mother and go on living. We were pierced together by the same shaft. But she didn't know that. Nor was I going to say anything unless she did' (132–3).

Despite the nervous breakdown she suffers shortly after her husband shares his 'heavy, untrue story' (139) with the narrator and Liam, the mother is more unyielding than Frank. She obdurately refuses to satisfy the narrator's curiosity about the past, although he feels certain that she knows more about what happened than any other living person. The narrator believes throughout the second half of *Reading in the Dark* that 'Staying loyal to my mother made me disloyal to my father' (236). When he is about 15, he finds an ingenious way—not unlike writing an autobiographical novel—to tell and not tell his secret at one and the same time. He writes out the story about Eddie as he understands it, painstakingly translates it into Irish (a language neither of his parents knows), and then, pretending to share an essay about 'local history' he has written for school, reads the Irish text to them. His father nods and smiles and says that 'it sounded wonderful', but the narrator credits his mother with greater understanding: 'I knew she knew what I was doing' (203).

The narrator's fixation on the buried past provokes a state of 'low-intensity warfare' (225) between his mother and himself as he nears the end of his secondary schooling. He yearns for her to confide in him, 'rehearsing conversations I would never have' to the effect that 'If you loved me more or knew how much I loved you and him, then you would say everything' (216–17). Simultaneously, though, he recognizes that there are many things that no one, his mother included, can know for sure ('like the way Eddie died, like who was there, like what exactly had happened') because 'everyone who had been there was dead or in exile or silenced one way or the other' (217). When his mother takes to lingering on the staircase again, the narrator sees her as communing with 'her ghosts', but 'Now the haunting meant something new to me—now I had become the shadow' (228).

The narrator is alienated from his father by what his father does not know that he does, but he is 'separated' (240) from his mother by the secrets they share: 'It wasn't just that she was trapped by what had happened. She was trapped by my knowing it' (234). He goes to Belfast for university, 'glad to be free of the immediate pressure' of living at home but 'sorry to have so mishandled everything that I had created a distance between my parents and myself that had become my only way of loving them' (236). Years later, 'as the Troubles came in October 1968', the mother suffers a stroke that robs her of her speech, which the narrator experiences as 'almost a mercy': 'I would look at her, sealed in her silence, and now she would smile slightly at me and very gently, almost imperceptibly, shake her head. I was to seal it all in too. Now we could love each other, at last' (242). As the violence intensifies outside the house, invading it periodically, the narrator contemplates his equally quiet parents and imagines that 'in her silence, in the way she stroked his hand, smiled crookedly at him, let him brush her hair, bowing her head obediently for him, she had told him and won his understanding' (243).

Critics who have written about *Reading in the Dark* tend to identify over-whelmingly with the narrator's attempt to discover what happened to Uncle Eddie, and they generally accept his version of his family's story despite its gaps, speculation, and details uncorroborated by any of the novel's other characters. They certainly do not question the value of the narrator's search, to which he remains committed throughout the book, or his determination to articulate the truth as he 'knows' it. The academic bias in favour of the narrator is not surprising: critics recognize in this precocious youth the qualities of intellect, curiosity, and persistence essential to a scholar. The novel ends, however, when the narrator is still a young man in his early thirties.[67] I wish to suggest that the middle-aged parent *writing* the book was willing to entertain a possibility that its critics have not taken seriously—the possibility, that is, that his parents might not have been wrong to want to consign aspects of their history to oblivion. Deane could, at least, sympathize with their desire to keep past traumas from infecting the present and future.

Reading in the Dark's narrator believes in learning and telling the truth, which he equates with the facts, and he proves adept at discovering things that his elders, for various reasons, would prefer remained hidden. His resourcefulness and skill typically impress readers. Deane himself, however, observed that what the narrator finds out is almost entirely 'damaging' to him. One moral of the novel is that repression has negative consequences—the mother's 'startling' mental break-down, for example (143–52). Deane's chronicle of what he called the narrator's 'sad search' for a 'master-story', however, suggests equally that people are often better off *not* knowing things and that telling some truths can endanger others.[68]

The novel centres on its most dramatic instance of truth-telling: the narrator's maternal grandfather's revelation that he mistakenly ordered Eddie's execution. Deane leads up to this gradually, with the boy, after the 'Roses' episode, being sent to live in Grandfather's house and to help Aunt Katie care for him in his final illness. Intrigued by his grandfather's cryptic comment about the 'ancient history' of Derry that his teachers 'couldn't teach and wouldn't if they could' (122), the narrator begins pumping him for information, only to be met with the statement that 'You're better not knowing' (123). It is, ironically, not long after this conversation that the grandfather tells the narrator's mother his shocking secret, an event that marks 'the beginning of her long trouble' (124). Despite his mother's horrified reaction to her father's confidence, the narrator burns with a desire to hear it himself, which he finally does. He stalks his grandfather for weeks, pretending that his mother has begun talking to him about Eddie but has sworn him to secrecy. Finally, after refusing the sacrament of confession that might have contained his disruptive truth, the grandfather tells the boy what he innocently longs to know—thereby further wrecking the narrator's relationships with both his parents, already strained by their refusal to speak about the topics of most urgent interest to him. As the novel clearly dramatizes, both sharing and withholding a truth like this one can have negative consequences.

The question of whether the narrator or his mother will ever tell his father that Eddie was erroneously killed at the command of his father-in-law-to-be and that his wife was once romantically involved with the real informer hangs over the rest of the book, suspense rendered poignant by the narrator's genuine uncertainty as to whether learning these truths would bring his father comfort or pain. His mother, determined to protect her husband, seems to have no doubt on the subject, wordlessly prohibiting any disclosure that might disturb Frank's peace of mind. The narrator, however, never comes to any final decision, although he continues to wonder 'Was nothing ever said…as their marriage mutated slowly around the secrets that she kept in a nucleus within herself and that he sensed, even though he also thought he was free of the one secret he knew, since he had told us, false as it was?' (241). He ultimately decides that his father 'knew something lay beyond him but he had no real wish to reach for it' and allows that perhaps this attitude was 'wise', 'for the whole marriage had been preserved by his not allowing the poison that had been released over all these years…to ever get to him in a lethal dose' (241).

Despite his awareness that knowledge can sometimes be a liability, there is little suggestion in the novel that the narrator would have preferred not to know the things he does. In any case, knowing them shapes (or deforms) his youth to such an extent that he would not be the same person without knowing them. In this sense, his personal story echoes the biblical account of the fall of man: once innocence is lost, there is no going back. Similarly, when the narrator uncovers the destructive way in which his parents' family histories intertwined years before they themselves met, he thinks their marriage 'should never have been allowed' (140). If it had not taken place, though, he would not exist—and how could he wish that?

Reading in the Dark raises philosophical questions about the value and cost of knowledge that relate to its theme of education. The narrator regrets that his father never had the opportunities he himself did for intellectual development, remarking in a passage describing his return from university that 'My father…would have loved to have been educated' (237). Seamus Deane, though, probably suspected that his mother could have done more with such training. The novel repeatedly stresses the similarities between the narrator and his mother in colouring and perception, and Deane commented that the mother is 'more intelligent than the father, more sensitive than he'. What might once have struck him unfavourably as her wilful withholding of vital information became, over the course of composition, a sign for him of her heroic self-sacrifice. As he told an interviewer the year after the novel's publication, 'what I was trying to say of the mother figure is that she is the one, ultimately, who takes the whole burden of knowledge upon herself'.[69]

In tribute to his own mother, Deane gave the narrator's mother the most forth-rightly political speech in *Reading in the Dark*. This appears in the second 'Sergeant Burke' vignette, dated December 1957—although the narrator makes a point of telling readers that his mother did not describe the encounter to him until several years later, when she was 'more assured of my silence, no matter what I knew' (212). The policeman, nearing retirement, had called on the mother, seeking, like the narrator himself, answers to questions about events of the 1920s that he thought she might be able to give him. 'Politics destroyed people's lives in this place,' he had observed, adding that 'People were better not knowing some things, especially the younger people, for all that bother dragged on them all their lives, and what was the point?' (215). He had nevertheless proposed, contradic-torily, that full disclosure (especially to her husband), offered the best way to put the past to rest: 'There has to be an end to it,' he had insisted, 'a separation from all that grief, a walking away from it, a settling' (212). Warning that 'the poison was spreading' to her children, he had asked, 'Isn't it about time it was all stopped? Did nobody want free of it? Why had it to go on and on and on?' (213). The nar-rator reports,

> Well, she told me, she let him know in quick order why. Injustice. The police themselves. Dirty politics. It's grand to say let it stop to people who have been the victims of it. What were they supposed to do? Say they're sorry they ever protested and go back to being unemployed, gerrymandered, beaten up by every policeman who took the notion, gaoled by magistrates and judges who were so vicious that it was they who should be gaoled, and for life, for all the harm they did and all the lives they ruined? He had no answer to that.   (213)

The mother's argument that the trauma of past conflict cannot be neutralized by accurate historical accounting until the conditions that gave rise to the conflict no longer exist had at least as much relevance in the 1960s, 1970s, 1980s, and 1990s as it had had in the 1950s. Her comments indicate that *Reading in the Dark* should be read as a post-conflict text as well as a postcolonial one. Deane ended his novel in July 1971, just before the rapid intensification of violence that followed the Northern Ireland government's introduction of internment without trial of suspected republican terrorists in August of that year.[70] When the book appeared in 1996, this exchange between Burke and the narrator's mother offered a reminder, as mental health professionals began to calculate the psychic effects of political and sectarian violence since the late 1960s, that there were still many people living in Ireland (Deane among them) for whom the Troubles of the 1920s remained an open wound. The partition-era violence reverberating decades later in *Reading in the Dark* took place *within* the Northern Catholic community, but this only underscores the extent of the damage done then.

Deane never solved to his own satisfaction the problem of what to do with 'bad history' (221), both personal and political, although he recognized that the issue did not lend itself to 'rational investigation'.[71] Perhaps for this reason, he continued to feel uneasy about *Reading in the Dark*, despite the international acclaim it received.[72] His siblings disapproved of his decision to publish the book, seeing it as family exposure, and he had struggled to write the last section of it. Bill Buford rejected six or seven attempts as overly sentimental before Deane finally settled on the published ending, a conclusion he described as less a resolution than a 'puncture' of the narrative. The difficulty, he reflected, probably stemmed from the fact that he was trying to find closure in a still-unsettled situation.[73] When an interviewer asked him in 2007 if he had felt a weight lifted from his shoulders after finishing the book, Deane sighed and said, 'I did then for a while. But…something was raised and then dismissed rather than realized for me in that novel.…It was an exploration that went further than I had gone before but it still didn't find anything. So, whatever North Pole I set off for, I never reached.'[74] Readers of the novel are likely to feel similarly deflated, as any expectations they might have of receiving definitive answers to the narrator's questions about the past—both what happened in it and how, or whether, to talk about it—go unfulfilled. The discomfort thus created, though, may be the book's profoundest comment on the after-effects of loss: lost time, lost opportunity, lost love, lost life.

4

Repeating

Bernard MacLaverty embarked on a novel in the autumn of 1994 mainly because he was contractually obliged to write one. The imprint that would publish the American edition of his latest short-story collection had agreed to do so on the condition that he promise them 'the next novel', but MacLaverty 'hadn't a clue' what to write about.[1] He had a reputation at the time as a 'misery-monger'. The protagonist of his first novel, *Lamb* (1980), kills a child in his care in an attempt to 'save' him, an act MacLaverty saw as a metaphor for what 'violent republicans' were doing to the Ireland they claimed to love. His second novel, *Cal* (1983), centres on a young man who falls obsessively in love with the widow of a reserve policeman whose murder he participated in as a driver for the IRA. MacLaverty allowed that both *Lamb* and *Cal* 'reflect the negativity, the disappointment, the gloom of the situation in Northern Ireland', but he insisted that he was not fundamentally 'a gloomy person'. The IRA cessation announced in August 1994 and the loyalist ceasefire declared that October contributed to MacLaverty's sense of 'the opening up of possibilities', freeing him to contemplate a more affirmative sort of novel.[2]

Born in Belfast in 1942, MacLaverty enjoyed what he called 'an excellent, happy childhood', until his father died when he was 12. He earned A-levels in English and Chemistry, but his grades were inadequate for admission to university as a student; instead, he found a job as a technician in a medical laboratory at Queen's University Belfast. Shortly after leaving school, though, MacLaverty read *The Brothers Karamazov*, developing an enthusiasm for literature in the process, and at the age of 19 or so he began writing short stories. After a lecturer in the English Faculty, Philip Hobsbaum, read one published in a campus medical magazine, MacLaverty was invited to join the Belfast Writers' Group, where he got to know talented contemporaries, including Stewart Parker, Seamus Heaney, and Michael Longley.[3]

MacLaverty enrolled at Queen's as a mature student after a decade in the lab and completed an English Honours degree in 1974, by which time the intensifying violence had negatively impacted his life. The events of the Troubles came as a shock to someone who had reached adulthood during what he remembered as a 'wholly peaceful time' in Northern Ireland. 'Before 1969', he recalled in 1995, 'there was conflict, but people didn't die. There was debate, but people weren't blown up.'[4] MacLaverty decided to leave Northern Ireland as a result of the Ulster Workers' Council (UWC) Strike of May 1974, when industrial action by Protestant

Getting to Good Friday: Literature and the Peace Process in Northern Ireland. Marilynn Richtarik, Oxford University Press.
© Marilynn Richtarik 2023. DOI: 10.1093/oso/9780192886408.003.0005

workers toppled a short-lived power-sharing government that represented the last truly promising political initiative there before the 1990s. Loyalist paramilitaries enforced the strike, while the population suffered power cuts lasting up to twelve hours, food shortages, school closures, disrupted social services, and threats to other utility systems.[5] MacLaverty, then preparing for his final exams, studied by candlelight because there was no electricity, in a house where only the transistor radio was working. He described

> coming down to the university where there were groups of guys with baseball bats and Balaclava helmets—it all looked very, very ugly. You would realize that the thing uppermost in your mind was, 'Will I get home alive? Will these guys kill me or beat me up?—but in the meantime I'll have to write this paper on Wordsworth'....Sometimes from the exam hall you could hear explosions or ambulances.[6]

MacLaverty and his wife, Madeline, resolved at that point to spend the foreseeable future somewhere else, and, after a one-year teacher training course, he applied for teaching jobs in Britain. In 1975, they moved with their four children to Scotland, where MacLaverty taught in Edinburgh and on the Isle of Islay before resigning in 1981 to devote himself full-time to writing. The family eventually settled in Glasgow, and by 1994 he had published four volumes of short stories in addition to his two novels.[7]

One of the first decisions MacLaverty made about his third novel was that its central character would be a woman. Looking through his unpublished work for inspiration, he had come across two short stories abandoned ten or fifteen years earlier that both had female protagonists ('one of them was having a baby, and the other one was someone who had the courage to break a relationship'); thinking about his novel, he 'realised' that these women 'were the same person'.[8] He incorporated elements of another story he had begun about an Irish woman mistakenly imprisoned for republican activity, explaining that 'as the book grew I subtracted the bars of the prison, and it became a prison of the mind'. Conscious of his penchant for writing father-son stories, MacLaverty deliberately set out to write a mother-daughter story this time, and he gave himself the further challenge of 'not really us[ing] any male characters'.[9] Men such as the protagonist's father, lover, and mentors would feature in the story but would be presented exclusively through her thoughts and memories.

A female friend, also a writer, 'sparked off' MacLaverty's writing process by observing that 'It's all right for you—you don't have to have the babies'. In this 'throwaway remark' he glimpsed 'the whole of the novel'. He decided to focus on what he later called 'the central life-event of birth, which is in the gift of women. But it's not a simple gift; there's a lot of pain and awfulness around it, and I wanted to get this across'.[10] MacLaverty heightened the conflict by making his heroine an artist struggling with both the unfamiliar demands of motherhood and post-natal depression, her ability to create new life interfering with her ability to create art.

Tillie Olsen's book *Silences*, on women and writing, influenced MacLaverty's thinking about biological and socially constructed barriers to female artistic achievement. Discussing the difficulties faced by female authors who happen to be mothers, Olsen writes,

> More than in any other human relationship, overwhelmingly more, motherhood means being instantly interruptable, responsive, responsible. Children need one *now*.... The very fact that these are real needs, that one feels them as one's own (love, not duty); *that there is no one else responsible for these needs*, gives them primacy. It is distraction, not meditation, that becomes habitual; interruption, not continuity; spasmodic, not constant toil.... Work interrupted, deferred, relinquished, makes blockage—at best, lesser accomplishment. Unused capacities atrophy, cease to be.[11]

The fear that her artistic reflex might cease to function owing to her new responsibilities as a mother afflicts MacLaverty's central character.

Despite the sex of its protagonist, however, the novel that became *Grace Notes* (1997) contains significant autobiographical elements. MacLaverty had a personal interest in the creative process and impediments to it, and he was just emerging from a period of writer's block partly brought on by the serious illness of one of his daughters. He had, in the past, overcome a similar obstacle by asking himself 'what can be worse than a writer who can't write?'—a question that inspired a story about a blind painter.[12] This time, he sought to express his own ideas about art by projecting them onto another 'creative person...in a different discipline', and, having been fascinated by music since he was about 16, he decided to make his central character a female composer. Like him, she would be a Northern Ireland native who had moved to Scotland and lived on Islay. 'You do write out of your own experience', MacLaverty acknowledged, but the thought of adopting a female perspective did not intimidate him. In any case, he believed, as he told himself during the planning stages of the book, that 'If something is to be written from a woman's point of view then she must constantly have the feeling that she is being treated as an inferior person. It will not be difficult to empathise with this—like a catholic in a Unionist world.'[13]

Religion, closely connected with art in MacLaverty's mind, also featured prominently in his thoughts about the novel from the start. He had been raised in what he described as an 'intensely religious household' where 'everyone got up early and went to mass daily' and 'the family rosary was said every night'. He himself served as an altar boy and was 'steeped in that religious tradition'. In retrospect, he saw this as 'a great upbringing' because 'Growing up Catholic, I took symbols and words to be immensely important.' As he matured, however, he came to doubt the dogma behind them and, like James Joyce before him, found in art a replacement for the Church. As he explained his conversion,

> All the ways in which we attempt to explore what we are as human beings can become some kind of substitute for religion. Religion says, 'This is the answer, you do this, you live your life according to this, and it will result in an afterlife of eternal happiness.' But when that doesn't exist for us any more, we examine life, seeing the cruelties and the awfulness, and the injustices. Art is a reflection of that, and that's really what's left to us.[14]

MacLaverty wanted to call his book *Credo* before he discovered that another novel with that title had already been published, and in early notes he asserted that humans celebrate the spiritual in their nature through 'art and music and words'. These works had previously 'been directed at God, but now they are for themselves they are no less spiritual'.[15]

One source of MacLaverty's distaste for institutionalized religion was his experience of living in Northern Ireland, especially after it descended into overt sectarian violence. Under these circumstances, he naturally saw religion as a 'divisive force'. For once, though, he did not feel compelled at first to write either directly or indirectly about the Troubles themselves. He even wondered early on whether the Northern Irish setting he envisaged for at least part of the book could be 'justified'.[16]

MacLaverty's notes towards the novel indicate that, in its initial planning stages, he wanted to explore issues affecting Catholics, especially Irish Catholics, more generally. These ideas centred on the Church's strictures regarding sex, which sceptical observers like MacLaverty found contradictory. In May 1992, an American named Annie Murphy revealed in the *Irish Times* her affair during the early 1970s with Eamonn Casey. Casey, then Bishop of Kerry, had gone on to become the popular and progressive Bishop of Galway. The relationship resulted in the birth of a child, whom Casey had failed to persuade his lover to give up for adoption. Over the years, he had avoided contact with Murphy and their son, offering only sporadic financial support, until she finally went public with her story. This exposé forced Casey's resignation and exile, and Murphy followed it with a sensational memoir in 1993. The saga riveted Irish Catholics everywhere. As novelist Colm Tóibín observed in the spring of 1995, 'the Casey scandal, as it unfolded, reminded us of how conservative and anachronistic our society remained, even as it exposed the hypocrisy of the Church's moral edicts'. This incident, he emphasized, was just one of many (including cases involving abortion, child sexual abuse, and homosexuality) that eroded the Catholic Church's authority in Ireland during the early 1990s.[17] MacLaverty, like his counterpart from the Republic, was fascinated by the fundamental shift in public perceptions of the Church in Ireland.[18] His original plan for the novel included a romance between the female composer and a Catholic priest who comes to share her atheism.

Although MacLaverty had no shortage of material or ambition for his third novel, he struggled to begin writing it. He had been thinking about and making notes towards the book for months by April 1995, when he lamented in his diary that 'Madeline is away in Ireland and I have the house to myself and I have a contract for a novel and I have a word processor and I am even typing on the fucking thing so why can't I do it? I think I'm afraid of doing it wrongly.'[19] Meanwhile, the hope that had accompanied the previous autumn's promising developments was fading by the day.

The 1994 ceasefires created great expectations, but there had been little political progress since they took effect. The British and Irish governments wanted to broker an agreement among the parties in Northern Ireland, but they saw the issues involved from starkly different points of view. The Irish government prioritized keeping militant republicans engaged in the peace process, while the British government worried more about unionist sensitivities. The unionist demand that the IRA 'decommission' its weapons before being allowed to participate in substantive talks about the future of Northern Ireland, a demand the IRA leadership rejected, overshadowed the year and a half following the IRA's suspension of military activity. As the stalemate continued, sectarian tensions in Northern Ireland rose sharply.

Problems became apparent immediately after the IRA's ceasefire announcement, when unionists and the British government complained that it failed to specify that the group's 'complete cessation of military operations' would be 'permanent'. SDLP leader John Hume dismissed such objections as 'nit-picking' and insisted that the way to make the ceasefire permanent would be to proceed as quickly as possible to talks including all parties with an electoral mandate, a position endorsed by Irish Taoiseach Albert Reynolds. First reactions among Northern Ireland's citizens similarly diverged: nationalists and republicans greeted the ceasefire with jubilation and relief, while unionists expressed anxiety and suspicion that the British government had done a secret deal with republicans.[20] During a two-day visit to Belfast in late October, Prime Minister John Major stated that he would make a 'working assumption' that the IRA cessation was permanent and that preliminary talks with Sinn Féin could begin before Christmas. However, his government undercut such overtures with conflicting signals. When Reynolds opened the Irish government-sponsored Forum for Peace and Reconciliation in Dublin barely a week after Major's speech, the British ambassador did not attend because Sinn Féin would be represented. Republicans began to develop a well-founded fear that the British government was seeking to reduce the momentum of the peace process.[21]

The first meeting in more than two decades between Sinn Féin representatives and British civil servants at Stormont did not take place until early December

1994, over three months after the IRA's ceasefire began, and it would be five more months before Sinn Féin met directly with a British minister in the Northern Ireland Office. During both discussions, British representatives insisted on the need for IRA decommissioning, while the Sinn Féin delegations sought 'parity of esteem' for their party and movement on issues important to republicans, including prisoner releases, Irish language rights, all-around 'demilitarisation', and the start of inclusive negotiations. It seemed obvious to Sinn Féin President Gerry Adams that 'British strategy was still focused on defeating republicans. The stalling and prevarication were about reducing expectations, diminishing hope and encouraging schisms among our ranks'—which, he allows, 'was always a danger'. From a republican perspective, as Adams explains, the IRA was just one of 'many armed groups' involved in the Troubles, and 'Removing weapons from Irish politics had to be a goal of the process, not a pre-condition.'[22]

The fall of the Reynolds government in November 1994 made republicans anxious because they had regarded Reynolds as a strong leader and ally. John Bruton of Fine Gael, known to be sympathetic to unionist concerns and strongly critical of the IRA, headed the next coalition government. Nevertheless, Bruton seemed to endorse Reynolds's assessment that requiring the IRA to hand in weapons was 'not a sensible precondition' for multilateral talks. He warned days after his election as Taoiseach that it would be unwise to let the peace process become deadlocked over decommissioning, and he met with Adams a few days later.[23]

It was unionists' turn to feel nervous a few months later, when the British and Irish governments published their Frameworks for the Future documents: one by the British government consisting of proposals for political structures in Northern Ireland, and one addressing 'the totality of relationships' involved in the conflict. The latter, often referred to loosely as 'the Framework Document' or 'the Frameworks Document', proved controversial. It expressed 'a shared understanding between the British and Irish Governments to assist discussion and negotiation involving the Northern Ireland parties' and built explicitly on the three-strand approach of the Brooke/Mayhew talks in 1991 and 1992: Strand One dealing with arrangements within Northern Ireland, Strand Two with possible North–South institutions, and Strand Three with relations between the islands and governments of Britain and Ireland. The joint Framework also incorporated the statements of principle laid out in the Downing Street Declaration of December 1993, including the governments' pledge to support 'self-determination by the people of Ireland', 'achieved and exercised with and subject to the agreement and consent of a majority of the people of Northern Ireland'.[24] This document encapsulated ten months' collaborative effort between British and Irish civil servants and ministers, and, as with the Downing Street Declaration, the Northern Ireland Office believed it had 'delivered an "Orange document in Green-speak".[25] Unionists, however, disagreed.

The governments unveiled the Frameworks on 22 February 1995, but the *Times* had printed extracts three weeks earlier with the comment that 'the British and

Irish Governments have drawn up a document that brings the prospect of a united Ireland closer than it has been at any time since partition in 1920'. Unionists were especially alarmed by the description of a North–South body designed to 'promote agreement among the people of the island of Ireland; to carry out on a democratically accountable basis delegated executive, harmonising and consultative functions over a range of designated matters to be agreed; and to serve to acknowledge and reconcile the rights, identities and aspirations of the two major traditions'. Most concerning for unionists was the governments' statement that the body's remit 'should be dynamic, enabling progressive extension by agreement of its functions to new areas'. Journalist Henry McDonald explains that this looked to many unionists 'like a United Ireland in embryo form'.[26]

Major observes that 'Sinn Fein would in reality have had great difficulty with the Framework Documents', but 'Gerry Adams had the wit to welcome them, so as to drive deeper the wedge between Unionists and the government'. A chasm had yawned between Major's administration and the hardline DUP for some time now (Major had ejected a DUP delegation from his office in early September 1994 after Paisley refused to accept his word that he had not made a secret deal with the IRA).[27] In contrast, the nine UUP MPs loomed large in a Parliament where the Conservative Party held a perilously slim majority, and Major records that considerations of '[w]hat the UUP might be persuaded to accept' ('a hard judgment to make when the UUP was riven into factions') dominated the Framework negotiations.[28] The controversy generated by the Frameworks revealed that the Prime Minister's team had underestimated unionist objections to any arrangement that appeared to dilute British sovereignty in Northern Ireland.

During the weeks and months that followed, the British government strove to mollify unionists by doubling down on the call for IRA decommissioning before Sinn Féin would be allowed into multilateral talks. In early March 1995, Secretary of State for Northern Ireland Patrick Mayhew announced that before Sinn Féin could join negotiations there must be 'willingness in principle to disarm progressively', agreement on 'what decommissioning would actually entail', and the 'actual decommissioning of some arms'. Major regarded this as an 'inherently reasonable' formulation representing 'a softening of the government's position' on the arms issue, but it failed either to persuade republicans or to appease unionists. Three days later, the UUP officially rejected the Frameworks proposals in their entirety.[29]

The Sinn Féin leaders, meanwhile, grew increasingly worried about the IRA ceasefire holding, given the lack of political movement. In an interview with the *Irish Times* in mid-June, Adams claimed, inaccurately, that the British government had never mentioned IRA decommissioning as a precondition to negotiations before 31 August 1994. Had it done so, he added, there might 'have been no IRA cessation on September 1 last year'. His colleague Martin McGuinness underlined the point later that month, stating that 'in reality there is not a snowball's chance in hell of any weapons being decommissioned this side of a negotiated settlement'.[30]

Mounting republican frustration and unionist fear made for an acrimonious marching season in 1995. Three thousand or so parades were held annually during the spring and summer in Northern Ireland at this time, most by Protestant organizations such as the Apprentice Boys of Derry and the Orange Order (named for William of Orange, who defeated the Catholic James II at the Battle of the Boyne in 1690). Unionists typically regarded these parades as street festivals celebrating Ulster Protestant history and culture, while nationalists viewed them as demonstrations of triumphalism. An overwhelming majority of marches took place peacefully, but a small number, perhaps fewer than a dozen, regularly gave rise to controversy, even violence. These problematic parades tended to be in areas previously home to one side that were now inhabited by the other. Historian Jeremy Smith explains that, in 1995, unionists' 'right to march across the hallowed earth of Ulster became a metaphor for their right to remain British', whereas nationalist communities 'for the first time felt empowered to challenge a tradition they had long held to be little more than celebrations of Protestant power and ascendancy'; republicans, moreover, 'had long ago realized that nothing strengthened the Nationalist cause in the south, in London and especially in America more than the sight of red-eyed Orangemen rampaging and rioting'. Nationalists won some early victories in April, when, after protests by local residents and Sinn Féin members, the RUC rerouted marches that had been scheduled to pass through the Catholic Lower Ormeau Road area of Belfast. Unionist anger at such restrictions came to a head in early July outside the Orange stronghold of Portadown.[31]

The 'siege of Drumcree' began on 9 July, when the RUC stopped Orange marchers from returning to Portadown via their traditional route after a church service just outside of town. There were nationalist housing estates along that stretch of the Garvaghy Road, and the local residents' group, led by a former IRA prisoner, opposed the parade passing through. The RUC, fearful that paramilitaries on both sides would infiltrate the area and start fighting each other, decided to bar the parade from the Garvaghy Road. The marchers, however, took this action as a provocation.[32] Ian Paisley, a seasoned rabble-rouser, appeared on the scene that evening to insist that the stand at Drumcree was 'a matter of freedom or slavery'. Local MP David Trimble had attended the Orange service and was already taking a leading role in the protest when Paisley arrived. Hitherto obscure outside unionist political circles, Trimble's actions at Drumcree would catapult him into the international spotlight.[33]

Two years younger than Bernard MacLaverty, Trimble, who entered the Northern Ireland civil service after leaving school, had also studied at Queen's University as a mature student. After earning a Bachelor of Law degree with first-class honours in 1968, he joined the law faculty at Queen's. Trimble took little interest in local politics until the early 1970s, when his daily bus trips to the university from his flat in north Belfast (a short walk from MacLaverty's child-hood home) became, in his words, 'a terror tour of the hot spots of the early Troubles'.[34] He became involved with Ulster Vanguard, a political movement founded in February 1972 by former Northern Ireland Minister of Home Affairs William Craig and described by Henry McDonald as 'a pan-unionist alliance of disgruntled members of the Unionist Party, former B Specials, Orangemen and various factions of the loyalist paramilitary underworld' that also attracted 'unionists who mistrusted the religious fundamentalism and blustering rhetoric of Ian Paisley'. Trimble shared Craig's belief that direct action was the only way to get results under direct rule, a system he described to Dean Godson as 'dictator-ship moderated by riot'.[35] Vanguard members, like other hardline unionists, hated the Sunningdale Agreement, especially its provision for a Council of Ireland, and in January 1974 Trimble proposed (not for the last time) an independent Northern Ireland as an alternative to a united Ireland.[36]

The UWC Strike featured as prominently in Trimble's life as it did in MacLaverty's, but for different reasons. While most politicians were slow to hop on board the UWC bandwagon, McDonald records that Trimble 'was an early and enthusiastic supporter of what was to become the most successful revolution against the British government since World War II'. He had even 'played an important back-room role in bringing down the last power-sharing administra-tion in Northern Ireland', co-editing the daily news bulletin of the strike commit-tee and providing the UWC with political and legal advice.[37] Trimble displayed his fondness for street theatre in July 1995 at Drumcree, where he first attempted to lead about eight hundred Orangemen past the RUC road block and later urged another group of loyalists assembled in Portadown to stand their ground. By the next day, ten thousand or more Orange supporters (from all the counties of Northern Ireland, from the Republic, and from Scotland) had gathered in and around Portadown to confront a thousand members of the RUC. Elsewhere in Northern Ireland, loyalists held protest rallies, blockaded roads, and shut down the busy port of Larne in 'scenes of mass disruption' reminiscent of the UWC Strike two decades earlier.[38]

Trimble helped negotiate a compromise by the early morning of 11 July whereby a limited but substantial number of Orangemen (all from Portadown District Lodge) were allowed to march down the Garvaghy Road without the loyalist bands that would normally accompany them; in exchange, they agreed not to march along the road the following day. Trimble, not a member of the local lodge, greeted the marchers at the end of their route. When members of the crowd called for him and Paisley to accept their thanks, Trimble strode onto the street, grabbed Paisley's hand, and lifted it into the air. McDonald notes that this 'triumphal image' of 'the two rival unionist MPs walking, their arms held aloft, between two lines of wildly cheering and clapping loyalists was transmitted by television cameras around the world', inspiring 'deep resentment among nationalists across Ireland'. However, the impression of unionist unity was mis-leading. Trimble, who despised Paisley and his fundamentalist politics, recalled later that he had aimed to prevent the older man from upstaging him: 'I thought to myself, "How do I make sure he doesn't walk in front of me?" So I grabbed his hand to keep him in his place'. The episode, however, 'planted an idea of Trimble as someone every bit as hard-line and belligerent as Ian Paisley' and led to his 'being depicted in the UK press as a bigot in a bowler hat'.[39]

Trimble's high profile at Drumcree factored in his election as UUP leader on 8 September 1995, replacing James Molyneux. He later allowed that, among those who supported him for the position, 'there were undoubtedly people who watched the events at Drumcree and thought I was going to be their man, "doing something"'. He insisted, though, that other members of the Ulster Unionist Council who voted for him saw a man 'who wasn't for going down Molyneaux's integrationist path, which he saw as being part of the "do nothing, let's dig our-selves into our trenches" policy—but was instead going for devolution. And everybody knew...that the need was to do a deal with nationalism. By 1995 the only question was the shape of the deal, if you were going to do one'. Thus, the UUC delegates 'would have known that the perception of me in the party was much more as a dangerous moderate than as a hard man'.[40]

As one of his biographers comments, 'a vote for Trimble was, paradoxically, a vote both for change and for cussed defiance of Ulster's many enemies'. Observers not intimately familiar with unionist politics, however, including most national-ists and republicans, took Trimble's election as leader to mean that the UUP's right wing was taking over. The Northern editor of the *Irish Times*, in a typical reaction, remarked that Trimble 'clearly regards compromise as a surrender, and that bodes ill for all-party talks'. The Dublin *Sunday Business Post* expressed the view that Trimble's victory 'has confirmed the fundamentally extreme nature of the politics favoured by the party's activists', and McDonald also records 'panic among nationalist opinion' in Northern Ireland at the time.[41]

Judging from his comments to a Spanish interviewer within a month of Trimble's becoming UUP leader, MacLaverty shared the general nationalist gloom about the immediate prospects of the peace process. He confided that 'This time last year I would have had more hope than at any time', but 'there has been such a struggle during this last year, and then we realize that we are not even at the start. Nobody has said anything to anybody else, there are no negotiations'. MacLaverty admitted that he regarded unionists as 'a problem'. He perceived 'a spectrum' of opinion among Northern Catholics, but on the other side all he saw was a 'huge block of Unionist-thinking people':

> The Catholic side has changed over the years but the Unionist has not. I suppose that they are besieged people and that they have to stick together and act as one....If people sit down and work out structures how they can live together

that's fine, that's what it should be. Neither a united Ireland nor an Ulster Unionist Northern Ireland, but some kind of sharing of power, of responsibility, of learning to live together. But...they haven't even sat down.[42]

Under the circumstances, he did not feel sanguine about Northern Ireland's future.

At around the same time, in late September, MacLaverty decided that his novel, which he had started writing in the spring or summer of 1995, was also headed in the wrong direction. He had, by then, drafted two large sections of the book and had begun work on a third. Part One depicted his protagonist's trip to Northern Ireland for her father's funeral; it focused on her tentative reconciliation with her mother, from whom she had been estranged for several years, and included her confession that she had given birth to a daughter and was suffering from post-natal depression. Part Two flashed back to the birth of the composer's baby and her decision to leave both her abusive partner and Islay. In Part Three, which MacLaverty abandoned unfinished, she returned to Northern Ireland to live with her mother, applied unsuccessfully for a job teaching music in a local Catholic school, and became friends, then lovers, with a young Catholic priest. This draft ended abruptly, in the middle of a scene in which they go to bed together for the first time. MacLaverty recalled after the novel was published that he had initially thought his heroine might be 'fulfilled by meeting someone and having a relationship or some other hopeful event' but later determined that 'her fulfilment must come from her own work'.[43] In the autumn of 1995, though, he was still ruminating on the question of how to conclude the book, and he suspended work for a few months to consider it as the political situation deteriorated further.

In conversation with a German interviewer on 5 October 1995, MacLaverty expressed frustration with the British government's demand for IRA decommissioning before Sinn Féin could participate in negotiations about the future of Northern Ireland. In his opinion, shared by most nationalists, the IRA's decommissioning its arms would mean nothing 'because they could go out and buy them again'. Honest communication was needed instead:

> Very, very few—if any—conflicts have been solved by the handing over of weapons. And to make this a pre-condition for people who are at loggerheads like the Unionists, like the Brits, like the IRA, like Sinn Fein is very foolish indeed. I think...there never was *any* justification for the IRA killing people and there is no justification for them to go back to killing people, but I can...see the insensitivity of the British government in what they are doing....The Unionists have always said, 'There isn't a problem,' and the British say, 'No, there isn't a problem here.' There *is* a problem and people need to sit down and talk about it. And for the British government to put a barrier or a hurdle like this in front of the talks seems to me amazingly obtuse....What you want is people to sit down and say, 'Okay, we have got a problem. How can we solve it?'[44]

By the summer of 1995, it was increasingly obvious that British insistence on prior decommissioning left the peace process at the mercy of hardliners in the IRA leadership who did not want it to succeed. Bruton and Major decided to build on an idea first proposed by the UUP's security spokesman for an international body to advise on the practical aspects of putting weapons beyond use. Major hoped such a body could 'help the Provisionals over the decommissioning hump', and Adams, who feared it would be used merely 'to process the British government's pre-condition', regarded the proposal with great suspicion. Most other interested parties saw the creation of an international commission on decommissioning as a tactic that might allow the British government to save face while backing away from its call for paramilitary disarmament before substantive talks.[45] Major had little room for manoeuvre on Northern Ireland, with nine UUP MPs and dozens of Conservative back-benchers scrutinizing his every move. Something clearly had to change, though. Riots and arson attacks by both sides in the North provoked increasingly urgent calls from the SDLP, Sinn Féin, and the Irish government for all-party talks to begin as soon as possible. The IRA used the first anniversary of its ceasefire, however, to reiterate its own position that 'there is absolutely no question of any IRA decommissioning at all, either through the back door or the front door'.[46]

The British and Irish governments wanted to get the peace process moving again on a 'twin-track' basis, with an international body studying the decommissioning issue while the governments convened preparatory talks with each of the parties in Northern Ireland. Unfortunately, an effort to launch the twin-track initiative in early September foundered amid reports of threatened republican violence.[47] Shortly after this setback, however, Major and Bruton met privately again and agreed to revive the idea of simultaneous progress on political issues and disarmament. Both prime ministers were pleasantly surprised at this juncture by Trimble's first major policy speech as UUP leader, in which he made 'a moderate proposal for an elected assembly, with limited powers, as the route to all-party talks'.[48] Trimble further impressed Bruton when he 'broke with recent Unionist tradition by going openly to Dublin on 2 October to meet him'; as Major notes, he 'was proving a more flexible and adept leader than we had imagined'.[49]

Despite their shared desire for speedy progress, the perspectives and priorities of the British and Irish governments differed significantly, and Major recalls 'intensive exchanges' in November over 'the precise wording of the communiqué' announcing the creation and brief of the International Body on Decommissioning. Bruton wished to launch the initiative before Bill Clinton's 30 November visit to Northern Ireland, the first by a sitting US President, and negotiations continued through the evening of 28 November. The 'easiest' decisions concerned the international body's membership. Major readily accepted the Irish government's suggestion that former US Senator George Mitchell should chair the commission: unionists disliked the idea of 'outside involvement in Northern Ireland' and distrusted the Clinton Administration, but the 'softly-spoken and patient' Mitchell 'had begun to win them over in his role as the President's Special Adviser for Economic Initiatives in Ireland', which he had filled since January. General John de Chastelain, chosen by the British government, was brought on as 'the military expert'; he had served two terms as Canada's Chief of the Defence Staff, separated by a year as Canadian ambassador to the US, and was about to retire. The third member of the commission, chosen by the Irish government, was Harri Holkeri, former Prime Minister of Finland, who possessed what Major terms an 'exquisitely neutral background'. The governments aimed to convene all-party talks by the end of February, so they engaged the commission members for six weeks, requesting their report by mid-January.[50]

The prime ministers used President Clinton's 1995 trip to Britain and Ireland to consolidate support for the peace process. During one long day, Clinton visited west Belfast, east Belfast, and Derry before returning to Belfast to switch on the city-centre Christmas lights. Greeted by large and rapturous crowds everywhere he went, he emphasized the hope afforded by the twin-track initiative. In west Belfast he declared, 'Here in Northern Ireland, you are making a miracle... In the land of the harp and the fiddle, the fife and the Lambeg drum, two proud tradi-tions are coming together in the harmonies of peace'. Several hours later, in Derry, Clinton cited the climactic Chorus speech from *The Cure at Troy*, explaining that Seamus Heaney's words 'for me capture this moment': '"History says don't hope on this side of the grave, but then, once in a lifetime the longed-for tidal wave of justice can rise up. And hope and history rhyme."' 'Well, my friends,' Clinton stated, 'I believe we live in a time of hope and history rhyming....The further shore of that peace is within your reach.'[51]

Mitchell, who had agreed to chair the International Body on Decommissioning because the job 'sounded like an interesting and challenging assignment that wouldn't take long', had probably already developed some private doubts on that score. He attended several events with Clinton in Northern Ireland, including his meetings with a few local political leaders. After consecutive late-night sessions with Paisley and Adams, which significantly exceeded the time allotted to them and consisted entirely of monologues relating mutually exclusive histories of Northern Ireland (Paisley's from a unionist perspective and Adams's from a republican one), Mitchell lay awake wondering 'how it was possible to have two such completely different views of the same society'.[52]

In early December, Mitchell and his colleagues officially began their work and soon learned there were three main positions on decommissioning. The British government and the mainstream unionist parties insisted that paramilitary groups must hand over their weapons before the parties associated with them could join multi-party negotiations; the parties representing paramilitaries on both sides maintained that there would be no disarmament before a negotiated agreement; and the Irish government, the SDLP, and other parties from both

Northern Ireland and the Republic, as well as businesspeople, religious figures, community leaders, and other representatives of civil society from across the political spectrum, wanted decommissioning but believed that making it a pre-condition to talks might mean 'there would never be negotiations'. Mitchell recalls in his memoir that he and his colleagues were told repeatedly that 'The British government had gotten itself on the hook of prior decommissioning,…and we had been brought in to get them off'. The most decisive testimony came from the chief constable of the RUC, who said that Adams did not have enough control over the IRA leadership to make them decommission before negotiations even if he wanted to do so—an impression corroborated by other top security officials on both sides of the Irish border.[53]

To the members of the Mitchell Commission, 'parallel decommissioning' (dis-armament and talks taking place simultaneously) seemed the obvious compromise between those arguing for decommissioning before talks could begin and those contending that any decommissioning would not happen until after negotiations ended. Major surprised them, however, by telling them directly that he would 'have to' reject their report if they recommended parallel decommissioning. This left Mitchell and his colleagues with a dilemma: 'The British wanted inclusive negotiations, and they wanted prior decommissioning—but clearly they could not have both. How could we help them see that? More importantly, what could we recommend in place of prior decommissioning that would provide the unionists with enough reassurance to enable them to enter into negotiations?'[54]

The Mitchell Commission's report, which rejected prior decommissioning as unworkable, consisted of three main parts: a recommendation that any party par-ticipating in negotiations should agree to adhere to six principles of democracy and non-violence (later known as the 'Mitchell Principles'); a suggestion that the governments 'consider parallel decommissioning'; and a description of 'a detailed process to achieve decommissioning'.[55] At the British government's urging, the commission also included a glancing reference to the part a possible 'elected body' might play in the negotiations: 'Elections held in accordance with demo-cratic principles express and reflect the popular will. If it were broadly acceptable, with an appropriate mandate, and within the three-strand structure, an elective process could contribute to the building of confidence.' Mitchell later recalled the rationale behind mentioning elections specifically: 'the British repeatedly told me that David Trimble was in a difficult position politically, that there's a political division in Unionism and we've got to help him work his way through that'.[56]

Major himself had a political balancing act to maintain when the Mitchell Commission published its report in late January 1996. The report did not deliver the endorsement of his prior decommissioning policy that he had expected, but neither did it endorse the republican attempt to erode the distinction between paramilitary weapons and those held by the security forces. Major thus accepted the report, knowing that parts of it (including some of the Mitchell Principles) would be at least as difficult for Sinn Féin to accept.[57] In doing so, though, he sidestepped its suggestion regarding parallel decommissioning, describing to the House of Commons two ways in which inclusive talks could get under way: 'the first is for the paramilitaries to make a start to decommissioning before all-party negotiations. They can—if they will. If not, the second is to secure a democratic mandate for all-party negotiations through elections specially for that purpose'. These elections would be to a new Northern Ireland Forum from which the actual negotiators would be drawn; as historian Smith explains, the elections would serve as a 'type of decontaminating process, a sort of democratic sheep-dip'.[58]

Trimble welcomed Major's proposal, which had originally been his, and called for elections in April or May. Hume bemoaned the delay that holding elections would entail, indirectly accusing Major of buying unionist votes to remain in office and asking him instead to set a firm date for the start of all-party talks. Adams remarked that Major had swapped one precondition for entry into negotiations for another. In essence, Adams was correct, but at least this new precondition was one Sinn Féin could meet on its own by participating in the elective process. Mitchell himself appreciated the 'political skill' with which Major handled the report: 'By focusing on elections, he provided the reassurance that the unionists needed, and he deflected attention away from his eventual abandonment of prior decommissioning.'[59]

The decommissioning debate turned academic when the IRA resumed its military campaign the following month. Major stresses in his autobiography that, throughout the IRA's cessation, 'intelligence from all sources...had shown that much of the Provisional movement dissented from Adams's "unarmed" strategy'. The same knowledge of strain within the republican movement had motivated the frequent calls by Hume, Adams, and the Irish and US governments for the start of inclusive all-party talks. Both sides' worst fears were realized on 9 February 1996, when the IRA ended its ceasefire with a bombing in London's Docklands which killed two people, injured more than a hundred others, and caused damage estimated at £100 million. The IRA blamed the attack on the British government's 'bad faith' in responding to their cessation, but Major stated that it merely confirmed 'the urgent need to remove illegal arms from the equation'. Unionists, too, felt justified in their belief that the IRA's ceasefire had been purely tactical. Bruton spoke for many nationalists when he declared that 'The British government made a mistake in its response to the Mitchell report. The Unionist parties made a mistake in not sitting down with Sinn Féin and asking them the hard questions face to face, but a comparison cannot be drawn between political mistakes and the response to those mistakes that took human life. Killing is never justified as part of the political process.'[60]

The Docklands bombing brought the British and Irish governments back into close cooperation. At the end of February, they announced that elections to the Northern Ireland Forum would be held in May and all-party talks would begin on 10 June, with Sinn Féin's participation contingent upon a new IRA ceasefire. Mitchell explains that unionists got the elected body they wanted, while nationalists ensured that this body would have no bearing on the negotiations themselves, apart from the fact that each party would choose its delegates to the talks from among those elected. In an 'ingenious' touch, the British government created a new electoral system that provided, 'in a society where there were five well-established parties' (the DUP, the UUP, Alliance, the SDLP, and Sinn Féin), that 'the top *ten* parties would be eligible'. Major acknowledges that the primary purpose of the 'very complicated electoral formula' used for the Forum elections, which guaranteed a minimum of two seats each to the ten parties receiving the most votes in Northern Ireland as a whole, was to keep the loyalist paramilitaries 'on-side and off terrorism' by ensuring their political representatives space at the negotiating table as long as they maintained their ceasefire. It also allowed two new parties into the talks: the Northern Ireland Women's Coalition and a Labour coalition.[61] Sinn Féin reluctantly agreed to participate in these elections after the SDLP announced that it would take part. Although republicans had no intention of taking their seats in the Forum, they won 15.5 per cent of the vote (42 per cent of the nationalist vote), which Adams interpreted as an endorsement of his party's 'peace strategy' and some other commentators read as approval of the IRA's bombing campaign. The DUP had also increased its share of the vote since the 1992 general election, while the UUP's fell more than 10 per cent. Smith notes that this 'drift to the "political extremes" within both communities' marked an ominous development: the 'centre ground, the only place where a political settlement could emerge, looked extremely fragile' just as the governments 'were about to launch the first multi-party talks since 1992'.[62]

Despite Sinn Féin's 'increased mandate', it would not be admitted to the talks until (or unless) the IRA renewed its ceasefire, but this did not deter Adams from leading a sizeable delegation to the office building where the talks were being held, for the express purpose of being turned away with maximum publicity. Inside, discussions began 'in the absence of the party around which much of [the] process leading to the negotiations had been woven'.[63] The governments had re-engaged the three members of the Mitchell Commission to chair the talks, but some of the unionist negotiators objected to Mitchell as chair of the plenary sessions on the grounds of his Irish ancestry. Mitchell, de Chastelain, and Holkeri spent two full days waiting across the hall in Mayhew's office while the negotiators debated Mitchell's role. When Mayhew finally seated the independent chairmen, in the wee hours of the third day, the DUP and United Kingdom Unionist Party (UKUP) delegations, led respectively by Paisley and Robert McCartney, walked out in protest. They returned later that day, but discussions proceeded at an agonizingly slow pace; Mitchell recalls that merely adopting rules of procedure—which should have taken a few days—required weeks of 'tedious and arcane debate'. Progress was not made any easier by continued IRA attacks, including a gigantic lorry bomb that destroyed much of Manchester city centre on 15 June, injuring two hundred people and causing damage initially estimated at £300 million.[64]

Throughout the first half of 1996, amid these discouraging developments, MacLaverty had been working anew on his novel. Once again, Northern Ireland was forcing itself to the forefront of his mind, edging out the scandalous love story he had intended to write in favour of a narrative about self-determination: specifically, that of his protagonist, now called Catherine McKenna. By the time he completed the first draft, in June 1996, MacLaverty had eliminated the plot line involving the priest and re-centred the novel on the first two parts of the version he had set aside the previous September.[65] In Part One, depicting Catherine's trip home for her father's funeral, the sympathetic young priest retains a vestigial presence but is merely one person among many in her hometown who try to make her feel welcome. Part Two, as in the original version, backs up to show the birth of Catherine's child and her escape from Islay and her irresponsible, violent partner. In this draft, however, as in the published novel, she goes to stay with her friend Liz in Glasgow rather than with her mother in Northern Ireland. MacLaverty had also added a climactic final scene to end Part Two (and the novel) by describing the debut performance of Catherine's first major symphonic work, entitled *Vernicle* after the badges worn by medieval pilgrims. As he had decided it must, Catherine's fulfilment is shown as stemming from her creative work, both as a mother and as a composer, rather than from a relationship with a man.

MacLaverty's worries about where the peace process was going, or if it was going anywhere at all, found expression in the novel's structure. He divided Catherine's story into two parts, and readers encounter the second half of it first. Thus, MacLaverty explained, 'you can end on a high note before you realise that the *actual* end has been in the middle of the book when she relapsed into another depression. But it wasn't as bad as what she first suffered, so some small progress has been made'. This formal device enabled him 'to end the book with hope although it doesn't end on a kind of an unreasonable level of hope; it is a very attenuated hope'.[66]

The June 1996 draft also marks the initial appearance of an important new character: Miss Bingham, Catherine's piano teacher. In MacLaverty's original version of the novel, the composer's parents were her first music teachers, with her father taking her to concerts in Belfast and her mother teaching her to play the piano and providing her first composition notebook. In this and subsequent drafts, Miss Bingham, who is marked as Protestant, takes over these roles.[67] This change helped MacLaverty to show how Catherine's vocation separates her from her parents, who love music but do not understand what goes into writing it. It also allowed him to include, in a realistic manner, an influential and encouraging Protestant character.

As Brian Friel had done during the composition of *Making History*, MacLaverty went out of his way to question his own stereotyped assumptions about Northern Protestants in writing and revising his novel. In this first full draft, for example, during a scene in which Catherine remembers watching and listening to Lambeg drummers with her father when she was a child, she muses that 'She could never work out why the Orangemen came out here. Were they being considerate? Not subjecting their neighbours to the noise of their practicing. People who played the pipes or trumpets had the same problem. Or were they beating their drums on rising ground above the town to let the Catholics know they had to behave themselves. The Protestants were in charge and this was a sign they were in charge.' Maintaining that self-questioning stance was about to become exponentially more challenging, however, and MacLaverty eliminated the first possible explanation from later drafts.

After the 'siege of Drumcree', many people expected another sectarian standoff there in 1996. Conflict began on 7 July, when the RUC once again barred the local Orange lodge from marching down the Garvaghy Road. Instead of dispersing when faced with 'armoured Land Rovers, barbed wire and RUC officers in full riot gear', the Orangemen vowed to remain at Drumcree 'for as long as it takes'.[68] Thousands of supporters rushed to join them, and loyalists engaged the police in violent exchanges of bottles and stones for plastic bullets and tear gas. The next day, the murder of a Catholic taxi driver by renegade members of the Portadown UVF raised fears that the loyalist ceasefire had ended (the UVF disbanded its Portadown unit the following month instead, but for weeks uncertainty lingered about the ceasefire's status). Trimble, Paisley, and McCartney announced that their parties would not participate in multi-party talks until the RUC left Drumcree; the Orange Order staged protests across Northern Ireland to show support for the Drumcree lodge and to strain the security forces; and loyalists put up roadblocks and barricades that disrupted daily life and cut off entire towns. In response, Major dispatched two extra battalions of soldiers to Northern Ireland to back the police, but the prospect of 'widespread and uncontrolled disorder' remained.[69] Reports of a mechanical digger fitted with armour plates to break through police lines, a slurry tanker filled with petrol to spray RUC members, and sixty thousand Orangemen and loyalists converging on the area prompted a crisis meeting at which the Army's General Officer in Command informed the RUC Chief Constable that he would need to use live ammunition to hold the line if the police could not.[70]

The chief constable ultimately reversed his original decision to reroute the Orange march, in what Major describes as 'a serious defeat for law and order, but a victory for common sense'. Nationalists, however, were incensed. Mitchell reports that 'The principal nationalist newspaper, the *Irish News*, summed up their attitude with a large, single-word headline: "BETRAYED." As unionist rioters victoriously left the streets, they were replaced by grim and angry nationalist rioters'. On 11 July, the police cleared the Garvaghy Road of nationalist protesters so they could force the Orange march through, 'with some rough-handling of residents captured in graphic detail by the television cameras', and Adams notes that the Lower Ormeau Road was 'effectively put under a state of martial law' in preparation for another Orange march there the following day.[71] Disturbances raged for several days in nationalist areas throughout Northern Ireland, and the SDLP withdrew permanently from the Northern Ireland Forum, reducing it to a unionist debating club. The end of the IRA ceasefire had brought the British and Irish governments closer, but apparent British capitulation to unionists helped to revive the pan-nationalist alliance, with Bruton commenting that 'a state can never yield to the threat of the use of force'. Sean Farren and Robert F. Mulvihill record in their study of the peace process a worrying shift in many Northern Catholics' outlook at this time, as a 'sense that might alone would prevail and that at least the IRA offered some form of redress, if not a solution, took hold amongst people who previously would never have countenanced violence'.[72]

Mayhew described the 1996 Drumcree standoff as 'without doubt, the worst setback for many years', and it left the two communities more polarized than they had been since the 1981 hunger strike. A senior police representative, speaking privately, discussed the danger in graphic terms: 'We were on the brink of all-out civil war. Letting the march through was bad but the alternative was a thousand times worse....We have the potential in this community to have a Bosnia-style situation.'[73] Mitchell, who had suspended negotiations during the crisis, called the participants back on 22 July in the mistaken belief that things 'had calmed down enough to permit a resumption of the talks'. During the 'long and very contentious' meeting that ensued, 'delegates hurled insults and invective at each other', and Mitchell 'learned a valuable lesson about the fragility of the process and the sensitivity of the participants to external violence'. He recalls in his memoir that 'The memory of this day was with me nearly two years later when, fearful of the effects of a new surge of violence, I decided to propose a final, rigid deadline for the talks.'[74]

Trimble attracted intense nationalist opprobrium for his actions at Drumcree. In a sense, his position resembled that of Gerry Adams at the funeral of the Shankill Road bomber in October 1993; Mayhew himself acknowledged to a Conservative back-bencher that 'Trimble can't afford not to be there.' Many members of his party disliked the fact that he had allowed Mitchell to be seated as talks chair, and he needed to be seen as actively defending the Orange cause in his own constituency. Concerns about Trimble's 'credibility after he took the risk of accepting Mitchell's chairmanship' may also have influenced the British government's back-pedalling on the parade issue, as one of his biographers explains: 'if the march did not go down the road, the UUP leader would have been destroyed' and, with him, 'any prospect of an inclusive settlement'.[75] Most damaging to his reputation outside unionist circles was the BBC's revelation on 15 July of discussions between Trimble and paramilitary leader Billy Wright five days earlier. Trimble said he feared that loyalists led by Wright were preparing to attack the security forces and that his only objective in talking with Wright was to try to calm the situation. Nationalists would have found this explanation more convincing, however, if the dispute at Drumcree had not hinged on the Portadown Orangemen's refusal to negotiate with the Garvaghy Road residents because the residents' chief spokesman, Brendan McKenna (or, in Irish, Breandan MacCionnaith), was a former IRA prisoner. Trimble claimed he talked with Wright but not McKenna because the IRA ceasefire had been broken and the loyalist one remained intact, yet, as another Trimble biographer notes, 'Everyone who gathered at the Drumcree stand-off knew that the local Portadown UVF', commanded by Wright, 'had been responsible for the killing just two days before Trimble met Wright'.[76] The incident seemed to nationalists to make a mockery of the UUP's supposedly principled stance against dealing directly with Sinn Féin.[77]

MacLaverty, like most nationalists, deplored the spectacle afforded by 'A race of people whose ambition it is to march unimpeded down streets where they are despised', musing that 'Maybe this could be in the novel in the voice of her father.' He himself regarded it as 'a mindless ambition': 'For intelligent people like David Trimble to pretend to see this as important is patronizing in the extreme. He is just humouring these people in return for their votes'.[78] Trimble had portrayed the Orangemen's demand to follow their traditional route as a matter of religious and civil liberty, but MacLaverty perceived a hypocritical disconnection between the display of dominance at Drumcree and Christianity itself: 'Where does the CHURCH come into all this. They march to and from CHURCH. Christian values don't get much of a look in there.' As a non-believer from Northern Ireland, MacLaverty saw religion itself as intimately connected with the problem of sectarianism. It was, moreover, hard for him to imagine what compromise might be possible in such a situation: 'It is like the KKK insisting on being able to parade in full regalia through a black area.'[79]

Throughout the rest of that summer, as Farren and Mulvihill note, 'Communal strife mounted as attempts were made, on the one hand, to prevent parades taking place and, on the other, to insist that the right to parade was above question. Schools, churches and other property clearly associated with either community became regular targets for arson', and 'several Catholic churches were picketed at mass times and church-goers subjected to physical and verbal abuse'. Unsurprisingly, the talks made little progress during this period, with negotiators barely managing to approve rules of procedure before breaking for the month of August. At that point, the best that could have been said about prospects for peace was that the situation remained radically unresolved.[80]

The next draft of MacLaverty's novel, dated 9 September 1996, is the first to be called *Grace Notes*. MacLaverty had several senses of the words in mind. He described grace notes in another context as 'ornaments in a musical work which add to its sound but do not make up its melody', 'incidentals', the 'tiniest optional details': 'Trills, turns, slurs and the like.'[81] He was also doubtless thinking about the theological implications of grace: the 'free and unmerited favour of God as manifested in the salvation of sinners and the bestowing of blessings' and the 'divine influence which operates in men to regenerate and sanctify, to inspire virtuous impulses, and to impart strength to endure trial and resist temptation'. Under the circumstances then obtaining in Northern Ireland, nothing less would have seemed necessary to induce the contending parties to reach an agreement. Grace as thanks or 'thanksgiving' could not have been far from his mind, either, and its obsolete sense of 'pardon or forgiveness' also seems relevant to a narrative focused on reconciliation. Given his preoccupation with how art could take the place of religion, MacLaverty was also fascinated by the process of conversion. Among his notes are several considering grace notes 'in terms of religion': 'This is turning one note into another by the smallest of changes in pitch.... How to turn one thing into another. How to convert?'[82] In the novel, Catherine's middle name is Anne, and her daughter is called Anna; both names derive from the Hebrew word for 'grace' or 'favour'.

Most elements of the published novel are present in MacLaverty's September 1996 draft. He produced four additional drafts in the course of finalizing the text, which he did by 4 December, but most of his changes in this period consisted of elaborating on or minutely adjusting existing scenes.[83] Multi-party talks continued inconclusively during the same months. Mitchell records that the parties settled upon an agenda by mid-October but quickly got stuck on its second item: agreement about how to make progress on decommissioning alongside the three-stranded negotiations. Unionists still wanted paramilitary decommissioning before the start of 'substantive negotiation', but the parties varied in how rigidly they were prepared to stick to this demand. Mitchell headed off an attempt by UKUP and the DUP to force a vote on the issue at the end of November, recognizing it as 'a part of the internal struggle within unionism' ('Paisley and McCartney were opposed to the very process in which they were participating.... Trimble, on the other hand, plainly wanted to keep it going'), but the talks adjourned in mid-December without reaching consensus on this touchy subject.[84]

Like *The Cure at Troy*, *Grace Notes* is an affirmative text written in defiance of its contemporary context. The novel is not set during the peace process; none of the characters alludes to negotiations, and there are references to continuing violence. Catherine finds her hometown, for example, 'hardly recognisable' after a bomb attack: 'Shop-fronts were covered in hardboard, the Orange Hall and other buildings bristled with scaffolding. Some roofs were covered in green tarpaulins, others were protected by lath and sheets of polythene.'[85] While writing the novel, MacLaverty imagined its action as taking place entirely during the 1980s.[86] Nevertheless, *Grace Notes* testifies to the period of its composition through its portrayal of strained and broken relationships and awkward conversations. These personal interactions serve as metaphors for the tense political situation and what would be required to improve it. If Catherine's symphonic work *Vernicle* represents the possibilities of reconciliation, the novel's interpersonal level encodes both its difficulty and its necessity if Northern Ireland is to progress.

Those working in conflict resolution have noted the role of narrative in changing destructive habits of mind and patterns of interaction. Robert Schreiter, a theologian and consultant to the Roman Catholic Church for reconciliation and peace-building programmes, identifies 'establishing a shared identity between the two aggrieved or separated parties' as a key part of the 'long and complex process' of 'social reconciliation'. This project involves both 'analysis of current identities' and 'adjudicating the different versions of history maintained by each party', and the purpose of this shared identity is 'not just to create a common past, but also to provide a platform for a different future'. Schreiter stresses that memory, 'an essential part of identity', hinges on 'the relationship of the present to things and events past' and 'is continually shaped by a dialectic of remembering and forgetting'. Thus, 'To forgive is not to forget...but to remember in a different way'.[87]

MacLaverty believed that 'Narrative is a way of thinking',[88] and his story about Catherine McKenna struggling to adjust to her changed circumstances and to renegotiate the terms of her relationships with important people in her life, as well as with her personal and communal histories, can be read as a case study in the process of reconciliation itself. Regarded in this light, the scenes in Part One depicting Catherine's tentative rapprochement with her mother acquire special significance. As readers, we might easily ignore Mrs McKenna or regard her disapproval of certain aspects of Catherine's behaviour as just one more barrier between the young composer and her pursuit of her art. The limited third-person narration encourages us to identify with Catherine's thoughts and emotions and to overlook her mother's. Yet the text provides us with enough information to see what motivates Mrs McKenna and to find in her concern for her daughter ground for a new affiliation between the two. Thus, subtly, MacLaverty shows the way forward for parties who have defined themselves by their differences.

The estrangement between Catherine and her parents has persisted for several years at the time of the novel's present. An only child, she had shared her parents' devout Catholic faith and fulfilled their expectations for her by graduating with a first-class degree from Queen's University, undertaking a year of postgraduate study in Glasgow, and winning a travel award to experience the music of other cultures. Catherine has always been independent-minded, but her self-assertion has typically taken the form of not doing things rather than of doing them—the biggest argument she ever had with her father centred on her twin failures to observe the Feast of the Immaculate Conception and to come home for Christmas the year she finished her course in Glasgow. Readers know that she had lost her faith some time before this, but her father had not, until then, grasped that she no longer believed. He could not be blamed for his ignorance, however, because Catherine had concealed her change of heart, keeping her real opinions to herself to avoid confrontation.

Readers gather that silence and secrecy have been Catherine's habitual defences against perceived opposition. Early in the novel she remembers defying her parents when, at 13, she lied to them to spend an afternoon with a slightly older boy. Her parents discovered the subterfuge, and her mother 'smacked her across the face with her open hand' when Catherine resisted her attempts to find out exactly what had happened, although right after this she 'walked to the other side of the room so that she wouldn't hit her again' (47). The incident and its aftermath were exceptional enough for Catherine to recall them vividly a dozen years later, but even in this case she had deceived her mother and father rather than face their disapproval.

It may have been *because* Catherine had always been close to her parents that she felt an obscure need to distance herself. She reflects in Part One that 'It was simpler to conform when she was at home. This was one of the reasons she'd left—if she'd stayed everything would have been done because it was the line of least resistance. It wasn't so much that she'd left—she just failed to come back after her postgraduate year in Glasgow.... It was a gut reaction and she evolved reasons for it later. She became the prodigal daughter' (40).

Catherine's desertion has taken various forms over the previous several years: she did not invite her parents to her graduation in Glasgow; she has not visited since the 'big falling out' on the telephone with her father, who ended their conversation by saying that 'he wouldn't care if she never came home again' (153–4); she last wrote to them during her scholarship travel three years earlier; and she has not kept them informed about anything that has happened in her life since then. She considered telling them that the BBC would broadcast *Vernicle* but 'delayed too long', with the uneasy recognition that 'A girl who doesn't tell her parents of her success is more estranged than one who conceals her mistakes' (268).

Readers know that Catherine has been preoccupied with her personal drama throughout the time in which she has not been in contact with her parents. She has trained as a teacher, travelled, launched her composing career, moved to Islay to take up a teaching position, become romantically involved with the Englishman Dave, got pregnant accidentally, had the baby, suffered from depression, and watched Dave turn from a heavy drinker into an alcoholic. We do not know what her parents have been doing during this time nor how they have explained her silence to themselves. Aware that they would condemn many of her decisions, beliefs, and actions, and unwilling or unable to defend them, she has merely stayed away.

Catherine believes that 'she, the daughter,...should have enough sense to mend fences. Her parents were set in their ways. She should forgive *them*' (156). Before Anna's birth she thinks about writing to let them know 'they soon would be grandparents' but loses her nerve. Later, she tells herself that her parents would be so distressed by her repudiation of religion that 'They would rather endure the pain of seeing her dead. At least then they would think of her as in heaven' (217–18). So things stand a few months before Catherine's father dies suddenly, and without this disruption they might have remained thus indefinitely.

The division between Catherine and her mother is on a different scale to that caused by sectarian murder, but the steps they take in Part One of *Grace Notes* to mend their relationship are not different in kind from those required to end a political conflict like Northern Ireland's. First, there must be a mutual desire to reconcile. MacLaverty's style is so economical that this goodwill is not always obvious, but it exists. Mrs McKenna has gone to great lengths to locate Catherine to inform her of her father's death, and Catherine returns for the funeral 'to comfort her mother' (29), despite having to borrow money and leave her baby with a friend to make the trip. By now, she has acknowledged to herself the wrong she did her parents, reflecting before the *Vernicle* premiere that 'It was unheard of. For an only child to walk out like that. An only girl' (268). Upon her arrival at home, however, her mother clearly indicates her desire to reconnect: ' "Catherine," she said. She opened her arms and stood like that. Her chin went lumpy and she began to cry. Catherine went to her and they held on to each other. Both women were crying' (12). Significantly, Catherine's first words to her mother are 'I'm sorry—I'm sorry' (13), but their initial conversation establishes that it will take more than remorse to fix what's wrong between them. 'That was terrible about the bomb', Catherine essays. 'I like the way you phoned to check we were all still alive', her mother retorts (15).

Reconciliation also requires that the parties both change and recognize each other as capable of change. Much of the transformation within Catherine has occurred before this reunion, and readers do not learn about most of it until the second half of the novel. There we encounter, for example, her response to Anna's birth:

> She felt she could fly—she felt light with love. For her girl, for herself. For all the other women in the world who had ever given birth. Especially for her own mother—the feeling was totally unexpected, came from nowhere into her. She wanted to be with her mother, they had both shared an experience which should unite them in love. She wanted to tell her as another mother, as an equal about her girl child who would some day, maybe, give birth to her own girl.   (164–5)

On the spot, Catherine had forgiven her mother 'for some of her anxieties which grew out of concern, grew out of love' (165). Catherine's troubles with Dave have also given her new insight into some of the burdens her mother has borne. While there's little indication in the novel that Catherine's publican father was an alcoholic, his drinking caused contention between himself and his wife (184). Because Catherine's depression has locked her into her own mind, MacLaverty leaves readers to imagine the changes her mother has undergone during the years of non-communication. However, signs of her alteration penetrate even Catherine's consciousness. Her first sight of Mrs McKenna shocks Catherine, as 'her hair had gone grey and she looked too old to be her mother' (12). Seemingly trivial details reinforce readers' perception that Catherine's mother has the capacity to surprise her; she notices, for instance, that her parents have purchased a CD player and had a shower installed.

In discussing what he terms the 'healing of memories' that makes reconciliation possible, Schreiter identifies three stages in the healing process: acknowledging loss, making connections, and taking new action, and he associates the first stage with mourning.[89] Early in *Grace Notes*, Catherine and her mother bond, literally, over the dead body of her father. As his coffin is removed from the house, 'Catherine looked at her mother and reached out and they held hands, a thing they had not done since she was a child' (55). Both women also hide behind his memory at first, however. Mrs McKenna tells Catherine her father had been 'very hurt' by her withdrawal (65), and she confides that he was 'terribly disappointed' to have missed the *Vernicle* broadcast (68). Later, when her mother says accusingly, 'You never came home once in five years', Catherine replies, 'I was told not to.' Mrs McKenna insists that 'He didn't really mean that. He was always saying things he regretted. And there was too much foolish man in him to take anything back.' Catherine just sighs heavily in response, and, rather than speaking on her own behalf, her mother follows up this comment with a question about why Catherine had not invited them to her graduation in Glasgow: 'That hurt him as well, missing that' (90).

The tension between Catherine and her mother rises with each of the four days of her visit, but this represents progress. As Schreiter explains, 'To acknowledge loss....is to allow the venting of anger, the feelings of betrayal and abandonment and violation. It is only in acknowledging loss that we can position ourselves to have a new relationship with the past.'[90] The night before her father's funeral, Catherine wonders how to tell her mother about Anna, speculating that 'Maybe it would be better to say nothing' (57)—a phrase that recalls the time-honoured Northern Irish strategy of coexistence, summed up in the expression 'whatever you say, say nothing' (106). Their conversation hardly conduces to such revelations, anyway, because every question Mrs McKenna asks that Catherine answers seems to give them more to disagree about. Catherine's mother cannot understand why she would leave a teaching job to collect the dole and write music; she is distressed when Catherine confirms her lack of faith and dismisses as blasphemy her daughter's current project of writing a mass. Nevertheless, she ends the discussion by urging Catherine to stay 'a day or two longer'. Catherine, still withholding the news that she has a child, says only that she must get back because 'there's people depending on me', but when she asks if 'somebody' can drive her to the airport the next day, her mother quickly promises to do so (88–91).

By the last morning of her visit, Catherine has lapsed more deeply into depression. Perhaps her knowledge that she will be leaving combines with her sense that things cannot get much worse to make her risk upsetting her mother further. When Mrs McKenna wakes Catherine for an appointment with her old piano teacher, she notices the bottle of tablets on the bedside table. Catherine does not immediately answer her mother's question about them but eventually reveals that they are anti-depressants (91–2).

Crucially, throughout her stay, Catherine answers her mother's queries truthfully, even when she knows Mrs McKenna will not like the answers—'truth-telling' is an essential part of the reconciliation process.[91] On this last morning, though, she does something new: she volunteers vital information. Having deflected an earlier question about why 'someone like you' would be depressed, Catherine pauses after the conversation has moved on and says, 'Mum, it's a kind of post-natal depression' (92, 94). This confession marks a major advance on Catherine's part, but her mother's initial reaction confirms her fears about sharing the facts of her current life. Mrs McKenna has been brushing her daughter's hair but, once she realizes Catherine is serious, moves away from her and stands up, declaring that 'I'm just glad your father's dead.... If the heart attack hadn't killed him, this certainly would' (94). Now she sees Catherine as 'dirty' and, after learning the baby's sex, predicts, 'She'll break her mother's heart—just like you're breaking mine' before bursting into tears and fleeing the room. Catherine, weeping, resolves to leave without speaking to her mother again.

This painful encounter between the two women proves cathartic, however. Admitting loss, in Schreiter's terms, allows 'a space' to open 'between ourselves and those whom we have lost and the displacement we have experienced from a certain kind of lived world'—a space in which 'new connections can begin to be made'.[92] As Catherine walks to Miss Bingham's house, willing herself not to think about her mother and feeling wholly alienated from her, she suddenly recalls that 'It was her mother who had started the whole music thing. She had asked Miss Bingham, when Catherine was ten, to call and give her piano lessons' (99). She still plans to avoid her mother when she gets home, though, not expecting her even to say goodbye. But Mrs McKenna has been doing some thinking of her own, and, before Catherine can slip out of the house with her luggage, she emerges from the kitchen 'with her own coat on'. 'I said I'd run you for three-thirty—so I will', she says, 'her face averted', and brushes off Catherine's protests that she can take a bus with the words 'You have to be there an hour before. And it'll take us the best part of an hour to get there. So we're all right. There's some more talking to be done' (114–15).

Overcoming their current impasse will require adjustment on both sides, along with a will to forge new connections. As the women initiate their revised relationship, they pass through the rebuilding underway in the town centre. 'So how am I supposed to react to your news?' Mrs McKenna asks, and Catherine replies, 'I don't know. That's for you to decide.' The narrator tells us that 'Having passed through all the dust and debris of the reconstruction the windscreen was dirty', and, while Mrs McKenna squirts water to clean it, she launches a series of clarifying questions about the baby and its father (115). Only at this juncture does she begin to speak solely for herself, instead of as a representative of her late husband, telling Catherine, 'I'm just very angry, very hurt about this' before commenting, 'Your father would have probably banned you from the house for ever and a day.' Catherine agrees, and the two fall 'silent' (116).

When Mrs McKenna breaks this silence, she demonstrates her readiness to move on to Schreiter's third stage of healing, characterized by 'a new vision' and 'new action'.[93] 'When am I going to get to see it?' she asks, and, when Catherine ignores the question, she hastily revises it: 'I mean her. When am I going to get to see her?' (116). 'I haven't thought all this out yet', she adds, 'but you must always remember that there's a home for you here. And your baby. And your man if it comes to that.' Catherine thanks her mother, while insisting that 'It would never work' (117), and the conversation rapidly devolves into wrangling about Anna's unbaptized state, but Mrs McKenna has proved that her love for Catherine is not conditional. By the end of their drive, she has already begun 'to remember in a different way', which Schreiter sees as the essence of forgiveness, musing that 'Your father was a grandfather for eighteen months and he died before he found out. I don't know which is worse. Him knowing or not knowing' (118).

MacLaverty is too much of a realist to imply that the relationship between Catherine and her mother can be redeemed easily or quickly. In the airport, Catherine's admission that 'The baby's father is no longer on the scene' prompts the discouraging response, 'Oh Jesus, Catherine—you're really making a mess of things' (118). Nonetheless, Mrs McKenna obtains Catherine's contact information, and Catherine promises to phone. Mrs McKenna repeats her offer, more tentatively: 'If you want to come home....I could get used to it. I would hate to lose you a second time' (118). And the women exchange gifts. Mrs McKenna gives Catherine a loaf of wheaten bread, symbolizing her desire to nurture her daughter and granddaughter. Catherine's offering to her mother is prospective. 'I'll write a piece of music for you someday', she vows, to which her mother humorously rejoins, 'The Tune the Oul Cow Died of.' Notably, neither woman utters the words 'I forgive you', and the other would probably angrily deny the need for them if she did. Instead, they hug, 'once', and Catherine hurries off to catch her plane (119). Their attempt at a new level of honest communication may not seem like much, but it offers hope that their future dealings with each other will not fall prey to established and unhealthy patterns of guilt and blame.

Throughout *Grace Notes*, Catherine's depression functions metaphorically as an image of Northern Ireland's Troubles. Waking to a familiar cycle of negative thoughts in Part One, she feels 'locked inside a wheel' that 'went round and round while she stayed in the same place. Each tread was the same, each thought was the same. Getting nowhere, yet she couldn't stop' (29). A passage in Part Two similarly portrays her mental illness as condemning her to fruitless repetition: 'Not only the days repeating but the everyday thoughts repeating. Endless loops. Like a refrain. Over and over again' (199). In this state, it seems to Catherine as if 'The only things which were real were in the past. The future didn't exist. She was forced to look back because it was impossible to look forward' (30). Critic Gerry Smyth describes repetition as 'the predominant characteristic of Nationalist and Unionist discourses in Northern Ireland, fixated as they both are with preserving the past through practices and rituals'. During the period when he was writing *Grace Notes*, the Drumcree standoffs in 1995 and 1996 presented MacLaverty with a vivid example of this compulsion to repeat. In the novel, Smyth notes, MacLaverty represents musical repetition by means of literary repetition, deploying both 'to reflect on a sectarian society that has traditionally fetishized the ability to repeat the past without transformation'.[94]

Like the peace process, Catherine's recovery from depression proceeds in fits and starts. Before her father died, 'she'd been so much better—was convinced she was improving'. '[S]lipping back was so awful', but 'Her new doctor had said it might be that way—two steps forward, one step back' (29). In another dynamic resembling that of the peace process, Catherine's progress towards mental health is driven at times, paradoxically, by the kind of shock that might be expected to worsen her troubles. Intensifying paramilitary violence in the early 1990s had made Northern Ireland's population more supportive of efforts to chart a path towards a negotiated settlement of the 'crisis' that had lasted for almost a quarter of a century; similarly, Dave's increasingly brutal treatment of Catherine drives her to change her circumstances: 'In a strange way it was *he* who'd helped *her*. The night he first hit her—she saw that time as a turning point' (238). Catherine spends most of the next day walking on the beach with Anna, and on this outing her depression begins to lift as mysteriously as it had descended.

During the walk, Catherine removes her wet skirt and leaves it high on the beach weighed down by a rock, to be collected 'on the way back...if she ever came back' (209). MacLaverty was keenly aware of 'the narrative possibility of a suicide with baby'. Instead of Catherine drowning herself and Anna, however, the day with her daughter becomes another 'fulcrum point', 'a kind of rebaptism' in which she 'bonds with the baby in the sea'.[95] By the water's edge, Catherine experiences two distinct moments of grace. As Anna sits splashing in the water, 'Suddenly from nowhere Catherine felt good. Were her tablets beginning to work—after all this time? Was it the weather? Or her hormones? Whatever it was she hadn't felt like this since the baby was born' (211). Soon, Catherine hears in her head the first notes of what will become *Vernicle*, a piece she dedicates to Anna. Later, she remembers with wonder that 'She had not asked for it, but the music had come.... She had found small gaps in each day to put down what she was hearing inside her head. And that in turn gave her the confidence to make this move—away from Dave' (231). Catherine's epiphany on the beach does not mark the end of her obsessive dwelling on 'thoughts which caused her pain' (215), but, like the 1994 ceasefires, it changes things decisively for the better.

Perhaps because of her Northern Irish upbringing, Catherine's creative imagination appears in the novel as essentially dualistic. One of her early works is entitled *A Canon for Ulster*: 'In places it was a mirror canon, two parts appearing simultaneously the right way up and upside down, one being the reflection of the other' (223). Her Latin mass in progress is designed to be sung by 'two small choirs' placed in different parts of the church or concert hall: 'Choirs which were mirror images of each other' (74). Catherine imagines 'two blocks of voices singing at and with each other in turn' (150). Her symphonic work, *Vernicle*, also employs a two-part structure: 'she hoped it would have the bilateral symmetry of a scallop shell' (273).

Grace Notes itself mirrors the structure of *Vernicle*, with two equal parts reflecting (and reflecting upon) each other.[96] MacLaverty explained that this gave him the opportunity to 'rhyme and chime things'. These 'things' range from the largest thematic elements to the smallest textual details. Part One, for example, ends with Catherine's joy in her daughter and Part Two with her joy in her music, although, because the music was inspired by her baby, the two are 'not separable'. The final section of Part One, which depicts Catherine rushing home from the airport to Anna, beginning to compose the *Credo* of her mass in the taxi, pairs with the section at the end of Part Two describing *Vernicle*. The passages are connected both by subject-matter (Catherine's love for her daughter *and* devotion to her music) and by form (the present tense of both differentiates them from the past tense of the rest of the novel). *Grace Notes* begins with the words 'She went down' and ends with the words 'She rose'; Part One ends with the word *Credo*, and Part Two begins with the words 'Day crow'.[97]

Among the elements mirroring each other in the two parts of *Grace Notes*, scenes involving Lambeg drums have special significance in a Northern Irish context. These gigantic drums often accompany Orange marches; for this reason, while many unionists view them as a vital part of Ulster Protestant culture, Catholics tend to associate them with threatening sectarian displays. In Part One, Catherine recalls witnessing, as a child, a drumming match between two Orangemen. MacLaverty explains that a drumming match is 'an event where one drummer defeats (or maybe deafens) his opponent' in a contest 'akin to boxing, wrestling, jousting', with an emphasis on 'strength and endurance and volume rather than musicality'. 'There are', he adds, 'as few women Lambeg drummers as there are women conductor/composers.'[98] In the novel, Catherine and her father had been out walking and noticed the drummers setting up. He told her, 'They're supposed to be able to play different rhythms, different tunes…but it all sounds the same to me.…On the Twelfth they thump them so hard and so long they bleed their wrists. Against the rim. Sheer bloody bigotry.…They practise out here above the town to let the Catholics know they're in charge.' Catherine, though, 'was thrilled by the sound, could distinguish the left hand's rhythm from the right.…There were slaps and dunts on the off-beats, complex rhythms she couldn't begin to write down—even now, never mind then' (8). Her father drew her away when the men surrounding the drummers 'turned to stare' at them, his tightening grip on her hand betraying his own discomfort: 'You're looking at a crowd whose highest ambition, this year and every year, is to march down streets where they're not wanted.…It's their right, their heritage.…The Orange dis-Order, I call them. And the politicians that lead them are ten times worse, for they should know better' (9).

Years later, Catherine includes Lambeg drums in *Vernicle*: a sign of what critics Liam Harte and Michael Parker term her 'refusal to be defined solely in terms of her native interpretive community'.[99] She writes the piece for a concert sponsored by the European Broadcasting Union, which had specified, inviting submissions, that it would give preference to works 'which included an instrument more asso- ciated with music of ethnic origins' (261). Performing the work requires the par- ticipation of actual Lambeg drummers, in the shape of 'four Orangemen from Portadown' (257). They seem 'sheepish' and 'a bit nervous' upon meeting Catherine; one, in a gesture that recalls the awkward handclasp between Mabel and Archbishop Lombard in *Making History*, reflexively 'rubbed his hand on the backside of his jeans after shaking Catherine's hand' (257–8). He later explains that fifes used to be played alongside Lambeg drums. 'The fife played the tune', while the drum beat along with it: 'Then over the years the fifing fell away.' When Catherine remarks that 'You're accompanying a tune which doesn't exist any more,' he allows that she 'might be right' but also informs her tartly after she looks for scars on his wrist that 'a good drummer's wrists never touch the rim.…That's Roman Catholic propaganda—to make us look like fanatics' (259).

Catherine considers various titles before settling on *Vernicle*, one of which, *Reconciliation*, could have served equally well as a title for MacLaverty's novel (214), as evidenced by the scenes discussed earlier portraying Catherine's efforts, in critic Richard Rankin Russell's words, 'to negotiate a better relationship with her mother'. Catherine also reconnects with other people from her past with whom she had lost touch (Miss Bingham, her childhood friend Geraldine, her parents' neighbours, her former flatmate Liz), illustrating the more general sense of reconciliation as 'restoring estranged people or parties to friendship'.[100] MacLaverty explores various obstacles to reconciliation, including words spoken in anger, negative experience, fixed attitudes, pride, shame, awkwardness, passiv- ity, and insufficient knowledge of the other. These can be overcome with mutual goodwill, but he also highlights two factors that prevent reconciliation: death

(Catherine has lost the opportunity to reconcile with her late father) and violence (she does not wish to mend her relationship with Dave).

Another rejected title, *Metamorphoses*, also gets at the heart of the novel (214). Most repetition in *Grace Notes* has a negative connotation. Catherine dislikes taped church bells, for instance, because they remind her of 'dogma': 'Always the same' (59). In *Vernicle*, however, repetition becomes transformation, 'the same sound but with a different meaning' (275), through a change in context. The long passage at the end of Part Two describing Catherine's piece during its perform-ance marks the novel's climax and highlights its relevance to contemporary Northern Ireland.[101] The European Broadcasting Union's sponsorship of the con-cert recalls the important role the European Union played in the peace process by facilitating face-to-face meetings between British and Irish prime ministers on the fringes of EU gatherings, in addition to providing shared regulations and regional funding opportunities. The concert venue, a deconsecrated church, sym-bolizes MacLaverty's desire to strip art of its religious connotations and Northern Ireland's cultural traditions of their sectarian associations. In his telling, the church building undergoes a *reconsecration*—another meaning of the word 'reconciliation'[102]—as a concert hall, complete with 'a BBC sacristy lamp' (267). The orchestral platform sits where 'the altar used to be' under 'two stained-glass windows' which, at night, are 'featureless and dead': 'To see them properly', the narrator notes, 'you would have to be outside the church' (266–7). Catherine finds it 'odd to be sitting like this, row upon row in the light': 'The only equivalent, she thought, was sitting in church. But this *was* church' (269).

Earlier in Part Two, in the throes of giving birth, Catherine had thought that 'it was a bit like composing music, really, parading the personal' (161). MacLaverty's description of *Vernicle* gathers motifs (words, phrases, and images) from through-out the novel, inviting readers to reflect anew upon Catherine's experience as transmuted into art. The first movement begins with a 'five-note phrase'—probably the one she wrote down the day after Anna's birth—and builds from the 'gentle tremolo of strings' she first heard in her head while on the beach with her daughter (172, 213, 269). 'Gradually the great arch of the movement begins to take shape' with more and more instruments joining in until 'the climactic point is reached', but 'there is no vista from the top'; instead 'everything is cut short by the entrance of the Lambegs' in a 'short burst—enough to kill and maim' (271). MacLaverty's description of the drums' sonic effects evokes, in addition to Orange triumphalism, Catherine's depression and her abuse by Dave. The other instru-ments attempt to rise above the 'din' as the 'black blood of hatred stains every ear', but 'after an intense struggle, the orchestra falls away section by section until only the drums are left pulsing' (272). When the drums finally stop, all that remains is 'a feeling of depression and darkness' (273).

The second movement, 'the other side of the arch', begins as 'quietly' as the first one but with an added measure of hesitancy, 'as if the orchestra has not forgotten what happened on the first side of the arch and are playing, looking over their shoulders, waiting for the reappearance of the Lambegs' (273–4). With the entrance of bells, which had not featured in the first movement, audience members know 'they are going somewhere' at last (274). As all the instruments take up the 'bell theme', the music 'grows in confidence and in volume' and 'the horror of the first movement falls away, is forgotten' (274). Once more, the music builds towards a climax, and the narrator pauses to explain that what follows is 'like an optical illusion in sound' by which 'The same thing could be two things':

> At the moment when the music comes to its climax, a carillon of bells and brass, the Lambegs make another entry at maximum volume. The effect this time is not one of terror or depression but the opposite.... The whole church reverberates. The Lambegs have been stripped of their bigotry and have become pure sound. The black sea withdraws. So too the trappings of the church—they have nothing to do with belief and exist as colour and form.... Exhilaration comes from nowhere. The bell-beat, the slabs of brass, the whooping of the horns, the battering of the drums. Sheer fucking unadulterated joy. Passion and pattern.
>
> (275–6).

As MacLaverty depicts the creative process in *Grace Notes*, a work of art represents a symbolic resolution of tensions in the artist's life which, in Catherine's case, stem from her origins in Northern Ireland's Catholic minority, as well as from her personal and familial circumstances. Critic Patrick Grant observes that, by including Lambeg drums in *Vernicle*, 'Catherine transforms the fears and residual bigotry inherited from her father, not by taming their power to excite strong feelings, but by placing them within a further set of relationships where that power communicates joy and celebration'. In presenting her work as he does, MacLaverty offers readers a memorable illustration of how artists can contribute to the ongoing enterprise of creating a more inclusive sense of Northern Irish identity. In Grant's words, 'What happens to the lambeg drums in the musical composition is what might happen also in a polity marked by a reconciliation of old and violent differences.'[103]

Northern Ireland was not such a society in 1996, when MacLaverty was writing and revising *Grace Notes*—nor is it such a society today. In the novel's uplifting conclusion, he envisions a possible future. The fact that the concert takes place before Catherine's trip home and her relapse into depression indicates his awareness that a non-sectarian Northern Ireland will not be easily or quickly achieved. However, the non-linear structure of the book also indicates what will be required to bring such a future within reach. In musical terms, *Grace Notes* ends with a virtual repeat sign that beckons readers to experience the novel again with the knowledge of what preceded Part One.[104] What looks like naïve realism upon a first reading of Part One reveals itself, in subsequent readings, to be ambitious literary fiction, so meticulously patterned that almost every detail has significance in the context of the entire novel. A reader who does not perform this act of reconsidering the present with knowledge of the past misses out on much of what *Grace Notes* has to offer. Making true reconciliation a reality will require a similar willingness on all sides to reconsider what one thinks one knows.

5

Drafting

'On Bloomsday 1997,' scholar Joseph Kelly recalls, 'Danis Rose set off a bomb in the Joyce community by publishing his "Reader's Edition" of *Ulysses*', in which he 'corrected all the mistakes that he found, even those made by Joyce, with the same license and authority that any editor would bring to bear on a manuscript submitted by a contemporary author'. The edition provoked an outraged reaction from Joyceans who hardly believed their idol capable of mistakes and were used to interpreting the novel's words and phrases as if there were profound intention behind each one. Seamus Deane took a comparatively tolerant view of Rose's enterprise, viewing it as 'one of the most important editions' of *Ulysses* 'in a long time'. As a leading Joyce scholar, Deane attended the book's launch and stood at ground zero of the controversy, but he found himself distracted by a literal rather than a metaphorical act of terror. In a crowded Dublin pub on 16 June, Deane heard 'fragments of TV news' about two policemen dead in Lurgan and thought 'it must be a program that was replaying old footage', but it 'nagged at' him that he could not recall any such incident: 'It was only at dinner afterward that I heard the details and the full realization dawned.' Journalist Deaglán de Bréadún recounts that two men had run up behind the policemen late that morning and 'shot them in the head at point-blank range', leaving 'five children under ten without fathers' and generating 'a wave of helplessness and apprehension in the community at large, heightened by the fact that the annual Drumcree church parade by the Orange Order in nearby Portadown was now only three weeks away'.[1]

The predictably 'anarchic' effect of these killings, de Bréadún explains, raised suspicion that 'a dissident element' within the IRA was 'trying to sabotage the peace process'.[2] This was the only explanation that made any sense. On 1 May, the British general election had resulted in a resounding win for the Labour Party, pleasing republicans frustrated with John Major's Conservative government. Sinn Féin had won two Westminster seats and 16 per cent of the overall vote—the third-highest share in Northern Ireland, ahead of the Democratic Unionist Party (DUP)—and the party had gained twenty-three seats in council elections three weeks later. The new British government, headed by Prime Minister Tony Blair, had indicated at once that the decommissioning issue would not be used to bar republicans from talks if the IRA renewed its ceasefire. Indeed, Sinn Féin delegations had already had two meetings with British officials in the Northern Ireland Office, the first such encounters in over a year. Furthermore, after a general election in the Republic on 6 June, Fianna Fáil's Bertie Ahern appeared likely to replace

Getting to Good Friday: Literature and the Peace Process in Northern Ireland. Marilynn Richtarik, Oxford University Press.
© Marilynn Richtarik 2023. DOI: 10.1093/oso/9780192886408.003.0006

John Bruton as Taoiseach, another change welcomed by republicans. Despite these promising developments at a time when, as Deane noted, 'any intelligent person would have given short odds on a new cease-fire', the IRA 'had killed two police-men, suddenly, with cruel efficiency'. Consequently, he continued, 'Guns are being unsheathed, bonfires prepared, city centers are emptying, fear is in the air tinging everything with a faint nausea. The I.R.A., or a faction within it, has made its lethally effective, strategically opaque contribution. The corpses of those dead policemen lie across the threshold of this oncoming summer.' Deane made these observations in the *New York Times*, surely mindful both of past Irish-American support for republicans' armed struggle and of the constructive role played by the United States more recently in support of the peace process—during a visit to London at the end of May, President Clinton had declared his belief that Sinn Féin should participate in multi-party talks but only after an IRA ceasefire, criti-cizing those who adopted the attitude that 'we'll talk when we're happy and shoot when we're not'.[3]

Deane admitted that the shootings and their likely implications made the 'harmlessness' of his own day's pursuits seem 'culpably infantile': 'The discussions of virtual text, copy text, isotext, hypertext, substantives, accidentals, apostrophes, vaporized in the news heat. One reviewer accused Danis Rose of "demagoguery" in promoting his "Reader's Edition." Did this reviewer ever hear a demagogue, ever see what political catastrophes a demagogue can create?' Yet, Deane asked, 'why surrender all fine or subtle discriminations, or even absurd eccentricities, to barbaric actions? Why yield to the killings by running for cover into the sanctuary of "culture" or by embracing that world of "action," which rebukes anything less savage than itself?'[4] The choice between these alternatives, he intimated, was a false one.

The notion that 'subtle discriminations' embodied in texts might themselves be marshalled against violent conflict would be tested in the months to come, as politicians and civil servants struggled to devise a written formula that could con-tain and transform old antagonisms. Deane's commentary points to the import-ance of writing and editing—and the careful distinctions these activities require and enable—in the ongoing effort to compose a new Northern Ireland. In his 2013 novel *TransAtlantic*, Colum McCann similarly highlights the role of writing in peace-making through his portrayal of independent chairman George Mitchell's role in the talks that resulted in the Belfast/Good Friday Agreement. Texts at various stages of composition feature prominently in *TransAtlantic*, with Mitchell, in his chapter, presented as a master of them. As he travels to Belfast for the final fortnight of negotiations, McCann's Mitchell feels

the weight of the days ahead, the changed minds, the semantical shuffling, the nervous search for equilibrium. He and his team have given them a deadline.... A finishing line. Otherwise the whole process will drag on forever. The rut of another thirty years. Clauses and footnotes. Systems and subsystems. Visions and revisions. How many times has it all been written and rewritten? He and his team have allowed them to exhaust the language. Day after day, week after week, month after month. To roil in their own boredom. To talk through the vitriol towards a sort of bewilderment that such a feeling could have existed at all.[5]

Viewed through the prism of Deane and McCann's insight about the importance of the right words in the right places, the historical record takes on a distinctly literary cast. Texts' centrality to the peace process leaps out from accounts by participants of events leading up to the 1998 Agreement, itself a crucially important document. These include first-person reminiscences by Blair, Ahern, Mitchell, Secretary of State for Northern Ireland Mo Mowlam, Blair's chief of staff Jonathan Powell, Sinn Féin president Gerry Adams, and Ulster Unionist Party (UUP) leader David Trimble, among others, as well as scholarly treatments of the inclusive talks written by members of various parties' delegations.[6] Through these diverse narratives, the writing process emerges as both the medium of and a metaphor for the peace process.

Blair's speech at the Royal Ulster Agricultural Show in Balmoral on 16 May 1997 had immediately signalled his attitude towards the intractable puzzle of Northern Ireland. As his first major policy declaration since his landslide victory, delivered during his first trip outside of London, Blair's speech demonstrated the new British government's commitment to resolving the conflict there. In opposition, Blair and his team had backed John Major's Northern Ireland policy; they had also privately noted what they saw as his mistakes—not welcoming Sinn Féin into all-party talks soon after the IRA's 1994 cessation and making decommissioning a precondition for republican participation—and vowed to avoid them. Their priority would therefore be getting the IRA to renew its ceasefire. Blair knew enough about Ulster Protestant sensitivities, however, to understand that keeping unionists from leaving the talks as soon as the republicans entered would require reassurance that he did not intend to hustle them into a united Ireland.[7] The 'quintessentially unionist' venue for the speech was chosen with this aim in mind, and Blair also consulted Trimble on its content.[8]

A professional diplomat who served as the prime minister's private secretary for foreign affairs under both Major and Blair wrote the first draft of the Balmoral speech, but Powell explains that 'As a former barrister [Blair] could only speak with feeling if he had written out what he was going to say in longhand himself, on foolscap paper with a fountain pen.' In this instance, Blair delivered the 'key words' so naturally that Trimble surmised afterwards that he 'had ad-libbed' them, but Powell insists that 'he had written them himself the day before and we had shown them to the Irish and the Americans'. These words included an explicit 'defence of the Union': 'My agenda is not a united Ireland....I believe in the United Kingdom. I value the Union.' These assertions, hardly surprising from the prime minister of that United Kingdom, would nonetheless disappoint republicans, who had long urged the British government to become a ' "persuader" for Irish unity' (a position shared by the Labour Party before Blair became leader). Instead, he 'went out of his way to make consent the centrepiece of the speech', as it would be central to his Northern Ireland policy, remarking that 'Northern Ireland is part of the United Kingdom because that is the wish of the majority who live here. It will remain part of the United Kingdom for as long as that remains the case.' Throughout his tenure as prime minister, Blair would argue to unionists that this consent principle should be regarded as 'fundamental', in contrast to the decommissioning issue ('transient' because any group that got rid of its weapons could easily obtain new ones). Not coincidentally, Powell writes, 'The principle of consent, which had been accepted by the Irish government in progressively stronger terms in the Sunningdale Agreement of 1973, the Anglo–Irish Agreement of 1985 and in the Downing Street Declaration of 1993, would be the most difficult concession for Republicans to make.'[9]

Blair had insisted on including one of the most memorable lines in the Balmoral speech, despite reservations expressed by a senior Irish government official. 'None of us in this hall today, even the youngest, is likely to see Northern Ireland as anything but a part of the United Kingdom' was, as Blair recalls, 'quite a bold pro-Union statement' given that 'some of those present were in their twenties'. This comment proved especially 'wounding' to republicans, but, as de Bréadún notes, 'about the only practical measure the speech contained' was 'the hugely important announcement that [Blair] was permitting his officials to meet Sinn Féin'. Having open contact with republicans in the absence of an IRA ceasefire marked a radical departure from previous British government policy, and Blair's pro-Union expressions were 'essentially a smokescreen' for this initiative.[10]

Blair's speech did not impress Adams, who felt it 'repeated much of the failed rhetoric of the past', but within an hour of its delivery the republican leader had received a fax from Mowlam inviting Sinn Féin to meet with officials in the Northern Ireland Office, an invitation promptly accepted by fax. This exchange initiated a flurry of texts of all types aimed at creating the conditions for all-party negotiations later that year. Following two encounters between Sinn Féin delegations and British civil servants, Blair sent republicans a 'written note' laying out 'the government's position regarding their entry into the talks'; officials called this document an 'aide-mémoire', according to Mowlam, 'to avoid the charge that we were negotiating'. The aide-mémoire stipulated that, if the IRA called a ceasefire, the government would decide whether it was genuine six weeks after the violence ended and, if so, invite Sinn Féin into all-party talks, which would conclude by May 1998—thus addressing key republican concerns about when they would be admitted to negotiations and how long those negotiations would be permitted to continue. Sinn Féin would have to accept the Mitchell Principles and promise to work in good faith towards implementing all of them, including the one committing the parties to 'the total disarmament of all paramilitary organizations'.[11]

Sinn Féin received the aide-mémoire on 13 June, just three days before the Lurgan murders. The British government suspended contact in the immediate aftermath of these, but, after receiving assurances from republicans that the killings had been unauthorized by the IRA leadership, publicized the conditions laid out in the document so that it could not be accused of making 'a secret deal with Sinn Féin'. Around the same time, on 24 June, the British and Irish governments presented a proposal to a plenary session of the talks that called for negotiations and decommissioning to proceed in parallel, along the lines suggested in the Mitchell Report. The following day, in a speech to the House of Commons, Blair reviewed the plan, including a 15 September deadline for the start of all-party talks, declaring that 'The settlement train is leaving, with or without Sinn Féin. If it wants to join it is absolutely clear what it has to do.'[12] From a republican perspective, though, the British position remained ambiguous, and de Bréadún mentions a 'huge debate' said to be raging within the movement over 'whether decommissioning really had been removed as an obstacle to Sinn Féin's participation in negotiations on an overall settlement'. In June, the IRA's 'most senior commanders' discussed the aide-mémoire 'at an all-night meeting', ultimately rejecting it as the basis for another ceasefire.[13]

Fortunately, there were two governments involved in the peace process, both willing to put their views in writing. Elected Taoiseach on 26 June, Bertie Ahern made the North his priority from the start. By the end of June, senior Irish civil servants from several departments, in close consultation with the Sinn Féin leadership, had drafted a 1,700-word document for the consideration of the IRA's Army Council, laying out the Irish government's commitments in the event of a new ceasefire. This text referenced the consent principle, the Mitchell Principles, and existing agreements between the British and Irish governments; however, it also included specific undertakings regarding prisoners and security, pledges of political support for the peace process, and a promise to maintain communication with Sinn Féin throughout the negotiations. Most important, the Irish government's stance towards the Mitchell Report's call for paramilitary decommissioning acknowledged that this would require the cooperation of those in possession of weapons and could not necessarily be delivered by the paramilitary-related parties themselves. Thus, the test to be met for Sinn Féin's participation in the talks would involve simply working in good faith to achieve decommissioning.[14]

The Irish government's textual intervention likely provided the impetus for the Army Council's decision to renew the 1994 ceasefire and accept the governments' terms for participation in multi-party negotiations. This vote was taken on 2 July but was kept secret, even from most IRA members, until more than two weeks later. In the meantime, a third confrontation between the Orange Order and

Catholic residents of the Garvaghy Road in Portadown strengthened republicans' hand in the international public relations competition. Drumcree 1997 was a dreary replay of Drumcree 1996, with the Orange march allowed down the road on 6 July, despite residents' objections, after police roughly dispersed 'several hundred protesters who were sitting down on the parade route'.[15] Days of rioting in republican areas across Northern Ireland followed, made worse by the 8 July publication of a leaked Northern Ireland Office document dated 20 June; this listed options for dealing with the Drumcree crisis, identifying a 'controlled march' as the 'least worst' of them. Mowlam describes this text as 'an innocuous enough briefing paper' but allows that 'its tone was unfortunate': 'The interpretation given by the media to the contents of the leaked document was that I had made up my mind what to do long before the final decision was made.' Adams recalls that 'On the streets of Portadown young nationalist street fighters chanted "No ceasefire! No ceasefire!" as they fought the RUC', an attitude shared by most IRA activists.[16]

Against this seemingly hopeless backdrop, Adams and John Hume issued a joint statement on 17 July 1997 welcoming actions taken by 'the new Irish and British governments' to eliminate the 'obstacles, erected by the previous British government, to an inclusive and meaningful negotiations process' and expressing their view that 'the peace process can be restored' and 'with political will on all sides we can move towards a new political agreement'. Mowlam felt intense excitement when this text became public because she knew, based on a similar statement released by Hume and Adams just before the 1994 ceasefire, that 'such a positive statement would not have come unless they knew it would provoke a positive response from within the IRA'. Sure enough, an announcement from the IRA leadership that it was restoring the 1994 ceasefire soon followed, although it restated traditional republican aims and retained, provocatively, the ambiguous wording of the previous ceasefire declaration: 'The Irish Republican Army is committed to ending British rule in Ireland.... We want a permanent peace and therefore we are prepared to enhance the search for a democratic peace settlement through real and inclusive negotiations.' To that end, the IRA would observe 'a complete cessation of military operations'. This time, the governments were not inclined to quibble about the absence of the word 'permanent' as a description of the ceasefire itself. 'Most observers', de Bréadún records, 'agreed the republican movement pulled a masterstroke by calling the ceasefire when it did. It badly wrong-footed the unionists, putting them in a position where, if they now rejected the Anglo–Irish joint document on decommissioning and walked out of the talks, they would be seen as unreasonable in the eyes of the world.'[17]

That very nearly happened, and the fact that it did not owed a great deal to a fax David Trimble had received from Sean O'Callaghan a few weeks earlier. O'Callaghan was a former IRA member who had served prison time for terrorist offences before changing sides, becoming an agent for the Irish police. He had met Trimble through Irish historian Ruth Dudley Edwards and acted on a voluntary basis as his independent adviser on Irish republicanism. O'Callaghan later recalled that, in the fax, he urged Trimble not to allow himself to be 'stampeded into doing something rash' but to 'stay in the process and open up dialogue with the Catholic Church, have consultations with his own party and other unionists and nationalists'. The IRA leadership, O'Callaghan argued, assumed that unionists would all leave the talks together once Sinn Féin came into them, which would suit them because they wanted the British government to impose a settlement on unionists. The best way to thwart their plan was thus to remain in the negotiations.[18] A couple of days after the IRA's cessation announcement, Ian Paisley and Robert McCartney withdrew their DUP and UKUP parties from the talks for good, to the relief of the other participants—parties, governments, and independent chairs alike.[19] Although Trimble initially opposed the governments' plan for dealing with decommissioning, he took O'Callaghan's advice, circumventing the hardliners in his own UUP to consult members of what Mowlam terms the 'broad unionist community' and Northern Ireland's 'civil society', an exercise that reinforced his own inclination to continue in the talks. The UUP's decision to stick with the process surprised many at the time, 'wrong-footing the republicans who had wanted to negotiate directly with the British throughout'.[20]

On 24 September, talks participants finally approved a 'detailed procedural motion' to establish sub-committees on arms decommissioning and confidence-building measures; political scientists Paul Bew and Gordon Gillespie explain that, although the motion described decommissioning as 'an indispensable part' of the negotiations, it had the effect of sidelining the issue. This text cleared the way for much-anticipated 'substantive negotiations' to begin in early October. At long last, parties representing the full spectrum of political opinion in Northern Ireland were present in the same room, even though two of them (the UUP and Sinn Féin) were arguably there to spite each other. Under the rule of 'sufficient consensus' adopted by the talks in July 1996, affirming any proposal required the support of parties representing simultaneously a majority of the overall electorate and a majority of both unionist and nationalist voters as measured by the results of the May 1996 Forum election, the approval of the British government for Strand One matters (related to the internal governance of Northern Ireland) and of both governments for measures related to Strands Two and Three (dealing, respectively, with relations between Northern Ireland and the Republic and those between Ireland and Britain), and the assent of a majority of the political parties present. The intention was to ensure that 'any agreement reached in the talks would have broad support'.[21]

In practical terms, the sufficient consensus rule meant that no agreement could be made without the Social Democratic and Labour Party (SDLP), which represented more than half of Northern nationalists, and the UUP plus at least one of the two small loyalist parties, which together could claim (barely) to speak for a majority of unionist voters. This gave the UUP an effective veto over the proceedings, which Trimble quickly cited to reassure anxious unionists. Because it was theoretically possible for unionists to make a deal with the SDLP alone, he argued that there was no need for him to talk with Sinn Féin delegates at all. Trimble would refuse to engage with Sinn Féin representatives throughout the talks, directing all questions and comments to them through the chair.[22] He later allowed, however, that unionists did not 'fully appreciate' another aspect of sufficient consensus. One of the Mitchell Principles that Sinn Féin had to affirm when it joined the talks a year after the rule's adoption was 'To agree to abide by the terms of any agreement reached in all-party negotiations and to resort to democratic and exclusively peaceful methods in trying to alter any aspect of that outcome with which they may disagree'—thus, when republicans entered the talks, 'they were binding themselves to accept the outcome of a process in which they had no veto', a fact that put considerable strain on the republican movement's unity.[23] Sinn Féin might not be essential to approving an agreement, but such an agreement would not result in peace unless republicans were committed to it.

During the remaining months of 1997, failed efforts to arrive at the first draft of an agreement dominated the talks. After the suspense and tension that had surrounded getting—and keeping—enough parties involved in the process to achieve a political settlement, about the only thing Trimble and Adams could have agreed upon once 'inclusive' negotiations began was that they were incredibly dull. Trimble remembers that the UUP delegation 'often joked when selecting the two or three talks team members to go up and take our front seats at the talks table that we were sending them in "to bore for Ulster"', and Adams found it 'impossible' to convey 'the tedium and the slowness' of this phase of the talks. John Hume had 'first dreamed of, and then helped assemble, international backing for inclusive government in Northern Ireland', as well as articulating the requirements for a settlement and the design of the talks themselves. He was frankly exhausted by the time they finally began, however, and delegated most of the actual negotiating to his SDLP colleagues. One observer remarked that there were 'hours, days and months when Hume might as well have been somewhere else. Head down on his arms while the discussion went on. Or he'd be in the room for a while and then missing for days', but this commentator added that 'If he'd been inside the room any longer, mind you, he'd have been swinging from the curtains.'[24]

No one was more frustrated by this stalemate than George Mitchell, who, by now, had been chairing the plenary sessions for almost a year and a half. He had married a woman much younger than himself in December 1994, just before accepting President Clinton's invitation to get involved in Northern Ireland, and she had given birth to their son on 16 October 1997. For personal as well as political reasons, Mitchell wanted rapid, concrete progress towards a settlement. He asked the parties for detailed position papers, with the aim of getting them to work together to 'prepare and agree on a document that would identify the key issues for resolution—essentially a more detailed comprehensive agenda', reasoning that 'Only when all of the issues were seen together could the parties get a sense of where the necessary trade-offs and compromises might be made.' At the meetings, though, delegates merely restated orally what they had submitted in writing, and Mitchell tried in vain to get 'a genuine negotiation underway.'[25]

Adams, who 'felt sorry' for Mitchell, recalls him saying, at the end of an especially vexing day, 'You have a life and this is it. I have a life and this isn't it.' On 16 December, the negotiations broke for Christmas with no accord reached on 'a detailed final agenda'. Mitchell later remarked that 'Much has been said and written about my patience. I do have a lot of it, but I felt that I had just about used it up.... For hundreds and hundreds of hours I had listened to the same arguments, over and over again. Very little had been accomplished.' On that day, he began dreaming about a deadline 'earlier than the one at the end of May that Blair had already set'. '[W]ithout a hard deadline', Mitchell realized, 'these people just would not decide anything: the decisions are so fraught with danger for them that they would just keep talking and talking and talking.'[26]

The failure of the parties to commit themselves in writing even to an account of what they still disagreed about forced the British and Irish governments to step into the writerly void. In truth, Mowlam observes, 'the parties were much happier working from something produced by the two governments': 'It meant that none of them had to be seen to make the first move or surrender the first compromise.'[27] The efforts by Blair and Ahern, together with their teams of advisers, ministers, and civil servants, to formulate a draft agreement capable of achieving 'sufficient consensus' illustrate the challenges of co-authorship (or, more precisely, writing by committee). The crucial task was finding a formula that could gain assent from both unionists and republicans, and, not for the first or the last time, the British and Irish governments acted as proxies for these perspectives.[28]

Ahern worried especially about an October 1997 split in the republican movement, which had resulted in the formation of a splinter group known as the Real IRA.[29] It joined existing republican splinter groups, including the Irish National Liberation Army (INLA) and the Continuity IRA, but Ahern's intelligence sources were telling him that 'the new group could draw off significant numbers'. Equally concerning was the fact that loyalist paramilitaries—people, in the words of loyalist political leader Gary McMichael, whose 'most instinctive form of expression was violence'—were also getting restless in the absence of obvious political progress. Tensions between the main loyalist groups led to the disbandment of the Combined Loyalist Military Command in October, imperilling the loyalist ceasefire, and loyalist prisoners announced in late December that they would be reviewing their support for the peace process because they regarded the British government as 'working to a republican agenda'.[30] On 27 December, the INLA's assassination of loyalist leader Billy Wright in the Maze Prison initiated a spate of sectarian killings by both loyalists and dissident republicans, the victims of which included people close to some of the talks participants. Mowlam managed to keep the peace process alive on 9 January by visiting the Maze in her official capacity as Secretary of State for Northern Ireland to meet in person with both loyalist and republican paramilitary prisoners and allay their concerns about where the talks were headed, but the situation both inside and outside of the negotiations remained extremely tenuous.[31]

In this atmosphere of crisis, the British and Irish governments produced a discussion paper entitled 'Propositions on Heads of Agreement', released on 12 January and described by one commentator as 'a first skeleton draft of what emerged as the Good Friday Agreement' which 'fitted on the front and back of an A4 page'.[32] This had originated in Downing Street with a unionist-leaning draft, to which the Irish government had responded with a more nationalist-flavoured one. After Trimble was shown the Irish draft and 'rejected it out of hand', he helped the governments arrive at a compromise version over the weekend of 10/11 January—a process which involved Blair's chief of staff Jonathan Powell managing 'an elaborate three-way discussion' between the Irish in Dublin, Blair in Tokyo (on an official visit to Japan), and Trimble. 'Propositions on Heads of Agreement' suggested changes to articles 2 and 3 of the Constitution of Ireland (which laid claim to the six counties of Northern Ireland) and to the (British) Government of Ireland Act. It also recommended a Northern Ireland Assembly with responsibility for local departments; a new 'British–Irish Agreement' to replace the Anglo–Irish Agreement (a long-standing unionist demand); an Intergovernmental Council of representatives from assemblies throughout Britain and Ireland; and a North–South Ministerial Council accountable to the Northern Ireland Assembly and the Dáil, with suitable 'implementation bodies' for policies this council agreed upon. Large differences remained among the negotiators, especially about the powers to be devolved to the Northern Ireland Assembly, whether or not there should be a Northern Ireland executive (the SDLP wanted one, while the UUP did not), and the extent and nature of cross-border cooperation. Nonetheless, most of the parties (despite their annoyance at being excluded from the governments' discussions after Trimble revealed that he had been consulted) were pleased to have, at last, something specific about which to negotiate.[33]

Republicans, however, greeted the governments' 'Propositions on Heads of Agreement' with 'fury'. All Sinn Féin's written contributions to the talks to date had assumed an all-Ireland context, reflecting, as Kate Fearon notes, 'a perspective utterly different from that of any other participant, including the Irish government' and leaving other negotiators to wonder just how seriously republicans were taking the process. Historian Thomas Hennessey writes of the 'Propositions' that 'Many of the more controversial details which the Irish had wanted to include, particularly on matters of power-sharing and British commitments on security and prisoners, were either deleted or watered down in order to secure Trimble's agreement' to the document. Because many of these 'details' were key republican objectives—a point the IRA reinforced with a statement explicitly rejecting the 'Propositions' as the basis for 'a lasting peace settlement'—the Sinn Féin leaders immediately began lobbying the Irish government for a new North–South paper 'at least' in line with the Framework Document.[34]

In response to the republican backlash, the British and Irish governments in late January put forth another discussion paper, dealing exclusively with North–South structures. By any measure, the parties were far apart on this subject, as de Bréadún explains, 'Unionists essentially wanted little more than a North–South version of the Rotary Club where ministers from Dublin and Belfast would meet perhaps once a month with their opposite numbers in a Northern Ireland administration to discuss entirely voluntary co-operation on matters of mutual interest. Republicans wanted at the very least an embryo governmental structure to facilitate the transition to a united Ireland in ten or fifteen years.' The format adopted for this paper was 'a series of questions aimed partly at outlining the views of the two governments but also at eliciting the real positions of the various parties, as distinct from the rhetoric reserved for press conferences'. The governments' submission had the intended effect of pleasing nationalists and republicans, but it did not achieve their goal of nudging the parties closer to consensus. The Irish had pushed hard for a statement in the paper reaffirming the governments' commitment to their previously agreed Framework Document, notwithstanding that it had been vehemently rejected by unionists following its publication early in 1995. Prominent UUP negotiator Jeffrey Donaldson scored points at 'a packed news conference' by announcing that 'We as a party will not put our hand to any agreement based on the Framework Document', while stagily destroying a copy of it.[35]

Adams comments, 'Rumour had it that [Donaldson] couldn't possibly have torn up the document without first having it already partially cut and sections of it removed. This provided light relief to talks insiders, but it did not detract from the serious message of intransigence he was delivering.' In an 8 March article for *Ireland on Sunday*, Adams himself appeared to outline an uncompromising position, asserting that his party's 'bottom line' included powerful cross-border bodies operating independently of a Northern Ireland Assembly, policing and a justice system under the control of new all-Ireland institutions, the disbanding of the RUC, the release of all paramilitary prisoners, the withdrawal of the British Army, and the retention of the territorial claim to Northern Ireland in the Constitution of Ireland.[36] However, this piece, like the Sinn Féin document entitled *A Bridge into the Future* which it previewed, resembled Blair's Balmoral speech in one important respect. Slipped in alongside the traditional republican agenda was the information that Sinn Féin would regard any agreement resulting from the talks as part of a 'transitional process' to unity: 'I felt that it was important to ensure that republicans especially understood that we did not expect these negotiations to produce a united Ireland by May that year', Adams recalls.[37] He clearly understood that no achievable settlement would deliver all (or even much) of what republicans wanted, but his article offered no clue as to what Sinn Féin's real 'bottom line' might be.

In December 1997, delegates representing all Northern Ireland parties in the talks had 'bet on how long the actual deal would take to be done', with the average wager being four days. By mid-March, however, most of the parties were still withholding their true positions—according to Mowlam, 'We all knew this was going to the wire, and no one was going to reveal their bottom lines until we got a lot closer to it.'[38] Mitchell's patience finally ran out by mid-March, and he decided to give talks participants what most writers both hate and need: 'an early, hard deadline'. 'As I studied the calendar', he remembers in his memoir, 'Easter week-end leaped out at me. It had historical significance in Ireland. It was an important weekend in Northern Ireland, a religious society.' Crucially, an agreement made by Easter would allow time for a referendum in late May and an assembly election in late June, 'before the peak of the marching season in early July'. Estimating that a deal could be made in 'two intense weeks', Mitchell counted back from Easter Sunday to 30 March, then decided to leave a 'margin for error' by moving the final deadline to midnight on the Thursday before Easter: 9 April 1998. Before putting this proposal in front of talks participants, Mitchell had discussed it thoroughly with each of them and knew 'it would be agreed to unanimously'.[39]

Even at 'this late stage' of the negotiations, Mowlam records, none of the parties 'had really moved very far from the positions they had adopted at the beginning of the year.... None of them wanted to be the first to move, the first to show their hand. It was going to be up to the two governments.' Mitchell shared in her 'frustration' about this reality: 'He could see the process slipping out of his hands and all being done between London and Dublin.' Mowlam suspected that Mitchell's irritation at being kept out of the loop motivated the detailed work plan he laid out on 25 March: from Monday, 30 March through Thursday, 2 April, the independent chairs would collect 'final comments on the content of an agreement' from the two governments and eight political parties involved in the negotiations; on Friday, 3 April, the chairs would present 'the first draft of a comprehensive accord', which the parties would review overnight; the chairs would then meet separately with each party on Saturday and Sunday 'to get their reactions to the first draft'; overnight Sunday the chairs would prepare 'a second, final draft' to be made available to the participants on Monday, 6 April; and the talks would end with 'four days and nights of final negotiations, culminating in an agreement' by midnight on 9 April.[40] Ultimately, and for reasons beyond Mitchell's control, little would unfold according to his plan, but this was the understanding with which the parties approached the final fortnight of negotiations.

The first attempt to present a comprehensive agreement in writing, planned for 3 April, was to be a synthesis of the governments' positions and the parties' ideas compiled by the independent chairs. This format gave the smaller parties an opportunity to ensure that their priorities were enshrined in the agreement, and Mowlam remembers that they were the most 'desperate' to make progress during the penultimate week of the talks. Sinn Féin and the UUP, she notes, 'turned up for meetings, a little more aggressive than their normal level, but with nothing much different to say apart from repeating what their outline positions were. The ones working away frantically were the British and Irish civil servants who were writing, rewriting and revising papers every day and long into the night.' It had often seemed to the members of the tiny Northern Ireland Women's Coalition (NIWC), a party formed to participate in the negotiations, that the position papers they had been writing since late autumn 'were being produced and going nowhere. But George Mitchell was a former judge who liked to have things on paper. So did the British and Irish civil servants. What the NIWC did not realise at the time was that many of their proposals were being banked, and would be processed, and re-presented in the name of others at future times.' The NIWC had 'placed some of the more detailed papers before the talks', and during this final stretch of the negotiations, 'they discovered that one party could set the agenda merely by putting in some time and producing a paper that would form the basis for discussion'.[41] In this way, ideas that had originated with them made it into the agreement.

In compiling the original draft of the accord, Mitchell's team 'worked off...a draft submitted jointly by the governments' which reflected their shared positions on most issues apart from matters of significant disagreement in Strands One and Two. The chairs, Mitchell explains, 'compared [the governments'] joint position with those which had been submitted by the parties and made changes that we thought would enhance the prospect of agreement', providing options for resolving the controversial issues that remained. Mitchell and his colleagues saw a comprehensive initial draft as 'a critical step in the process' because it would allow talks participants, for the first time, to 'see all of the issues laid out in a single document', enabling them to 'evaluate the trade-offs involved and determine whether they, and their constituents, could accept them'.[42]

The failure of the British and Irish governments to deliver a Strand Two text on schedule, however, thwarted the chairs' desire to give the parties a complete draft by Friday evening. By the middle of that penultimate week, Mowlam recalls, 'the main action was all between No. 10 and the Taoiseach's office': Ahern had travelled to London on Wednesday, and he and Blair were negotiating directly about potential North–South institutional arrangements, 'working better together with just the two of them, with a few officials on hand to take notes and give advice'. By Friday afternoon, Mitchell grew 'tense', as the hours passed with no agreed language on Strand Two, which everyone knew would be the most contentious aspect of the agreement.[43]

Mitchell 'regarded the two-draft process as essential to eventual success', reasoning that 'There had to be the opportunity for the negotiators to react to the first document, to let off steam, then hopefully move on to the final draft.' He was thus deeply disappointed when the prime ministers informed him early Friday evening that they were still working on the Strand Two section. They encouraged him to circulate a partial draft of the agreement, providing only an 'oral summary on Strand Two' without 'anything on it in writing', a suggestion rejected by Mitchell, his colleagues, and the parties—the first draft needed to be complete to serve its intended purpose. Mitchell reluctantly agreed to wait until Sunday evening for Strand Two. In fact, as British negotiator Jonathan Powell reveals, this section dealing with North–South relations was already 'basically agreed, apart from a few passages in square brackets for further discussion', but Blair and Ahern 'decided to leave it unfinished for the moment'. The prime ministers 'feared that if they gave it to George Mitchell for circulation too early, the parties would pull it to pieces over the weekend'. This strategic delay fitted into Blair's plan to use the impending deadline 'to rush the parties into an agreement without allowing them to stop and think too much'.[44]

Mitchell and his colleagues agreed to accept blame for missing the Friday deadline, but they hesitated when the governments, delivering the Strand Two section on Sunday, asked them to assume authorship as well and insert it into the agreement 'as *our* draft, not theirs'. Moreover, the prime ministers wanted the independent chairs to 'include in our comprehensive document what they had agreed on *without any changes*. They did not want a single word or a single comma altered'. This represented a fundamental departure from the process the chairs had followed in compiling the rest of the draft agreement, and they seriously considered refusing. The prospect was especially worrying, Mitchell recalls, because he knew 'instantly' upon reading the section that 'it would not be acceptable to the unionists'. In the end, the chairs acceded to the request, motivated chiefly by fear that the governments might 'split over this issue': 'It was imperative that they stay united and that we all mount the last drive for agreement together, even though the route they had chosen disquieted us'.[45]

Mitchell was 'jolted' again on Monday by the revelation that the governments had yet to negotiate annexes to their Strand Two paper detailing 'possible areas of co-operation' between Northern Ireland and the Republic, 'in various categories of importance and certainty'—hardly 'simple, noncontroversial issues', he notes drily. These annexes 'were to be lists of subject areas [such as tourism, education, agriculture, and fisheries] in categories that corresponded to the words of the Frameworks Document: executive, harmonizing, and consultative'. The Irish negotiators sought 'to hew as closely as they could to the Frameworks Document' and 'make the annexes as comprehensive as possible', while the British team 'recognized that the greater the fidelity to the Frameworks Document the less likely it was that the Ulster Unionists would accept the annexes and the agreement to which they were to be attached'. Mitchell did not receive the text of the annexes until very late Monday night, at which point his team could finally assemble a comprehensive draft.[46]

The resultant 'Mitchell paper', as Mowlam explains, was thus 'a hybrid', in which 'the George bits left both sides enough room to manoeuvre' and 'the Strand Two part did not'. Mitchell had the words 'Draft Paper for Discussion' added to the top of each page before copying the document for distribution to the party leaders after midnight, and he appended 'a covering memorandum explicitly describing it as just that'. He also 'begged' the parties to keep the draft confidential, taking the additional precaution, Adams remembers, of claiming that 'subtle changes in each text would allow the chairs to identify which party leaked the paper, if any appeared in the press'. The document did not leak, but on Tuesday, in Mowlam's words, the 'unionist family revolted en masse'; Mitchell admits that even he 'had underestimated how negative the reaction would be'.[47]

All the unionist parties (including the cross-communal Alliance Party, which rejected the unionist label for itself) opposed the Strand Two proposals. UUP negotiator Thomas Hennessey explains that their objections centred on 'the source of authority for the implementation bodies': 'The transfer of functions, by London and Dublin, to the North–South Council clearly made it the source of authority for North–South co-operation and therefore it would, in Unionist eyes, be acting as a third level of government in Ireland.' Because the North–South Council would be established through legislation by the two governments, the Northern Ireland Assembly would not have the power to determine what and how much coordination would occur. Instead, 'Unionists were being given a preordained range of implementation bodies and told precisely where North–South co-operation would be conducted.'[48]

From Trimble's perspective, the Strand Two section of the draft agreement 'was just essentially the Frameworks proposals again'. He surmised that 'the Irish government were focussed on nationalist demands, especially Sinn Fein's repeated insistence that they would not support an accord that departed from Frameworks', but he did not understand why Blair had yielded on this issue, especially after the corresponding parts of the governments' 'Propositions on Heads of Agreement' had, 'at my insistence, and with Ahern's agreement,' been revised to make them acceptable to unionists. Trimble could only conclude that Blair had 'decided to prioritise keeping republicans in the process'. This seems a reasonable inference given the tone of Sinn Féin's written submission to the talks in late March, which described the arrangements the party would be prepared to accept as 'part of a transitional process to Irish unity and independence' in terms that must have read to unionists like a nightmarish embodiment of their suspicions about cross-border institutions as the means to unify Ireland by stealth: 'Powerful all-Ireland bodies, exercising significant and meaningful executive and harmonising powers alongside consultative functions,…with the range of functions to be discharged or overseen initially designated by the two governments, operating independently, immune from the veto of any proposed six county institutions, with no limit on the nature and extent of their functions, with the dynamic and ability to grow'.[49]

Mitchell and his colleagues informed the governments on Tuesday morning that the only way to salvage the talks would be for the prime ministers to renegotiate the Strand Two section—otherwise, the unionists, united for once, would simply walk out. The independent chairs and the British and Irish officials working in Belfast agreed unanimously on the need to get the prime ministers on site as soon as possible. Blair arrived on Tuesday evening; Ahern joined him on Wednesday, although his mother had died suddenly that Monday (Ahern travelled to Belfast on Wednesday morning, flew to Dublin for her midday funeral, and returned on Wednesday afternoon). Mitchell met with Blair on Tuesday and Ahern on Wednesday to tell them that 'the one thing I wanted from them was an absolute commitment to the deadline': 'When we start on Thursday morning, it has to be clear to everyone that we'll continue until we finish, one way or the other. There can be no discussion of a pause or a break.... We'll either get an agreement or we'll fail to get an agreement. Then we'll all go out together and explain to the press and the waiting world how we succeeded or why we failed.' Both 'agreed, without hesitation'. Ahern now opposed the idea of Mitchell's team producing a second draft before the deadline. With the two prime ministers present in the talks building, Mowlam writes, 'the real hard negotiations started'.[50]

Mitchell emphasizes that Blair and Ahern, aided by their 'warm personal relationship', 'didn't just supervise the negotiations; they conducted them. Word by word, sentence by sentence, paragraph by paragraph, the compromise came together.' The two men had gotten to know each other when they were both in opposition. Blair requested a meeting with Ahern after the breakdown of the IRA ceasefire in February 1996, and they had agreed, Ahern remembers, 'that if elected Prime Minister and Taoiseach we would take a hands-on role about the North': 'We were always direct and, over the years, we would say things to each other that were tough. But there was always a sense that from our own different national interests we wanted to get this sorted.' Anxious to prevent officialdom from interfering with their 'personal rapport', Ahern suggested that they should keep in touch using their personal mobile phones, and he estimates that they 'spoke several times a week' throughout the time Blair headed the British government. Blair regarded Ahern as 'a true friend', describing him as 'smart, cunning in the best sense, strong and, above all, free of the shackles of history'. Despite his family's 'firm republican credentials' and his own leadership of the Fianna Fáil party, Ahern undertook the rewrite of Strand Two to allay unionist fears—as Powell observes, 'There would have been no agreement in Northern Ireland if it had not been for his unadorned common sense.'[51]

The tug-of-war between unionist and republican positions on Strand Two during the final days of the talks replayed their struggle during and after the writing of the governments' 'Propositions on Heads of Agreement', only this time the latter had won the first round. Ahern reluctantly agreed on Wednesday that the 'text could be revisited', although he insisted 'the substance had to be maintained'. Overall, he didn't really understand why the unionists were so exercised about North–South collaboration, commenting to Blair that 'It's not like we're not already doing it in the EU.' Ultimately, the crucial concession was Ahern's willingness to revise in and of itself. By late Thursday, the UUP and the Irish government had agreed upon a compromise. Trimble had learned from the Northern Ireland Office (NIO) that it would take almost a year to devolve power from London to any new Northern Ireland institutions created by an agreement, during which transitional period the Assembly would operate in 'shadow mode'. He suggested using 'the shadow period to solve the problem' by letting the shadow Assembly negotiate with the Irish government and the NIO 'what co-operation schemes there should be and how they should be structured', after which the NIO could 'use its powers to legislate by Order in Council to give effect to the Assembly's decisions'. Unionists could rest assured that 'the Assembly would clearly be in control of the northern end of the negotiation', but 'the safeguard for the Irish government was that this would all have to be done before devolution': 'if we did not agree to a council and worthwhile co-operation, then there would be no Assembly'. Blair termed this feature of the agreement 'mutually assured destruction'.[52] In addition, the three Strand Two annexes detailing over sixty 'subject areas' for cross-border cooperation were reduced to one illustrative list of twelve.[53]

On Thursday morning, Blair had stressed to Trimble that Ahern's 'pragmatism' should make it possible to arrive at language acceptable to unionists on Strand Two, but 'Trimble should not push his luck on other issues', advice the UUP leader apparently heeded. The compromise on Strand Two, Powell records, 'unlocked negotiations on Strand One'. The UUP quickly consented to most SDLP proposals for new Northern Ireland institutions, including an executive consisting of ten ministers chosen according to the d'Hondt method (a complex system of proportional representation named for its Belgian inventor), a First Minister and a Deputy First Minister elected jointly on a cross-community basis, and a 108-member Assembly operating under a version of sufficient consensus for key decisions to ensure cross-community support. These were, according to Powell, 'all ideas that the Unionists had been rejecting for years'. As de Bréadún remarks, 'in the shotgun wedding between unionism and nationalism, the Strand Two draft was the shotgun'.[54]

Trimble explains that he was guided largely by 'political considerations': 'If the new administration was to work successfully, it would require a good working relationship between ourselves and the SDLP', but the SDLP would be vulnerable to attacks from Sinn Féin on Strand One if they could not demonstrate 'that they had not surrendered nationalists to unionist domination'. Trimble remembers that 'at the very end' of the UUP's negotiations with the SDLP on Strand One, 'they asked if we could revert to using the term "Minister" for the person exercising executive power, rather than the more modern "Secretary". After a brief consultation, we agreed, to be surprised at their rather emotional reaction': it 'almost seemed that this word meant more' to the nationalists than 'everything else'. SDLP leader John Hume had served as minister for commerce in the short-lived power-sharing government brought down in May 1974 by the loyalist strike David Trimble had supported logistically, a fact that probably had something to do with his party's insistence on this semantic point.[55]

During negotiations on Strands Two and Three, Mitchell's midnight Thursday deadline passed with little comment, but the process almost foundered again in the wee hours of Friday morning—and would have ended without a viable agreement had it not been for crucial editing performed by Mo Mowlam. Trimble had insisted throughout the talks that Sinn Féin was 'marginal to the process' because, under the rule of sufficient consensus, it was technically possible for unionists to conclude a deal with the SDLP alone. As everyone understood, however, Sinn Féin's importance to the negotiations did not rely solely on its much-vaunted 'electoral mandate'. Any agreement that did not enjoy republican support would not eliminate political violence in Northern Ireland. Blair recalls that when a Sinn Féin spokesman on Thursday evening 'told the waiting hordes of media there would be no agreement, collective hysteria broke out' among the British government negotiators: 'The result, as no doubt Gerry and Martin intended, was that we had to scuttle off to them and try to bring them back.' Blair advised the Sinn Féin leaders to suggest specific amendments that might render the draft agreement acceptable to them but was 'aghast' when they 'came back with forty pages of detailed changes'. He had earlier reminded the British team that Adams and McGuinness were 'negotiating with at least a modicum of worry someone will come along and blow their brains out if they go too far', and their presentation of such a long list of amendments 'at the last minute' made him worry that 'they were getting nervous about doing a deal at all'.[56]

Throughout most of that final week of negotiations, Mowlam had seen it as her role to 'keep talking to everyone' while the prime ministers focused on 'the big issues with the main players', but her knowledge of republican psychology, politics, and tactics proved vital in the pre-dawn Friday negotiations with Sinn Féin. Specifically, she knew how they, like all the Northern Ireland parties, used 'lists of demands' as 'bargaining chips in the negotiations, to try and get the best deal they could before allowing progress to be made' and to reinforce their members' faith in the peace process. Confronted with Sinn Féin's last-minute list, Blair 'assumed all [items on it] were to be taken seriously, and needless to say, they would have made Unionist hair curl'. Mowlam, however, 'took receipt of the document' and 'then ignored the overwhelming majority of the points, focusing on the one or two things that might matter': 'It seemed very odd to me, but it worked.'[57]

Sinn Féin's main concern centred on prisoners. The republicans argued, with Mowlam's support, that all paramilitary prisoners whose organizations approved the agreement should be released within one year instead of the three years offered by the British government. Blair eventually agreed to commit publicly to two years, assuring Adams orally that he would release the prisoners in one year if circumstances allowed (they didn't). Mowlam records that, because early prisoner release was insisted upon by the two loyalist parties as well as by Sinn Féin, 'none of the other parties could reject it and hope to get agreement'.[58]

Sinn Féin also pushed hard on the agreement's wording with respect to decommissioning. Adams recounts that 'The unionists were trying to secure a procedural linkage within the agreement between actual decommissioning and holding office in an executive', but the governments 'both knew that we weren't negotiating for the IRA, and that there was no possibility of us signing up to something we couldn't deliver'. In the end, the governments 'opted for a good conflict resolution answer to this vexed question' by calling 'on all parties to use their influence to achieve decommissioning in the context of the implementation of the overall agreement'. Sinn Féin's leaders were not authorized to approve any settlement before its members had an opportunity to vote on it; by breakfast-time on Friday, though, Adams and McGuinness had informed Mitchell and the governments that they 'were prepared to go to our party with a draft agreement, but only if there were no further changes'.[59]

The agreement had been evolving continuously since talks participants received Mitchell's complete draft after midnight on Monday, with parties afforded only intermittent glimpses of what was happening to it in the meantime. For the Northern Ireland Women's Coalition, the Mitchell draft offered 'the negotiating opportunity they had been waiting for for two years'. Soon after it was distributed, 'all the members of the NIWC delegation had a copy of the first draft, and were poring over the details, outlining questions, suggesting word changes, highlighting words in ink or fluorescent marker'. 'At this point', NIWC talks participant Kate Fearon observes, 'delegates came to realise the primacy of the written word in politics. For all the extra-tabular discussions, if it wasn't written down, it didn't exist.' During the final days of the negotiations, the good relations the women had developed over time with the chairs and the British and Irish officials doing the drafting paid dividends for them, as they worked to ensure that their priorities were reflected in the agreement. The NIWC proposed, for example, adding 'the right of women to full and equal political participation' to the document's list of 'Human Rights' affirmed by the parties. When one of the women went to raise the issue with Mowlam, she found access to her target's office 'jealously guarded by her officials'. The NIWC representative hung around in the corridor until Mowlam appeared, told her she needed to speak with her urgently, then shared a cubicle with her in the women's toilets to discuss the provision. After this amendment was added to the document, 'no one dared take it out'.[60]

Once a party succeeded in getting something into the agreement, it had to keep tabs on what happened to the draft after that, a task complicated by the fact that delegates had no direct access to it. 'Bizarrely,' Fearon remarks, 'each party would throw its amendments into a pot upstairs, and only the British government, the secretariat and the chairs could see the full picture at any one time.' Members of the NIWC delegation 'literally sat outside civil servants' doors until they came out for air, waiting to see whether there were still brackets around certain clauses' to indicate that 'they were still on the table, but not yet agreed'. Such tactics were necessary because 'after the first draft had been completed, the only copy of the draft agreement was on disk', and it was constantly changing.[61]

One of the NIWC's most significant contributions to the final agreement was a section on 'Reconciliation and Victims of Violence'. Throughout the talks, the cross-communal NIWC had been the only party to advocate for both prisoners and victims. During the final negotiations, the NIWC strove 'to communicate the importance of having a strong section on provision for victims and victims' rights' as a 'counterpoise to a liberal section on prisoner releases'. None of the other parties seemed to see this as important at first: 'The one small paragraph on the topic in the draft was only there because the NIWC had been putting the issue on the agenda at every available opportunity over the previous two years', but the women believed that the agreement's language on victims 'had to be right not only for the participants, but for those who would be voting on it, and for those who would be influencing the vote'. The NIWC prepared a detailed amendment on victims but discovered upon proposing it that 'the most recent draft had written out victims altogether'. The party 'had to push hard to get a new, extended version back in'. 'Subsequently,' Fearon notes, 'prisoner releases, decommissioning and the role of victims became the linked issues on which the referendum on the Good Friday Agreement was fought.'[62]

Women's Coalition members were not the only ones guarding the provisions of the draft agreement which were most important to them. On Thursday, according to de Bréadún, the talks building began to fill with a 'new type of talks delegate...more used to doing business in rather more robust ways than polite conversation across a table'. 'As the night wore on,' Powell recalls, 'the security people told us that among those coming into the building were an increasing number of hard-core IRA members, presumably to be consulted, since Adams and McGuinness could not leave to talk to them'. The loyalist Progressive Unionist Party (PUP) and Ulster Democratic Party (UDP) were similarly 'accompanied in their rooms' by the leaderships of the paramilitaries they represented, the Ulster Volunteer Force (UVF) and Ulster Defence Association (UDA) respectively, and the parties also regularly relayed developments to loyalist prisoners. UDP leader Gary McMichael remembers that 'We had the [UDA] Inner Council in the room with us because you weren't allowed to take anything out of the building, so we had to bring them in to see the documents.'[63] The UVF commander had been part of the PUP delegation all along, but other UVF leaders joined that party's deliberations at the end of the negotiations. Prominent PUP negotiator Billy Hutchinson developed doubts about the Strand Two compromise during the last stage of these, driven by fear that 'we weren't seeing all the bits of paper'. The UVF's Number Two, however, persuaded him 'that I needed to show unity and not create a split in the camp'. From that paramilitary leader's perspective, 'We had seen drafts of the document and had a pretty good idea of what the final document would look like.... We had been over every detail and processed every sentence, so we were confident there would be no surprises in the final outcome. There was a consensus amongst the entire leadership on this and they were all in the building during those last hours'.[64]

Although these sentiments were widely shared by participants, the talks weathered a final crisis on Friday. All the parties received 'the new text of the agreement' by late morning, at which point, Powell records, 'all hell broke loose'. 'Most of the parties hadn't seen any text since Monday and big sections of it must have come as a surprise', Powell allows, but it was Trimble's UUP delegation ('swollen by this time as supporters piled in') that delayed a planned noon plenary for hours while they debated the document amongst themselves. Powell comments, 'I suppose that, confronted with a document that put Sinn Féin in government with no guarantee of decommissioning, with prisoners being released, doubts about the future of the RUC, a new relationship with Dublin, with nationalists holding a veto in the Assembly over major issues, and without preparation from their leaders on any of these points, it was not so surprising they had difficulties.' It seemed obvious to him that 'Trimble had failed to pave the way for an inclusive agreement, believing that Sinn Féin would not be able to swallow the principle of consent and would therefore not sign'.[65]

Advocating the agreement to his party, Trimble distinguished between constitutional and policy issues in a manner reminiscent of a textual editor's distinction between 'substantives', an author's words and their meanings, and 'accidentals' like spelling and punctuation. In Trimble's judgement, Hennessey explains, 'The UUP...had entered the talks to secure the constitutional future of the Union. They had achieved those objectives. All of the other distasteful aspects of the Agreement—prisoners, the commission on policing—were *policy* issues which any British Government could introduce at any time.' Trimble remembers arguing that 'The former, the constitutional changes, the north/south structures, the Assembly were generally acceptable. These matters, I pointed out, would be permanent and they represented a good deal for unionism against the background of the hated Anglo–Irish Agreement and what might happen if we were unable to make a deal. On the other hand the policy matters were within the responsibility of the government, whether we made a deal or not. The government would almost certainly proceed with them even if we refused to agree to the proposed agreement.' Despite Trimble's efforts to convince his wavering colleagues, however, 'two key problems' remained: 'prisoner release and the linkage of decommissioning to holding office'. Trimble suggested appealing to Blair one last time but warned that 'to have any hope of success we should prioritise'. He recalls 'an immediate consensus that decommissioning was more important'—no doubt partly because the early release of prisoners was as significant to the loyalist parties as it was to Sinn Féin, and the UUP needed the support of at least one of them to claim to speak for the majority of unionists.[66]

Yet another document, Blair's (in)famous 'side letter', finally broke the deadlock in the UUP delegation. Trimble recounts that, after listening to the concerns of the five senior UUP members who appealed to the prime minister, 'Blair's response was, not unexpectedly, that he could not unilaterally change the text that was agreeable to the other parties and that it was not realistic to try to restart the negotiations at that late hour. I then mooted the idea of a letter from [the British government] containing some helpful commitments on the matter.'[67] After the UUP representatives left his office, Blair dictated such a letter to Powell, who typed it 'at top speed' on his laptop. This document acknowledged the UUP's worry that the agreement required 'decisions on those who should be excluded or removed from office in the Northern Ireland Executive to be taken on a cross-community basis', pledging 'that if, during the course of the first six months of the shadow Assembly or the Assembly itself, these provisions have been shown to be ineffective, we will support changes to these provisions to enable them to be properly effective in preventing such people from holding office'. Blair, who told none of the other parties about his side letter, remarks that its wording 'was very typical of the intricate nuance of the negotiation: we didn't say we *would* exclude, we said we would support changing the agreement so as to exclude'.[68]

Powell writes that, as soon as he finished typing the letter, 'I snatched it off the printer and raced down to give it to Trimble. There was no time to lose because we feared he was about to walk out. But down on the Unionist floor, I was confronted by a locked door. They were debating whether or not to accept the agreement inside, and I couldn't get in'. Powell finally pushed a note under the door to alert the UUP to his presence, and Trimble took delivery of the letter. He read it with his deputy John Taylor 'looking over his shoulder', and Powell recalls Taylor saying, 'almost instantly, "That's fine, we can run with that." ' Even so, Powell records, 'there was a tense hour before we got an official acceptance'. Trimble read out Blair's letter on exclusion during the press conference later that day, confiding afterwards his worry 'that the ink would run in the rain'. Powell adds, 'Little did he know that, if it had, we would not have been able to give him another copy. In the rush I had omitted to save the letter on the computer or keep a copy and it wasn't until the NIO eventually plucked up the courage to ask the UUP for a duplicate a few years later that we had a record of what we'd written'. Adams disparaged Blair's side letter when he learned of its existence ('Although it had no status, the letter clearly breached the terms of the agreement'). During the interminable afternoon spent waiting for the UUP to decide whether or not to endorse the agreement, however, he had himself faced the realization that everybody's hard work 'might yet all come to nothing if the UUP did not come on board', an experience which likely mitigated his annoyance with the prime minister.[69]

The British government under Blair had tried deliberately 'to surprise the parties into an agreement'. Up until the final plenary, convened fifteen minutes after Trimble informed Mitchell that the UUP was 'ready to do the business', uncertainty about the status of the agreement remained. A Mitchell aide informed members of the other parties waiting to enter the session that 'Everyone needed to get into the chamber, agree to the thing as a whole, and leave. There could be no debating time in which Trimble could change his mind.' When Mitchell surveyed the assembled delegations, each party leader replied, 'For the agreement' or 'Agree'—the only exceptions were Adams, who said 'Agree subject to consultation', and Trimble, who replied, significantly, 'Yes.'[70] Right after this vote, Powell recalls, 'There was no applause, just stunned silence.' Blair and Ahern left the plenary before it ended, so they could be the first to explain the deal to the media. Afterwards, Ahern remembers, they retired to a room 'set aside so that we could sign the agreement immediately, again to make sure that no one would try to reopen the negotiations'. British civil servants had entitled the document 'The Belfast Agreement', but Ahern dubbed it at once, with Blair's approval, the 'Good Friday Agreement'. Eventually, he reports, 'it got the official title, "The Belfast Agreement signed on Good Friday". But to this day, it is known around the world as the Good Friday Agreement.'[71]

There is reason to believe that both sides were, indeed, surprised to have an agreement. Adams describes a conversation he had with Mitchell amid the fraught hours of waiting for the UUP's decision: ' "The problem for David Trimble is that he didn't think you were serious," the Senator told me. "He expected Sinn Féin to blink first. He expected you to walk out. You haven't. And he is running out of time." ' Trimble biographer Henry McDonald points out, however, that Sinn Féin similarly anticipated that unionists would balk at the accord:

> SDLP and Irish government sources have since confirmed that up until the last moment Sinn Fein [sic] expected the Ulster Unionists to reject the package in its entirety and thus plunge the entire political process into crisis—a crisis, republicans hoped, which would be blamed on the UUP. Now that Trimble had accepted the Agreement and they were locked into an essentially partitionist solution, Sinn Fein found itself in the difficult situation of having to overturn its century-old constitution barring the party from entering a Northern Ireland Parliament. Sinn Fein was as lukewarm about the outcome as some in the UUP but far more adept than Trimble's team at masking dissent and, in public at least, repressing their own anxieties.

Quite possibly, then, both republicans and unionists assented to the agreement in the belief that the other did not want them to do so; such a belief may even have provided decisive motivation for so doing. The fact that neither necessarily expected there to *be* an agreement, let alone that they themselves would be required to uphold their end of it, would present significant challenges when negotiation gave way to implementation. The hopes and expectations of Northern Irish people in general, as opposed to politicians, however, were well summed up in the NIWC's closing statement, which referenced the women's 'obstinate optimism' in declaring that 'Northern Ireland owed it to those who had died in the past three decades to build a society that would stand as a living testimony to the victims of the Troubles.'[72]

Colum McCann likewise sought to embody a hard-won optimism about humanity's ability to survive catastrophe, even disasters of its own making, in his novel *TransAtlantic* (2013), which ends with words spoken by a woman on the verge of losing her family home: 'We have to admire the world for not ending on us' (300). Born in Dublin in 1965, McCann had lived abroad since his early twenties, settling in New York City in the mid-1990s. Before he began writing *TransAtlantic*, he had published two collections of short fiction and five novels; his last novel, *Let the Great World Spin*, had won the National Book Award, celebrating 'the best literature in America', in 2009, the same year McCann was inducted into Aosdána, an honour 'acknowledging his contributions to the arts in Ireland'. He set out in *TransAtlantic* to explore the 'incredible' links between Ireland and the United States, a country that, he has said, 'means more to Ireland than any other nation', functioning for many Irish people as 'a dream place'.[73]

The novel originated in McCann's compulsion to write about Frederick Douglass, the fugitive slave turned autobiographer and pro-abolition orator whose lecture tour of Ireland in 1845/46 coincided with the start of the Great Famine, which accelerated Irish immigration to the US in the mid-nineteenth century.[74] 'I was taken by Douglass', McCann recalled shortly after *TransAtlantic*'s publication, 'but I knew that I didn't want to write a historical novel' (or, at least, not one that 'would be labeled "historical"'). In fact, seeing parallels between Douglass and then US President Barack Obama, whose 2011 state visit to Ireland is the last major public event alluded to in *TransAtlantic*, he 'wanted to push it up against the present': 'And if I actually shoved anything of the Present up against anything as monumental as an African American slave being in Ireland, it had to be something monumental now.'[75] McCann, who spent summers during his childhood on his mother's family's farm in Northern Ireland, immediately thought of the peace process in which Senator George Mitchell ('the best politician of our time') had played a vital role. Wanting something to bridge the gap between the sojourns in Ireland of these 'two great American statesmen', McCann 'discovered, or 're-remembered' the story of Jack Alcock and Teddy Brown, who in 1919 completed the first transatlantic flight, starting in Newfoundland and landing 'in a bog in Ireland'.[76]

For some time, McCann 'was operating on the fumes of those stories, not quite sure where it was I would go'.[77] The journeys of Douglass, Alcock and Brown, and Mitchell were 'what we classically call nonfiction', but he also wanted to investigate the unrecorded aspects of 'human history'. Where, McCann wondered, were 'the women who...suffered it and endured it and created it in many ways?' He found them in the margins of what he had already written, as women 'appeared in minor ways in the male narratives'. Although they were fictional characters, 'the premise of them was inherently real. There would have been a maid in the house where Douglass stayed. And there probably would have been a journalist observing the Alcock and Brown flight. And there certainly would have been a mother/grandmother pairing who were enormously indebted to Senator Mitchell'. When he conceived of them, McCann regarded these women as 'partly "me"— the observer character, sitting on the edge, watching, wondering what was about to unfold'. At an advanced stage of the writing process, it occurred to him that the stories of these women could function as the 'glue' holding together the stories of the men.[78]

In the published novel, the women at the edges of the famous men's stories presented in Book One are revealed in Book Two to be generations of the same matrilineage. Lily, the maid from the Douglass chapter, is inspired by his visit to emigrate from Ireland to the US. Her daughter, Emily, becomes a pioneering female journalist who writes about Alcock and Brown's flight. Emily's daughter, Lottie, a photographer, meets her future husband when she and her mother travel to Europe in 1929 in pursuit of subjects for magazine features; the couple settle permanently in Belfast, his hometown. Book Three, the only one written in the first person, is narrated by Lottie's daughter, Hannah, who in 2011 still acutely misses her son, Tomas, killed in Troubles-related violence in 1978. 'I wanted the women to own the novel', McCann told fellow novelist Elizabeth Strout. Thus, although they are peripheral characters in Book One, the women move to the foreground in Book Two as the men portrayed in Book One become bit players in *their* lives. 'There's a symmetry in the book', McCann commented: 'three male "nonfiction" narratives, three female "fiction" narratives, and then a lone voice at the end, almost as if she has been narrating the whole novel'. Part of his purpose in *TransAtlantic*, he confided, was 'to question the gulf between what is "real" and what is "imagined." Is there any difference at all? Can the imagined be considered real? And vice versa?' To his mind, 'A story is a story whether it is based on real-life characters or not', and in the novel he aimed 'to braid the tapestry together so that "fiction" and "nonfiction" get confused'.[79]

In the case of Mitchell, however, McCann's 'nonfictional' subject was not only still alive but resided just a short walk away from his home in New York City.

McCann wrote to Mitchell and his wife, Heather, asking for permission to tell the story of Mitchell's time in Northern Ireland, which they were happy to give because they had enjoyed some of his previous work. When Heather replied to his letter by asking when he would like to interview her husband, McCann explained that he preferred to imagine Mitchell's experience first, talking with him only after he had drafted the chapter. Heather, a literary agent, understood the creative process well enough to leave him to it. McCann, at this point, had read Mitchell's peace process memoir but otherwise knew him only through the media. Nonetheless, Heather was impressed by the accuracy of his insights, although she pointed out some factual errors in his first three drafts. It was only after he had completed the fourth draft that, 'with great trepidation', McCann allowed Mitchell to read it and sat down for an interview with him that lasted four or five hours. He was willing to edit his text in accordance with Mitchell's suggestions ('A journalist would obviously never do this', McCann remarks, 'But I was writing fiction. I'm interested in truth!'). However, 'there was nothing really that Senator Mitchell wanted to change'.[80]

McCann has said of *TransAtlantic* that 'I knew I wanted to write about peace', and the focus on Mitchell himself was secondary: 'I wanted people to feel what it was like to be a man dedicating his life to the notion of peace'. McCann saw nothing 'soft' about this pursuit, and he wanted readers, too, to view it as 'something muscular, something tough'. The novel's Mitchell chapter is entitled 'Para Bellum' in reference to the Latin epigram *Si vis pacem, para bellum* (106): 'If you want peace, prepare for war'. Mitchell literally risks his life by taking a prominent part in the negotiations, a fact mentioned glancingly throughout the chapter—most directly in Heather's worry 'that he will become the flesh at the end of an assassin's bullet' (103). Her husband dismisses this possibility but lives in fear that something— 'Bombing? Murder? Broken ceasefire?' (120)—will happen to disrupt the talks. Like Frederick Douglass in the nineteenth century, Mitchell is a celebrity on both sides of the Atlantic, but, unlike Douglass, he seeks 'The refuge of the anonymous' (124). For the most part, as critic Charles I. Armstrong points out, 'We are presented with an individual playing an unglamorous and demanding role under no little pressure'.[81] McCann's Mitchell conceives of himself less as a diplomat than as a warrior:

He dislikes the praise, the glad-handing, the false backslaps, the gestures to his patience, his control. It's the tenacity of the fanatic that he wants to pitch himself against. There is, he knows, something akin to his own form of violence in the way he wants to hang on and fight. The way the terrorist might hide himself in a wet ditch all night....He would like to outlast that man in the ditch, outwait the cold and the rain and the filth, and the opportunity for a bullet, remain down in the reeds, underwater, in the dark, breathing through a hollow piece of grass.... Match him breath for breath. Let the gunman grow so cold that he cannot pull the trigger and then allow the silhouette to trudge dejected over the hill. To filibuster the son of a bitch, and then watch him climb out the ditch and to thank him and shake his hand and escort him down the high-brambled lane-way with the senatorial knife in his back.   (112–13)

Most of the high colour in the novel's Mitchell chapter appears in passages like this one depicting his interiority.

'Para Bellum' takes place during the two weeks leading up to the Good Friday Agreement; these final days, as other narratives of the negotiations demonstrate, abounded in drama, suspense, and action, but a reader who did not already know a great deal about the events of this fortnight would learn little about their specifics from McCann's text. Much of the chapter is set in transit. McCann devotes half of it to an account of Mitchell's journey from New York City to Belfast on Sunday and Monday, 29/30 March 1998, inserting an oblique reminder of the punishing schedule this man in his mid-sixties has endured for too long: 'Almost two hundred flights over the past three years. One every three days' (101). McCann regularly interrupts the description of this trip, however, with excursions into his protagonist's thoughts, feelings, and memories. The most fully fleshed-out characters in the chapter, apart from Mitchell himself, are fictional ones representing his dealings with the ordinary people of Northern Ireland. The major players and elements of the peace process are dispensed with via a ubiquitous use of lists: 'Strand One, Strand Two, Strand Three' (112); 'The paramilitaries, the politicians, the diplomats, the civil servants' (113); 'The Unionists, the Nationalists, the Loyalists, the Republicans, the Planters, the Gaels.... The alphabet soup of the terrorists' (117); 'Hume. Trimble. Adams. Mowlam. Mallon. McMichael. Cooney. Hill. Donoghue. McWilliams. Sager' (131); 'On the phone he talks to Blair and Ahern. President Clinton, too. A letter of best wishes arrives from Nelson Mandela. A handwritten note from Václav Havel' (139). There is no climactic scene depicting the plenary session, chaired by Mitchell, at which the Agreement was formally approved. Instead, McCann conveys the ultimate success of the negotiations indirectly, through the sounds of 'cheers along the corridor growing louder' that Mitchell hears while waiting in his office (148). These sounds of celebration intrude upon a reverie induced by 'taps on the pane' made by the rain outside the window, reminiscent of the 'light taps upon the pane' that falling snow makes at the end of James Joyce's story 'The Dead', which call to the protagonist's mind 'all the living and the dead'.[82]

McCann's treatment of the peace process in *TransAtlantic* accords with autobiographical and historical accounts of it in the emphasis placed upon textual issues, however. Unsurprisingly, given his own preoccupations, McCann was favourably impressed by Mitchell's skills as a reader and writer. He asserted in a 2013 interview that, during the peace process, language was everything. And George Mitchell was in the heart of things. The Irish people used language and flung their stories against him. But Mitchell's great beauty was that he operated like the great carnivorous reader you're always hoping you find, if you're a writer. He allowed the text to work upon him. And when they exhausted themselves and said everything they could possibly say, he turned around and said, 'Okay, you told me all your stories. Now it's time to achieve some peace.' And that was great because they were mangling the language. And he knew it was time to create a whole new language, or a new allowance for language.[83]

Mitchell's ability to wield words struck other sophisticated observers similarly. Deaglán de Bréadún, who reported on the talks for the *Irish Times*, describes the prose style of Mitchell's press statements as 'one of short, declarative sentences' but notes that 'there was often a subtle political ambiguity there when it came to controversial issues. He had a way of providing comfort to both sides of an argument...while appearing at the same time to take a simple and clearcut stance.' During the final fortnight of talks, Mitchell's deadline proved 'crucial', as his role changed 'from the apparently passive auditor of the various points of view to the dynamic chairman injecting momentum into the process and pushing the parties closer together'. Mitchell's draft agreement, despite the Strand Two problems not of his making, moved the negotiations forward decisively because 'Having built a reputation with all sides for impartiality he was able to act as a clearinghouse for ideas, whether from governments or political parties. Plans and proposals lost their partisan taint by being routed through Mitchell who made it possible to consider them on their merits rather than their origins.'[84]

Aware as he has become of 'the geography that went into words' and the 'history behind every syllable', the only thing that keeps McCann's Mitchell going at times is what the narrator, besting W. B. Yeats, terms 'fascination with the impossible' (118).[85] When the journey that opens 'Para Bellum' finally ends at the talks building, the narrator's description of the Mitchell draft in the process of being assembled has a striking materiality: 'What they have is a sixty-page draft, two governments, ten political parties, little less than two weeks. Strand One. Strand Two. Strand Three. None of the strands yet set in stone. The incredible weave of language. All the little tassels still hanging down' (127).

For all the craftsmanship that Mitchell has poured into this document, however, 'It does not belong to him: it is the property of others' (143). 'Para Bellum' comes closest to the historical record in its description of the Strand Two crisis from Mitchell's perspective: 'When the diplomatic pouch arrives from London on Sunday night—two days late—his heart falls through his chest....He knows the very moment he reads it that it will not work' and yearns, on his own behalf, to 'knock an absolute simplicity into the process. Take it or leave it' (139). This, of course, is not an option, and at the press conference later he suppresses his anger at the prime ministers and takes the blame for the delay, reflecting afterwards that 'What they need are the signatures. After that, they will negotiate the peace. Years of wrangling still to come, he knows. No magic wand. All he wants is to get the metal nibs striking against the page' (140). A vignette of Mitchell watching Blair and Ahern work at four in the morning a few days later underscores his essential outsider status: 'They are stuck now on a point of language. The British and their words. The Irish and their endless meanings. How did such a small sea ever come between them?' (147). Earlier in the chapter, the narrator similarly calls attention to Mitchell's distance from the main action through an image of the independent chairs watching the performance of a play from offstage, both separate from and part of the theatrical event: 'Paisley. Adams. Trimble. McGuinness. Throw a word in their midst and watch them light the fuse. Ahern. Blair. Clinton. Mowlam. Hume. Robinson. Ervine. Major. Kennedy. McMichael. A fine cast. Shakespearean almost. And he sits in the wings, with de Chastelain and Holkeri, waiting for the moment for the cast to bring out their spears. Or not' (112).

McCann's Mitchell does have a role to play in the drama of the peace process, though, one akin to that of the Chorus in classical Greek drama: he represents the people of Northern Ireland as a whole, as distinct from the discrete segments of the population represented by the politicians. In Armstrong's words, *TransAtlantic* conveys 'the sense that Mitchell is not merely a neutral party in the talks, but also understands and represents the will of the Northern Irish people'. More specifically, Mitchell's interactions with fictional women in the novel—including, most notably, the elderly Lottie, who, her daughter Hannah remembers, cried 'happy tears' when 'what she called George Mitchell's peace' was concluded (268)—depict him as a vehicle for their deepest desires. Hannah notes that she herself spent 'a decade in the Women's Coalition' (252), a reminder that the real-life Mitchell worked hard to ensure that NIWC members were treated with the respect they deserved during the negotiations, structuring the final stages of these in such a way that the women were able to make an impact.[86] McCann's Mitchell regrets that he has been more absent than present during his son Andrew's first five months of life: 'How many hours has he sat in the stark chambers listening to men argue about a single comma, or the placement of a period, when all he wanted was to return to the surprise of his very young child?' Disheartened by the 'cramped maleness' that dominates the room, he 'wishes that he could empty the chambers of the men, fill the halls instead with women' (114–15). His last act before embarking on his return transatlantic journey at the end of the chapter is a press conference at which he delivers remarks based on the real Mitchell's press statement announcing the Agreement: 'The ordinary people own it now. We could not have found peace unless the desire for it was already here....No, it doesn't take courage to shoot a policeman in the back of the head. What takes courage is to compete in the arena of democracy....It was not an expectation, no. It was a conviction. Generations of mothers will understand this' (150).[87]

Conclusion

Truth-Seeking

In its management of Northern Ireland's peace process, British Prime Minister Tony Blair's government did not attempt to resolve the political issues that had given rise to the conflict—an approach that would be easy to mock were it not for the fact that it succeeded where countless other efforts had failed.[1] Chief British negotiator Jonathan Powell explained that 'In essence the Good Friday Agreement was an agreement to disagree.' Unionists still wanted Northern Ireland to remain in the United Kingdom; nationalists still sought a united Ireland, but all parties to the negotiations pledged to pursue their aims only through peaceful and democratic means. 'Both sides were surprised to end up with an agreement the other side could sign up for', Powell remembered, but 'neither side had wanted to get the blame for collapsing the process'. A problem that dogged Blair's government throughout the rest of its existence, however, was that 'constructive ambiguity', which had made an agreement possible, became progressively less helpful as time passed.[2]

It took nine years to implement the Agreement fully, with the process foundering repeatedly. Obstacles included the reluctance of some hardliners in the republican movement to commit themselves exclusively to politics through the symbolic act of decommissioning arms, as well as divisions within unionism reflected in the ambivalence or outright hostility of unionist political leaders towards the Agreement's provisions regarding power-sharing, police reform, and the early release of paramilitary prisoners. More than a year and a half elapsed between Good Friday 1998 and the establishment of the power-sharing executive, and the British government suspended the devolved institutions in Northern Ireland more than once after that—shutting them down on one occasion, beginning on 15 October 2002, for more than four and a half years. Blair glossed over this period in his autobiography with the comment that 'I could go through, by chronology, all the tortured and tortuous steps between June 1998 and May 2007, but you can be grateful that I won't.'[3] Those seeking details of the successive rounds of negotiation can consult Powell's memoir or one of the fine journalistic narratives of the peace process.[4] Along the way, politics in Northern Ireland became ever more polarized between extremes in both main ethnonational groups, with Sinn Féin overtaking the Social Democratic and Labour Party (SDLP) as the dominant party on the nationalist side and the Democratic Unionist Party (DUP) displacing

Getting to Good Friday: Literature and the Peace Process in Northern Ireland. Marilynn Richtarik, Oxford University Press.
© Marilynn Richtarik 2023. DOI: 10.1093/oso/9780192886408.003.0007

the Ulster Unionist Party (UUP) as the majority voice of unionism after the Northern Ireland Assembly elections of November 2003. This immediate post-Agreement phase of the peace process would conclude, improbably, with the swearing-in of Ian Paisley and Martin McGuinness as First and Deputy First Ministers of Northern Ireland on 8 May 2007.[5] In the meantime, though, many people both in and outside of Northern Ireland wondered if the Agreement had heralded yet another false dawn, as conflict continued in the realms of culture (evidenced, for example, by persistent disputes over the Irish language and Orange marches) and historical interpretation.

Powell ended his 2008 account of the peace process by expressing his belief that 'before the two sides become truly reconciled they need to find a way to deal with the past': 'The trauma of IRA murders, security-force collusion and loyalist sectarian violence needs to be exorcised' because, otherwise, Northern Ireland's people risk being 'dragged back into the morass from which they are trying to escape'.[6] Because analysing the Troubles could only be controversial, discussions leading up to the Belfast/Good Friday Agreement had mostly avoided the subject, and the Agreement itself contains only oblique references to coping with the con-flict's aftermath. The toughest issues related to the legacy of the violence, includ-ing paramilitary decommissioning and the reform of policing and the criminal justice system, were deferred to the post-Agreement period and, in the cases of decommissioning and policing, delegated to independent commissions. Other efforts to grapple with Northern Ireland's divisive past were led by a variety of state and non-state actors and were frequently contentious. For instance, the 1998 report of a Victims Commission established by the British government empha-sized practical support for victims but drew criticism from nationalists for down-playing specific concerns raised by the families of people killed by state forces. Many of the first victims' groups were predominantly nationalist and demanded formal inquiries into deaths caused by the RUC and the British Army, including cases of suspected collusion between the security forces and loyalist paramilitar-ies; after the Agreement was approved, new victims' groups advocating for the victims of paramilitary (especially republican) violence proliferated in response to the early release of paramilitary prisoners. The British government, responding to public pressure, funded several official investigations, including the Saville Inquiry into the events of Bloody Sunday in Derry and the Stevens and Cory inquiries into allegations of state involvement in paramilitary killings. Attempting to boost public confidence in the reformed police, the Police Service of Northern Ireland launched the Historical Enquiries Team in 2006 to reinvestigate Troubles-related deaths; this was plagued, however, by accusations of inefficiency, incompetence, and partiality. Community initiatives, such as the Ardoyne Commemoration Project, took the lead in oral history and commemoration projects.[7] In a study of memory formation researched mainly between July 1999 and August 2001 and published in 2007, cultural historian Graham Dawson observed that Northern

Irish 'efforts to deal with the recent past in the context of the peace process have tended to be conducted within rather than between the two political communities', so that 'the terrain of the past has remained a battlefield'.[8]

In such a context—especially given the prominence accorded in international news reports to South Africa's post-apartheid Truth and Reconciliation Commission (TRC), which issued the first five volumes of its report in October 1998—it was natural that people should wonder if a formal and comprehensive truth-seeking mechanism might be appropriate for Northern Ireland. Truth commissions had become so common in situations of post-conflict transition over the previous three decades or so that, as sociologists Patricia Lundy and Mark McGovern remarked in a 2008 article, 'the North stands out internationally as a rare instance of contemporary conflict resolution where an overarching truth recovery process has not been part of the move towards peace'.[9] The diverse goals of such bodies have included establishing an authoritative record of past human rights abuses, helping victims to heal, making recommendations for reform, providing accountability, promoting reconciliation, and drawing a line between a troubled past and the present/future.[10]

Despite truth commissions' ubiquity, however, critics have noted the scarcity of empirical evidence that they actually achieve their aims.[11] Because 'truth is not monolithic', legal scholar Erin Daly asserts, 'no commission can realistically expect to produce a single accounting of events' that will command the belief of all, and 'a report is taken as authoritative by those who are predisposed to accepting the truth it tells and by those whose minds are open to change based on new information, but not by those who are committed to a different understanding of past events'. Thus, ironically, 'truth commissions are likely to work the least where they are needed most'. Daly also questions the notion that truth commissions necessarily help victims, given the relatively small numbers who actually get to testify about their experience, the typical lack of psychological support to help ensure that telling their stories does not merely retraumatize them, and the disappointment felt by victims in situations where perpetrators, once identified, are not subsequently prosecuted. 'More often than not', in reality, 'the disclosure of the truth in a commission report or by another means results not in accountability but in impunity'. Daly finds the assumption that truth and reconciliation are 'complementary' to be especially dubious, suggesting that 'at worst, truth may actually impede reconciliation' because 'The evil is often so ghastly that it is unlikely to be mitigated by a greater understanding of the details.'[12]

The question of whether or not Northern Ireland should have a truth commission provoked much debate in the opening years of the new millennium. Following extensive public consultation, the independent cross-community group Healing Through Remembering made recommendations in 2002 on strategies for dealing with the past in Northern Ireland. In addition to advocating for a network of commemoration projects, a Day of Reflection, a collective storytelling process, and a memorial museum, the group suggested that a 'unique truth recovery process' might be appropriate, but only after 'all organizations and institutions that have been engaged in the conflict, including the British and Irish states, the political parties and Loyalist and Republican paramilitaries', had 'honestly and publicly' acknowledged 'responsibility for past political violence due to their acts of omission and commission'.[13] Others argued that 'resolution' regarding the past was a necessary precondition for political progress.[14] In 2003, the Northern Ireland Human Rights Commission expressed the view that 'sooner or later, some sort of mechanism will have to be put in place to deal with the recovery of the truth' about the Troubles but worried that 'the time is not right at the moment' and called for further study of approaches tried elsewhere.[15]

Brandon Hamber, a South African psychologist who had conducted extensive research on post-conflict transition in both South Africa and Northern Ireland, warned against a wholesale adoption of the South African model. The TRC had solicited testimony from victims and their loved ones which created 'an unforgettable record of the atrocities committed', making it impossible for most white South Africans to continue to deny the harm done under the apartheid system. In addition, perpetrators could apply for amnesty conditional on disclosing the full details of their crimes. The South African TRC, Hamber argued, had been 'plagued' from the start by 'the question of whether the TRC was a quasi-legal process of truth recovery and rigorous investigation, or fundamentally a mechanism about the attainment of reconciliation and healing'. In his view, 'By placing amnesty with reconciliation, its bedfellow, at the core of the South African TRC, the real benefits of the truth commission have been sidelined in South Africa, and in much subsequent international debate.' Many of the victims who participated in the South African TRC process were ultimately disappointed because 'Healing...cannot be separated from the social and political process of dealing with the past', including 'justice'.[16]

In May 2004, then Secretary of State for Northern Ireland Paul Murphy visited South Africa to learn more about that country's post-conflict transition. His visit occasioned much commentary, with many worried that the government might adopt a similar amnesty policy for Troubles-related offences, but a senior civil servant reported afterwards that the people they had met doubted that a South African-style truth commission would work in Northern Ireland. Unlike in South Africa, there had been no clear victor there to insist upon a reckoning, and paramilitaries on both sides (not known for leaving a clear paper trail) had been responsible for more killings than the government.[17] The Northern Ireland Affairs Committee of the British Parliament similarly considered legacy issues in 2005. Although various people who made submissions to or testified before the committee raised the possibility of an overall truth-recovery process, and some members expressed interest in the idea, its reports concluded that the 'peace is as yet too fragile, the scars of the conflict too fresh, the co-operation of parts of

Northern Ireland's population is not assured, the political conditions are not yet sufficiently settled, the conflict in the estimation of many people is not yet finally over'. Moreover, assuming that such a thing as an authoritative record of the Troubles could be established, Northern Ireland's divided society was not yet prepared to share an 'official version of historical truth', and 'such an initiative should only be undertaken when there is a realistic possibility that this will happen'.[18]

Public opinion on truth recovery, as on most issues in Northern Ireland, tended to divide along sectarian and political lines. Because it was associated with the first victims' rights groups, truth recovery was distrusted by many unionists and loyalists as reflecting a 'republican agenda' that would interfere with the prosecution of those who had engaged in terrorism and would instead focus criticism on the forces of law and order. Groups like the police that had been directly engaged in the fight against the IRA emphasized their members' 'suffering and sacrifice' and expressed fears that a formal truth-recovery process would only be used to attack them and the government. Nationalists and republicans, on the other hand, generally supported the idea of a formal truth-recovery process, although republicans were realistic enough to understand that their own actions, as well as the state's, would inevitably come under scrutiny.[19]

Conducted between October 2004 and February 2005, a survey of 1,800 adults, chosen randomly to reflect the population of Northern Ireland, included specific questions about attitudes towards a truth commission. Results revealed a high degree of ambivalence. Only 25 per cent of respondents were familiar with the concept of a truth commission, and most of those who were had South Africa's TRC in mind. While 50 per cent felt that a truth commission would be important for Northern Ireland, 65 per cent agreed with the statement that there were better ways to deal with the past than such a commission. Although the largest group of respondents believed that the primary aim for a truth commission should be to get at the truth, more than 80 per cent agreed with the statement that 'you wouldn't necessarily get the truth from a truth commission' and thought there were better uses for public funds. Respondents rejected most candidates to administer such a commission: 92 per cent would not trust the British government to do so, 89 per cent distrusted the Northern Ireland Assembly, and 97 per cent the Irish government. The most support was expressed for an international commission run by an organization like the United Nations, although even this option appealed to only 48 per cent of respondents.[20]

There appeared to be as much anxiety as hope regarding what a Northern Irish truth commission might accomplish, with 45 per cent worrying that it might do 'more damage than good', 48 per cent concerned that it could create 'greater tension', and 42 per cent afraid that it might 'start people fighting again'—although the most commonly expressed fear was that it would be 'a waste of money' (52 per cent). In short, although Northern Irish people were intrigued by the idea of a truth commission, there was no consensus regarding its desirability and there was a severe shortage of the political will that would be required to implement one. At the end of her 2007 book *Truth Recovery and Justice after Conflict*, which includes a detailed and clear-eyed description of the political landscape in Northern Ireland during the opening years of the twenty-first century, Marie Breen Smyth expressed the view that politicians with responsibility for Northern Ireland had a choice between 'a comprehensive, contained and relatively orderly process of managing the truth' or an ongoing 'situation where political and personal life is regularly punctuated by a series of new disclosures about the tragedies of the past'.[21] Essentially, they opted for the latter.

Around 2004, amid public speculation about the possibility of a truth commission for Northern Ireland, David Park embarked on a thought experiment in the form of a novel. Born in 1953 and raised in an evangelical Protestant family in east Belfast, Park had earned a degree in English at Queen's University and accepted a post as a schoolteacher immediately afterwards. He began writing fiction years later out of 'desperation' to engage his adolescent pupils with material that seemed more relevant to their lives than the texts in the prescribed curriculum. They liked his first effort, 'Killing a Brit' (about a boy who witnesses the aftermath of a shooting on his way home from school), so he kept producing short stories, collected in his first book, *Oranges from Spain* (1990).[22] He followed that work with five well-received novels, all published between 1992 and 2004. Despite critical success, however, Park was still teaching full-time, as he had been for the past thirty years, when he began writing the book that would become *The Truth Commissioner* (2008). He worked on his novel at night and during school holidays, with no time to spare for research apart from reading *Country of My Skull*, Afrikaner poet Antjie Krog's memoir, first published in 1998, of her work reporting on South Africa's Truth and Reconciliation Commission for radio.[23] Otherwise, in describing the workings of a fictional Northern Ireland Truth and Reconciliation Commission, Park relied on his imagination and knowledge of current events to produce what fellow novelist Glenn Patterson described at the book's launch in February 2008 as 'a feat of empathy as well as choreography, of novelist's craft allied to an attentive citizen's ear'.[24]

The question that preoccupied Park, along with many others at the time and since, was that of how to 'deal with the past in a way that does not damage or destabilise the future'. He made the 'risky' decision to set his novel in Northern Ireland—a fictional version of it that differed from the actual one only in the cast of characters—in the immediate future. The gamble paid off, as Park's created world proved utterly recognizable to the book's initial readers. Poet Ciaran Carson, in a review for the *Independent*, remarked that 'in Northern Ireland we are great sticklers for authenticity' and 'David Park's account reads true'. Patterson hailed Park's 'bravery' in having the action take place 'no later than the day after tomorrow', courting the danger of its being 'overtaken by—outdated by—events', and marvelled at how much Park had got right, pointing out that, at the time of composition, 'there was no guarantee that the Stormont Executive would ever be up again'.[25]

In *The Truth Commissioner*, Park alludes several times to two events that finally prompted, in July 2005, an unambiguous declaration from the IRA that its war was over, thus making the odd coalition between Sinn Féin and the DUP possible in 2007: one was the attacks on the United States on 11 September 2001, which eliminated any remaining tolerance for terror tactics among Irish republicans' American allies, and the second was the theft, attributed to the IRA, of £26.5 million from the Northern Bank's Belfast headquarters on 20 December 2004, which threatened relations between the Sinn Féin leadership and Tony Blair's administration.[26] In writing *The Truth Commissioner*, Park assumed both restored devolution and the continuity of the British government's policy regarding Northern Ireland. A character attends 'one of the new Prime Minister's first public speeches', noting that 'the mouth delivering the words may have changed but not the hands of the writers' and 'feeling he has overdosed on sugar as he endures the endless references to healing and closure' (49). Reviewing the book for the *Culture Northern Ireland* website, Kiran Acharya observed that 'Park's reminder of the forgotten, the human, is a brave move in the current-day climate of official optimism'.[27]

One of the first decisions Park made about his novel concerned its structure. It would be narrated from the perspectives of four men (a former IRA commander who is now a member of the Northern Ireland Executive, a retired police chief from Northern Ireland, a cosmopolitan English lawyer, and a manual labourer in Florida) who seem utterly distinct in the present but are linked by an event in the past. He knew from the start that these four lives would come together by the end, for better or worse. In keeping with his conception of a book as an essentially 'moral' undertaking, Park thought of his four male protagonists as 'four images of one everyman'.[28] Above all, he wanted them to be fully developed human beings, rather than mere representatives of political positions. For him, the novel was primarily about people, and he got to know them through writing their stories. When he began the work of composition, his notes towards the book, which could probably have fitted on a notecard, consisted almost entirely of characters' names. In the absence of any detailed plan for the novel, the image he kept in mind of his work was of walking through a heavy snowstorm unable to see what lay ahead.[29]

Park made his fictional truth commission an international one, including among its members a South African and a Finn: a nod to the real-life Finnish and South African citizens who advanced the peace process in Northern Ireland by chairing negotiations, helping the British and Irish governments find creative ways of handling the decommissioning issue, and advising British officials and members of the parties' negotiating teams (because each commissioner hears cases separately, readers see only the British member in action). The body aims 'to give a voice to the victims of the violence, to remember those who have died or suffered and to try to help those who grieve to take the difficult and painful steps towards healing', as well as 'to try to initiate a process of [societal] healing through the establishment of truth and openness'. It can compel people to testify about their involvement in past human rights abuses, and it offers amnesty in exchange for 'a full and truthful account of the incident' in question (317). Witnesses called before the commission are entitled to legal representation and other support, but the commission is not a court of law: 'People have to admit their own guilt, put the truth in their own words', and they do not have 'the normal protection of the law to fall back on' (313). Naturally, all parties to the conflict are eager to ensure that 'their' people appear in the best light while others are discredited, and they go to great lengths, convincingly dramatized by Park, to coach witnesses. The novel's portrayal of a Northern Irish truth commission reflects Park's suspicion that a formal truth-recovery process in Northern Ireland would be less likely to result in 'truth and reconciliation' than in 'truth and recrimination'.[30]

Park's fictional TRC holds its hearings in a Belfast city-centre building that was 'formerly Church property'.[31] The stained-glass windows remain because they were 'protected by a preservation order', but everything else has been 'neutralised': the ceiling and walls are 'painted in creams and whites', 'specially commissioned desks and chairs are made from a light-coloured ash', and 'there's a new sound system and facilities for translation into Irish and Ulster Scots if required' (28)—a sly allusion to the language question, with its perennial, and largely symbolic, arguments about 'culture' in the overwhelmingly English-speaking North of Ireland. The commission also has a state-of-the-art storage facility in the refurbished drawing office of the shipyard where Park's grandfather, a riveter, had worked on *Titanic*.[32] The pristine, ultra-modern surroundings contrast starkly with the records they house, case files that 'wear the marks of their age and use and are badged with grubbiness', a physical manifestation of the sordid past the commissioners are somehow supposed to 'shape…into meaning' (23–4).

The case readers follow in *The Truth Commissioner*—that of a fifteen-year-old police informant named Connor Walshe who was kidnapped, killed, and secretly buried by the IRA—shows nobody involved in a positive light. Critic Stefanie Lehner explains that such victims in Northern Ireland, known as 'the Disappeared', were usually murdered 'as part of the IRA's internal "policing" system'. These victims were often suspected of treachery, so stigma, shame, and fear afflicted their families, manifested in 'the silencing that has taken place in the aftermath of their disappearance'. There are fewer than twenty known cases: a small number with an outsized psychological impact because the uncertainty about a disappeared person's fate is itself a torture for those left behind. Lehner writes, 'As "absent presences," these figures have haunted the peace process: their legacy remains one of the most emotive and unsettling of the many issues…unresolved from the conflict'.[33]

The Truth Commissioner opens with a short chapter that functions like the first scene of a television mystery, in which viewers are given direct access to the facts of a case without the context needed to make sense of them. The perspective belongs to an adolescent petty thief, whom readers will later recognize as Connor. Like the rest of the novel, this section is narrated in the third person limited and in the present tense, giving the action a vivid immediacy. The first sentence, 'He's never been anywhere he's never been', establishes the boy's lack of experience and knowledge of the world. Despite the limits of his life, though, 'all he really wants' is 'to be someone' (1). When his captors take him to a house in the country to question him more and more aggressively, he lies about his activities because he knows instinctively that they will not accept 'the truth that he did it because just for a while it made him someone' (4).

Connor swears that he 'never did it for the money':

> Sometimes he thinks he never did anything for the money. Even the breaking into houses, even the thieving. Not really for the money. There was something he liked about being in other people's houses, about stepping into someone else's world, touching their things, seeing what they had, how they lived. Sometimes taking things was only his way of justifying to himself what he was doing and the risks he was running. (5)

In this self-reflexive passage, Park signals his approach to truth-seeking, rooted in the effort to understand, and to help readers understand, who his protagonists are as people and what has brought each one to the point at which he enters the action. Throughout the novel, Park finds points of contact between his characters and himself, understanding that he is not 'the judge' of them.[34] Here, at the outset, he reveals the impulses motivating a juvenile delinquent and a novelist to be startlingly similar. In the eight chapters that follow, he inserts readers into the metaphorical 'houses' of the four men whose lives will intersect in the book, allowing them to view the world through each one's eyes in turn on two separate occasions before merging the narrative strands in a chapter describing the TRC hearing on the Connor Walshe case.

In writing the novel, Park found himself fascinated by the character most different from himself in politics and temperament: Francis Gilroy, the former IRA commander recently appointed Minister with responsibility for Children and Culture in the Northern Ireland Executive. Initially, Park felt 'a slight temptation to do a hatchet job on him', but the character 'grew into this complexity of fidelity to a political faith' and ended up being, in Park's opinion, 'the most fully formed in terms of his inner life'.[35] Gilroy bears a more than passing resemblance to Martin McGuinness, one-time IRA chief of staff, who served as education minister in the first power-sharing executive established after the Good Friday Agreement, performing the role 'with every sign of having found his true mission in life'.[36]

Although Park denied that any of the characters in the novel were based on real people, he admired McGuinness for the kind of 'statesmanship' displayed all too rarely by Northern Ireland's politicians. Journalist Fionnuala O Connor noted in 2002 that republicans before the Good Friday Agreement would have denounced the Northern Ireland Assembly as a 'partitionist' body with no 'legitimacy', so their taking positions in the new government was regarded by the British, Irish, and US governments as a significant concession, but 'the essence of modern republicanism' was 'to move away from tradition with a smile, as though this was triumph not compromise, much less failure'. Sinn Féin members were so good at projecting assurance and pleasure at their new part in the administration of Northern Ireland that many unionists were persuaded that they themselves had been the losers in the April 1998 accord. Nonetheless, republican politicians like McGuinness, who had reframed participation in Northern Ireland's institutions as a new phase of the struggle that would result, eventually, in a united Ireland, were uncomfortably aware that, from the point of view of dissident republicans like Bernadette Sands McKevitt (spokesperson for the 32-County Sovereignty Committee and sister of the late hunger-striker Bobby Sands), the Agreement had offered only a 'modernised version of partition', and the consent principle, according to which the constitutional status of Northern Ireland would not change until the majority of its citizens voted to change it, amounted to nothing more than 'a unionist veto, dressed up in another way'.[37]

In an early review of *The Truth Commissioner*, novelist Joseph O'Connor pointed out that the surname Gilroy means 'servant of the king', an authorial choice that focuses attention on the contradictions in contemporary Irish republicanism.[38] Because readers form their impressions of Gilroy from his thoughts, emotions, and perceptions, the tensions inherent in his position are much clearer than they would be if he were encountered solely through his public persona. On the one hand, he understands and appreciates 'how far they have come and the magnitude of what has been achieved', and he feels pride in these accomplishments: 'Pride for himself, the son of a sign-painter, pride for his people—the second-class citizens—who now through him sit at the very top table.' On the other hand, everything about the Stormont Parliament seems 'designed to make you feel small', from the 'aggressive defiance' of Edward Carson's statue in front of the building, 'with his outstretched arm which always makes Gilroy think the Unionist icon is giving him the finger', to 'the sparkling white urinals that you can't use without having to think of the people who have stood in the same place' (88–9, 94). Sometimes he finds himself wondering 'what it has been all about':

> For the people? For Ireland? It is a strange thought but several times during the last few months he has been afflicted by the idea that Ireland does not exist. Like God it's just perhaps some concept that has no meaning apart from the one you construct in your head. He feels the shame of his thoughts, the traitorous

serpent of doubt snaking through his lifetime of commitment, trying to under-
mine all that he has achieved.   (82)

For Gilroy, the pain of such heretical musings is compounded by his inability to
share them with anyone.

Given his education and culture portfolio, Gilroy feels self-conscious about the
fact that he left school at 16. He reads poetry secretly, trying 'to crack it', because
he views his ignorance as a personal weakness and is 'determined to do something about it', although he hesitates to ask for help for fear of revealing his inse-
curity (73). This quandary highlights Gilroy's isolation at Stormont. The hostility
of most other politicians in the Assembly and Executive largely goes unremarked.
He is, however, acutely conscious of the scrutiny to which he is subjected by
punctilious civil servants, including those attached to his own department. He
works hard at his job, striving to discharge his duties to a professional standard and
understanding that he needs the civil servants' 'knowledge about legal issues, about
how best to frame the legislation and shape it into a coherent whole, because if there
is a flaw or a single weak spot they can be sure that the wolves in the Assembly will
fasten their teeth on it and tear and tear until it collapses in ridicule' (72). This kind
of labour, though, runs against the grain of his personality and experience, and he
contemplates a typical workday without enthusiasm: 'Meeting after meeting, a
torrent of talk channelled through the rigid sides of procedures and agendas. Why
is it not possible any more to just sit down and have a talk, sort things out over a
slow drink?' (79). Sometimes, 'the only people in the room he recognises as people
are the women who serve the tea'. He longs to connect with them on the basis of
shared working-class identity, but 'because they come from the Protestant estates
up the road, he knows they probably still think of him as the Antichrist' (80).

Like their real-life Sinn Féin counterparts, Gilroy and his right-hand man, Ricky
Sweeney, are obsessed with security. Gilroy is always aware of 'the permanent
possibility of a hit' by 'some maverick', 'one of the dissidents', or 'some unknown
relative of a forgotten victim who has never forgotten' (69). He and Sweeney survived the conflict together, including countless 'nights on the run' and time spent
in prison, and they maintain 'the enforced habits of a lifetime's struggle' (79, 69).
The 'youngsters', however, do not understand 'the need for vigilance, the constant
need for caution' (68). Gilroy worries that his driver does not keep a careful
enough watch on the car when they are not in it, reminds him to make sure that
nobody is following them, and has a panic attack when the young chauffeur
heedlessly enters the drive-through of a McDonald's.[39] Sweeney manages Gilroy's
schedule with a handwritten diary and a tape recorder, avoiding computers as a
matter of principle because they can be hacked into. They regularly check Gilroy's
Stormont offices for listening devices, avoid using the phones for anything
'important', and talk at Clonard Monastery (an important site throughout the
peace process for secret meetings involving republicans) when the subject is especially sensitive (89–90, 268).

These seemingly paranoid precautions have a perfectly rational basis, as *The Truth Commissioner*'s original Northern Irish readers knew. Journalist Patrick Radden Keefe explains that 'the IRA was, in actual fact, hopelessly penetrated by double agents'. In May 2003, the identity of one of the British Army's highest-ranking paid informants became public: a man named Freddie Scappaticci, who headed an IRA unit called the Nutting Squad—charged, ironically, with the identification and punishment of spies. Even after the IRA adopted a cellular structure in the late 1970s, Keefe writes, its 'security unit was like a junction box for the whole organization, and for most of the Troubles, the British had a man placed right inside it'. Scappaticci worked for the British for twenty-five years and was personally linked to as many as fifty murders, most of fellow IRA members suspected of treason.[40]

Scappaticci was hardly the only highly placed agent the British had in the republican movement. A major factor behind the suspension of Northern Ireland's devolved institutions in October 2002 had been a police investigation into allegations of Sinn Féin spying that uncovered sensitive government documents on computers in the party's Stormont offices. In December 2005, however, the Public Prosecution Service abruptly announced that it was dropping charges against the three men arrested in connection with the spy ring, 'in the public interest'. One of them, Denis Donaldson, was an ex-IRA leader who had worked as Sinn Féin's head of administration at Stormont. A week later, Sinn Féin President Gerry Adams announced that Donaldson had admitted to being a paid informer for the security forces over the previous two decades. Following the exposure of his dual role, Donaldson retired to the Donegal countryside, where, unsurprisingly, he was found dead a few months later.[41] When, in *The Truth Commissioner*, Sweeney prepares Gilroy for the news that Connor Walshe's case will soon come before the Truth Commission, Gilroy jokes, 'Hell's bells, Ricky, you're not about to tell me you've been working for the Brits for the last twenty years?' Sweeney answers, 'No, I'm probably the only one who hasn't been' (269).

Park understood that it was exceedingly hard for republicans to renounce the armed struggle—so many of them had sacrificed so much to it that they needed to believe it had served a purpose.[42] Gilroy's conscious feelings of guilt regarding his activities during the Troubles centre on the effect his paramilitary involvement had on his family. Now that he has become a mainstream politician, he regrets the 'years which he should have spent with his children', the period of his life when he could not 'take his family downtown or anywhere public' (82). Gilroy must strive to accept his only daughter's engagement to a cricket-playing English advertising executive. When he learns on her wedding day that she is pregnant, he blames himself 'for not having looked after her properly, for not being there for her', despite his wife's assurances that their daughter *wants* to get married (110). Giving her away at the church, he recognizes that 'he was never the provider of safety but rather the person who put her at risk, the father who always put her needs second to what he saw as the bigger needs of the cause' and 'silently promises himself that he will atone for the past through the love and time he will give to her child' (115). After the ceremony, he makes an affirmative speech, suggesting that 'We are building a new future for our children and perhaps this marriage which spans two nations is a symbol of this new understanding' (122). In the weeks that follow, however, he feels drained. In 'every soundbite for the radio or television', he talks about the future, but 'increasingly he wants to lie down in the comfort of the past': a past 'shaped and nurtured by his imagination', in which 'he's a family man with all his children safely round him' (261). Gilroy's regrets about his parental failings, like his anxiety about his ministerial responsibilities, remain private, however. In public, he projects optimism and confidence.

While Gilroy's star has been rising as he becomes part of the new Northern Ireland establishment, that of former police chief constable James Fenton has been falling. If the ex-IRA leader turned government minister was an emblematic figure in post-conflict Northern Ireland, so, too, was the alienated ex-police officer. The Royal Ulster Constabulary, or RUC, had never been an ordinary British police force. Established to enforce partition in 1922, it had a paramilitary character, had always been large in relation to Northern Ireland's population, and was overwhelmingly associated with one side of its divided society. Nationalists had historically hesitated to join the RUC because they feared harassment and ostracism from their own community if they did so and because they opposed the state the police defended. From the mid-1970s on, the British government had pursued a policy of 'police primacy', in which the RUC led the fight against the IRA. This made policemen prime targets for republican paramilitaries, which also had a negative effect on relations between the RUC and nationalists. By the 1990s, Catholics made up only 8 per cent of the force, which was widely perceived as being biased against them. Unionists had long sought the devolution of policing to Northern Ireland, but nationalists and republicans would never agree to this without thorough police reform. The negotiators of the Belfast/Good Friday Agreement deliberately deferred this incendiary issue, stipulating that an independent commission would be established to make proposals aimed at ensuring that 'policing arrangements, including composition, recruitment, training, culture, ethos and symbols, are such that...Northern Ireland has a police service that can enjoy widespread support from, and is seen as an integral part of, the community as a whole'.[43]

The Independent Commission on Policing, headed by Chris Patten, a Conservative politician who had served as a junior minister in the Northern Ireland Office in the 1980s and as the last British Governor of Hong Kong from 1992 to 1997, delivered its report in September 1999. Patten had told Jonathan Powell earlier that year that 'he aimed to achieve balance between the two sides by changing the name and symbols of the RUC while making sure that enough remained of the old force to prevent republicans claiming it had been abolished'. The commission's report pointed to the fact that nationalists associated the police 'with unionism and the British state' as the 'main problem' for policing in Northern Ireland, recommending 'that the police be made representative, nationally-impartial, accountable, decentralised and demilitarised', to the extent allowed by the security situation. It called for 'a focus on human rights at the heart of policing and for the police to behave as a "service" working with the community rather than a "force" policing it', for measures to increase recruitment of Catholics, and for a downsizing of the police 'from 11,400 to 7,500 full-time officers, through attrition and generous early retirement packages'. The Patten Commission further proposed 'that the name and symbols of the police be freed from "any association with either the British or Irish states"' and replaced with neutral ones.[44] The British government ultimately accepted most of the commission's advice. Powell deemed the recommendations ('for a smaller, more modern, more accountable police force, with some changes to the symbols, but with an emphasis on the fact that the RUC was not being disbanded') to be 'very sensible'; as often before, however, Blair's team 'failed to reckon with the curious nature of Northern Ireland politics where symbols can be more important than substance'.[45]

The immediate, and outraged, unionist reaction to the report took Patten by surprise—he had expected the backlash to come from republicans, but they (taking their cue from the unionist anger) joined the SDLP in endorsing the Patten Commission's proposals. The vehement unionist response to these, political scientist John McGarry comments, merely 'confirmed the Commission's analysis that the central problem was that Unionists regarded the RUC as "their" police'. Over the more than three decades since the late-twentieth-century Troubles began, a significant percentage of Northern Ireland's unionist population had served in the RUC, and, as journalist Dean Godson notes, all of them 'had friends and relations in a very tight-knit community'. In 2004, then UUP leader David Trimble observed that the 'substance' of the Patten Commission's report largely conformed with the RUC's own plan for how to 'take an anti-terrorist force back to being a normal police force again'. He criticized, however, its 'complete and deliberate insensitivity' in failing 'to acknowledge the achievements and sacrifice of the RUC', admitting that many of his own electoral difficulties after 1999 stemmed from the Patten Commission's blueprint for police reform and 'the hurt in the policing family': 'The leadership of the police and the Police Federation, and ostensibly the senior officers, acquiesced. But...they felt bad about it, and especially those who took early retirement, they and their families felt bitter about it'. 'On the doorsteps', he recalls, UUP campaigners 'were getting more hassle over policing than over Sinn Féin'.[46]

The Police Service of Northern Ireland (PSNI) officially replaced the RUC in November 2001, although, as Trimble pointed out, the police remained largely 'the same men wearing much the same uniform enforcing exactly the same law'.[47] The change did, however, entail significant depletion of the upper ranks, and Park's character James Fenton lost his position as RUC Chief Constable because of this reorganization. Fenton resents his early expulsion from the pinnacle of his career and takes offence at the notion that wholesale reform was necessary: 'Like all his generation he has accepted the pension and the pay-off deals that were too generous to be refused, even though it stuck in his throat to have to acknowledge that he was considered part of the corporate embarrassment, part of a past that had to be quietly replaced' (127). At low moments, Fenton feels 'dirty' and

> knows the job's to blame, tells himself that it's not possible to spend over thirty years rubbing up against dirt and not be stained by it.... He has witnessed it over the years in his colleagues, the experiences that gradually coarsen and degrade.... He tries to show through his life rather than his words that they need a higher code to live by, otherwise things get blurred, harder to know where the difference is between right and wrong. He knows, too, for some, that difference has so shrunk that it's hardly visible any more, replaced by what they can get away with and what they can't.   (143)

Sometimes Fenton even wonders if the British government might have been 'right after all' in assuming that 'too many of them were too damaged to be part of a future supposed to be cleaner.' Reluctant to include himself as a member of this group, however, he calls on wrath as a defence against his feeling of having been dishonoured: 'No longer to be called a force but a service as if they hadn't served before and as he thinks of it he can't assuage the familiar anger, the sense of his own shame at taking the money and walking away cap in hand' (143). Anger, indeed, has become the dominant emotion of this proud, consciously upright man.

Fenton keeps himself busy in retirement through his church, taking on volunteer work and fundraising for a Romanian orphanage—a place that, like Northern Ireland, is transitioning from a horror-filled past to what will, he hopes, be a better future. He has also taken up hill-walking and finds the mountains 'purer than anything he's ever known' (124). The way Fenton thinks about them reflects his aspiration for himself: 'there is honesty in the mountains—they have no pretensions to prettiness but only a rugged bleakness and he likes their disdainful indifference to who, or what, he is' (124). Despite his 'active days', though, 'it feels as if nothing has been shed, that nothing has left him'. Fenton's past is still 'there in his dreams, in the snatches of conversation that replay constantly in his head as if on a loop, in the sudden sour taste in his mouth', 'all of which seem able to clutch his consciousness at will and squeeze out the life of the present and deaden any vision of the future' (127).

Like Gilroy, Fenton remains hyper-alert and security-conscious, haunted by all the occasions on which he has felt fear: 'Stepping into the bar after it was sprayed. Hearing the news coming in that a colleague has been shot. Sometimes just turning on the ignition of the car. Afterwards when he told himself that he was alive, that it was someone else who hadn't survived, it brought no sense of relief but only a sense of fragility, of things hanging by a thread. The randomness of fate' (163).

Gilroy and Fenton have much in common, although this fact would probably not be evident to either of them. Both, for example, have been happily married for thirty-five years. Whereas Gilroy has four adult children, though, Fenton and his wife are childless, and at times 'he blames the absence of children in his marriage' for his inability 'to move on' (127). (In a political context in which demographics are regarded as destiny, Park may be commenting obliquely on the long-term prospects of republicanism and unionism.) Fenton also relates his sense of incompleteness to his sacrifices as a police officer. He and his wife had to leave their first house at a day's notice when their address fell into 'the wrong hands': 'That was the first and only time she asked him to find a different job', and, years later, 'she let it slip to him that she thought that if they had stayed in that first home they would have had a baby' (285). Fenton originally got involved with the orphanage in the hope of adopting one of the children, but now 'even that dream is undermined' because they are too old to be considered even if international adoptions by non-relatives were still allowed (155).

Fenton and Gilroy share more than family values. They both jealously regard younger people who, in Gilroy's eyes, resemble 'a bunch of vultures waiting for the first sign of weakness', having done nothing 'in the struggle' to dirty their hands because they were 'busy getting their university education and all their fancy degrees' (96). Fenton trains his envy on Alec, the one-time colleague 'who has now acquired his former post on a fraction of the experience', ambitious and fortunate 'to be in the right place at the right time, the perfect candidate with a good degree, youth and…no baggage' (126, 129). Both Fenton and Gilroy also disapprove of the Truth and Reconciliation Commission and seek to avoid testifying before it. For Gilroy, the commission was 'a bloody stupid idea' that republicans agreed to only 'Because we sang so loud about having the truth on everything they ever did that we stumbled blindly into the net and then it was too late to get ourselves out when they turned round and asked for our truth' (97). Upon being told that Connor's relatives want to learn about 'the circumstances surrounding his disappearance', Fenton retorts that everyone knows the IRA shot him as 'a tout' and disposed of his body. When Alec informs him that 'important people', presumably British secret service operatives, want Gilroy 'kept out of the frame' to protect 'the institutions', Fenton explodes in anger: 'They took the badge, they took the name, any kind of respect that was owed, and now they want to take the truth and twist it into whatever shape they think suits them best?' (133–4).

Fenton recruited Connor as an informant (a risky occupation for anyone) and Gilroy commanded the IRA unit that abducted him, but neither man feels personally responsible for Connor's murder. Fenton believes that Gilroy is to blame: 'He may not be the one who pulled the trigger but he was the one who gave the order, the one who arranged it' (134). Gilroy alone knows that Connor was never supposed to die. The intention was for the boy to be questioned and to record a confession, then to explain at a press conference how he was paid to spy for the police. Rafferty, a senior man from 'the border brigade' whose younger brother had been killed six months earlier, defied 'Belfast orders' by beating Connor, rendering him unfit to present to journalists, and then, when he tried to escape, shot him (341–3).

Although neither Gilroy nor Fenton thinks he has done anything wrong, the narrative hints that both may subconsciously labour under a burden of guilt. Gilroy 'no longer fully trusts' his body (79), feels exhausted, and worries that he might be 'in the first stages of some serious illness' (111). Fenton seeks peace in solitude but, after learning that the Connor Walshe case will be coming before the Truth Commission, repeatedly flashes back to his interactions with the boy. Even before his conversation with Alec about the case, Fenton's habit of hiking alone betrays an uncharacteristic carelessness about his own safety that may reflect his negative judgement on his life.

The previous Boxing Day, Fenton had slipped and fallen on an icy patch of rock near a mountain stream, landing flat on his back and hitting his head against the stone but somehow escaping major injury. After the shock of the impact passed, 'he had lain there, curiously calm, and into his mind had come an image that would repeat itself many times in the future' of 'him drifting into unconsciousness and then slowly slipping from the polished slab into the narrow rush of water where he is carried and cribbed by the stone sides of the grey granite until his body is borne to the sea. Then and now, there's no fear in the image but only a sense of calm, an acceptance of his inability to resist or stop the flow' (125–6). If Fenton did not, at that point, actively seek death, he also did not seem to find the prospect of it unwelcome, and his frequent recollection of this incident says a great deal about his general state of mind. Each of the four protagonists in *The Truth Commissioner* dwells lovingly on water, and Park attributes this imagery to his Baptist upbringing and water's religious association with cleansing and purifying.[48]

The protagonist who feels guiltiest about what happened to Connor is arguably the least culpable. Michael Madden, who goes by the name of Danny in Florida, was only a few years older than Connor when he joined the IRA after loyalists set fire to his family's home. As a low-ranking volunteer, he mostly ran errands until the night he helped lure Connor into the trap set for him. He prepared food for the men interrogating the boy at the safe house, sat guard over him for a while, and was among those pursuing him after he squeezed through a window and fled. Traumatized by the night's events, Madden left Northern Ireland soon afterwards and has been living illegally in the US ever since. Throughout 'Danny's' introductory chapter, readers know nothing about any of this because he strives to banish all traces of the past from his present life, even from his thoughts, 'telling himself that the longer things endure, the less chance there is of everything he now thinks [of] as his being snatched away from him' (181). For him, truth lies in the future, where he promises always to be a good father to the baby that he and his partner, Ramona, are expecting, although recent conversations about wedding planning are raising awkward questions about his family back in Belfast.

All Madden has ever wanted is to feel 'safe', and he believes that living 'in the moment' will carry him through (230, 208); he comes to realize the limitations of this approach when a member of the IRA's Army Council tracks him down to deliver a summons to appear before the Northern Ireland Truth and Reconciliation Commission. To shield Gilroy, the republican leadership has designated Madden as the one who will take the blame for killing Connor. If Madden makes this 'ritual' appearance, he will be supported by the movement; if he fails to do so, republicans will use their connections in the US government to ensure his deportation (237–8). Madden complies because he has no choice, but in Ramona's eyes he becomes 'another man who's lied to her and abused her love'. She disappears the day after he reveals his true identity, and he does not even know where to begin looking for her because 'he knows almost as little about her past life as she knew about his': 'He didn't need or want to hear beyond what she chose to reveal because always he wanted them to live only in a shared future' (291). Of the three protagonists involved in Connor's death, only Madden thinks sympathetically about the boy's family members and how long they have waited to learn what happened to him; he is also the only one to believe there might be 'a release in truth' (240).

The fourth protagonist, British Truth Commissioner Henry Stanfield, seems designed to cast doubt on the British government's claims to be 'a neutral facilitator' of the peace process.[49] Ironically, he displays less integrity in his personal and professional life than any of the perpetrators presented in the novel. Unlike Gilroy, Fenton, and Madden—all committed monogamists—Stanfield cheated repeatedly on his late wife and has been estranged from his adult daughter, Emma, since her mother died five years ago. He accepted the position of Truth Commissioner for its generous salary and the prospect of writing a book about the experience, and he refuses to admit, even to himself, that Emma's residence in Northern Ireland influenced his decision. The most educated and cultured of the four protagonists, Stanfield nonetheless specializes in self-delusion, trying to convince himself that his many affairs are prompted by love and that he has 'no personal or political baggage' in connection with Northern Ireland, 'despite spending the first twelve years of his life in a leafy suburb in Belfast' with an English Protestant father and an Irish Catholic mother (33, 19).

Stanfield, who thinks that 'truth rarely makes anything better and often makes it worse' (66), approaches his job in a wholly cynical fashion. He regards the Troubles as a 'pathetic and primitive tribal war', and his image for the truth and reconciliation process is that of 'an old manged, flea-infested dog returning to inspect its own sick' (25). Stanfield almost pities his idealistic young staff, who believe they are playing 'an important part in constructing the way out of the morass, in building a new bridge to healing and forgiveness', and he wonders how they would feel 'if he were to tell them now that it's all been for the optics, that what will happen and how it will happen has already been agreed, mapped out, and the fixity of the main boundaries established like every continent after every war' (17). Shadowy British securocrats resort to both bribes and threats to persuade him to prioritize the stability of Northern Ireland's institutions in his work, but neither of these tactics is strictly necessary because Stanfield has a firm grasp of his intended role from the start. Emma has asked him to do everything he can to help Connor's sister, who works with her, but Stanfield never has any intention of summoning Francis Gilroy to testify, as the Walshe family has requested.

Notwithstanding Stanfield's modest expectations of the Truth and Reconciliation Commission, things go 'more badly than he could ever have anticipated', with two violent attacks and 'regular examples of verbal abuse and threats shouted with an intensity that he's never heard before' (245–6). There are occasional high points, some stories that 'take on the mysterious power to…touch the quick of everyone who hears them', even moments when antagonists are driven 'briefly towards each other like Priam kneeling to kiss Achilles's hand' (247). Such moments, though, are rare and exceptional. For the most part, Stanfield

> has presided over some truth but little reconciliation and as each day goes by it becomes increasingly obvious that what the plaintiffs want is truth and the justice that they feel they've been denied.…Instead they get some formulaic, pre-learned response that expresses a vague regret for the pain caused and then presents the get-out-of-jail card that avoids personal guilt or moral culpability by stating that they believed they were fighting in a war. When it's all over, Stanfield sees, too, the void opening up inside the bereaved, when they understand that this is all they are to be given and they realise it's not enough.   (246)

Within weeks of taking up his position, he is making plans to resign 'before the whole gimcrack edifice tumbles like a house of cards' (244).

Most of what readers witness of the TRC's workings confirms Stanfield's jaded view of it. Park presents the commission as a forum for political theatre intended to deliver the illusion of truth without its messy repercussions. Having introduced the four main characters in separate chapters, Park allots each one a second chapter before, in the climactic chapter depicting the hearing on Connor's disappearance, combining all their perspectives: moving from one point of view to another from section to section, paragraph to paragraph, and eventually even within paragraphs. As the novel enacts the communal drama of the TRC, Park's diction and imagery underscore the performative nature of the proceedings. Stanfield, who has given up on repairing his relationship with Emma and intends to post his resignation letter as soon as the hearing is over, braces himself for what is to come with the thought that, one last time, 'he has to become a ringmaster in a three-ring circus and this is the day when he must perform better than any other day' (309). As the hearing gets underway, he hopes that, in this case, 'everything will go according to the script' (316). Fenton 'just wants to say his piece and be gone, let those who took the boy face the spotlight and acknowledge their guilt' (312); on the way to the hearing, his Police Federation adviser and legal representative coach him on how to walk from the car to the hearing room and on the advisability of sticking to 'the agreed outline' (312–13). Madden, awaiting his turn to testify, contends with stage fright as he 'rehearses his words in his head, the words he's been given, and tries to calm himself, to bring his focus exclusively on what it is he has to say' (323).

The carefully produced illusion of full disclosure is dramatically ruptured by two intrusions of real life on the action. In the first, the Walshe family's advocate plays Connor's tape-recorded confession of his spying activities, thus exposing as a lie of omission Fenton's failure to mention the times he paid the boy for what paltry information he could provide. In the second plot twist, Madden, seized by 'a sudden spin of anger' (336) at the way he has been treated by the IRA in both the past and the present, rejects his assigned story, in which Connor is shot accidentally while tussling with himself. Instead, he tells the truth as he understands it, naming Francis Gilroy as Connor's killer. Thus, according to critic Matt McGuire, '*The Truth Commissioner* actively disrupts the republican/loyalist standoff...whereby a Northern Irish truth commission is regarded as either a panacea for all ills or yet another concession to a group of unrepentant...murderers'.[50]

Ironically, however, both these apparent incursions of inconvenient truth into the TRC's workings are false. In his statement to his captors, Connor admits that he spied for the police but also lies about RUC threats to his family that he claims forced him to do so. Madden, having heard the shot that killed Connor but not seen it, does not actually know what happened. When he arrived on the scene, he saw 'the two senior men' (339) standing over Connor's body, with Gilroy holding the gun, but he does not realize that Gilroy had just taken it from Rafferty (343). If the main purpose of a truth commission is to determine the facts about what happened in the past, then, as McGuire observes, Park's novel 'encourages us to lower our expectations about what a Northern Irish truth commission might achieve, should one ever be realized'.[51]

While allowing that Park's fictional truth commission 'becomes a theatre of self-interest rather than a space of reconciliation', critic Lisa Propst takes a more optimistic view of such a body's potential in Northern Ireland to 'create the groundwork for societal change by driving people to question their previous frameworks for understanding themselves and others, even if those questions are never articulated within the spaces of the commission or in any verbal form'. Although both Fenton and Gilroy 'refuse any public acknowledgment of the harms they have done', Propst argues that 'they come to question their previous assumptions about how they fit into the violence of the Troubles and what they owe to whom'. The former 'begins to recognize that he stood *in loco parentis* to the adolescent Connor, not through any legal obligation but simply by virtue of the boy's vulnerability and need'. The latter, attending a cross-community performance by schoolchildren while Connor's hearing takes place, 'replays Connor's death in his mind in a stream of consciousness where...pronouns replace proper names', and Propst asserts that 'The ambiguity in Gilroy's account...implies that even if he did not fire the shot that killed the boy, he recognizes his complicity'.[52]

Although such mental adjustments have value, they are achieved in *The Truth Commissioner* at a cost that many readers will find excessive. As journalist Malachi O'Doherty commented in a review of the novel, Park 'creates characters that we care about and...ruthlessly puts them into the worst circumstances they could imagine for themselves'. After Connor's hearing, the protagonists disperse, and each has a final chapter devoted to him. Park leaves all these (like every other chapter in the novel) open-ended, enabling readers to imagine the characters' future. Any realistic denouement, though, would probably be more negative than positive. In what he described as a 'moment of weakness', Park allowed Madden to retrieve his passport from the safe house and head for the airport, but, as critic Shameem Black points out, he is likely condemned to 'endless global exile'.[53] Gilroy, at the very least, will lose his ministerial post, and Northern Ireland will be deprived of a talented and dedicated politician. Fenton, his anger over the way he has been pushed aside replaced with shame, points his own gun to his head following the hearing; the fact that he does not pull the trigger within the confines of the novel does not mean that he will not soon find some less obvious way to end his life.[54] Even Stanfield, who is 'rewarded for the service he didn't give' (367) when Emma allows him to hold his newborn grandson, will be thereby compelled to spend most of the next two years completing his truth commissioner term in Northern Ireland, a prospect that just hours earlier he had regarded as 'a slow death' (360).

If the aim of truth-seeking is to encourage private reassessment of what one thinks one knows, then a novel can achieve that goal more effectively than a public hearing. Northern Ireland may never have a truth commission, but it does have *The Truth Commissioner*, a fiction that, in Glenn Patterson's words, 'deals as eloquently and movingly with the past in its 372 pages as any government instituted body could in many, many millions more'. Novelist Joseph O'Neill remarked in his review of the book that 'the novel can itself be a kind of truth commission'. This metaphor makes each individual reader into a truth commissioner. Park's protagonists co-exist in the same space but inhabit separate worlds. The novel constructs a collective narrative, in which readers can observe what the four men have in common, although these characters cannot see themselves in each other.

In the end, Park commented, the only 'truth' the novel espouses is that the protagonists share a 'flawed humanity' worthy of compassion.[55]

South Africa's Truth and Reconciliation Commission explicitly acknowledged that 'truth', especially in a divided society, is a complex concept. Its report identified four distinct 'notions of truth' informing its work: 'factual or forensic truth', 'personal or narrative truth', 'social or "dialogue" truth', and 'healing and restorative truth'. Factual truth uses 'corroborated evidence' and 'accurate information' to answer questions such as 'what happened to whom, where, when and how, and who was involved?' Personal truth admits a subjective element, and the TRC had tried 'to contribute to the process of reconciliation by ensuring that the truth about the past included the validation of the individual subjective experiences of people who had previously been silenced or voiceless' and had aimed 'to capture the widest possible record of people's perceptions, stories, myths and experiences'. Social truth, in contrast to personal truth's individual emphasis, is 'established through interaction, discussion and debate'; in pursuing this kind of 'dialogue' truth, the TRC sought 'to transcend the divisions of the past by listening carefully to the complex motives and perspectives of all those involved'. Healing truth, finally, moves beyond a binary notion of truth as either objective or subjective to posit 'the kind of truth that places facts and what they mean within the context of human relationships'.[56]

Brian Friel's *Making History* demonstrates that literature should not be relied upon for 'factual' truth. However, literary texts *can* serve as valuable sources of personal, social, and 'restorative' truths, as I hope this book has illustrated. Friel's play, for example, presents the social truth of 'Gaelic' and 'settler' traditions in the North of Ireland in productive tension with each other and shows the negative effects of eliminating that connection. Deirdre Madden's *One by One in the Darkness* and Seamus Deane's *Reading in the Dark* centre the unspoken suffering of many victims and survivors of Northern Ireland's twentieth-century Troubles in indelible expressions of narrative truth. Bernard MacLaverty's *Grace Notes* metaphorically points the way to social reconciliation through an estranged mother and daughter's efforts to reach 'dialogue' truth and a Catholic composer's musical embrace of Lambeg drums. David Park's *The Truth Commissioner* comprehends the disparate personal truths of its protagonists in a gripping enactment of social truth about the troubled past they share. And Michael Longley's 'Ceasefire' and Seamus Heaney's *The Cure at Troy* offer affirmative visions of the healing truth that can be found on 'the far side of revenge'.[57]

Colum McCann's *TransAtlantic* suggests that the peace in Northern Ireland was made, literally, through writing—an insight I have come to share. While working on *Getting to Good Friday*, I followed the example of the authors whose texts feature in it by questioning my own preconceptions about my subject and writing towards an understanding of different perspectives and experiences.

I hope that reading this book might help others to do the same. Throughout the peace process, creative writers have contributed to the ongoing project of imagining a Northern Irish identity capacious enough to earn the allegiance of all who live there. As Northern Ireland continues to work towards a more affirmative, future-focused peace, I have no doubt that literary writers will continue to offer what Belfast writer Stewart Parker believed they were uniquely qualified to provide: 'a working model of wholeness by means of which this society can begin to hold up its head in the world'.[58]

Notes

Introduction

1. Lucy Caldwell, *All the Beggars Riding* (London: Faber and Faber, 2013), 19–20. Further references to this book will be given in parentheses in the text.
2. Christian Ganter, 'Bernard MacLaverty, Glasgow, in Interview', *Anglistik* 7.2 (1996), 17.
3. Marilynn Richtarik, *Acting Between the Lines: The Field Day Theatre Company and Irish Cultural Politics 1980–1984* (Oxford: Oxford University Press, 1994) and *Stewart Parker: A Life* (Oxford: Oxford University Press, 2012).
4. Marilynn J. Richtarik, 'The Personal is Political: Bernard MacLaverty's *Grace Notes* as a Peace Process Novel' in Richard Rankin Russell (ed.), *Bernard MacLaverty: New Critical Readings* (London: Bloomsbury, 2014), 101–16.
5. Maurice Fitzpatrick, *John Hume in America: From Derry to DC* (Newbridge, Co. Kildare: Irish Academic Press, 2017), 188. In a study of the pivotal role John Hume played in the revision of Irish nationalism, political scientist Peter McLoughlin pays particular attention to the ways in which 'Hume contributed to, helped to refine, and…successfully articulated a new nationalist discourse'. P. J. McLoughlin, *John Hume and the Revision of Irish Nationalism* (Manchester: Manchester University Press, 2010), xvii.
6. Fintan O'Toole, 'The Man From God Knows Where: An Interview with Brian Friel', *In Dublin* (28 October 1982), 21, 23.
7. Eugene McNamee, 'Fields of Opportunity: Cultural Invention and "The New Northern Ireland"' in Peter D. Rush and Olivera Simić (eds), *The Arts of Transitional Justice: Culture, Activism, and Memory After Atrocity*, Vol. 6 of the Springer Series in Transitional Justice (New York: Springer, 2014), 13, 2, 15.
8. Dennis O'Driscoll, *Stepping Stones: Interviews with Seamus Heaney* (New York: Farrar, Straus and Giroux, 2008), 353, 176–7. At Hume's invitation, both Heaney and Friel accompanied him on St Patrick's Day 2000 to a White House gathering hosted by US President Bill Clinton. Brian Friel, letter to Seamus Heaney, 4 January 2000, Rose Library, MS 960, box 39, file folder 10.
9. McGuinness recalled Deane as a 'great' teacher who 'was gentle, kind and never raised his voice at all'. Martin Doyle, 'Seamus Deane, leading Irish writer and critic, has died aged 81', *Irish Times*, 13 May 2021: https://www.irishtimes.com/culture/books/seamus-deane-leading-irish-writer-and-critic-has-died-aged-81-1.4564018 (accessed 27 January 2022).
10. Fintan O'Toole, 'The Meanings of Union', *New Yorker* (27 April/4 May 1998), 56.
11. Albert Reynolds with Jill Arlon, *My Autobiography* (London: Transworld Ireland, 2009), 209, 218.
12. Reynolds, 209, 311.

13. Michael Longley, *Sidelines: Selected Prose 1962–2015* (London: Enitharmon Press, 2017), 386, 396.

14. See Feargal Cochrane, *Northern Ireland: The Fragile Peace*, rev. ed. (New Haven: Yale University Press), 283–308 for a comprehensive overview of the threat posed by Brexit to the peace deal, summed up in his observation that 'whether you take a unionist, nationalist or non-aligned position on Northern Ireland's political identity, Brexit re-weaponized the partition of Ireland and the "constitutional question" which had been quietly parked by the terms of the GFA [Good Friday Agreement] since 1998' (297).

15. Ian McBride, 'The Truth About the Troubles' in Jim Smyth (ed.), *Remembering the Troubles: Contesting the Recent Past in Northern Ireland* (Notre Dame, Indiana: University of Notre Dame Press, 2017), 24. Robin Wilson's *The Northern Ireland Experience of Conflict and Agreement: A Model for Export?* (Manchester: Manchester University Press, 2010) makes illuminating and depressing reading along these lines. Similarly sceptical about the tendency to regard Northern Ireland's conflict as primarily ethnic in nature, Cillian McGrattan also emphasizes a negative continuity between the attitudes and behaviour of both nationalist and unionist political elites before and after the Agreement. Cillian McGrattan, *Northern Ireland 1968–2008: The Politics of Entrenchment* (Basingstoke: Palgrave Macmillan, 2010).

16. Colin Coulter, Niall Gilmartin, Katy Hayward, and Peter Shirlow, *Northern Ireland a Generation After Good Friday: Lost Futures and New Horizons in the 'Long Peace'* (Manchester: Manchester University Press, 2021), 18–19, 30.

17. Jude Webber, 'Donaldson Gambles by Pulling the Plug on Northern Ireland's Executive', *Financial Times*, 7 February 2022: https://www.ft.com/content/70a1db58-369e-4e90-9e85-fcb67ea6bc0f (accessed 7 February 2022).

18. Coulter, et al., 2.

19. Siobhan Fenton, *The Good Friday Agreement* (London: Biteback Publishing, 2018), 130.

20. Fenton, 334.

21. Coulter, et al., 1–2.

22. Readers seeking a longer historical perspective on Northern Ireland's Troubles and peace process might begin with Marc Mulholland's *Northern Ireland: A Very Short Introduction* (Oxford: Oxford University Press, 2002).

Chapter 1

1. For a narrative account of Field Day's formative years, see Marilynn Richtarik, *Acting Between the Lines: The Field Day Theatre Company and Irish Cultural Politics 1980–1984* (Oxford: Oxford University Press, 1994). Criticism of the company became markedly more political after it began publishing pamphlets in 1983, a circumstance that also changed the context in which its theatrical productions were received. For details of some of the controversy provoked by Field Day in the early to mid-1980s, see *Acting*, 140–90 and 239–55.

2. Charles Fitzgerald, 'City Without Theatre Making Stage History', *News Letter*, 21 September 1988.

3. Mary Holland, 'A Field Day for Irish Theatre', *Observer* (magazine section), 29 October 1988.

4. See, for example, Christopher Murray, 'Brian Friel's *Making History* and the Problem of Historical Accuracy' in Geert Lernout (ed.), *The Crows Behind the Plough: History and Violence in Anglo-Irish Poetry and Drama* (Amsterdam: Rodopi, 1991), 61–77; Sean Connolly, 'Translating History: Brian Friel and the Irish Past' in Alan Peacock (ed.), *The Achievement of Brian Friel* (Gerrards Cross, Buckinghamshire: Colin Smythe, 1993), 149–63; and Anne Fogarty, 'The Romance of History: Renegotiating the Past in Thomas Kilroy's *The O'Neill* and Brian Friel's *Making History*', *Irish University Review* 32.1 (2002), 18–32.

5. Marilynn Richtarik, *Stewart Parker: A Life* (Oxford: Oxford University Press, 2012), 269.

6. James Joyce, *A Portrait of the Artist as a Young Man*, ed. Seamus Deane (New York: Penguin, 1993), 276.

7. Fintan O'Toole, 'The Man From God Knows Where: An Interview with Brian Friel', *In Dublin* (28 October 1982), 22.

8. For a discussion of this experiment in self-government for Northern Ireland, the strike by loyalist workers that forced its abandonment, and the repercussions of these events, see Jonathan Bardon, *A History of Ulster* (Belfast: The Blackstaff Press, 1992), 701–14, and Robert Fisk, *The Point of No Return: The Strike Which Broke the British in Ulster* (London: André Deutsch, 1975).

9. Richard Kearney, 'Myth and Motherland', *Ireland's Field Day*, Field Day Theatre Company (London: Hutchinson, 1985), 68. See Paul Bew and Gordon Gillespie, *Northern Ireland: A Chronology of the Troubles 1968-1999* (Lanham, Maryland: The Scarecrow Press, 1999), 143–59, for a detailed description of events during the period of the hunger strikes, and Bardon, 741–6, for an account of the progress of the strikes and their lasting effects. The group originally known as the Provisional IRA was responsible for most of the violence on the republican side during the protracted late-twentieth-century Troubles in Northern Ireland. The term 'Provisional' in its name was intended to distinguish it from the old 'Official' IRA, which had decided to recognize the constitutional status quo and devote itself to democratic politics by the end of 1969. The political party associated with the Provisional IRA, Provisional Sinn Féin, similarly had its origin in a split from the then-mainstream republican movement in favour of a more militant approach. The Provisional IRA was frequently referred to as 'the Provisionals,' 'the Provos', or 'the PIRA'. By the period covered in this book, the once-dissident 'provisional' groups represented the mainstream of the republican movement. I will refer to them simply as 'the IRA' and 'Sinn Féin', which is how they referred to themselves.

10. Brian Friel, letter to the new Field Day directors, 21 September 1981, Brian Friel papers, National Library of Ireland (NLI), Dublin, Ireland, MS 37, 181/1.

11. Bew and Gillespie, 157.

12. Bardon, 743, 746, 749–50.

13. John Hume, *A New Ireland: Politics, Peace and Reconciliation* (Boulder, Colorado: Roberts Rinehart Publishers, 1996), 62; Jeremy Smith, *Making the Peace in Ireland* (London: Longman, 2002), 123.

14. Hume, 109–10.

15. O'Toole, 'The Man From God Knows Where', 20, 22–3.

16. Richtarik, *Acting*, 191–203; minutes of the Field Day board meeting of 5 June 1983, Tom Paulin papers, Stuart A. Rose Manuscript, Archives, and Rare Book Library, Emory University, Atlanta, Georgia, MSS 880, box 52/folder 1.

17. Richtarik, *Acting*, 148–50.

18. Richtarik, *Acting*, 157–64, 184–90; Brian Friel, letter to Seamus Deane, 21 June 1984, Seamus Deane papers, Rose Library, MSS 1210, b1/f11.

19. Minutes of the Field Day board meeting of 8/9 September 1984, Rose Library, MSS 880, b52/f1; 'The Protestant Idea of Liberty', *Derry Journal*, 21 May 1985.

20. Minutes of the Field Day board meeting of 6 August 1986, Rose Library, MSS 880, b52/f1; Richtarik, *Stewart Parker*, 305, 321–4; minutes of the Field Day board meeting of 19/20 January 1988, Field Day papers, NLI, MS 47, 112/7.

21. Seamus Deane, 'Civilians and Barbarians', *Ireland's Field Day*, 31–42. Each director had the opportunity to read all three pamphlets before the board met on 5 June 1983.

22. According to Anthony Roche, Friel first read O'Faolain's book at age 23. Roche, *Brian Friel: Theatre and Politics* (Basingstoke: Palgrave Macmillan, 2011), 163.

23. Sean O'Faolain, *The Great O'Neill: A Biography of Hugh O'Neill, Earl of Tyrone, 1550–1616* (Dublin: The Mercier Press, 1992), vi, 4–5. O'Faolain's biography of O'Neill was first published in 1942, reissued in 1970, and reprinted several times thereafter.

24. O'Faolain, 43.

25. O'Faolain, 11–13, 93; Brian Friel, *Making History* (London: Faber and Faber, 1989), 26.

26. O'Faolain, 94, 92, 169–70; Hiram Morgan, *Tyrone's Rebellion: The Outbreak of the Nine Years War in Tudor Ireland* (Woodbridge, Suffolk: The Boydell Press, 1993), 102.

27. Brian Friel, notes towards *Making History*, 13 December 1983 and 15 December [1983], NLI, MS 37, 100/1. In quotations, the underlining is Friel's.

28. O'Faolain, 170–1.

29. Friel, notes towards *Making History*, 26 January 1984, NLI, MS 37, 100/1.

30. O'Faolain, 243–5.

31. O'Faolain, 177, 279.

32. The following account of *Making History*'s composition is based, unless otherwise indicated, on Friel's notes towards the script held at the National Library in Dublin: MS 37, 100/1. In addition to O'Faolain, Friel consulted, among other sources, the *Itinerary* of Fynes Moryson, a travelogue and eyewitness account of the Nine Years War written by an Englishman who served as personal secretary to the English commander (Lord Mountjoy) who finally defeated O'Neill; *Elizabeth's Irish Wars* by Cyril Falls; *Tudor and Stewart Ireland* by Margaret MacCurtain; and Constantia Elizabeth Maxwell's *Irish History from Contemporary Sources (1509–1610)*.

33. O'Faolain, vi, 274–81.

34. O'Faolain, 69–70, 101, 116–19, 121.

35. Nicholas Canny, letter to Brian Friel, 4 April 1986, NLI, MS 37, 100/2, and *Making Ireland British, 1580–1650* (Oxford: Oxford University Press, 2001), 81.

36. Friel, notes towards *Making History*, 27 February and 29 March 1984, NLI, MS 37, 100/1.

37. Friel, notes towards *Making History*, 15 January 1985, NLI, MS 37, 100/1.

38. Friel, notes towards *Making History*, 26 February 1984, NLI, MS 37, 100/1.

39. Bew and Gillespie, 171, 174.

40. Friel, notes towards *Making History*, 29 March 1984, NLI, MS 37, 100/1.

41. Friel, notes towards *Making History*, 5 April [1985], NLI, MS 37, 100/1.

42. Friel, notes towards *Making History*, March 1985, NLI, MS 37, 100/1.

43. Friel, notes towards *Making History*, 21 November 1985, NLI, MS 37, 100/1.

44. The following discussion of the Anglo–Irish Agreement and reactions to it is based primarily on Bardon, 754–72; Bew and Gillespie, 189–211; Smith, 123–40; and Hume, 64–70.

45. Bew and Gillespie, 191.

46. Hume, 68.

47. Seamus Heaney, 'Applying the Yeats Challenge to the Anglo–Irish Agreement', *Boston Globe*, 27 June 1988.

48. Hayden White, 'Between Science and Symbol', *Times Literary Supplement* (31 January 1986), 109–10.

49. Two especially cogent critiques came from John Andrews and Brian McAvera. See Brian Friel, John Andrews, and Kevin Barry, 'Translations and A Paper Landscape: Between Fiction and History' (edited version of an exchange between Friel and Andrews hosted by the Interdisciplinary Seminar at St. Patrick's College, Maynooth, on 20 January 1983), *Crane Bag* 7.2 (1983), 118–24, and Brian McAvera, 'Attuned to the Catholic Experience', *Fortnight* (3 March 1985), 19–20.

50. 'Translations and A Paper Landscape', 124, 123.

51. Friel, notes towards *Making History*, 4 March 1986, NLI, MS 37, 100/1.

52. Bardon, 766–7, 772–3; Bew and Gillespie, 201–3; O'Faolain, 162–6.

53. Bardon, 764; Bew and Gillespie, 201.

54. Roche, 164.

55. Friel, notes towards *Making History*, 7 January 1987, NLI, MS 37, 100/1.

56. Mabel and Harry, the characters in the play closest to O'Neill, are identified throughout the script of *Making History* by their first names.

57. Friel, *Making History*, 19. Further references to this book will be given in parentheses in the text.

58. O'Faolain, 122.

59. Morgan, 4.

60. Constantia Maxwell, *Irish History from Contemporary Sources (1509–1610)* (London: Allen & Unwin, 1923), 187–8.

61. O'Faolain, 132–7.

62. O'Faolain, 268–9.

63. John Vidal, 'Stronger Than Fiction', *Guardian*, 5 December 1988.

64. Brian Friel, programme note for *Making History* (Field Day Theatre Company, 1988), collection of the author.

65. Connolly, 160.

66. It is worth remembering that characters in the play do not allude to specific dates. These are provided only in stage directions, and audiences attending the Field Day production would not have seen them unless they bought the programme. All anyone merely watching the play would know or need to know is that Act I is set before the debacle at Kinsale and Act II after it, which may help to explain why there was little appreciable outcry at the time of the play's première about its misrepresentation of history. Thus, Friel's obvious manipulation of chronology and his strange little programme note were aimed at a specific intellectual segment of his public, and it is unlikely that he was either surprised or dismayed by the later academic critique of *Making History*.

67. Friel himself compiled a list of 'Historical Errors' in the front of the notebook containing his 'final' draft of the play, as if to purge himself of any remaining qualms on this score. Brian Friel, 'Final Version' of *Making History*, NLI, MS 37, 101/4.

68. Connolly, 160.

69. Austin Currie, quoted in Bew and Gillespie, 208.

70. Brian Friel, notecard with notes towards *Making History*, NLI, MS 37, 100/5.

71. 'History in the Making', *Ulster Herald*, 15 October 1988.

72. Roche, 166.

73. Friel, notes towards *Making History*, NLI, MS 37, 100/1.

74. O'Faolain, 121–2, 282.

75. O'Faolain, 33.

76. Mabel's argument about Queen Elizabeth's willingness to bargain with O'Neill finds support in Nicholas Canny's analysis of the 1603 settlement, which emphasizes its surprising generosity. The terms offered did present O'Neill with a better opportunity to preserve his own power and Gaelic culture than exile did because they 'involved a categorical rejection…of the Dublin official view that colonisation should inevitably follow upon conquest'. The Flight of the Earls, in contrast, 'led inexorably to plantation in Ulster'. Canny, *From Reformation to Restoration: Ireland, 1534–1660* (Dublin: Helicon, 1989), 146–9, 163.

77. See, for example, F. C. McGrath, *Brian Friel's (Post)Colonial Drama: Language, Illusion, and Politics* (Syracuse: Syracuse University Press, 1999), 220.

78. Roche, 168.

79. Murray, 74–5.

80. Seamus Heaney, letter to Brian Friel, 22 January 1988, NLI, MS 37, 102/1.

81. 'History in the Making'; Kevin O'Sullivan, 'Making History—Compelling but with One Slight Flaw', *City Tribune*, 28 November 1988; Declan Hasset, 'Making History…Rewriting History', *Cork Examiner*, 24 November 1988; Timothy O'Grady, 'Courage and Pain of a Man with a Foot in Two Worlds', *Evening Press*, 24 September 1988.

82. Nicholas Canny, 'Making History', *Galway Advertiser*, 27 October 1988.

83. Jim Patton, 'A Gripping New Drama', *Belfast Telegraph*, 21 September 1988; Charles Fitzgerald, 'Playwrights Can Change History Too', *News Letter*, 23 September 1988; 'Friel's Cavan Delight', *Cavan Leader*, 28 October 1988.

84. Jane Coyle, 'Friel Play's Touch of First Night Nerves', *Sunday Press*, 25 September 1988; 'History in the Making'; 'Friel's Cavan Delight'; Brian Brennan, 'The Reinvention of Hugh O'Neill', *Sunday Independent*, 25 September 1988.

85. Milton Shulman, 'Shaping the Past', *Evening Standard*, 6 December 1988; Michael Billington, 'History Kisses the Blarney Stone', *Guardian*, 7 December 1988.

86. Seamus Heaney, 'A Field Day for the Irish', *The Times*, 5 December 1988; Stephen Rea, quoted in Vidal.

87. Irving Wardle, 'Language a Key to Life', *The Times*, 6 December 1988; Michael Coveney, 'Making History', *Financial Times*, 6 December 1988.

88. O'Grady; Richard Pine, *The Diviner: The Art of Brian Friel* (Dublin: University College Dublin Press, 1999), 234.

89. Fintan O'Toole, 'A Hesitant Move Into Unknown Territory', *Irish Times*, 24 September 1988, and 'Marking Time: From *Making History* to *Dancing at Lughnasa*' in Peacock, 211.

90. Pine, 234, 285, 317; McGrath, 230–1; Ulf Dantanus, 'O'Neill's Last Tape: Self, Failure and Freedom in Friel and Beckett' in Richard Harp and Robert C. Evans (eds), *A Companion to Brian Friel* (West Cornwall, Connecticut: Locust Hill Press, 2002), 121; Aidan O'Malley, *Field Day and the Translation of Irish Identities: Performing Contradictions* (Basingstoke: Palgrave Macmillan, 2011), 42, 199.

91. Yvonne Lysandrou, 'Hugh O'Neill as "Hamlet-Plus": (Post)colonialism and Dynamic Stasis in Brian Friel's *Making History*', *Irish Studies Review* 14.1 (2006), 91.

92. Minutes of the Field Day board meeting, 12 August 1988, NLI, 37, 181/2. To put this aim into perspective, a comparison with Field Day's 1990 tour of Seamus Heaney's Sophocles adaptation *The Cure at Troy* is illuminating. Although Heaney was not an established playwright like Friel, he was certainly a household name in 1990, so a play by him would reasonably have been expected to attract attention and audiences. At a post-production meeting on that tour, Friel observed that the budget estimate for ticket sales had been based on 70 per cent houses, which he considered unrealistically high—the actual figure had been closer to 50 per cent. Minutes of the Field Day board meeting, 13 April 1991, NLI, MS 37, 181/2.

93. Attendance figures for the Field Day production of *Making History*, Field Day papers NLI, MS 46, 912/1.

94. Eamonn Nolan, letter to Brian Friel, 28 May 1989, NLI, MS 37, 102/1.

95. Brian Friel, letter to Stephen Rea [copied to all Field Day directors], 31 July 1989, Seamus Heaney papers, Rose Library, MSS 960, b39/f9.

Chapter 2

1. Seamus Heaney, letter to Brian Friel, 22 January 1988, quoted in Marilynn Richtarik, 'Reality and Justice: Seamus Heaney's *The Cure at Troy*', *Estudios Irlandeses* 13 (2018), 99.

2. Gerry Adams, *Hope and History: Making Peace in Ireland* (London: Brandon, 2003), 57–8.

3. Martin McKeever, *One Man, One God: The Peace Ministry of Fr Alec Reid C.Ss.R.* (Dublin: Redemptorist Communications, 2017), 113, 23, 115–16.

4. McKeever, 117–18; Adams, *Hope and History*, 42; Mark Durkan, 'Shaping the Peace' in Seán Farren and Denis Haughey (eds), *John Hume: Irish Peacemaker* (Dublin: Four Courts Press, 2015), 127. Durkan would later be a key member of the SDLP's negotiating team during the talks that resulted in the Good Friday Agreement, after which he served in Northern Ireland's assembly and power-sharing government. He eventually followed in Hume's footsteps both as leader of the SDLP and as an elected member of the British parliament. Farren and Haughey (eds), 213–14.

5. Adams, *Hope and History*, 43. Adams describes his first meeting with Hume as taking place considerably earlier than others who have chronicled the peace process maintain. In his 1997 biography of Hume, Paul Routledge writes that Father Reid sent a letter to Hume early in 1987 and met with the SDLP leader several times later that year, and he identifies Hume's 11 January 1988 meeting with the Sinn Féin president as 'his first meeting of the Irish Peace Initiative with Gerry Adams'. Routledge, *John Hume: A Biography* (London: HarperCollins, 1997), 214–17. Durkan also dates Father Reid's initial approach to 'early 1987' (126). However, a 2017 book about Father Reid's

peace ministry by a fellow Redemptorist priest includes the text of Reid's first letter to Hume, dated 19 May 1986 (McKeever, 112–29). Because various accounts agree that Hume's response to Reid was both prompt and positive, I find Adams's narrative plausible and speculate that the discrepancy with other versions of the story stems from the fact that their earliest meetings were held in secret, with information about them withheld even from Hume's closest SDLP colleagues. At any rate, unlike others who have commented on this first meeting, Adams attended it.

6. Paul Bew and Gordon Gillespie, *Northern Ireland: A Chronology of the Troubles 1968–1999* (Lanham, Maryland: The Scarecrow Press, 1999), 189; Adams, *Hope and History*, 43–4.

7. Adams, *Hope and History*, 44; Jonathan Bardon, *A History of Ulster* (Belfast: The Blackstaff Press, 1992), 775; Bew and Gillespie, 207–10.

8. Seán Farren (ed.), *John Hume: In His Own Words* (Dublin: Four Courts Press, 2018), 19, 25–6; Dennis O'Driscoll, *Stepping Stones: Interviews with Seamus Heaney* (New York: Farrar, Straus and Giroux, 2008), xxi, 176–7.

9. Durkan, 128; Bardon, 778; Bew and Gillespie, 215; Adams, *Hope and History*, 67–70, 73.

10. O'Driscoll, 258; Seamus Heaney, 'Applying the Yeats Challenge to the Anglo–Irish Agreement', *Boston Globe*, 27 June 1988; Fintan O'Toole, 'Seamus Heaney: Beyond the Normal Niceties', *Colour Tribune*, 10 April 1988.

11. Adams, *Hope and History*, 77–82; Durkan, 130–1.

12. Minutes of the Field Day board meeting of 9/10 November 1985, Tom Paulin papers, Stuart A. Rose Manuscript, Archives, and Rare Book Library, Emory University, Atlanta, Georgia, MSS 880, box 52/folder 1; Brian Friel, postcard to Seamus Heaney, [1 May] 1989, Seamus Heaney papers, Rose Library, MSS 960, b39/f9; Barry White, ' "Troy" is the Setting for Heaney's First Play', *Belfast Telegraph*, 29 September 1990; O'Driscoll, 420–1; Flyer from the Field Day production of Seamus Heaney's *The Cure at Troy* (1990), collection of the author.

13. See, for example, Alan Peacock, 'Mediations: Poet as Translator, Poet as Seer' in Elmer Andrews (ed.), *Seamus Heaney: A Collection of Critical Essays* (New York: St. Martin's Press, 1992), 233–55; Richard Rankin Russell, *Seamus Heaney's Regions* (Notre Dame, Indiana: University of Notre Dame Press, 2014), 279–309; and Michael Parker, 'Back in the Republic of Conscience: Seamus Heaney's *The Cure at Troy*, Its Politics, Ethics and Aesthetics', *Textual Practice* 31.4 (2017), 747–81. Peacock discusses *The Cure at Troy* as a key step in Heaney's development of a public poetic voice, Russell relates the play to the entire body of Heaney's work through analysis of intertextual references to the writings of Yeats and Wilfred Owen, and Parker offers a detailed and convincing reading of Heaney's drama, with special attention to those places where Heaney does most to 'colonize' the Sophocles text.

14. John Walsh, 'Bard of Hope and Harp', *Sunday Times*, 7 October 1990. Heaney told Walsh that the public aspect of theatre's production and reception had taken him aback as a writer accustomed to the privacy of poetry: 'I wrote the words in a study at Harvard, just concentrating on being faithful to the text, thinking abstractly: "This must be speakable." That was all.'

15. For examples of politicians' citation of *The Cure at Troy*, see Hugh Denard, 'Seamus Heaney, Colonialism, and the Cure: Sophoclean Re-Visions', *PAJ: A Journal of*

Performance and Art 22.3 (September 2000), 1–2, and Matt McGuire, 'Tragedy and Transitional Justice: Seamus Heaney's *The Cure at Troy*' in Chris Andrews and Matt McGuire (eds), *Post-Conflict Literature: Human Rights, Peace, Justice* (New York: Routledge, 2016), 26. Adams's peace process memoir, published in Europe as *Hope and History: Making Peace in Ireland* and in the United States as *A Farther Shore: Ireland's Long Road to Peace* (the latter title a slight misquotation of a late Chorus speech in Heaney's play), also contained an epigraph consisting of lines from *The Cure at Troy*.

16. I was researching my Field Day book in 1990 and saw the company's production of *The Cure at Troy* at several of the smaller Northern Irish venues, where this question was a popular topic of conversation.

17. Robert Fitzgerald (trans.), *The Iliad* of Homer, introd. by Gregory Nagy (New York: Knopf, 1992), 59.

18. Oscar Mandel, *Philoctetes and the Fall of Troy: Plays, Documents, Iconography, Interpretations* (Lincoln, Nebraska: University of Nebraska Press, 1981). I cannot prove that Heaney read Mandel's book. However, Harvard's Widener Library owned a copy, and it would be surprising if Heaney (an anxious first-time playwright as well as a scrupulous scholar) did not at least peruse it.

19. Mandel, 3–45.

20. Mandel, 95–103.

21. Mandel, 103.

22. Mandel, 110, 112, 113–14; Denard, 6–7, 17–18. Nathan Wallace records that the connection with *The Tempest* was noted even by the first reviewers of *The Cure at Troy*. Wallace, *Hellenism and Reconciliation in Ireland from Yeats to Field Day* (Cork: Cork University Press, 2015), 117.

23. O'Driscoll, 420; Seamus Heaney, quoted in Marianne McDonald, 'Seamus Heaney's *Cure at Troy* Politics and Poetry', *Classics Ireland* 3 (1996), 137.

24. Seamus Heaney, 'A Postcard from North Antrim', *Field Work* (New York: Noonday, 1989), 19; O'Driscoll, 222–3; Jeremy Smith, *Making the Peace in Ireland* (London: Longman, 2002), 147–52; Durkan, 132.

25. Parker, 762; Seamus Heaney, programme note for *The Cure at Troy* (Field Day Theatre Company, 1990), collection of the author.

26. Seamus Heaney, '*The Cure at Troy*: Production Notes in No Particular Order' in Marianne McDonald and J. Michael Walton (eds), *Amid Our Troubles: Irish Versions of Greek Tragedy*, introd. Declan Kiberd (London: Methuen, 2002), 173, 175; Edmund Wilson, *The Wound and the Bow: Seven Studies in Literature* (Cambridge, Massachusetts: Houghton Mifflin, 1941), 283.

27. Mandel, 115. The authority he cites on this point is Classics scholar H. D. F. Kitto.

28. Mandel, 115.

29. Seamus Heaney, draft of *The Cure at Troy*, Seamus Heaney papers, National Library of Ireland, MS 49, 493/233, Notebook 1. The first draft of the Chorus speech appears opposite a page dated 3 February 1990.

30. Seamus Heaney, *The Cure at Troy* (London: Faber and Faber, 1990), 1. Further page references to this book will be given in parentheses in the text.

31. Heaney, 'Production Notes', 175, and quoted in McDonald, 137.

32. See, for example, Heaney's comments in 'Production Notes', 173–4.

33. White. This last reading proved attractive even to some of *The Cure at Troy*'s most knowledgeable commentators. Seamus Deane, for example, argues that 'Troy's "meaning" in the play's system of political reference is ostensibly clear; it refers to Northern Ireland. But there is the problem that it also refers to a place that is finally sacked and that this prelude to the final battle, which seems to be about a miraculous change, is not in any coherent sense really about an alteration that will bring reconciliation. Instead, it will bring victory to one side and defeat to the other.' Deane, 'Field Day's Greeks (and Russians)' in McDonald and Walton (eds), 159.

34. Denard, 5, 15.

35. Heaney, 'Production Notes', 175; Durkan, 125.

36. Bew and Gillespie, 191; Wallace, 118.

37. See, for example, Shaun Richards, '"A Solution to the Present Crisis"? Seamus Heaney's *The Cure at Troy*', *Études irlandaises* 20.2 (1995), 77–85.

38. Heaney, in an interview shortly before the Field Day opening, said the play was 'about the nature of being betrayed': 'The better half of your intelligence and nature says "I know I have been betrayed but you have to keep moving. For life's sake this has to be swallowed, ingested, and we must proceed."' He acknowledged, though, that 'it isn't so easy'. White.

39. Parker, 749, 752.

40. Adams, *Hope and History*, 92; Durkan, 125; Denard, 4. Gerry Adams could have identified with Philoctetes literally as well as metaphorically. In *Hope and History* he describes his recovery after an assassination attempt in March 1984 in which he was hit by five bullets. This proceeded well apart from 'a nagging pain' in his upper left arm, which he learned upon returning to the hospital was caused by a bullet that had been left inside him. When the senior surgeon sliced open his arm to remove it, 'we were both almost overcome by the odious smell which immediately arose from the poisoned wound' (20–7).

41. Seamus Heaney, 'John Hume's Derry', *Hibernia* (21 November 1969), 7; Adams, *Hope and History*, 79–80; Cathy Gormley-Heenan, 'Political Leader' in Farren and Haughey (eds), 197; Fionnuala O Connor, *Breaking the Bonds: Making Peace in Northern Ireland* (Edinburgh: Mainstream Publishing, 2002), 24.

42. In tragedies, the use of one actor was standard until Aeschylus added a second; later, Sophocles revised the form by adding a third actor. Lee A. Jacobus (ed.), *The Bedford Introduction to Drama*, 2nd ed. (Boston: Bedford Books, 1993), 36.

43. Although most reviewers praised Des McAleer as Philoctetes, the performances of the other two male actors were seen by many (including me) as inadequate. The Chorus, however, was outstanding. For what I would term an accurate description of the Field Day production, see Colin Meir, 'Theatre', *Linen Hall Review* 17.3/4 (Winter 1990), 12–13.

44. Eileen Battersby, 'Sometimes a Great Notion', *Irish Times*, 29 September 1990; Michael Coveney, review of *The Cure at Troy* by Seamus Heaney, *Observer*, 7 October 1990; Walsh.

45. Quoted in Marilynn Richtarik, *Acting Between the Lines: The Field Day Theatre Company and Irish Cultural Politics 1980–1984* (Oxford: Oxford University Press, 1994), 6; Seamus Deane, 'Oranges and Lemnos', *New Statesman* (5 April 1991), 19.

46. Heaney, 'Production Notes', 178; O'Driscoll, 421.

47. Bew and Gillespie, 229, 243, 255.

48. Gerry Adams, *A Farther Shore: Ireland's Long Road to Peace* (New York: Random House, 2003), 35, and *Hope and History*, 18–19; Smith, 131–2; Bew and Gillespie, 244.

49. Farren (ed.), 203–4.

50. Smith, 133, 146; Adams, *Hope and History*, 95; David McKittrick and David McVea, *Making Sense of the Troubles: A History of the Northern Ireland Conflict*, rev. ed. (London: Viking Penguin, 2012), 329.

51. Bew and Gillespie, 188, 227–9, 238; 'Nauseating' (leader), *Derry Journal*, 27 July 1990.

52. Bew and Gillespie, 236.

53. Bew and Gillespie, 236; Adams, *Hope and History*, 45–7.

54. David McKittrick, 'IRA Uses Human Bombs', *Independent*, 25 October 1990; David Hearst, '"Human Bombs" Kill 7', *Guardian*, 25 October 1990.

55. James Dalrymple and Liam Clarke, '"Satanic" IRA Men Denounced by Bishop', *Sunday Times*, 28 October 1990; Hearst.

56. Smith, 162–3, 158–9; Adams, *Hope and History*, 93–9.

57. Maurice Fitzpatrick, *John Hume in America: From Derry to DC* (Newbridge, County Kildare: Irish Academic Press, 2017), 150–1.

58. Adams, *Hope and History*, 95, 115.

59. Bew and Gillespie, 243–4; Adams, *Hope and History*, 101.

60. Bew and Gillespie, 269, 256. For a vivid account of this time in Northern Ireland, see Bardon, 810–17.

61. Bardon, 816; Bew and Gillespie, 266, 270–1.

62. See, for example, 'NIO Hoist With Own Petard' (leader), *News Letter*, 13 January 1988.

63. Smith, 123–31, 147–57; Bew and Gillespie, 267.

64. Adams, *Hope and History*, 115–17; Bew and Gillespie, 270; Smith, 164. It emerged later that the British government had believed itself to be responding to a message from republicans which had really been manufactured by the Derry contact to try to bring the two sides together. The message stated that 'The conflict is over but we need your advice on how to bring it to an end. We wish to have an unannounced cease-fire in order to hold dialogue leading to peace.' Adams, *Hope and History*, 141–5; Smith, 164. For a concise description of back-channel communication between the IRA and the British government via the Derry link from its inception until 1993, see Jonathan Powell, *Great Hatred, Little Room: Making Peace in Northern Ireland* (London: The Bodley Head, 2008), 66–73.

65. Adams, *Hope and History*, 116–17; Smith, 164; Bew and Gillespie, 272; 'Grief and Rage Greet Litter-bin Atrocity', *News Letter*, 22 March 1993; John Cassidy, 'No Let-up in Bloody War', *News Letter*, 26 March 1993; Paul Connolly, 'Violence Poll Support Shock', *News Letter*, 1 April 1993.

66. Bardon, 775–7; Bew and Gillespie, 210.

67. Mervyn Pauley, 'Stop the Killing Is Senator's Plea', *News Letter*, 26 March 1993.

68. 'IRA Lecture for Wilson', *News Letter*, 8 April 1993; Richard Sullivan, 'Critics Proved Right as Wilson Plea Fails', *News Letter*, 9 April 1993.

69. John Cassidy, 'Internment Call Grows', *News Letter*, 12 April 1993; Adams, *Hope and History*, 107, 105–6.

70. McKittrick and McVea, 330; Adams, *Hope and History*, 108, 111.

71. Fitzpatrick, 149; '"Secret Talks Offer Little Hope of Peace"', *News Letter*, 12 April 1993; Adams, *Hope and History*, 119.

72. Fitzpatrick, 149.

73. 'SF Talks Outrage', *News Letter*, 13 April 1993; Fitzpatrick, 150; 'Meeting Challenges to End Violence', *Irish News*, 12 April 1993.

74. Adams, *Hope and History*, 120; Durkan, 136; Bew and Gillespie, 273; Farren (ed.), 249.

75. Durkan, 138. See the prime ministers' autobiographies for their perspectives and details of the actions, both public and private, taken by them and by the British and Irish governments in this period: John Major, *The Autobiography* (New York: HarperCollins, 1999) and Albert Reynolds (with Jill Arlon), *My Autobiography* (London: Transworld Ireland, 2009).

76. Durkan, 138; Adams, *Hope and History*, 127; Bew and Gillespie, 275; Smith, 166–7.

77. Farren (ed.), 253; Adams, *Hope and History*, 133–5. Then Taoiseach Albert Reynolds asserted in his autobiography that this mysterious Hume–Adams document consisted merely of 'a few paragraphs that reiterated all the old aspirations that had formed the substance of a statement Hume and Adams had already published—nothing new whatsoever of any value or worth, no kind of a "breakthrough" as had been intimated to the press'. From his point of view, their intervention at this critical time did more harm than good: 'rather than progressing the situation it served only to thwart it' because 'there was no way that the British government could be seen to be dealing with Sinn Féin' if it hoped to appeal to unionists. Reynolds, 268, 270, 274.

78. Adams, *Hope and History*, 134; Farren (ed.), 255; David McKittrick, 'Belfast Bomb Kills Nine', *Independent on Sunday*, 24 October 1993; Bew and Gillespie, 276–8.

79. Adams, *Hope and History*, 138–9; Reynolds, 280–1; Paul Routledge, 'Blast Kills Peace Hopes', *Independent on Sunday*, 24 October 1993; Bew and Gillespie, 278.

80. Adams, *Hope and History*, 141; Reynolds, 281–2.

81. Bew and Gillespie, 278; Adams, *Hope and History*, 139.

82. McKittrick and McVea, 227; Adams, *Hope and History*, 145–6; Bew and Gillespie, 279; Durkan, 139.

83. Durkan, 139. See Reynolds, 275–7 and 288–93, for details of some of his contacts with Northern Protestants around this time.

84. Smith, 168; Bew and Gillespie, 279.

85. Adams, *Hope and History*, 147; Bew and Gillespie, 279–82; Smith, 169.

86. Bew and Gillespie, 282–5.

87. Smith, 170.

88. Durkan, 139; Smith, 169; Bew and Gillespie, 286.

89. Bew and Gillespie, 283; Adams, *Hope and History*, 164.

90. Adams, *Hope and History*, 150; Bew and Gillespie, 286–7.

91. Durkan, 139–40; Adams, *Hope and History*, 157–9; Nancy Soderberg, 'In America' in Farren and Haughey (eds), 170–8. See Bill Clinton, *My Life* (New York: Vintage Books, 2005), 578–81, for an account of this episode from his point of view.

92. Adams, *Hope and History*, 162, 164–5; Bew and Gillespie, 288.

93. Bew and Gillespie, 288; Adams, *Hope and History*, 166–7.

94. 'Processed Peace?' (arts feature), *Fortnight* (March 1994), 35–42.

95. 'Processed Peace?', 40.

96. 'Processed Peace?', 41. Heaney also admired Auden: the published version of *The Cure at Troy* includes an epigraph consisting of two stanzas of his poem 'As I Walked Out One Evening', ending with the command to 'love your crooked neighbour / With your crooked heart'.

97. John Brown, *In the Chair: Interviews with Poets from the North of Ireland* (Cliffs of Moher, County Clare: Salmon Poetry, 2002), 87–96; Michael Longley, conversation with the author (Belfast, 1 March 2017), *Tuppenny Stung: Autobiographical Chapters* (Belfast: Lagan Press, 1994), and *Sidelines: Selected Prose 1962–2015* (London: Enitharmon Press, 2017). In *Sidelines*, see especially the three interviews (with Robert Johnstone, Peter McDonald, and Jody Allen Randolph).

98. Longley, interview with Randolph, *Sidelines*, 412.

99. Adams, *Hope and History*, 167; Fitzpatrick, 175.

100. Adams, *Hope and History*, 167; David McKittrick, 'IRA Ceasefire Branded Cynical', *Independent*, 31 March 1994; Bew and Gillespie, 289–90.

101. McKittrick, 'IRA Ceasefire Branded Cynical'; Adams, *Hope and History*, 171.

102. Bew and Gillespie, 292; Adams, *Hope and History*, 173–4.

103. Adams, *Hope and History*, 174, 176–7.

104. Adams, *Hope and History*, 178; Leonard Doyle, 'Americans "Could Persuade IRA It's Time to Change"', *Independent*, 21 August 1994.

105. David Sharrock, 'Britain Faces US Rift On IRA', *Guardian*, 22 August 1994; 'The Crucial Need For a Farewell to Arms' (leader), *Guardian*, 22 August 1994; Mary Holland, 'Ceasefire Talk Breathes Life Into Battered Hopes', *Observer*, 28 August 1994.

106. Tom McGurk, 'Why the IRA Is Committed To Making the September Truce a Permanent One', *Sunday Business Post*, 28 August 1994; Sarah Broom, 'Interview with Michael Longley', *Metre* 4 (1998), 21.

107. Fran Brearton, *Reading Michael Longley* (Tarset, Northumberland: Bloodaxe Books, 2006), 188–9. Brearton notes in the same passage that an invitation in 1992 to contribute to an anthology of contemporary poems based on stories from the *Metamorphoses* and edited by Michael Hofmann and James Lasdun solidified this thematic focus in *The Ghost Orchid* by sparking Longley's mid-life love affair with Ovid.

108. Broom, 'Interview with Michael Longley', 19; Longley, interview with McDonald, *Sidelines*, 392; Longley, *Sidelines*, 324.

109. Brearton, 207; Broom, 'Interview with Michael Longley', 20; Longley, interview with Randolph, *Sidelines*, 413.

110. Brearton, 207.

111. Eileen Battersby, 'Observing the Sons of Ulster', *Irish Times*, 9 March 2000; Geordie Schimmel, 'An Interview with Michael Longley', *Libertas* (20 February 1997), 10; Michael Longley, conversation with the author, 1 March 2017. Longley told Michael Parker that he composed 'Ceasefire' on 26 August 1994. Parker, *Northern Irish Literature: The Imprint of History, Volume 2: 1975–2006* (Basingstoke: Palgrave Macmillan, 2007), 164, 268.

112. Longley, conversation with the author, 1 March 2017, and *Songs for Dead Children: Poetry in Violent Times* (English PEN/Faber and Faber, 2017), 10–11.

113. Longley, conversation with the author, 1 March 2017, and 'Ceasefire', *The Ghost Orchid* (London: Jonathan Cape, 1995), 39.
114. Niall McGrath, 'Michael Longley: The Interview', *Poetry Life: People, Poets and Publishing* 6 (Spring 1996), 15; Longley, interview with Randolph, *Sidelines*, 405; Broom, 'Interview with Michael Longley', 21.
115. Longley, 'Memory and Acknowledgement' [text of a talk given in June 1995], *Irish Review* 17/18 (Winter 1995), 158, and interview with McDonald, *Sidelines*, 393.
116. Michael Longley, interview with the author, Belfast, 19 November 2017; Simone Weil, *The Iliad or the Poem of Force*, trans. Mary McCarthy (Wallingford, Pennsylvania: Pendle Hill, 1956), 3, 11, 14.
117. Weil, 15–18, 22, 27, 29.
118. Richmond Lattimore, 'Introduction' in Richmond Lattimore (trans. and introd.), *The Iliad of Homer* (Chicago: University of Chicago Press, 1951), 17, 21. Further references to this edition of the *Iliad* will be given in parentheses in the text.
119. Weil, 22–3. Patrick Radden Keefe offers vivid examples of this kind of pain as it was suffered by several prominent IRA members who regarded the peace process itself as a betrayal. Keefe, *Say Nothing: A True Story of Murder and Memory in Northern Ireland* (New York: Anchor Books, 2020).
120. Richard Rankin Russell, *Poetry and Peace: Michael Longley, Seamus Heaney, and Northern Ireland* (Notre Dame, Indiana: University of Notre Dame Press, 2010), 124; Sarah Broom, 'Learning about Dying: Mutability and the Classics in the Poetry of Michael Longley', *New Hibernia Review* 6.1 (Spring 2002), 110.
121. Broom, 'Learning about Dying', 111; Russell, *Poetry and Peace*, 118; Brearton, 207.
122. Lorna Hardwick, '"Murmurs in the Cathedral": The Impact of Translations from Greek Poetry and Drama on Modern Work in English by Michael Longley and Seamus Heaney', *Yearbook of English Studies* 36.1 (2006), 206.
123. Bew and Gillespie, 292–3; Adams, *Hope and History*, 180–1.
124. Bew and Gillespie, 293; Adams, *Hope and History*, 182–3.
125. Broom, 'Interview with Michael Longley', 21.

Chapter 3

1. Paul Bew and Gordon Gillespie, *Northern Ireland: A Chronology of the Troubles 1968-1999* (Lanham, Maryland: The Scarecrow Press, 1999), 295, 297; Seamus Heaney, 'Light Finally Enters the Black Hole', *Sunday Tribune*, 4 September 1994. The phrase 'inflicted and endured' comes from the climactic Chorus speech in Heaney's play *The Cure at Troy* (London: Faber and Faber, 1990), 77. This work is analysed in Chapter Two.
2. Michael Longley, *Songs for Dead Children: Poetry in Violent Times*, The PEN Pinter Prize Lecture 2017 (PEN/Faber and Faber, 2017), 12, 15. See Chapter Two for a discussion of 'Ceasefire'. The phrase 'each neighbourly murder' appears in Heaney's poem 'Funeral Rites'.
3. Robin Wilson, 'No Elegies', *Fortnight* (October 1994), 47.
4. Marie Smyth, 'Healing Emotional Scars', *Fortnight* (October 1994), 18–20.

5. See David Bolton, *Conflict, Peace and Mental Health: Addressing the Consequences of Conflict and Trauma in Northern Ireland* (Manchester: Manchester University Press, 2017).

6. Lyra McKee, 'Suicide of the Ceasefire Babies', *Mosaic Science*, 19 January 2016: https://mosaicscience.com/story/conflict-suicide-northern-ireland/ (accessed 19 November 2019).

7. Michael Parker, 'Shadows on a Glass: Self-Reflexivity in the Fiction of Deirdre Madden', *Irish University Review* 30.1 (Spring/Summer 2000), 95; Deirdre Madden, conversation with the author, Dublin, 19 June 2017, and *One by One in the Darkness* (London: Faber and Faber, 1997), 60. Further references to this edition of the novel will be given in parentheses in the text.

8. See Chapter Two for a discussion of this initiative and what was publicly known about it at various times.

9. Deirdre Madden, conversation with the author, 19 June 2017.

10. Deirdre Madden, conversation with the author, 19 June 2017, and e-mail to the author, 17 June 2019.

11. The rural Catholic heritage and mid-Ulster territory they share make comparisons between Madden and Heaney virtually obligatory. This passage reminds me most insistently of Heaney's poem 'Keeping Going' from *The Spirit Level* (published in 1996, the same year as *One by One in the Darkness*), which contrasts the experiences of the speaker, who has left Northern Ireland, and his brother, who has stayed.

12. Deirdre Madden, 'Looking for Home: Time, Place, Memory', *Canadian Journal of Irish Studies* 26.2/27.1 (Fall 2000/Spring 2001), 29–30.

13. Parker, 97.

14. Parker, 97–8.

15. For details on these historical events, see Bew and Gillespie, as well as Jeremy Smith, *Making the Peace in Ireland* (London: Longman, 2002) and Jonathan Bardon, *A History of Ulster* (Belfast: The Blackstaff Press, 1992).

16. As Parker explains, Brian's 'attempts to justify and contextualize the atrocity confirm his Sinn Féin credentials, whereas Peter and Charlie's contempt for his argument and condemnation of all forms of violence suggest they align themselves with the more moderate nationalism of the SDLP'. Parker also points out that Madden gives more prominence to Bloody Friday than to Bloody Sunday in her narrative, probably because this gave her an opportunity to draw attention to different reactions on the nationalist side: 'Bloody Friday drew a divided response from nationalists, whereas Bloody Sunday was met with universal condemnation' (98).

17. Geraldine Higgins, '"A Place to Bring Anger and Grief": Deirdre Madden's Northern Irish Novels', *Writing Ulster* 6 (1999), 147.

18. James Simmons, 'Too Happy, Too Soon', *Spectator* (8 June 1996), 35; Higgins, 148, 155–6, 158.

19. Patricia Craig, 'A Cabinet in Co Clare', *Times Literary Supplement* (24 May 1996), 26; Jayne Steel, 'Politicizing the Private: Women Writing the Troubles' in Brian Cliff and Éibhear Walshe (eds), *Representing the Troubles: Texts and Images, 1970–2000* (Dublin: Four Courts Press, 2004), 55–7.

20. Daniel W. Ross, 'An Uncanny Home: Deirdre Madden's *One by One in the Darkness* and the 1994 Ceasefire' in Alison O'Malley-Younger and John Strachan (eds), *Ireland at War and Peace* (Newcastle upon Tyne: Cambridge Scholars Publishing, 2011), 190–2; Elmer Kennedy-Andrews, *Fiction and the Northern Ireland Troubles Since 1969: (De-)Constructing the North* (Dublin: Four Courts Press, 2003), 155.

21. Madden, conversation with the author, 19 June 2017.

22. Her decision turned out to be a prudent one. By the time the novel was published in the spring of 1996, the IRA ceasefire had broken down and the political situation in Northern Ireland looked stagnant once more. Bew and Gillespie, 320–3.

23. Madden, conversation with the author, 19 June 2017.

24. McKee, 'Suicide of the Ceasefire Babies'.

25. Liam Harte, *Reading the Contemporary Irish Novel, 1987–2007* (Chichester, West Sussex: John Wiley, 2014), 174; 'Seamus Deane' (biography), *The Field Day Anthology of Irish Writing*, volume 3 (Derry: Field Day, 1991), 1434; Joe Cleary, 'Dark Fields of the Republic: Seamus Deane's Sundered Provinces', *boundary 2* 37.2 (Summer 2010), 1.

26. For a detailed survey of Deane's major literary and cultural criticism, see Cleary, 'Dark Fields of the Republic', 1–68. For a discussion of his contributions to the Field Day Theatre Company and their reception, see Marilynn Richtarik, *Acting Between the Lines: The Field Day Theatre Company and Irish Cultural Politics 1980–1984* (Oxford: Oxford University Press, 1994) and 'Brian Friel and Field Day' in Nicholas Grene and Chris Morash (eds), *The Oxford Handbook of Modern Irish Theatre* (Oxford: Oxford University Press, 2016), 357–71.

27. Bill Buford, letter to Seamus Deane, 20 September 1984, and Seamus Deane, draft letter to Bill Buford, 28 October 1994, Seamus Deane papers, MSS 1210, box 3, file folder 5 and box 4, file folder 1, Stuart A. Rose Manuscript, Archives, and Rare Book Library, Emory University, Atlanta, Georgia.

28. For details regarding the institutional challenges of Field Day's publishing projects in the 1980s and early 1990s, see Richtarik, 'Brian Friel and Field Day', 367–70.

29. Bill Buford, letters to Seamus Deane, 20 September, 11 October, and 10 December 1984, Rose Library, MSS 1210, b3/f5.

30. Seamus Deane, 'The Famous Seamus', *New Yorker* (20 March 2000), 54–79.

31. Seamus Deane, 'Haunted', *Granta* 18 (March 1985), 221–35. This piece contains versions of material that would feature in eight sections of Deane's novel: 'Stairs', 'Eddie', 'My Father', 'The Fort', 'Roses', 'Pistol', 'Accident', and the first 'Grandfather' vignette (dated December 1948).

32. Deane, 'Haunted', 228–30.

33. Bill Buford, letters to Seamus Deane, 22 January, 5 February, 8 May, and 29 May 1985 and 7 January 1986, Rose Library, MSS 1210, b3/f5 and b3/f6.

34. Bill Buford, letters to Seamus Deane, 1 May and 18 September 1986, Rose Library, MSS 1210, b3/f6; Seamus Deane, telephone conversation with the author, 9 August 2015.

35. Bill Buford, letter to Seamus Deane, 18 January 1988, referring to a recent meeting in person, and handwritten notes made by Buford and Deane about Deane's book, Rose Library, MSS 1210, b3/f7.

36. Bill Buford, letters to Seamus Deane, 12 February 1988, and 4 January, 28 March, 26 April, and 10 May 1989, Rose Library, MSS 1210, b3/f7.

37. Caroline Michel, letter to Seamus Deane, 6 April 1990, and Angus McKinnon, letters to Seamus Deane, 4 April and 14 May 1990, Rose Library, MSS 1210, b4/f1.

38. Bill Buford, letters to Seamus Deane, 11 June, 24 July, and 6 August 1990; Caroline Michel, letter to Seamus Deane, 19 July 1990; Seamus Deane, draft letter to Bill Buford, 23 August 1990; Bill Buford, faxes to Seamus Deane, 17 August and 22 October 1990, Rose Library, MSS 1210, b4/f1.

39. Richtarik, *Acting Between the Lines*, 257, 262; Catriona Crowe, 'Testimony to a Flowering', *Dublin Review* 10 (Spring 2003): https://thedublinreview.com/article/testimony-to-a-flowering (accessed 12 March 2021).

40. In September 1991, the plan was to publish the novel either in November or early in 1992. Finola O'Doherty, conversation with the author, Buncrana, County Donegal, 17 September 1991.

41. Crowe; Nuala O'Faolain, 'The Voice that Field Day Didn't Record', *Irish Times*, 11 November 1991.

42. See Richtarik, *Acting Between the Lines*, 256–69; Aidan O'Malley, *Field Day and the Translation of Irish Identities: Performing Contradictions* (Basingstoke: Palgrave Macmillan, 2011), 175–81; and Crowe for detailed examination of the controversy over the anthology and its consequences.

43. O'Malley, 176.

44. Crowe.

45. Bew and Gillespie, 201; Linden Peach, *The Contemporary Irish Novel: Critical Readings* (Basingstoke: Palgrave Macmillan, 2004), 236; Seamus Deane, letter to Brian Friel, 30 September 1992, National Library of Ireland, Brian Friel Papers, MS 37, 181/7.

46. Dympna Callaghan, 'An Interview with Seamus Deane', *Social Text* 38 (Spring 1994), 50.

47. Seamus Deane, draft letter to Bill Buford, 28 October 1994, Rose Library, MSS 1210, b4/f1.

48. Sonia Land, letters to Seamus Deane, 3 February 1995 and 13 March 1996, Rose Library, MSS 1210, b4/f1 and 2; Karin Davies, 'Reluctant American Takes on The New Yorker', AP, 4 February 1995: https://apnews.com/article/1cfe07dc69e2437682de69e2b4e36bc1 (accessed 15 March 2021).

49. Stephen Regan, review of *Reading in the Dark, Irish Studies Review* 19 (Summer 1997), 35; Deane, quoted in Nick Fraser, 'A Kind of Life Sentence', *Guardian*, 28 October 1996; '*Reading in the Dark*: An Interview with Seamus Deane', *English & Media Magazine* 36 (Summer 1997), 18; John Brown, *In the Chair: Interviews with Poets from the North of Ireland* (Cliffs of Moher, County Clare: Salmon Poetry, 2002), 98, 97.

50. '*Reading in the Dark*: An Interview with Seamus Deane', 18.

51. Marilynn Richtarik, 'The Other James: James Joyce, Henry James, and Seamus Deane's *Reading in the Dark*', *Texas Studies in Literature and Language* 64.4 (Winter 2022), 416–36.

52. Eileen Battersby, 'Six for the Booker', *Irish Times*, 2 October 1996: https://www.irishtimes.com/culture/six-for-the-booker-1.91645 (accessed 21 December 2021).

53. '*Reading in the Dark*: An Interview with Seamus Deane', 17–18.

54. Seamus Deane, *Reading in the Dark* (New York: Vintage International, 1998), 132. I am citing the 1998 international edition rather than the first edition because it incorporates significant corrections authorized by Deane. Further references to this book will be given in parentheses in the text.

55. Gerry Smyth, *Space and the Irish Cultural Imagination* (Basingstoke: Palgrave, 2001), 132.

56. Examples include Dermot Kelly, 'Joycean Epiphany in Seamus Deane's *Reading in the Dark*' in Wim Tigges (ed.), *Moments of Moment: Aspects of the Literary Epiphany* (Amsterdam: Rodopi, 1999), 435–43; Liam Harte, 'History Lessons: Postcolonialism and Seamus Deane's *Reading in the Dark*', *Irish University Review* 30.1 (Spring/Summer 2000), 149–62; Kennedy-Andrews, 215–23; Tom Herron, 'Derry *Is* Donegal: Thresholds, Vectors, Limits in Seamus Deane's *Reading in the Dark*', *Études irlandaises* 29.2 (2004), 165–83; Michael Parker, *Northern Irish Literature: The Imprint of History, Volume 2: 1975–2006* (Basingstoke: Palgrave Macmillan, 2007), 183–92; Conor Carville, '"Ne Pas Céder Son Désir": Symptom and Fantasy in Seamus Deane's *Reading in the Dark*', *Irish Studies Review* 15.4 (2007), 411–23; Robert F. Garratt, *Trauma and History in the Irish Novel: The Return of the Dead* (Basingstoke: Palgrave Macmillan, 2011), 97–112; and Stefanie Lehner, 'The Irreversible and the Irrevocable: Encircling Trauma in Contemporary Northern Irish Literature' in Oona Frawley (ed.), *Memory Ireland, Volume 3: The Famine and the Troubles* (Syracuse: Syracuse University Press, 2014), 272–92.

57. Maurice Fitzpatrick, 'An Interview with Seamus Deane', *Journal of Irish Studies* 22 (2007), 90. Deane also told Fitzpatrick that he regarded *Reading in the Dark* as closely connected to his poetry collection *Rumours* (91).

58. Fintan O'Toole, 'The Man From God Knows Where: An Interview with Brian Friel', *In Dublin* (28 October 1982), 22.

59. Carol Rumens, 'Reading Deane' [interview with Seamus Deane], *Fortnight* (July/August 1997), 30.

60. '*Reading in the Dark*: An Interview with Seamus Deane', 19; Marilynn Richtarik, *Stewart Parker: A Life* (Oxford: Oxford University Press, 2012), 7; Fitzpatrick, 86.

61. Seamus Deane, 'Haunted', 227, and 'The Birthday Gift', *Rumours* (Dublin: The Dolmen Press, 1977), 14–15. *Rumours* is dedicated 'In Memoriam Frank Deane (1905–75)'.

62. Regan, 35.

63. See Elizabeth Butler Cullingford, 'British Romans and Irish Carthaginians: Anticolonial Metaphor in Heaney, Friel, and McGuinness', *PMLA* 111.2 (March 1996), 222–39.

64. James Joyce, *Ulysses*, ed. Hans Walter Gabler (New York: Random House, 1986), 17.

65. Richard Kearney, 'Myth and Motherland' in *Ireland's Field Day*, Field Day Theatre Company (London: Hutchinson, 1985), 63.

66. Micheál MacDonncha, 'Operation Harvest—50 Years On', *An Phoblacht*, 14 December 2006: https://www.anphoblacht.com/contents/16187 (accessed 28 March 2021).

67. The novel's final section, 'After', is dated July 1971 but spans the decade following the narrator's completion of his university degree in June 1961.

68. Deane, telephone conversation with the author, 9 August 2015; Rumens, 30.

69. Rumens, 30.

70. See Bardon, 681–6, and Bew and Gillespie, 36–7, for a discussion of internment's consequences, prominent among them an increase in Northern Catholic alienation and an upsurge in recruitment to the Provisional IRA.

71. Deane, telephone conversation with the author, 9 August 2015.

72. *Reading in the Dark* was short-listed for the 1996 Booker Prize, won that year's *Guardian* Fiction Prize, and, in 1997, garnered both the *Irish Times* Irish Literature

Prize for Fiction and the *Irish Times* International Fiction Prize. It has been translated into more than twenty languages and attracted significant critical attention.

73. Deane, telephone conversation with the author, 9 August 2015.
74. Fitzpatrick, 90.

Chapter 4

1. Bernard MacLaverty, e-mail to the author, 25 February 2013.
2. Tom Adair, 'Waiting for Waite', *Scotland on Sunday*, 5 June 1994; Bernard MacLaverty, *Lamb* (London: Penguin, 1981), 152; Marisol Morales Ladrón, ' "Writing Is a State of Mind Not an Achievement": An Interview with Bernard MacLaverty', *Atlantis* 23.2 (2001), 208, 206; Liam Harte and Michael Parker, 'Reconfiguring Identities: Recent Northern Irish Fiction' in Liam Harte and Michael Parker (eds), *Contemporary Irish Fiction: Themes, Tropes, Theories* (Basingstoke: Macmillan, 2000), 251.
3. Christian Ganter, 'Bernard MacLaverty, Glasgow, in Interview', *Anglistik* 7.2 (1996), 5–7; Rosa González, 'Bernard MacLaverty' in Jacqueline Hurtley, Rosa González, Inés Praga, and Esther Aliaga, *Ireland in Writing: Interviews with Writers and Academics* (Amsterdam: Rodopi, 1998), 22–3; Jeremy Hodges, 'Author Bernard MacLaverty Regrets the Loss of Old Family Values', *Daily Mail*, 12 October 1999.
4. González, 23–4; Ganter, 6, 21.
5. For a concise description of the UWC Strike, see Marilynn Richtarik, *Stewart Parker: A Life* (Oxford: Oxford University Press, 2012), 127–33. Stewart Parker's Field Day play, *Pentecost* (1987), is set during the UWC Strike and conveys the emotions of that time. Richtarik, 304–15.
6. Hodges; Ganter, 9.
7. Ganter, 9, 6, 22; Ladrón, 201.
8. Harte and Parker, 250–1; Ladrón, 203.
9. Sharon Monteith and Jenny Newman, 'Bernard MacLaverty' in Sharon Monteith, Jenny Newman, and Pat Wheeler, *Contemporary British and Irish Fiction: An Introduction Through Interviews* (London: Arnold, 2004), 110; Ladrón, 209, 206.
10. Monteith and Newman, 110; Helen Meany, 'Lost in Music', *Irish Times*, 3 July 1997.
11. Bernard MacLaverty, notes towards *Grace Notes*, Bernard MacLaverty Papers, National Library of Ireland (NLI), Dublin, MS 6474, box 19; Tillie Olsen, *Silences* (New York: Delacorte Press/Seymour Lawrence, 1978), 18–19.
12. Adair; Meany. This story, 'The Drapery Man', appeared in MacLaverty's third collection, *The Great Profundo and Other Stories* (1987).
13. Bernard MacLaverty, 'An Interview with Richard Rankin Russell', *Irish Literary Supplement* 26.1 (Fall 2006), 22; Ganter, 16; MacLaverty, notes towards *Grace Notes*.
14. Bernard MacLaverty, radio script for *Grace Notes* 7 ('Childhood'), NLI, MS 6474, box 4; Ganter, 10; Monteith and Newman, 105–6.
15. Bernard MacLaverty, radio script for *Best of 3* 12, NLI, MS 6474, box 4; MacLaverty, notes towards *Grace Notes*.
16. MacLaverty, notes towards *Grace Notes*.
17. Colm Tóibín, 'Dublin's Epiphany', *New Yorker* (3 April 1995), 45–53.

18. See, for example, his comments on the Bishop of Galway affair and other contemporary shocks in two interviews he gave in the autumn of 1995: González, 35; Ganter, 11.

19. Bernard MacLaverty, e-mail to the author (quoting a diary entry dated 7 April 1995), 26 February 2013.

20. Paul Bew and Gordon Gillespie, *Northern Ireland: A Chronology of the Troubles 1968–1999* (Lanham, Maryland: The Scarecrow Press, 1999), 293; Seán Farren (ed.), *John Hume: In His Own Words* (Dublin: Four Courts Press, 2018), 266–7; Sean Farren and Robert F. Mulvihill, *Paths to a Settlement in Northern Ireland* (Gerrards Cross, Buckinghamshire: Colin Smythe, 2000), 171; David McKittrick and David McVea, *Making Sense of the Troubles: A History of the Northern Ireland Conflict*, rev. ed. (London: Viking/Penguin, 2012), 236.

21. Bew and Gillespie, 299–300. McKittrick and McVea note that 'Within weeks of the cessation, in fact, the British government had made a private assessment that the start of all-inclusive round-table negotiations was probably two years away' (236).

22. Bew and Gillespie, 301, 307; Gerry Adams, *Hope and History: Making Peace in Ireland* (London: Brandon, 2003), 200–1, 208–9, 214.

23. Adams, 196–8; Bew and Gillespie, 301.

24. The Framework Documents, 22 February 1995: https://cain.ulster.ac.uk/events/peace/docs/fd22295.htm (accessed 12 July 2021).

25. John Major, *The Autobiography* (New York: HarperCollins, 1999), 464; Dean Godson, *Himself Alone: David Trimble and the Ordeal of Unionism* (London: HarperCollins, 2004), 124.

26. Bew and Gillespie, 303–4; Henry McDonald, *Trimble* (London: Bloomsbury, 2000; paperback ed. 2001), 143.

27. Major, 467; Bew and Gillespie, 295.

28. Major, 307, 380–4, 464.

29. Major, 474; Bew and Gillespie, 305.

30. Major, 470–2; Bew and Gillespie, 308.

31. Mo Mowlam, *Momentum: The Struggle for Peace, Politics and the People* (London: Hodder and Stoughton, 2002; Coronet paperback ed. 2003), 87–8; Adams, 220; George Mitchell, *Making Peace* (New York: Knopf, 1999), 57; Jeremy Smith, *Making the Peace in Ireland* (London: Longman, 2002), 185; Bew and Gillespie, 306; Godson, 129.

32. Bew and Gillespie, 309; Adams, 222; Godson, 129–32, 134.

33. Major, 477; Godson, 131; Smith, 185–6.

34. Richard Rankin Russell, *Bernard MacLaverty* (Cranbury, New Jersey: Bucknell University Press, 2009), 12; Ganter, 6; McDonald, 13, 20, 22, 24–5, 30.

35. Bew and Gillespie, 46; McDonald, 34; Godson, 143.

36. McDonald, 46–7.

37. McDonald, 50, 5, 52–3.

38. Godson, 133, 136; Bew and Gillespie, 309; McDonald, 149.

39. Godson, 138–9; Bew and Gillespie, 309; McDonald, 150–1. For Trimble's opinion of Paisley, see McDonald, 76–7.

40. Bew and Gillespie, 312; McDonald, 156–7; Frank Millar, *David Trimble: The Price of Peace* (Dublin: The Liffey Press, 2004), 46, 45.

41. Godson, 153; McDonald, 158.

42. González, 37.

43. Bernard MacLaverty, original (incomplete) version of the novel that became *Grace Notes*, NLI, MS 6474, Box 19, and notes on the writing of *Grace Notes*, attached to an e-mail to the author, 21 February 2013.

44. Ganter, 20–1.

45. Smith, 191; Major, 477; Adams, 223; Godson, 192.

46. McDonald, 165; Bew and Gillespie, 308–11.

47. Major, 478–9; Bew and Gillespie, 311–12. See Adams, 223–9, for an account of Sinn Féin's frantic (and largely unsuccessful) behind-the-scenes efforts to influence the brief given to the international body by the two governments.

48. Major, 480. See also Godson, 168–9, for a discussion of Trimble's remarks and their reception.

49. Major, 480.

50. Major, 482–4; Mitchell, 10, 27.

51. Major, 484; Bew and Gillespie, 316; Bill Clinton, 'Remarks by the President to the Citizens of Londonderry', 30 November 1995: https://cain.ulster.ac.uk/events/peace/docs/pres2.htm (accessed 23 July 2021). *The Cure at Troy* is discussed in Chapter Two.

52. Mitchell, 26–8.

53. Mitchell, 29–30.

54. Mitchell, 30–2.

55. Mitchell, 35. See Mitchell, 35–6, for the complete text of the Mitchell Principles.

56. Mitchell, 38; Godson, 195.

57. See Godson, 196–7, for detailed discussion of a memo by Mayhew outlining the British government's options for dealing with the Mitchell Commission's report.

58. Bew and Gillespie, 318–19; Smith, 193.

59. Bew and Gillespie, 319; Farren (ed.), 283–4; Mitchell, 39–40.

60. Major, 488; McDonald, 166; Bew and Gillespie, 321, 325.

61. Bew and Gillespie, 326; Mitchell, 43–4; Major, 490. This Labour party was unrelated to the British Labour Party.

62. Adams, 246, 251; Bew and Gillespie, 329; Smith, 198–9.

63. Adams, 251, 254–6; Farren and Mulvihill, 177.

64. Mitchell, 46–50, 56–7; Bew and Gillespie, 330; Adams, 257.

65. The following descriptions of and quotations from MacLaverty's various drafts of the novel are based on copies held in the Bernard MacLaverty papers in the NLI, MS 6474, Box 9. The June 1996 draft is 183 pages.

66. Monteith and Newman, 109; Ladrón, 206–7.

67. The June 1996 draft contains a passage cut from later versions of the text, in which Miss Bingham complains that she no longer plays the piano, owing to arthritis: '"I've lost all my flexibility." She moved her fingers slowly. "But then you'd say I'm an Ulster Protestant and hadn't got any in the first place."'

68. Bew and Gillespie, 330; McKittrick and McVea, 246.

69. Bew and Gillespie, 331–2; Mitchell, 58–9; McDonald, 170; McKittrick and McVea, 246.

70. Godson, 233–4, 237; Major, 491.

71. Major, 491; Mitchell, 59; McKittrick and McVea, 247; Adams, 260.

72. Bew and Gillespie, 331; Godson, 238–9; Farren and Mulvihill, 179.

73. Godson, 238; McDonald, 173; McKittrick and McVea, 247.

74. Mitchell, 61.

75. Godson, 231, 240, 237.

76. Bew and Gillespie, 332; McDonald, 171–2.

77. Godson, 239.

78. Bernard MacLaverty, notes towards *Grace Notes*, NLI, MS 6474, Box 19. Although MacLaverty did not date individual notes, I believe, based on passages added to the novel between June 1996 and the draft dated 9 September 1996, that these comments on 'Orange heritage' were made in response to the 1996 Drumcree crisis.

79. Adams, 259; MacLaverty, notes towards *Grace Notes*.

80. Farren and Mulvihill, 179; Mitchell, 54–69.

81. Bernard MacLaverty, draft of *Grace Notes* dated 9 September 1996 (197 pages), NLI, MS 6474, Box 9, and script for *Grace Notes* 1, [1999] (BBC Radio Scotland), NLI, MS 6474, Box 4.

82. *Oxford English Dictionary* (http://www.oed.com), 'grace' (noun), definitions 11a, 11b, 19 and 15a (accessed 19 February 2013); MacLaverty, notes towards *Grace Notes*.

83. The third draft (216 pages) is undated; the fourth (229 pages) is dated 12 November 1996; the fifth (229 pages) is dated 14 November; and the sixth (230 pages) is dated 4 December. Significant additions to the third draft include passages about one of Catherine's mentors, a Chinese composer named Huang Xaio Gang, and references to a symphony Shostakovich wrote in response to the Nazi massacre of Kiev's Jews, together with Catherine's musings about 'the places of death in her own country'.

84. Mitchell, 84–7.

85. Bernard MacLaverty, *Grace Notes* (London: Jonathan Cape, 1997), 9. Additional references to the novel will be given in parentheses in the text. Other signs of the ongoing Troubles include special security for air travellers to Northern Ireland (5) and the narrator's account of a BBC local news report: 'Nobody had been killed' (45).

86. Bernard MacLaverty, 'A Calendar of Events Grace Notes', sent as an attachment to an e-mail to the author, 25 February 2013. MacLaverty compiled this chronology after completing a draft of the novel to help himself check the details of his 'mosaic'. In it, he identified the present of the novel (Catherine's trip home for her father's funeral) as January 1988, with the concert performance of *Vernicle* taking place in December 1987. However, this 'Calendar' is a private document; no specific dates are mentioned in the novel itself.

87. Robert Schreiter, 'Establishing a Shared Identity: The Role of the Healing of Memories and of Narrative' in Sebastian C. H. Kim, Pauline Kollontai, and Greg Hoyland (eds), *Peace and Reconciliation: In Search of Shared Identity* (Aldershot: Ashgate, 2008), 7, 9–11.

88. Ganter, 17.

89. Schreiter, 13.

90. Schreiter, 13.

91. Schreiter, 8–9, 16–17.

92. Schreiter, 13.

93. Schreiter, 14, 13.

94. Gerry Smyth, ' "The Same Sound but with a Different Meaning": Music, Repetition, and Identity in Bernard MacLaverty's *Grace Notes*', *Éire-Ireland* 37.3/4 (2002), 18.

95. MacLaverty, notes towards *Grace Notes*.

96. MacLaverty recalled that the structure of *Grace Notes* was also influenced by the two-part structure of Beethoven's Piano Sonata No. 32 in C minor, Op.111. Bernard MacLaverty, e-mail to the author, 10 January 2022.

97. Ladrón, 203–4.

98. Bernard MacLaverty, e-mail to the author, 10 January 2022.

99. Harte and Parker, 243.

100. Russell, 97; *Oxford English Dictionary* (http://oed.com), 'reconciliation' (noun), definition 1b (accessed 31 October 2012).

101. The concert scene of *Grace Notes* has inspired much insightful commentary. In addition to the works already cited by Richard Rankin Russell, Liam Harte and Michael Parker, and Gerry Smyth, see Patrick Grant's discussion of it in *Literature, Rhetoric and Violence in Northern Ireland, 1968–98: Hardened to Death* (Basingstoke: Palgrave, 2001), 144–51.

102. *Oxford English Dictionary* (http://oed.com), 'reconciliation' (noun), definition 2 (accessed 31 October 2012).

103. Grant, 149.

104. I am obliged to Mary Grace Elliott for the image of the 'repeat sign', which she used to describe the ending of Joyce's *Ulysses*. My agent, Jonathan Williams, adds that this would be a repeat sign *da capo*.

Chapter 5

1. Joseph Kelly, 'A Defense of Danis Rose', *James Joyce Quarterly* 35.4/36.1 (Summer/Fall 1998), 811–12; Sarah Lyall, ' "Ulysses" in Deep Trouble Again: A New Edition Purges What May Have Been Joyce's Errors and Enrages Critics', *New York Times*, 23 June 1997; Seamus Deane, 'A Cruelly Efficient Act', *New York Times*, 23 June 1997; Deaglán de Bréadún, *The Far Side of Revenge: Making Peace in Northern Ireland*, rev. ed. (Cork: The Collins Press, 2008), 47. See Chapter Four for discussion of the Drumcree standoffs in 1995 and 1996.

2. de Bréadún, 49.

3. de Bréadún, 38–9, 42–7; Deane; Paul Bew and Gordon Gillespie, *Northern Ireland: A Chronology of the Troubles 1968–1999* (Lanham, Maryland: Scarecrow, 1999), 342.

4. Deane.

5. Colum McCann, *TransAtlantic* (New York: Random House, 2013; trade paperback ed. 2014), 109. Further references to this book will be given in parentheses in the text.

6. Among autobiographical accounts, see Tony Blair, *A Journey: My Political Life* (New York: Knopf, 2010); Bertie Ahern with Richard Aldous, *Bertie Ahern: The Autobiography* (London: Hutchinson, 2009); David Trimble, 'Antony Alcock Memorial Lecture' (University of Ulster, 24 April 2007: http://www.ricorso.net/rx/az-data/authors/t/Trimble_D/xtra.htm); Mo Mowlam, *Momentum: The Struggle for Peace, Politics and the People* (London: Hodder and Stoughton, 2002; Coronet paperback ed. 2003); Jonathan Powell, *Great Hatred, Little Room: Making Peace in Northern Ireland* (London: The Bodley Head, 2008); George Mitchell, *Making Peace* (New York: Knopf, 1999); and Gerry Adams, *Hope and History: Making Peace in Ireland*

(London: Brandon, 2003). For scholarly works by talks participants, see Kate Fearon, *Women's Work: The Story of the Northern Ireland Women's Coalition* (Belfast: The Blackstaff Press, 1999); Thomas Hennessey, *The Northern Ireland Peace Process: Ending the Troubles?* (New York: Palgrave, 2001); and Sean Farren and Robert F. Mulvihill, *Paths to a Settlement in Northern Ireland* (Gerrards Cross, Buckinghamshire: Colin Smythe, 2000). Fearon was a member of the NIWC delegation during the negotiations, Hennessey a part of the UUP talks team, and Farren a leading SDLP negotiator.

7. Powell, 8–10. Blair's mother came from Donegal, one of three Ulster counties ceded to the new Irish state after partition, and her family were Protestant farmers. His maternal grandfather had been Grand Master of an Orange lodge, and his maternal grandmother, who suffered from Alzheimer's at the time and barely recognized him, had once urged Blair, whatever else he did, never to marry a Catholic. Unbeknownst to her, he had recently begun dating the (Catholic) woman who would become his wife and the mother of his children, who would be raised as Catholics. As a child, Blair visited Ireland every summer until the Troubles erupted in 1969. Blair, 155–7.

8. Powell, 9; Blair, 164.

9. Powell, 8, 11–13.

10. Powell, 11; Blair, 164; de Bréadún, 42.

11. Adams, 282–3; Mowlam, 77; Powell, 13–14; Mitchell, 35.

12. Powell, 14. The Mitchell Commission and its report are discussed in Chapter Four.

13. de Bréadún, 50; Ed Moloney, *A Secret History of the IRA*, 2nd ed. (London: Penguin, 2007), 462.

14. Ahern, 195; Moloney, 463–5; Adams, 295–6.

15. Moloney, 467; de Bréadún, 54.

16. Bew and Gillespie, 344; Mowlam, 98; Adams, 294.

17. Seán Farren (ed.), *John Hume In His Own Words* (Dublin: Four Courts Press, 2018), 290–1; Mowlam, 112–13; Adams, 301; Ahern, 196; de Bréadún, 55.

18. Henry McDonald, *Trimble* (London: Bloomsbury, 2000; paperback ed. 2001), 69, 180–1.

19. Scholars often cite George Mitchell's comment on this development: 'The decision by Paisley and McCartney to quit the talks was predictable. . . . Yet, if their objective was, as they repeatedly insisted, to end this process, then their walkout was a fateful error. Reaching agreement without their presence was extremely difficult; it would have been impossible with them in the room.' Mitchell, 110.

20. Mowlam, 118–19; Fearon, 82.

21. Bew and Gillespie, 348; Mitchell, 120, 62, 68.

22. de Bréadún, 64–6; Mitchell, 121, 123. Adams repeatedly requested a meeting with the UUP leader and attempted to strike up conversations with him in neutral places like the canteen and the men's toilet, but he claims that the only response he ever received was one admonition to 'grow up'. Adams, 311, 365.

23. Mitchell, 36; Trimble.

24. Trimble; Adams, 315; Fionnuala O Connor, *Breaking the Bonds: Making Peace in Northern Ireland* (Edinburgh: Mainstream Publishing, 2002), 26, 31. Despite Hume's withdrawal during many of the public sessions, he likely played an important part behind the scenes, talking individually with talks participants. Gerry Adams notes,

for example, that Hume was one of the few people to call regularly on the Sinn Féin delegation. Adams, 352.

25. Mitchell, 10, 121, 123.

26. Adams, 321; Mitchell, 125–6.

27. Mowlam, 194.

28. The SDLP often felt taken for granted during the negotiations, with, Blair admits, some justification: ' "If we had weapons you'd treat us more seriously" was their constant refrain. There was some truth in it. The big prize was plainly an end to violence, and they weren't the authors of the violence.' Moreover, for strategic reasons, the SDLP had decided not to enter any government with unionists unless Sinn Féin 'were at the table too', to prevent republicans from accusing them of selling out. Blair, 170–1. However, the very 'structure and agenda for the negotiations', based on the SDLP's analysis of the Northern Ireland problem and its potential solution (guaranteeing both unionists and nationalists 'effective political, symbolic and administrative expression of their identity, ethos and way of life') indicated that, from their perspective, the important arguments had been made and won long ago: their 'focus had already been adopted and no longer had to be argued for in any essential manner'. Farren and Mulvihill, 188–9.

29. Ahern, 211–12. This split, prompted by the Army Council's decision to renew the ceasefire and by the Sinn Féin leadership's acceptance of the Mitchell Principles, marked the culmination of a struggle within the IRA that had been going on for at least a year. Adams downplays this development, 316–17, but see Moloney, 442–54 and 468–79, for more detailed discussion of these serious internal challenges to Sinn Féin's peace strategy.

30. Ahern, 212; Graham Spencer, *The State of Loyalism in Northern Ireland* (Basingstoke: Palgrave Macmillan, 2008), 160; Bew and Gillespie, 349, 352.

31. Bew and Gillespie, 352–3; Mowlam, 180–90; Adams, 327–8; Fearon, 96; Ahern, 212; Powell, 28–9; Spencer, 160–1.

32. Fearon, 97.

33. Powell, 25–8; Bew and Gillespie, 353; Hennessey, 117–19.

34. Hennessey, 117, 119–20; Fearon, 99–100; Adams, 330.

35. de Bréadún, 100–2. See Chapter Four for discussion of the governments' joint Framework Document and its reception in 1995.

36. Adams, 333; Bew and Gillespie, 355.

37. de Bréadún, 106–7; Adams, 338.

38. Fearon, 96; Mowlam, 202. Adams reveals in his peace process memoir that he knew by the autumn of 1997 that 'a Northern assembly would be part of any future political institutions', although he confided this belief only to Martin McGuinness; his aim in the 'real negotiation' would be 'the best assembly possible, firmly locked into and interdependent on the all-Ireland institutions'. Trimble, for his part, admits that he 'had long known, without ever actually saying so', that the UUP would have to abandon its 'executive committee model' in favour of 'the ministerial model' for the Northern Ireland executive preferred by 'virtually every other participant' in the talks. Adams, 315, 334; Trimble.

39. Mitchell, 143–4.

40. Mowlam, 207–8; Mitchell, 145.
41. Mowlam, 206; Fearon, 89.
42. Mitchell, 150–1.
43. Mowlam, 209.
44. Mitchell, 151–6; Powell, 90, 31.
45. Mitchell, 156, 159–62.
46. Mitchell, 162–4.
47. Mowlam, 212–13; Adams, 354; Mitchell 165.
48. Hennessey, 164–5.
49. Trimble; Hennessey, 136–7.
50. Mitchell, 166–73; Adams, 356; Mowlam, 214.
51. Mitchell, 175; Ahern, 178, 200–1; Blair, 168; Powell, 93–4.
52. Ahern, 221–2; Trimble; Powell, 32–3. Powell's account of the final Strand Two negotiations differs in significant respects from Trimble's and provides detail on the governments' parallel negotiations with nationalists on Strand Two (96–8). See also Hennessey, 166–7, Blair, 168–71, and Mitchell, 175–6, on the Strand Two negotiations.
53. de Bréadún, 126.
54. Powell, 97–8; de Bréadún, 124. Powell notes that Blair's threat in January 1998 'that if the parties did not agree then the governments would put their proposals to a referendum in Ireland North and South in May' had proved such an effective means of 'galvanising' them that it became 'our perennial Plan B'. Powell, 31–2.
55. Trimble. See David McKittrick and David McVea, *Making Sense of the Troubles: A History of the Northern Ireland Conflict*, rev. ed. (London: Viking/Penguin, 2012), 104–24, for discussion of the last serious attempt at a Northern Ireland settlement, in 1973/74.
56. Hennessey, 111; Blair, 172–3; Alastair Campbell and Richard Stott (eds), *The Blair Years: Extracts from the Alastair Campbell Diaries* (London: Hutchinson, 2007), 293, 296. Campbell served as Blair's chief press secretary and official spokesman; see 287–98 for his notes on the final week of negotiations in April 1998. Made at the time or immediately afterwards, these give a visceral sense of the chaotic nature of the proceedings, the way multiple things were always happening at once, how changes made to keep one party on board would usually create an imbalance that had to be corrected by concessions to another party, and the emotional ups and downs of the British government's negotiating team.
57. Mowlam, 217, 164–5; Blair, 173. Blair makes this process sound considerably easier than it was. Fearon provides two poignant glimpses of Mowlam's activity during the first hours of 10 April (113–14, 117).
58. Mowlam, 220–1; Adams, 359–60; Powell, 100–1.
59. Adams, 361–3.
60. Fearon, 104–7.
61. Fearon, 107.
62. Fearon, 112–13.
63. de Bréadún, 128; Powell, 100; Spencer, 165.
64. Henry Sinnerton, *David Ervine: Uncharted Waters* (Dingle, Co. Kerry, Ireland: Brandon, 2002), 211; Spencer, 171, 174.

65. Powell, 104; Fearon, 118–19; Adams, 363–5. See also de Bréadún, 135–9, for a discussion of the UUP's 'meeting from hell'.

66. Hennessey, 169; Trimble. Sinn Féin attracted much greater electoral support than either the PUP or the UDP, making it the only one of the paramilitary-related parties with a realistic prospect of gaining one or more ministerial posts; hence, the issue of decommissioning as a precondition for serving in the Northern Ireland Executive was of more immediate importance to republicans than to loyalists.

67. Trimble. As Blair and Powell tell the story, the letter idea was Blair's rather than Trimble's. See Blair, 176, and Powell, 105.

68. Powell, 105; Trimble; Blair, 176.

69. Powell, 105; Trimble; Adams, 364–5.

70. Powell, 32; Mitchell, 180; Fearon, 120–1. Unionists had, by 1998, a well-earned reputation as nay-sayers. Their most memorable slogan against the hated Anglo–Irish Agreement had been 'Ulster Says "No." '

71. Powell, 106; Ahern, 228–9. Many unionists continue to call it the Belfast Agreement, while nationalists (and most international commentators) refer to the Good Friday Agreement.

72. Adams, 365; McDonald, 212; Fearon, 121. The women's sentiment recalls ideas expressed at the end of Stewart Parker's 1987 play *Pentecost*, when the central character, Marian, declares that the dead are 'not our masters, they're only our creditors, for the life they never knew. We owe them at least that—the fullest life for which they could ever have hoped'. Parker, quoted in Marilynn Richtarik, *Stewart Parker: A Life* (Oxford: Oxford University Press, 2012), 314.

73. Earl G. Ingersoll and Mary C. Ingersoll (eds), *Conversations with Colum McCann* (Jackson: University Press of Mississippi, 2017), xv–xvi; nationalbook.org; James Santel, 'Funambulism: An Interview with Colum McCann', *Los Angeles Review of Books* (12 June 2013): https://lareviewofbooks.org/article/funambulism-an-interview-with-colum-mccann/ (accessed 3 January 2022).

74. Synne Rifbjerg, 'Do What Is Most Difficult' (2013 interview with Colum McCann) in Ingersoll and Ingersoll, 181. Caused by the potato crop's failure over several years, the Famine resulted in Ireland losing a fifth of its population to hunger, disease, and emigration between 1845 and 1851. See S. J. Connolly (ed.), *Oxford Companion to Irish History*, 2nd ed. (Oxford: Oxford University Press, 2002; paperback ed. 2004), 238–40.

75. Santel; Rifbjerg, 182.

76. Joseph Lennon, ' "A Country of the Elsewheres": An Interview with Colum McCann', *New Hibernia Review* 16.2 (Summer 2012), 98; John Cusatis, ' "Embracing the World by Inventing the World": The Literary Journey of Colum McCann' (2012) in Ingersoll and Ingersoll, 132; Rifbjerg, 182.

77. Santel.

78. Rifbjerg, 183; Santel.

79. 'A Conversation with Colum McCann and Elizabeth Strout' in *TransAtlantic* (New York: Random House, 2014 trade paperback edition), 309–10.

80. Colum McCann, conversation with the author, New York City, 1 November 2019; Michael Lackey, 'Colum McCann: Contested Realities in the Biographical Novel' (interview), *Éire-Ireland* 53.1/2 (Spring/Summer 2018), 141; Santel.

81. Lackey, 141; Cécile Maudet, 'Two Interviews with Colum McCann' (2013 and 2014) in Ingersoll and Ingersoll, 173; Charles I. Armstrong, '"George Mitchell's Peace": The Good Friday Agreement in Colum McCann's Novel *TransAtlantic*' in Charles I. Armstrong, David Herbert, and Jan Erik Mustad (eds), *The Legacy of the Good Friday Agreement: Northern Irish Politics, Culture and Art after 1998* (Cham, Switzerland: Palgrave Macmillan, 2019), 65.

82. James Joyce, *Dubliners*, ed. Terence Brown (New York: Penguin, 1993), 225. Lily in *TransAtlantic*, who with her female descendants holds the novel together, takes her name from the servant girl whose perspective governs the opening paragraph of the 'The Dead' and who discomfits the protagonist, Gabriel, with her bitter response to his attempt at small talk. Alec Michod, 'The Rumpus Interview with Colum McCann' in Ingersoll and Ingersoll, 143.

83. Michod, 140.

84. Deaglán de Bréadún, 'US Senator George Mitchell and The Good Friday Agreement', *IrishCentral*, 10 April 2020: https://www.irishcentral.com/roots/irishamerica/good-friday-agreement-george-mitchell (accessed 6 October 2021). This article originally appeared in April 1999 in *Irish America Magazine*.

85. Yeats expressed frustration about his theatre work in a poem entitled 'The Fascination of What's Difficult'.

86. Armstrong, 67; Mitchell, 44: Fearon, chapters 3 and 4.

87. See Mitchell, 181–2, for the text of his announcement.

Conclusion

1. See Graham Spencer, 'Managing a Peace Process: An Interview with Jonathan Powell', *Irish Political Studies* 25.3 (September 2010), 437–55.

2. Jonathan Powell, *Great Hatred, Little Room: Making Peace in Northern Ireland* (London: The Bodley Head, 2008), 108–9.

3. Powell, 165, 209; David McKittrick and David McVea, *Making Sense of the Troubles: A History of the Northern Ireland Conflict*, revised ed. (London: Viking/Penguin, 2012), 352–62; Tony Blair, *A Journey: My Political Life* (New York: Knopf, 2010), 180.

4. In addition to McKittrick and McVea, see Deaglán de Bréadún, *The Far Side of Revenge: Making Peace in Northern Ireland*, revised ed. (Cork: The Collins Press, 2008).

5. McKittrick and McVea, 358, 362. Even more incredibly, Paisley and McGuinness struck up a public friendship in their new roles and quickly became known as the 'Chuckle Brothers'. Novelist Glenn Patterson commented of 'the Ian Paisley/Martin McGuinness double act, and barely suppressed love affair' that Northern Ireland's inhabitants were thereafter living 'not at the End of History, but the End of Surprise'. McKittrick and McVea, 282–3; Marilynn Richtarik and Kevin Chappell, 'An Interview with Glenn Patterson', *Five Points: A Journal of Literature & Art* 13.2 (2010), 51.

6. Powell, 308.

7. For more detailed discussion of these initiatives and others, see Patricia Lundy and Mark McGovern, 'Truth, Justice and Dealing with the Legacy of the Past in Northern Ireland, 1998–2008', *Ethnopolitics* 7.1 (2008), 177–93, and Colin Coulter, Niall Gilmartin, Katy Hayward, and Peter Shirlow, *Northern Ireland a Generation after Good Friday:*

Lost Futures and New Horizons in the 'Long Peace' (Manchester: Manchester University Press, 2021), 70–103.

8. Graham Dawson, *Making Peace with the Past? Memory, Trauma and the Irish Troubles* (Manchester: Manchester University Press, 2007), xix, 84.

9. Lundy and McGovern, 179–80. See Priscilla B. Hayner, *Unspeakable Truths: Transitional Justice and the Challenge of Truth Commissions*, 2nd ed. (New York: Routledge, 2011) for an extensive discussion of truth commissions in their various forms and a chart listing forty such bodies established during the last quarter of the twentieth century and the first decade of the twenty-first.

10. Erin Daly, 'Truth Skepticism: An Inquiry into the Value of Truth in Times of Transition', *International Journal of Transitional Justice* 2 (2008), 23–41.

11. See, for example, David Mendeloff, 'Truth-Seeking, Truth-Telling, and Postconflict Peacebuilding: Curb the Enthusiasm?', *International Studies Review* 6.3 (2004), 355–80, and Daly.

12. Daly, 25, 38, 36–7.

13. Brandon Hamber, 'Rights and Reasons: Challenges for Truth Recovery in South Africa and Northern Ireland', *Fordham International Law Journal* 26.4 (April 2003), 1088–9.

14. See, for example, Ryan Gawn, 'Truth Cohabitation: A Truth Commission for Northern Ireland?', *Irish Political Studies* 22.3 (2007), 339–61.

15. Quoted in Gawn, 341.

16. Hamber, 1076–7, 1081, 1083, 1092.

17. Gawn, 341–3.

18. These passages come from reports published by the Northern Ireland Affairs Committee in April and October 2005, quoted in Gawn, 344. However, see Chapter 7 of Marie Breen Smyth, *Truth Recovery and Justice after Conflict: Managing Violent Pasts* (London: Routledge, 2007), 108–42, for analysis of the unionist bias of the NIAC (owing, in no small part, to the fact that Sinn Féin members elected to the British Parliament continued to pursue a policy of abstentionism, refusing to take their seats at Westminster).

19. Lundy and McGovern, 183; Smyth, 156–67.

20. Lundy and McGovern, 185, 190; Gawn, 346–51.

21. Lundy and McGovern, 187; Smyth, 181.

22. David Park, conversation with the author, Belfast, 5 April 2017; Ian Sansom, 'David Park: A Life in Books', *Guardian*, 20 April 2012; Sue Leonard, 'Interview. David Park' (originally published in the *Irish Examiner* in February 2008): http://journalistsueleonard.blogspot.com/2008/07/interview-david-park.html (accessed 14 October 2021).

23. Antjie Krog, *Country of My Skull: Guilt, Sorrow, and the Limits of Forgiveness in the New South Africa* (New York: Three Rivers Press, 2000); David Park, conversation with the author, Belfast, 22 July 2013.

24. Glenn Patterson, 'David Park', *Irish Pages* 4.2 (2008), 162.

25. Leonard, 'Interview. David Park'; Park, conversation with the author, 5 April 2017; Ciaran Carson, 'The Truth Commissioner', *Independent*, 28 February 2008; Patterson, 163.

26. David Park, *The Truth Commissioner* (New York: Bloomsbury, 2008), 21, 94, 129, 187, 265. Further references to this book will be given in parentheses in the text. On the connections between 11 September, the Northern Bank robbery, and the IRA's

announcement, see Powell, 310, 262–8; McKittrick and McVea, 359–60; and Feargal Cochrane, *Northern Ireland: The Fragile Peace*, rev. ed. (New Haven: Yale University Press, 2021), 232–4.

27. Kiran Acharya, 'The Truth Commissioner', *Culture Northern Ireland* (26 February 2008): https://www.culturenorthernireland.org/features/literature/truth-commissioner (accessed 18 October 2021).

28. Park, conversation with the author, 5 April 2017; Sansom; David Park, e-mail to the author, 22 April 2014.

29. Park, conversations with the author, 5 April 2017 and 22 July 2013.

30. Park, conversation with the author, 5 April 2017.

31. I picture the Spires Mall and Conference Centre: originally a church, it later served as the headquarters of the Presbyterian Church in Ireland before being converted for more commercial purposes in the early 1990s. Like the concert scene at the end of Bernard MacLaverty's novel *Grace Notes*, discussed in Chapter Four, the climax of *The Truth Commissioner* takes place in a de-/re-consecrated church.

32. Park, conversation with the author, 22 July 2013.

33. Stefanie Lehner, ' "Absent and yet Somehow Still Present": Representing the Irish Disappeared in Contemporary Photography and Fiction' in Chris Andrews and Matt McGuire (eds), *Post-Conflict Literature: Human Rights, Peace, Justice* (New York: Routledge, 2016), 31–2. See Ed Moloney, *A Secret History of the IRA*, 2nd ed. (London: Penguin, 2007), 122–5, and Patrick Radden Keefe, 'Where the Bodies are Buried', *New Yorker* (16 March 2015), 42–61, for divergent accounts of the most (in)famous and controversial such case: that of Jean McConville, a widowed mother of ten suspected by the IRA of informing on republicans for the British Army and 'disappeared' by them in December 1972—her body was finally found in 2003. I was teaching *The Truth Commissioner* in the spring of 2014 when the Police Service of Northern Ireland, investigating allegations that he had given the order for McConville's abduction, questioned Sinn Féin President Gerry Adams for four days. Park's novel, eerily prophetic upon its publication in 2008, still read like it had been ripped from the headlines six years later.

34. Park, conversation with the author, 5 April 2017.

35. Park, conversation with the author, 22 July 2013; Leonard, 'Interview. David Park'.

36. Fionnuala O Connor, *Breaking the Bonds: Making Peace in Northern Ireland* (Edinburgh: Mainstream Publishing, 2002), 78. Throughout the peace process, Gerry Adams and Martin McGuinness denied that they even belonged to the IRA, let alone held any sort of leadership role in it, but journalist Ed Moloney, in a well-informed book about the organization, writes that McGuinness served as chief of staff for about four and a half years between February 1978 and the autumn of 1982, giving up the position to devote himself more fully to politics. He also served as chairman of the Army Council and as the IRA's Northern commander during many of the peace process years. Moloney, 173, 215, 613, 697.

37. Park, conversation with the author, 22 July 2013; O Connor, 79, 75–6; de Bréadún, 74–5, 84–5.

38. Joseph O'Connor, 'Public Men and Private Troubles', *Guardian*, 8 February 2008.

39. In February 2008, the same month *The Truth Commissioner* was published, a former Sinn Féin driver was taken into protective custody following reports that he had

worked as an informer. At the novel's launch, Glenn Patterson praised Park's 'foresight' in creating 'a cameo for the driver of his prominent Sinn Féin politician'. McKittrick and McVea, 363; Patterson, 163.

40. Patrick Radden Keefe, *Say Nothing: A True Story of Murder and Memory in Northern Ireland* (New York: Anchor Books, 2020), 317–22. The British government also had high-ranking informants in the loyalist paramilitaries. The most notorious, Brian Nelson, was likewise implicated in about fifty murders. In 2012, then British Prime Minister David Cameron acknowledged 'frankly shocking levels of state collusion'. Keefe, 322–6. See also Moloney, 574–9.
41. Powell, 208–9; Moloney, 579–83; Keefe, 321–2; McKittrick and McVea, 360.
42. Park, conversation with the author, 22 July 2013.
43. See John McGarry, 'Police Reform in Northern Ireland', *Irish Political Studies* 15.1 (2000), 173–82.
44. de Bréadún, 419; Dean Godson, *Himself Alone: David Trimble and the Ordeal of Unionism* (London: HarperCollins, 2004), 476; Powell, 157; McGarry, 173, 177–8.
45. Frank Millar, *David Trimble: The Price of Peace* (Dublin: The Liffey Press, 2004), 99; Powell, 157.
46. Powell, 157; McGarry, 179–80; Godson, 486; Millar, 93, 95, 98.
47. McKittrick and McVea, 356; Millar, 94.
48. Park, conversation with the author, 5 April 2017. Gilroy longs to retire to the west coast of Ireland, by the Atlantic Ocean; Henry Stanfield, the British truth commissioner, spends a great deal of time sitting near the window of his 'luxurious apartment overlooking the river' (20); and former IRA member Michael Madden begins and ends each day in Florida on the shore of a lake near his home. Critic Stefanie Lehner, likewise noting the prevalence of 'water metaphors' for the characters' lives in *The Truth Commissioner*, observes that water can also be 'an image of erasure': 'In Greek mythology the river Lethe is said to induce forgetting of the previous life', something each of the protagonists desires. Lehner, 'Post-Conflict Masculinities: *Filiative Reconciliation in Five Minutes of Heaven* and David Park's *The Truth Commissioner*' in Caroline Magennis and Raymond Mullen (eds), *Irish Masculinities: Reflections on Literature and Culture* (Dublin: Irish Academic Press, 2011), 72–3.
49. Powell, 312.
50. Matt McGuire, 'The Trouble(s) with Transitional Justice: David Park's *The Truth Commissioner*', *Irish University Review* 47 supplement (2017), 517.
51. McGuire, 525.
52. Lisa Propst, 'Truth Commissions and Unspoken Narratives in Gillian Slovo's *Red Dust* and David Park's *The Truth Commissioner*', *The Comparatist* 41 (2017), 297–301. Propst believes that the 'slippage of pronouns' in Gilroy's recollection of Connor's killing 'renders the identity of the shooter unclear' (301) and that Gilroy 'may have pulled the trigger' (297), and a surprising number of critics (as well as my students) seem to agree. I would not go so far as that, nor did Park intend the fact of who pulled the trigger to be in doubt: in his mind, Rafferty killed Connor. David Park, conversation with the author, 5 April 2017.
53. Malachi O'Doherty, 'The Past Catches Up', *Fortnight* (July/August 2008), 27; David Park, conversation with the author, 5 April 2017; Shameem Black, 'Truth Commission Thrillers', *Social Text 107* 29.2 (Summer 2011), 62.

54. In *Country of My Skull*, Antjie Krog includes a letter she received from a policeman's wife, describing her reactions to the South African TRC hearings. The woman reported catching her husband 'turning his gun over and over in his lap' and hearing him say, 'They can give me amnesty a thousand times. Even if God and everyone else forgives me a thousand times—I have to live with this hell. The problem is in my head, my conscience. There is only one way to be free of it. Blow my own brains out. Because that's where my hell is' (195). Fenton would likely agree.

55. Patterson, 163; Joseph O'Neill, 'The Informer', *New York Times*, 30 March 2008; Park, conversation with the author, 5 April 2017.

56. Truth and Reconciliation Commission of South Africa, *Truth and Reconciliation Commission of South Africa Report*, Volume 1 (1998), 110–14: https://www.justice.gov.za/trc/report/finalreport/Volume%201.pdf (accessed 12 February 2022).

57. Seamus Heaney, *The Cure at Troy* (London: Faber and Faber, 1990), 77.

58. Stewart Parker, *Dramatis Personae & Other Writings*, ed. Gerald Dawe, Maria Johnston, and Clare Wallace (Prague: Litteraria Pragensia, 2008), 26. In 1973, Parker taught a creative writing class at Long Kesh prison camp, where one of his brightest students was Gerry Adams. Marilynn Richtarik, *Stewart Parker: A Life* (Oxford: Oxford University Press, 2012), 123–4.

References

Archives Consulted

In researching this book, I drew heavily on literary archives held by the National Library of Ireland (NLI) in Dublin, Ireland, and the Stuart A. Rose Manuscript, Archives, and Rare Book Library (Rose Library) of Emory University in Atlanta, Georgia, USA. NLI collections cited include: the Field Day papers (MS 46 and 47), the Brian Friel papers (MS 37), the Seamus Heaney papers (MS 49), and the Bernard MacLaverty papers (MS 6474). Rose Library collections consulted include: the Seamus Deane papers (MSS 1210), the Seamus Heaney papers (MSS 960), the Michael Longley papers (MSS 744), and the Tom Paulin papers (MSS 880). The final element in Rose Library citations refers to box and file folder numbers. I also consulted my own collection of Field Day material, assembled in the late 1980s and early 1990s through research conducted at the Field Day Theatre Company's office in Derry. This personal archive consists of copies of press clippings and memorabilia, such as flyers and theatre programmes. In Belfast, I read newspaper and magazine articles in Belfast Central Library's Newspaper Library and the Linen Hall Library's Northern Ireland Political Collection.

Unpublished Sources

Unpublished Papers and Correspondence

Buford, Bill, Letter to Seamus Deane, 20 September 1984, Rose Library, MSS 1210, b3/f5.
Buford, Bill, Letter to Seamus Deane, 11 October 1984, Rose Library, MSS 1210, b3/f5.
Buford, Bill, Letter to Seamus Deane, 10 December 1984, Rose Library, MSS 1210, b3/f5.
Buford, Bill, Letter to Seamus Deane, 22 January 1985, Rose Library, MSS 1210, b3/f5.
Buford, Bill, Letter to Seamus Deane, 5 February 1985, Rose Library, MSS 1210, b3/f5.
Buford, Bill, Letter to Seamus Deane, 8 May 1985, Rose Library, MSS 1210, b3/f5.
Buford, Bill, Letter to Seamus Deane, 29 May 1985, Rose Library, MSS 1210, b3/f5.
Buford, Bill, Letter to Seamus Deane, 7 January 1986, Rose Library, MSS 1210, b3/f6.
Buford, Bill, Letter to Seamus Deane, 1 May 1986, Rose Library, MSS 1210, b3/f6.
Buford, Bill, Letter to Seamus Deane, 18 September 1986, Rose Library, MSS 1210, b3/f6.
Buford, Bill, Letter to Seamus Deane, 18 January 1988, Rose Library, MSS 1210, b3/f7.
Buford, Bill, Handwritten notes about a draft of Seamus Deane's *Reading in the Dark*, January 1988, Rose Library, MSS 1210, b3/f7.
Buford, Bill, Letter to Seamus Deane, 12 February 1988, Rose Library, MSS 1210, b3/f7.
Buford, Bill, Letter to Seamus Deane, 4 January 1989, Rose Library, MSS 1210, b3/f7.
Buford, Bill, Letter to Seamus Deane, 28 March 1989, Rose Library, MSS 1210, b3/f7.
Buford, Bill, Letter to Seamus Deane, 26 April 1989, Rose Library, MSS 1210, b3/f7.
Buford, Bill, Letter to Seamus Deane, 10 May 1989, Rose Library, MSS 1210, b3/f7.
Buford, Bill, Letter to Seamus Deane, 11 June 1990, Rose Library, MSS 1210, b4/f1.
Buford, Bill, Letter to Seamus Deane, 24 July 1990, Rose Library, MSS 1210, b4/f1.
Buford, Bill, Letter to Seamus Deane, 6 August 1990, Rose Library, MSS 1210, b4/f1.

Buford, Bill, Fax to Seamus Deane, 17 August 1990, Rose Library, MSS 1210, b4/f1.

Buford, Bill, Fax to Seamus Deane, 22 October 1990, Rose Library, MSS 1210, b4/f1.

Canny, Nicholas, Letter to Brian Friel, 4 April 1986, NLI, MS 37, 100/2.

Deane, Seamus, Handwritten notes towards *Reading in the Dark*, January 1988, Rose Library, MSS 1210, b3/f7.

Deane, Seamus, Draft letter to Bill Buford, 23 August 1990, Rose Library, MSS 1210, b4/f1.

Deane, Seamus, Letter to Brian Friel, 30 September 1992, NLI, MS 37, 181/7.

Deane, Seamus, Draft letter to Bill Buford, 28 October 1994, Rose Library, MSS 1210, b4/f1.

Field Day Theatre Company, Attendance figures for the Field Day production of Brian Friel's play *Making History* (1988), NLI, MS 46, 912/1.

Field Day Theatre Company, Attendance figures for the Field Day production of Seamus Heaney's play *The Cure at Troy* (1990), NLI, MS 46, 926/1.

Field Day Theatre Company, Minutes of the Field Day board meeting, 5 June 1983, Rose Library, MSS 880, b52/f1.

Field Day Theatre Company, Minutes of the Field Day board meeting, 8/9 September 1984, Rose Library, MSS 880, b52/f1.

Field Day Theatre Company, Minutes of the Field Day board meeting, 9/10 November 1985, Rose Library, MSS 880, b52/f1.

Field Day Theatre Company, Minutes of the Field Day board meeting, 6 August 1986, Rose Library, MSS 880, b52/f1.

Field Day Theatre Company, Minutes of the Field Day board meeting, 19/20 January 1988, NLI, MS 47, 112/7.

Field Day Theatre Company, Minutes of the Field Day board meeting, 12 August 1988, NLI, MS 37, 181/2.

Field Day Theatre Company, Minutes of the Field Day board meeting, 13 April 1991, NLI, MS 37, 181/2.

Friel, Brian, Letter to the new Field Day directors, 21 September 1981, NLI, MS 37, 181/1.

Friel, Brian, Letter to Seamus Deane, 21 June 1984, Rose Library, MSS 1210, b1/f11.

Friel, Brian, Notes towards *Making History*, NLI, MS 37, 100/1.

Friel, Brian, Notecard with notes towards *Making History*, NLI, MS 37, 100/5.

Friel, Brian, 'Final Version' of *Making History*, NLI, MS 37, 101/4.

Friel, Brian, Postcard to Seamus Heaney, [1 May] 1989, Rose Library, MSS 960, b39/f9.

Friel, Brian, Letter to Stephen Rea (copied to all Field Day directors), 31 July 1989, Rose Library, MSS 960, b39/f9.

Friel, Brian, Letter to Seamus Heaney, 4 January 2000, Rose Library, MSS 960, b39/f10.

Heaney, Seamus, Letter to Brian Friel, 22 January 1988, NLI, MS 37, 102/1.

Heaney, Seamus, Draft of *The Cure at Troy*, NLI, MS 49, 493/233, notebook 1.

Land, Sonia, Letter to Seamus Deane, 3 February 1995, Rose Library, MSS 1210, b4/f1.

Land, Sonia, Letter to Seamus Deane, 13 March 1996, Rose Library, MSS 1210, b4/f2.

McKinnon, Angus, Letter to Seamus Deane, 4 April 1990, Rose Library, MSS 1210, b4/f1.

McKinnon, Angus, Letter to Seamus Deane, 14 May 1990, Rose Library, MSS 1210, b4/f1.

MacLaverty, Bernard, Notes towards *Grace Notes* (novel), NLI, MS 6474, box 19.

MacLaverty, Bernard, Original (incomplete) version of the novel that became *Grace Notes*, NLI, MS 6474, box 19.

MacLaverty, Bernard, Drafts of *Grace Notes* (novel), NLI, MS 6474, box 9.

MacLaverty, Bernard, Radio script for *Best of Three* 12, NLI, MS 6474, box 4.

MacLaverty, Bernard, Radio script for *Grace Notes* 1, NLI, MS 6474, box 4.

MacLaverty, Bernard, Radio script for *Grace Notes* 7 ('Childhood'), NLI, MS 6474, box 4.

Michel, Caroline, Letter to Seamus Deane, 6 April 1990, Rose Library, MSS 1210, b4/f1.
Michel, Caroline, Letter to Seamus Deane, 19 July 1990, Rose Library, MSS 1210, b4/f1.
Nolan, Eamonn, Letter to Brian Friel, 28 May 1989, NLI, MS 37, 102/1.

Interviews and Conversations with the Author

Deane, Seamus, Telephone conversation with the author, 9 August 2015.
Longley, Michael, Conversation with the author, Belfast, 1 March 2017.
Longley, Michael, Interview with the author, Belfast, 19 November 2017.
McCann, Colum, Conversation with the author, New York City, 1 November 2019.
Madden, Deirdre, Conversation with the author, Dublin, 19 June 2017.
O'Doherty, Finola, Conversation with the author, Buncrana, County Donegal, 17 September 1991.
Park, David, Conversation with the author, Belfast, 22 July 2013.
Park, David, Conversation with the author, Belfast, 5 April 2017.

Written Communication with the Author

MacLaverty, Bernard, E-mail to the author, 21 February 2013.
MacLaverty, Bernard, E-mail to the author, 25 February 2013.
MacLaverty, Bernard, E-mail to the author, 26 February 2013.
MacLaverty, Bernard, E-mail to the author, 10 January 2022.
Madden, Deirdre, E-mail to the author, 17 June 2019.
Park, David, E-mail to the author, 22 April 2014.

Published Sources

Acharya, Kiran, 'The Truth Commissioner', *Culture Northern Ireland* (26 February 2008): https://www.culturenorthernireland.org/features/literature/truth-commissioner (accessed 18 October 2021).
Adair, Tom, 'Waiting for Waite', *Scotland on Sunday*, 5 June 1994.
Adams, Gerry, *Hope and History: Making Peace in Ireland* (London: Brandon, 2003).
Adams, Gerry, *A Farther Shore: Ireland's Long Road to Peace* (New York: Random House, 2003).
Ahern, Bertie, with Richard Aldous, *Bertie Ahern: The Autobiography* (London: Hutchinson, 2009).
Andrews, Chris and Matt McGuire (eds), *Post-Conflict Literature: Human Rights, Peace, Justice* (New York: Routledge, 2016).
Andrews, Elmer (ed.), *Seamus Heaney: A Collection of Critical Essays* (New York: St. Martin's Press, 1992).
Anon., 'The Protestant Idea of Liberty', *Derry Journal*, 21 May 1985.
Anon., 'NIO Hoist With Own Petard' (leader), *News Letter*, 13 January 1988.
Anon., 'History in the Making', *Ulster Herald*, 15 October 1988.
Anon., 'Friel's Cavan Delight', *Cavan Leader*, 28 October 1988.
Anon., 'Nauseating' (leader), *Derry Journal*, 27 July 1990.
Anon., 'Grief and Rage Greet Litter-bin Atrocity', *News Letter*, 22 March 1993.
Anon., 'IRA Lecture for Wilson', *News Letter*, 8 April 1993.
Anon., 'Meeting Challenges to End Violence', *Irish News*, 12 April 1993.
Anon., ' "Secret Talks Offer Little Hope of Peace" ', *News Letter*, 12 April 1993.
Anon., 'SF Talks Outrage', *News Letter*, 13 April 1993.
Anon., 'Processed Peace?' (arts feature), *Fortnight* (March 1994), 35–42.

Anon., 'The Crucial Need For a Farewell to Arms' (leader), *Guardian*, 22 August 1994.

Anon., '*Reading in the Dark*: An Interview with Seamus Deane', *English & Media Magazine* 36 (Summer 1997), 17–20.

Armstrong, Charles I., '"George Mitchell's Peace": The Good Friday Agreement in Colum McCann's Novel *TransAtlantic*' in Charles I. Armstrong, David Herbert, and Jan Erik Mustad (eds), *The Legacy of the Good Friday Agreement: Northern Irish Politics, Culture and Art after 1998* (Cham, Switzerland: Palgrave Macmillan, 2019), 57–71.

Bardon, Jonathan, *A History of Ulster* (Belfast: The Blackstaff Press, 1992).

Battersby, Eileen, 'Sometimes a Great Notion', *Irish Times*, 29 September 1990.

Battersby, Eileen, 'Six for the Booker', *Irish Times*, 2 October 1996: https://www.irishtimes. com/culture/six-for-the-booker-1.91645 (accessed 21 December 2021).

Battersby, Eileen, 'Observing the Sons of Ulster', *Irish Times*, 9 March 2000.

Bew, Paul and Gordon Gillespie, *Northern Ireland: A Chronology of the Troubles 1968–1999* (Lanham, Maryland: The Scarecrow Press, 1999).

Billington, Michael, 'History Kisses the Blarney Stone', *Guardian*, 7 December 1988.

Black, Shameem, 'Truth Commission Thrillers', *Social Text 107* 29.2 (Summer 2011), 47–66.

Blair, Tony, *A Journey: My Political Life* (New York: Knopf, 2010).

Bolton, David, *Conflict, Peace and Mental Health: Addressing the Consequences of Conflict and Trauma in Northern Ireland* (Manchester: Manchester University Press, 2017).

Brearton, Fran, *Reading Michael Longley* (Tarset, Northumberland: Bloodaxe Books, 2006).

Brennan, Brian, 'The Reinvention of Hugh O'Neill', *Sunday Independent*, 25 September 1988.

Broom, Sarah, 'Interview with Michael Longley', *Metre* 4 (1998), 17–26.

Broom, Sarah, 'Learning About Dying: Mutability and the Classics in the Poetry of Michael Longley', *New Hibernia Review* 6.1 (Spring 2002), 94–112.

Brown, John, *In the Chair: Interviews with Poets from the North of Ireland* (Cliffs of Moher, County Clare: Salmon Poetry, 2002).

Caldwell, Lucy, *All the Beggars Riding* (London: Faber and Faber, 2013).

Callaghan, Dympna, 'An Interview with Seamus Deane', *Social Text* 38 (Spring 1994), 39–50.

Campbell, Alastair, and Richard Stott (eds), *The Blair Years: Extracts from the Alastair Campbell Diaries* (London: Hutchinson, 2007).

Canny, Nicholas, '*Making History*', *Galway Advertiser*, 27 October 1988.

Canny, Nicholas, *From Reformation to Restoration: Ireland, 1534–1660* (Dublin: Helicon, 1989).

Canny, Nicholas, *Making Ireland British, 1580–1650* (Oxford: Oxford University Press, 2001).

Carson, Ciaran, 'The Truth Commissioner', *Independent*, 28 February 2008.

Carville, Conor, '"Ne Pas Céder Son Désir": Symptom and Fantasy in Seamus Deane's *Reading in the Dark*', *Irish Studies Review* 15.4 (2007), 411–23.

Cassidy, John, 'No Let-up in Bloody War', *News Letter*, 26 March 1993.

Cassidy, John, 'Internment Call Grows', *News Letter*, 12 April 1993.

Cleary, Joe, 'Dark Fields of the Republic: Seamus Deane's Sundered Provinces', *boundary 2* 37.2 (Summer 2010), 1–68.

Clinton, Bill, 'Remarks by the President to the Citizens of Londonderry', 30 November 1995: https://cain.ulster.ac.uk/events/peace/docs/pres2.htm (accessed 23 July 2021).

Clinton, Bill, *My Life* (New York: Vintage Books, 2005).

Cochrane, Feargal, *Northern Ireland: The Fragile Peace*, rev. ed. (New Haven: Yale University Press, 2021).

Connolly, Paul, 'Violence Poll Support Shock', *News Letter*, 1 April 1993.

Connolly, Sean, 'Translating History: Brian Friel and the Irish Past' in Alan Peacock (ed.), *The Achievement of Brian Friel* (Gerrards Cross, Buckinghamshire: Colin Smythe, 1993), 149–63.

Connolly, S. J. (ed.), *Oxford Companion to Irish History*, 2nd ed. (Oxford: Oxford University Press, 2002; paperback ed. 2004).

Coulter, Colin, Niall Gilmartin, Katy Hayward, and Peter Shirlow, *Northern Ireland a Generation after Good Friday: Lost Futures and New Horizons in the 'Long Peace'* (Manchester: Manchester University Press, 2021).

Coveney, Michael, 'Making History', *Financial Times*, 6 December 1988.

Coveney, Michael, Review of *The Cure at Troy* by Seamus Heaney, *Observer*, 7 October 1990.

Coyle, Jane, 'Friel Play's Touch of First Night Nerves', *Sunday Press*, 25 September 1988.

Craig, Patricia, 'A Cabinet in Co Clare', *Times Literary Supplement* (24 May 1996), 26.

Crowe, Catriona, 'Testimony to a Flowering', *Dublin Review* 10 (Spring 2003): https://thedublinreview.com/article/testimony-to-a-flowering/ (accessed 12 March 2021).

Cullingford, Elizabeth Butler, 'British Romans and Irish Carthaginians: Anticolonial Metaphor in Heaney, Friel, and McGuinness', *PMLA* 111.2 (March 1996), 222–39.

Cusatis, John, '"Embracing the World by Inventing the World": The Literary Journey of Colum McCann' (2012) in Earl G. Ingersoll and Mary C. Ingersoll (eds), *Conversations with Colum McCann* (Jackson: University Press of Mississippi, 2017), 123–39.

Dalrymple, James and Liam Clarke, '"Satanic" IRA Men Denounced by Bishop', *Sunday Times*, 28 October 1990.

Daly, Erin, 'Truth Skepticism: An Inquiry into the Value of Truth in Times of Transition', *International Journal of Transitional Justice* 2 (2008), 23–41.

Dantanus, Ulf, 'O'Neill's Last Tape: Self, Failure and Freedom in Friel and Beckett' in Richard Harp and Robert C. Evans (eds), *A Companion to Brian Friel* (West Cornwall, Connecticut: Locust Hill Press, 2002), 107–32.

Davies, Karin, 'Reluctant American Takes on The New Yorker', AP, 4 February 1995: https://apnews.com/article/1cfe07dc69e2437682de69e2b4e36bc1 (accessed 15 March 2021).

Dawson, Graham, *Making Peace with the Past? Memory, Trauma and the Irish Troubles* (Manchester: Manchester University Press, 2007).

Deane, Seamus, *Rumours* (Dublin: The Dolmen Press, 1977).

Deane, Seamus, 'Civilians and Barbarians' in *Ireland's Field Day*, Field Day Theatre Company (London: Hutchinson, 1985), 31–42.

Deane, Seamus, 'Haunted', *Granta* 18 (March 1985), 221–35.

Deane, Seamus, 'Oranges and Lemnos', *New Statesman* (5 April 1991), 18–19.

Deane, Seamus (ed.), *The Field Day Anthology of Irish Writing*, Volume 3 (Derry: Field Day, 1991).

Deane, Seamus, 'A Cruelly Efficient Act', *New York Times*, 23 June 1997.

Deane, Seamus, *Reading in the Dark* (New York: Vintage International, 1998).

Deane, Seamus, 'The Famous Seamus', *New Yorker* (20 March 2000), 54–79.

Deane, Seamus, 'Field Day's Greeks (and Russians)' in Marianne McDonald and J. Michael Walton (eds), *Amid Our Troubles: Irish Versions of Greek Tragedy*, introd. by Declan Kiberd (London: Methuen, 2002), 148–64.

de Bréadún, Deaglán, *The Far Side of Revenge: Making Peace in Northern Ireland*, rev. ed. (Cork: The Collins Press, 2008).

de Bréadún, Deaglán, 'US Senator George Mitchell and The Good Friday Agreement', *IrishCentral*, 10 April 2020: https://www.irishcentral.com/roots/irishamerica/good-friday-agreement-george-mitchell (accessed 6 October 2021).

Denard, Hugh, 'Seamus Heaney, Colonialism, and the Cure: Sophoclean Revisions', *PAJ: A Journal of Performance and Art* 22.3 (September 2000), 1–18.

Doyle, Leonard, 'Americans "Could Persuade IRA It's Time to Change"', *Independent*, 21 August 1994.

Doyle, Martin, 'Seamus Deane, leading Irish writer and critic, has died aged 81', *Irish Times*, 13 May 2021: https://www.irishtimes.com/culture/books/seamus-deane-leading-irish-writer-and-critic-has-died-aged-81-1.4564018 (accessed 27 January 2022).

Durkan, Mark, 'Shaping the Peace' in Seán Farren and Denis Haughey (eds), *John Hume: Irish Peacemaker* (Dublin: Four Courts Press, 2015), 120–42.

Farren, Seán (ed.), *John Hume: In His Own Words* (Dublin: Four Courts Press, 2018).

Farren, Seán and Denis Haughey (eds), *John Hume: Irish Peacemaker* (Dublin: Four Courts Press, 2015).

Farren, Seán and Robert F. Mulvihill, *Paths to a Settlement in Northern Ireland* (Gerrards Cross, Buckinghamshire: Colin Smythe, 2000).

Fearon, Kate, *Women's Work: The Story of the Northern Ireland Women's Coalition* (Belfast: The Blackstaff Press, 1999).

Fenton, Siobhan, *The Good Friday Agreement* (London: Biteback Publishing, 2018).

Field Day Theatre Company, *Ireland's Field Day* (London: Hutchinson, 1985).

Field Day Theatre Company, Flyer for the Field Day production of Seamus Heaney's play *The Cure at Troy* (Field Day Theatre Company, 1990).

Fisk, Robert, *The Point of No Return: The Strike Which Broke the British in Ulster* (London: André Deutsch, 1975).

Fitzgerald, Charles, 'City Without Theatre Making Stage History', *News Letter*, 21 September 1988.

Fitzgerald, Charles, 'Playwrights Can Change History Too', *News Letter*, 23 September 1988.

Fitzgerald, Robert (trans.), *The Iliad* of Homer, introd. by Gregory Nagy (New York: Knopf, 1992).

Fitzpatrick, Maurice, 'An Interview with Seamus Deane', *Journal of Irish Studies* 22 (2007), 84–92.

Fitzpatrick, Maurice, *John Hume in America: From Derry to DC* (Newbridge, County Kildare: Irish Academic Press, 2017).

Fogarty, Anne, 'The Romance of History: Renegotiating the Past in Thomas Kilroy's *The O'Neill* and Brian Friel's *Making History*', *Irish University Review* 32.1 (2002), 18–32.

The Framework Documents, 22 February 1995: https://cain.ulster.ac.uk/events/peace/docs/fd22295.htm (accessed 12 July 2021).

Fraser, Nick, 'A Kind of Life Sentence', *Guardian*, 28 October 1996.

Friel, Brian, Programme note for *Making History* (Field Day Theatre Company, 1988).

Friel, Brian, *Making History* (London: Faber and Faber, 1989).

Friel, Brian, John Andrews, and Kevin Barry, 'Translations and A Paper Landscape: Between Fiction and History', *Crane Bag* 7.2 (1983), 118–24.

Ganter, Christian, 'Bernard MacLaverty, Glasgow, in Interview', *Anglistik* 7.2 (1996), 5–22.

Garratt, Robert F., *Trauma and History in the Irish Novel: The Return of the Dead* (Basingstoke: Palgrave Macmillan, 2011).

Gawn, Ryan, 'Truth Cohabitation: A Truth Commission for Northern Ireland?', *Irish Political Studies* 22.3 (2007), 339–61.

Godson, Dean, *Himself Alone: David Trimble and the Ordeal of Unionism* (London: HarperCollins, 2004).

González, Rosa, 'Bernard MacLaverty' in Jacqueline Hurtley, Rosa González, Inés Praga, and Esther Aliaga, *Ireland in Writing: Interviews with Writers and Academics* (Amsterdam: Rodopi, 1998), 21–38.

Gormley-Heenan, Cathy, 'Political Leader' in Seán Farren and Denis Haughey (eds), *John Hume: Irish Peacemaker* (Dublin: Four Courts Press, 2015), 193–202.

Grant, Patrick, *Literature, Rhetoric and Violence in Northern Ireland, 1968–98: Hardened to Death* (Basingstoke: Palgrave, 2001).

Hamber, Brandon, 'Rights and Reasons: Challenges for Truth Recovery in South Africa and Northern Ireland', *Fordham International Law Journal* 26.4 (April 2003), 1074–94.

Hardwick, Lorna, '"Murmurs in the Cathedral": The Impact of Translations from Greek Poetry and Drama on Modern Work in English by Michael Longley and Seamus Heaney', *Yearbook of English Studies* 36.1 (2006), 204–15.

Harte, Liam, 'History Lessons: Postcolonialism and Seamus Deane's *Reading in the Dark*', *Irish University Review* 30.1 (Spring/Summer 2000), 149–62.

Harte, Liam, *Reading the Contemporary Irish Novel, 1987–2007* (Chichester, West Sussex: John Wiley, 2014).

Harte, Liam and Michael Parker, 'Reconfiguring Identities: Recent Northern Irish Fiction' in Liam Harte and Michael Parker (eds), *Contemporary Irish Fiction: Themes, Tropes, Theories* (Basingstoke: Macmillan, 2000), 232–54.

Hasset, Declan, '*Making History* ... Rewriting History', *Cork Examiner*, 24 November 1988.

Hayner, Priscilla B., *Unspeakable Truths: Transitional Justice and the Challenge of Truth Commissions*, 2nd ed. (New York: Routledge, 2011).

Heaney, Seamus, 'John Hume's Derry', *Hibernia* (21 November 1969), 7.

Heaney, Seamus, *Field Work* (1979) (New York: Noonday, 1989).

Heaney, Seamus, 'Applying the Yeats Challenge to the Anglo–Irish Agreement', *Boston Globe*, 27 June 1988.

Heaney, Seamus, 'A Field Day for the Irish', *The Times*, 5 December 1988.

Heaney, Seamus, Programme note for *The Cure at Troy* (Field Day Theatre Company, 1990).

Heaney, Seamus, *The Cure at Troy* (London: Faber and Faber, 1990).

Heaney, Seamus, 'Light Finally Enters the Black Hole', *Sunday Tribune*, 4 September 1994.

Heaney, Seamus, *The Spirit Level* (London: Faber and Faber, 1996).

Heaney, Seamus, '*The Cure at Troy*: Production Notes in No Particular Order' in Marianne McDonald and J. Michael Walton (eds), *Amid Our Troubles: Irish Versions of Greek Tragedy*, introd. by Declan Kiberd (London: Methuen, 2002), 171–80.

Hearst, David, 'Human Bombs Kill 7', *Guardian*, 25 October 1990.

Hennessey, Thomas, *The Northern Ireland Peace Process: Ending the Troubles?* (New York: Palgrave, 2001).

Herron, Tom, 'Derry *Is* Donegal: Thresholds, Vectors, Limits in Seamus Deane's *Reading in the Dark*', *Études irlandaises* 29.2 (2004), 165–83.

Higgins, Geraldine, '"A Place to Bring Anger and Grief": Deirdre Madden's Northern Irish Novels', *Writing Ulster* 6 (1999), 142–61.

Hodges, Jeremy, 'Author Bernard MacLaverty Regrets the Loss of Old Family Values', *Daily Mail*, 12 October 1999.

Holland, Mary, 'A Field Day for Irish Theatre', *Observer* (magazine section), 29 October 1988.

Holland, Mary, 'Ceasefire Talk Breathes Life Into Battered Hopes', *Observer*, 28 August 1994.

Hume, John, *A New Ireland: Politics, Peace and Reconciliation* (Boulder, Colorado: Roberts Rinehart Publishers, 1996).

Ingersoll, Earl G. and Mary C. Ingersoll (eds), *Conversations with Colum McCann* (Jackson: University Press of Mississippi, 2017).

Jacobus, Lee A., *The Bedford Introduction to Drama*, 2nd ed. (Boston: Bedford Books, 1993).

Joyce, James, *Dubliners* (1914), ed. Terence Brown (New York: Penguin, 1993).

Joyce, James, *A Portrait of the Artist as a Young Man* (1916), ed. Seamus Deane (New York: Penguin, 1993).

Joyce, James, *Ulysses* (1922), ed. Hans Walter Gabler (New York: Random House, 1986).

Kearney, Richard, 'Myth and Motherland' in *Ireland's Field Day*, Field Day Theatre Company (London: Hutchinson, 1985), 59–80.

Keefe, Patrick Radden, 'Where the Bodies Are Buried', *New Yorker* (16 March 2015), 42–61.

Keefe, Patrick Radden, *Say Nothing: A True Story of Murder and Memory in Northern Ireland* (New York: Anchor Books, 2020).

Kelly, Dermot, 'Joycean Epiphany in Seamus Deane's *Reading in the Dark*' in Wim Tigges (ed.), *Moments of Moment: Aspects of the Literary Epiphany* (Amsterdam: Rodopi, 1999), 435–43.

Kelly, Joseph, 'A Defense of Danis Rose', *James Joyce Quarterly* 35.4/36.1 (Summer/Fall 1998), 811–24.

Kennedy-Andrews, Elmer, *Fiction and the Northern Ireland Troubles Since 1969: (De-) Constructing the North* (Dublin: Four Courts Press, 2003).

Krog, Antjie, *Country of My Skull: Guilt, Sorrow, and the Limits of Forgiveness in the New South Africa* (New York: Three Rivers Press, 2000).

Lackey, Michael, 'Colum McCann: Contested Realities in the Biographical Novel' (interview with Colum McCann), *Éire-Ireland* 53.1/2 (Spring/Summer 2018), 134–49.

Ladrón, Marisol Morales, '"Writing Is a State of Mind Not an Achievement": An Interview with Bernard MacLaverty', *Atlantis* 23.2 (2001), 201–11.

Lattimore, Richmond, *The Iliad of Homer*, trans. and introd. Richmond Lattimore (Chicago: University of Chicago Press, 1951).

Lehner, Stefanie, 'Post-Conflict Masculinities: *Filiative* Reconciliation in *Five Minutes of Heaven* and David Park's *The Truth Commissioner*' in Caroline Magennis and Raymond Mullen (eds), *Irish Masculinities: Reflections on Literature and Culture* (Dublin: Irish Academic Press, 2011), 65–76.

Lehner, Stefanie, 'The Irreversible and the Irrevocable: Encircling Trauma in Contemporary Northern Irish Literature' in Oona Frawley (ed.), *Memory Ireland, Volume 3: The Famine and the Troubles* (Syracuse: Syracuse University Press, 2014), 272–92.

Lehner, Stefanie, '"Absent and yet Somehow Still Present": Representing the Irish Disappeared in Contemporary Photography and Fiction' in Chris Andrews and Matt McGuire (eds), *Post-Conflict Literature: Human Rights, Peace, Justice* (New York: Routledge, 2016), 31–42.

Lennon, Joseph, '"A Country of the Elsewheres": An Interview with Colum McCann', *New Hibernia Review* 16.2 (Summer 2012), 98–111.

Leonard, Sue, 'Interview. David Park' (originally published in the *Irish Examiner* in February 2008): http://journalistsueleonard.blogspot.com/2008/07/interview-david-park.html (accessed 14 October 2021).

Longley, Michael, *Tuppenny Stung: Autobiographical Chapters* (Belfast: Lagan Press, 1994).

Longley, Michael, *The Ghost Orchid* (London: Jonathan Cape, 1995).

Longley, Michael, 'Memory and Acknowledgement', *Irish Review* 17/18 (Winter 1995), 153–9.

Longley, Michael, *Sidelines: Selected Prose 1962–2015* (London: Enitharmon Press, 2017).

Longley, Michael, *Songs for Dead Children: Poetry in Violent Times* (London: English PEN/Faber and Faber, 2017).

Lundy, Patricia and Mark McGovern, 'Truth, Justice and Dealing with the Legacy of the Past in Northern Ireland, 1998–2008', *Ethnopolitics* 7.1 (2008), 177–93.

Lyall, Sarah, '"Ulysses" in Deep Trouble Again: A New Edition Purges What May Have Been Joyce's Errors and Enrages Critics', *New York Times*, 23 June 1997.

Lysandrou, Yvonne, 'Hugh O'Neill as "Hamlet-Plus": (Post)colonialism and Dynamic Stasis in Brian Friel's *Making History*', *Irish Studies Review* 14.1 (2006), 91–106.

McAvera, Brian, 'Attuned to the Catholic Experience', *Fortnight* (3 March 1985), 19–20.

McBride, Ian, 'The Truth About the Troubles' in Jim Smyth (ed.), *Remembering the Troubles: Contesting the Recent Past in Northern Ireland* (Notre Dame, Indiana: University of Notre Dame Press, 2017), 9–43.

McCann, Colum, *TransAtlantic* (New York: Random House, 2013; trade paperback ed. 2014).

McDonald, Henry, *Trimble* (London: Bloomsbury, 2000; paperback ed. 2001).

McDonald, Marianne, 'Seamus Heaney's *Cure at Troy* Politics and Poetry', *Classics Ireland* 3 (1996), 129–40.

McDonald, Marianne and J. Michael Walton (eds), *Amid Our Troubles: Irish Versions of Greek Tragedy*, introd. by Declan Kiberd (London: Methuen, 2002).

MacDonncha, Micheál, 'Operation Harvest—50 Years On', *An Phoblacht*, 14 December 2006: https://www.anphoblacht.com/contents/16187 (accessed 28 March 2021).

McGarry, John, 'Police Reform in Northern Ireland', *Irish Political Studies* 15.1 (2000), 173–82.

McGrath, F. C., *Brian Friel's (Post)Colonial Drama: Language, Illusion, and Politics* (Syracuse: Syracuse University Press, 1999).

McGrath, Niall, 'Michael Longley: The Interview', *Poetry Life: People, Poets and Publishing* 6 (Spring 1996), 14–16.

McGrattan, Cillian, *Northern Ireland 1968–2008: The Politics of Entrenchment* (Basingstoke: Palgrave Macmillan, 2010).

McGuire, Matt, 'Tragedy and Transitional Justice: Seamus Heaney's *The Cure at Troy*' in Chris Andrews and Matt McGuire (eds), *Post-Conflict Literature: Human Rights, Peace, Justice* (New York: Routledge, 2016), 19–30.

McGuire, Matt, 'The Trouble(s) with Transitional Justice: David Park's *The Truth Commissioner*', *Irish University Review* 47 supplement (2017), 515–30.

McGurk, Tom, 'Why the IRA Is Committed To Making the September Truce a Permanent One', *Sunday Business Post*, 28 August 1994.

McKee, Lyra, 'Suicide of the Ceasefire Babies', *Mosaic Science* (19 January 2016): https://mosaicscience.com/story/conflict-suicide-northern-ireland/ (accessed 19 November 2019).

McKeever, Martin, *One Man, One God: The Peace Ministry of Fr Alec Reid C.Ss.R.* (Dublin: Redemptorist Communications, 2017).

McKittrick, David, 'IRA Uses Human Bombs', *Independent*, 25 October 1990.

McKittrick, David, 'Belfast Bomb Kills Nine', *Independent on Sunday*, 24 October 1993.

McKittrick, David, 'IRA Ceasefire Branded Cynical', *Independent*, 31 March 1994.

McKittrick, David and David McVea, *Making Sense of the Troubles: A History of the Northern Ireland Conflict*, rev. ed. (London: Viking/Penguin, 2012).

MacLaverty, Bernard, *Lamb* (London: Penguin, 1981).

MacLaverty, Bernard, *Grace Notes* (London: Jonathan Cape, 1997).

MacLaverty, Bernard, 'An Interview with Richard Rankin Russell', *Irish Literary Supplement* 26.1 (Fall 2006), 21–2.

McLoughlin, P. J., *John Hume and the Revision of Irish Nationalism* (Manchester: Manchester University Press, 2010).

McNamee, Eugene, 'Fields of Opportunity: Cultural Invention and "The New Northern Ireland"' in Peter D. Rush and Olivera Simić (eds), *The Arts of Transitional Justice: Culture, Activism, and Memory After Atrocity*, Vol. 6 of the Springer Series in Transitional Justice (New York: Springer, 2014), 1–24.

Madden, Deirdre, *One by One in the Darkness* (London: Faber and Faber, 1997).

Madden, Deirdre, 'Looking for Home: Time, Place, Memory', *Canadian Journal of Irish Studies* 26.2/27.1 (Fall 2000/Spring 2001), 25–33.

Major, John, *The Autobiography* (New York: HarperCollins, 1999).

Mandel, Oscar, *Philoctetes and the Fall of Troy: Plays, Documents, Iconography, Interpretations* (Lincoln, Nebraska: University of Nebraska Press, 1981).

Maudet, Cécile, 'Two Interviews with Colum McCann' (2013 and 2014) in Earl G. Ingersoll and Mary C. Ingersoll (eds), *Conversations with Colum McCann* (Jackson: University Press of Mississippi, 2017), 145–80.

Maxwell, Constantia, *Irish History from Contemporary Sources (1509-1610)* (London: Allen & Unwin, 1923).

Meany, Helen, 'Lost in Music', *Irish Times*, 3 July 1997.

Mendeloff, David, 'Truth-Seeking, Truth-Telling, and Postconflict Peacebuilding: Curb the Enthusiasm?', *International Studies Review* 6.3 (2004), 355–80.

Michod, Alec, 'The Rumpus Interview with Colum McCann' (2013) in Earl G. Ingersoll and Mary C. Ingersoll (eds), *Conversations with Colum McCann* (Jackson: University Press of Mississippi, 2017), 140–4.

Millar, Frank, *David Trimble: The Price of Peace* (Dublin: The Liffey Press, 2004).

Mitchell, George, *Making Peace* (New York: Knopf, 1999).

Moloney, Ed, *A Secret History of the IRA*, 2nd ed. (London: Penguin, 2007).

Monteith, Sharon, and Jenny Newman, 'Bernard MacLaverty' in Sharon Monteith, Jenny Newman, and Pat Wheeler, *Contemporary British and Irish Fiction: An Introduction Through Interviews* (London: Arnold, 2004), 103–18.

Morgan, Hiram, *Tyrone's Rebellion: The Outbreak of the Nine Years War in Tudor Ireland* (Woodbridge, Suffolk: The Boydell Press, 1993).

Mowlam, Mo, *Momentum: The Struggle for Peace, Politics and the People* (London: Hodder and Stoughton, 2002; Coronet paperback ed. 2003).

Mulholland, Marc, *Northern Ireland: A Very Short Introduction* (Oxford: Oxford University Press, 2002).

Murray, Christopher, 'Brian Friel's *Making History* and the Problem of Historical Accuracy' in Geert Lernout (ed.), *The Crows Behind the Plough: History and Violence in Anglo-Irish Poetry and Drama* (Amsterdam: Rodopi, 1991), 61–77.

O Connor, Fionnuala, *Breaking the Bonds: Making Peace in Northern Ireland* (Edinburgh: Mainstream Publishing, 2002).

O'Connor, Joseph, 'Public Men and Private Troubles', *Guardian*, 8 February 2008.

O'Doherty, Malachi, 'The Past Catches Up', *Fortnight* (July/August 2008), 26–7.

O'Driscoll, Dennis, *Stepping Stones: Interviews with Seamus Heaney* (New York: Farrar, Straus and Giroux, 2008).

O'Faolain, Nuala, 'The Voice that Field Day Didn't Record', *Irish Times*, 11 November 1991.

O'Faolain, Sean, *The Great O'Neill: A Biography of Hugh O'Neill, Earl of Tyrone, 1550–1616* (Dublin: The Mercier Press, 1992).

O'Grady, Timothy, 'Courage and Pain of a Man with a Foot in Two Worlds', *Evening Press*, 24 September 1988.

Olsen, Tillie, *Silences* (New York: Delacorte Press/Seymour Lawrence, 1978).

O'Malley, Aidan, *Field Day and the Translation of Irish Identities: Performing Contradictions* (Basingstoke: Palgrave Macmillan, 2011).

O'Neill, Joseph, 'The Informer', *New York Times*, 30 March 2008.

O'Sullivan, Kevin, 'Making History—Compelling but with One Slight Flaw', *City Tribune*, 28 November 1988.

O'Toole, Fintan, 'The Man From God Knows Where: An Interview with Brian Friel', *In Dublin* (28 October 1982), 20–3.

O'Toole, Fintan, 'Seamus Heaney: Beyond the Normal Niceties', *Colour Tribune*, 10 April 1988.

O'Toole, Fintan, 'A Hesitant Move Into Unknown Territory', *Irish Times*, 24 September 1988.

O'Toole, Fintan, 'The Meanings of Union', *New Yorker* (27 April/4 May 1998), 54–62.

O'Toole, Fintan, 'Marking Time: From *Making History* to *Dancing at Lughnasa*' in Alan Peacock (ed.), *The Achievement of Brian Friel* (Gerrards Cross, Buckinghamshire: Colin Smythe, 1993), 202–14.

Oxford English Dictionary: https://www.oed.com.

Park, David, *The Truth Commissioner* (New York: Bloomsbury, 2008).

Parker, Michael, 'Shadows on a Glass: Self-Reflexivity in the Fiction of Deirdre Madden', *Irish University Review* 30.1 (Spring/Summer 2000), 82–102.

Parker, Michael, *Northern Irish Literature: The Imprint of History, Volume 2: 1975–2006* (Basingstoke: Palgrave Macmillan, 2007).

Parker, Michael, 'Back in the Republic of Conscience: Seamus Heaney's *The Cure at Troy*, Its Politics, Ethics, and Aesthetics', *Textual Practice* 31.4 (2017), 747–81.

Parker, Stewart, *Dramatis Personae & Other Writings*, ed. Gerald Dawe, Maria Johnston, and Clare Wallace (Prague: Litteraria Pragensia, 2008).

Patterson, Glenn, 'David Park', *Irish Pages* 4.2 (2008), 162–4.

Patton, Jim, 'A Gripping New Drama', *Belfast Telegraph*, 21 September 1988.

Pauley, Mervyn, 'Stop the Killing Is Senator's Plea', *News Letter*, 26 March 1993.

Peach, Linden, *The Contemporary Irish Novel: Critical Readings* (Basingstoke: Palgrave Macmillan, 2004).

Peacock, Alan, 'Mediations: Poet as Translator, Poet as Seer' in Elmer Andrews (ed.), *Seamus Heaney: A Collection of Critical Essays* (New York: St. Martin's Press, 1992), 233–55.

Peacock, Alan (ed.), *The Achievement of Brian Friel* (Gerrards Cross, Buckinghamshire: Colin Smythe, 1993).

Pine, Richard, *The Diviner: The Art of Brian Friel* (Dublin: University College Dublin Press, 1999).

Powell, Jonathan, *Great Hatred, Little Room: Making Peace in Northern Ireland* (London: The Bodley Head, 2008).

Propst, Lisa, 'Truth Commissions and Unspoken Narratives in Gillian Slovo's *Red Dust* and David Park's *The Truth Commissioner*', *The Comparatist* 41 (2017), 288–308.

Regan, Stephen, Review of *Reading in the Dark*, *Irish Studies Review* 19 (Summer 1997), 35–40.

Reynolds, Albert, with Jill Arlon, *My Autobiography* (London: Transworld Ireland, 2009).

Richards, Shaun, ' "A Solution to the Present Crisis"? Seamus Heaney's *The Cure at Troy*', *Études irlandaises* 20.2 (1995), 77–85.

Richtarik, Marilynn, *Acting Between the Lines: The Field Day Theatre Company and Irish Cultural Politics 1980–1984* (Oxford: Oxford University Press, 1994).

Richtarik, Marilynn, *Stewart Parker: A Life* (Oxford: Oxford University Press, 2012).

Richtarik, Marilynn, 'The Personal is Political: Bernard MacLaverty's *Grace Notes* as a Peace Process Novel' in Richard Rankin Russell (ed.), *Bernard MacLaverty: New Critical Readings* (London: Bloomsbury, 2014), 101–16.

Richtarik, Marilynn, 'Brian Friel and Field Day' in Nicholas Grene and Chris Morash (eds), *The Oxford Handbook of Modern Irish Theatre* (Oxford: Oxford University Press, 2016), 357–71.

Richtarik, Marilynn, 'Reality and Justice: Seamus Heaney's *The Cure at Troy*', *Estudios Irlandeses* 13 (2018), 98–112.

Richtarik, Marilynn and Kevin Chappell, 'An Interview with Glenn Patterson', *Five Points: A Journal of Literature & Art* 13.2 (2010), 44–56.

Rifbjerg, Synne, 'Do What Is Most Difficult' (2013) in Earl G. Ingersoll and Mary C. Ingersoll (eds), *Conversations with Colum McCann* (Jackson: University Press of Mississippi, 2017), 181–92.

Roche, Anthony, *Brian Friel: Theatre and Politics* (Basingstoke: Palgrave Macmillan, 2011).

Ross, Daniel W., 'An Uncanny Home: Deirdre Madden's *One by One in the Darkness* and the 1994 Ceasefire' in Alison O'Malley-Younger and John Strachan (eds), *Ireland at War and Peace* (Newcastle upon Tyne: Cambridge Scholars Publishing, 2011), 189–99.

Routledge, Paul, 'Blast Kills Peace Hopes', *Independent on Sunday*, 24 October 1993.

Routledge, Paul, *John Hume: A Biography* (London: HarperCollins, 1997).

Rumens, Carol, 'Reading Deane' [interview with Seamus Deane], *Fortnight* (July/August 1997), 29–30.

Russell, Richard Rankin, Interview with Bernard MacLaverty, *Irish Literary Supplement* 26.1 (Fall 2006), 21–2.

Russell, Richard Rankin, *Bernard MacLaverty* (Cranbury, New Jersey: Bucknell University Press, 2009).

Russell, Richard Rankin, *Poetry and Peace: Michael Longley, Seamus Heaney, and Northern Ireland* (Notre Dame, Indiana: University of Notre Dame Press, 2010).

Russell, Richard Rankin, *Seamus Heaney's Regions* (Notre Dame, Indiana: University of Notre Dame Press, 2014).

Sansom, Ian, 'David Park: A Life in Books', *Guardian*, 20 April 2012.

Santel, James, 'Funambulism: An Interview with Colum McCann', *Los Angeles Review of Books* (12 June 2013): https://lareviewofbooks.org/article/funambulism-an-interview-with-colum-mccann/ (accessed 3 January 2022).

Schimmel, Geordie, 'An Interview with Michael Longley', *Libertas* (20 February 1997), 10–11.

Schreiter, Robert, 'Establishing a Shared Identity: The Role of the Healing of Memories and of Narrative' in Sebastian C. H. Kim, Pauline Kollontai, and Greg Hoyland (eds), *Peace and Reconciliation: In Search of Shared Identity* (Aldershot: Ashgate, 2008), 7–20.

Sharrock, David, 'Britain Faces US Rift On IRA', *Guardian*, 22 August 1994.

Shulman, Milton, 'Shaping the Past', *Evening Standard*, 6 December 1988.

Simmons, James, 'Too Happy, Too Soon', *Spectator* (8 June 1996), 35.

Sinnerton, Henry, *David Ervine: Uncharted Waters* (Dingle, Co. Kerry: Brandon, 2002).

Smith, Jeremy, *Making the Peace in Ireland* (London: Longman, 2002).

Smyth, Gerry, *Space and the Irish Cultural Imagination* (Basingstoke: Palgrave, 2001).

Smyth, Gerry, '"The Same Sound but with a Different Meaning": Music, Repetition, and Identity in Bernard MacLaverty's *Grace Notes*', *Éire-Ireland* 37.3/4 (2002), 5–24.

Smyth, Marie, 'Healing Emotional Scars', *Fortnight* (October 1994), 18–20.

Smyth, Marie Breen, *Truth Recovery and Justice after Conflict: Managing Violent Pasts* (London: Routledge, 2007).

Soderberg, Nancy, 'In America' in Seán Farren and Denis Haughey (eds), *John Hume: Irish Peacemaker* (Dublin: Four Courts Press, 2015), 168–79.

Spencer, Graham, *The State of Loyalism in Northern Ireland* (Basingstoke: Palgrave Macmillan, 2008).

Spencer, Graham, 'Managing a Peace Process: An Interview with Jonathan Powell', *Irish Political Studies* 25.3 (September 2010), 437–55.

Steel, Jayne, 'Politicizing the Private: Women Writing the Troubles' in Brian Cliff and Éibhear Walshe (eds), *Representing the Troubles: Texts and Images, 1970–2000* (Dublin: Four Courts Press, 2004), 55–66.

Strout, Elizabeth, interview with Colum McCann ('A Conversation with Colum McCann and Elizabeth Strout') in *TransAtlantic* (New York: Random House, 2014 trade paperback ed.), 307–15.

Sullivan, Richard, 'Critics Proved Right as Wilson Plea Fails', *News Letter*, 9 April 1993.

Tóibín, Colm, 'Dublin's Epiphany', *New Yorker* (3 April 1995), 45–53.

Trimble, David, 'Antony Alcock Memorial Lecture' (University of Ulster, 24 April 2007): http://www.ricorso.net/rx/az-data/authors/t/Trimble_D/xtra.htm (accessed 3 January 2022).

Truth and Reconciliation Commission of South Africa, *Truth and Reconciliation Commission of South Africa Report*, vol. 1 (1998): https://www.justice.gov.za/trc/report/finalreport/Volume%201.pdf (accessed 12 February 2022).

Vidal, John, 'Stronger Than Fiction', *Guardian*, 5 December 1988.

Wallace, Nathan, *Hellenism and Reconciliation in Ireland from Yeats to Field Day* (Cork: Cork University Press, 2015).

Walsh, John, 'Bard of Hope and Harp', *Sunday Times*, 7 October 1990.

Wardle, Irving, 'Language a Key to Life', *The Times*, 6 December 1988.

Webber, Jude, 'Donaldson Gambles by Pulling the Plug on Northern Ireland's Executive', *Financial Times*, 7 February 2022: https://www.ft.com/content/70a1db58-369e-4e90-9e85-fcb67ea6bc0f (accessed 7 February 2022).

Weil, Simone, *The Iliad or the Poem of Force*, trans. Mary McCarthy (Wallingford, Pennsylvania: Pendle Hill, 1956).

White, Barry, '"Troy" is the Setting for Heaney's First Play', *Belfast Telegraph*, 29 September 1990.

White, Hayden, 'Between Science and Symbol', *Times Literary Supplement* (31 January 1986), 109–10.

Wilson, Edmund, *The Wound and the Bow: Seven Studies in Literature* (Cambridge, Massachusetts: Houghton Mifflin, 1941).

Wilson, Robin, 'No Elegies', *Fortnight* (October 1994), 47.

Wilson, Robin, *The Northern Ireland Experience of Conflict and Agreement: A Model for Export?* (Manchester: Manchester University Press, 2010).

Index

For the benefit of digital users, indexed terms that span two pages (e.g., 52–53) may, on occasion, appear on only one of those pages.